Oxford Socio-Legal Studies

Lawyers and the Rise of
Western Political Liberalism

LAWYERS AND THE RISE OF WESTERN POLITICAL LIBERALISM

Europe and North America from
the Eighteenth to Twentieth Centuries

edited by
TERENCE C. HALLIDAY & LUCIEN KARPIK

CLARENDON PRESS · OXFORD
1997

Oxford University Press, Great Clarendon Street, Oxford OX2 6DP
Oxford New York
Athens Auckland Bangkok Bogota Bombay
Buenos Aires Calcutta Cape Town Dar es Salaam
Delhi Florence Hong Kong Istanbul Karachi
Kuala Lumpur Madras Madrid Melbourne
Mexico City Nairobi Paris Singapore
Taipei Tokyo Toronto Warsaw
and associated companies in
Berlin Ibadan

Oxford is a trade mark of Oxford University Press

Published in the United States
by Oxford University Press Inc., New York

British Library Cataloguing in Publication Data
Data available

Library of Congress Cataloging in Publication Data
Data available
ISBN 0-19-826288-4

1 3 5 7 9 10 8 6 4 2

Typeset by Hope Services (Abingdon) Ltd.
Printed in Great Britain
on acid-free paper by
Bookcraft Ltd., Midsomer Norton, Somerset

To Mavis Halliday, Katherine, Pamela, and Jennifer

T.C.H.

To Nathalie, Pierre, and Emmanuelle

L.K.

General Editor's Introduction

The original essays published here emphasize the central role played by the legal profession in the emergence of modern political liberalism. This book is premised on a series of arguments: in particular, that current views of the role of lawyers and the professions neglect the role of politics, fail to do justice to a detailed and systematically historical perspective, and have created a literature rather dominated by Anglo-American conceptions of professionalism which themselves tend to emphasize the centrality of the market. The result is a collection that challenges many of the generally accepted ideas about the legal profession and presents a series of critical analyses that display the range of lawyers' activities which have contributed to the development of the liberal state.

The editors of this volume have planned and organized it with exceptional care, and the papers themselves represent an extraordinary international collaborative effort. Their stimulus was the work of a number of scholars who have been part of the Working Group on Comparative Studies of Legal Professions of the International Sociological Association. The resultant collection is comprised of essays by leading academics in a number of countries, and their focus is the legal professions in France, England, Germany, and the United States. Each country is represented by a pair of papers, one historical, one sociological. These papers are in turn introduced and set in a common theoretical framework by the editors, who also complete the collection with a substantial concluding reflection. The result is an impressive symmetry in the structure of the work which grants it an internal coherence rare in such edited works. The book is a model of what a collection of original pieces by different authors should be.

This volume has a number of new and significant things to say about the political importance of lawyers and their part in the rise of modern, liberal societies. Socio-legal scholars, and especially those interested in the legal profession, will find here a book that is full of important insights and new ideas.

Keith Hawkins

Table of Contents

Preface

For two decades a debate has raged among scholars over the meaning of professions for modern societies and institutions. This book enters that debate with a new interpretation centred on lawyers and politics. What sociological state of play do we challenge? What historical interpretations do we contest? What concept of lawyers do we counterpose to prevailing views? The Preface briefly answers these questions. We identify the issues at stake, and the challenges in meeting them. We set out our common theoretical point of view and provide a brief overview of each of the contributions to our collective project.

The sociological study of professions cannot be divorced from the major scholarly conflict that broke out in the 1970s. Nor can it be detached from either the issues joined in that conflict or those that were excluded. Functionalist theory, in its British and American manifestations, dominated sociological studies of professions from the 1930s to the 1960s, and has continued to brood over the debate of the last twenty-five years. While it is no longer a dominant school of thought, it is a central player. Even when ostensibly ignored, it remains an invisible presence partially framing the rhetoric of its own critique.

Functionalism had two faces. On the one side, like every theoretical perspective, it was a sophisticated theory with strong limitations. Professions were without conflict, without markets, without history. On the other hand, it celebrated the virtues of professional communities, professional norms, professional practices, and the mobilization of professional knowledge for political and economic ends. While none of the leading writers in this school was entirely innocent of professions' vices, they and their circles in Britain and North America variously looked to professionalism as an ideal and practice that could help salve the wounds of modern economics, inform the process of democratic politics, and bind together with relative distinterestedness the centrifugal forces of progressively differentiated advanced industrial, and then post-industrial, societies.

As insurgent scholars entered the field in the 1960s, the sociological waters became muddied. Research cast increasing doubt on the homogeneity of professional communities, the probity of professional practice, and the effectiveness of professional regulation. Empirical studies found that higher reaches of professions used ethics and regulatory apparatuses to discipline lower strata of professionals with whom they seemed to have very little in common—whether by class of recruitment, religion, clients, or forms of practice. Professionals responsible for self-regulation seldom allowed the heavy hand of professional sanctions to fall on those too like themselves. Segments of professions struggled with each other in the workplace and in rival professional associations. Functionalism, said the revisionists of the late 1960s and early 1970s, confused reality with professional ideology and effectively propagated an illusory account of professions in modern societies.

Larson's book, *The Rise of Modern Professions*, published in 1976, brought disparate attacks into the first coherent, general critique of modern professions by a sociologist.[1] In a bravura turn, she deftly fused elements of neo-Marxist thought with Polanyi's historical interpretation of capitalist development. In contrast to most, Larson took a long view. Modern professions arose, she said, with modern capitalism, and cannot be understood without a recognition of the ways that all professional institutions serve a particular form of economy. Indeed, professions' collective representation of themselves serve practically to shield the exploitative undercurrents of modern capitalism from unmasking. In return for their faithful service to the capitalist order, the professions get to take home monopoly rents. But Larson also recognized that professions advance aspirations beyond material interests: they strive collectively for a secure and preferably rising mobility in the class system, and its rewards are not only material but symbolic. This double project engaged professions in a complex process that involved the market, professional knowledge, the university, and the state.

Larson's bold combination of a long historical account of market transformation and collective action wrought a major reinterpretation of the professions' 'complex' in modern societies: markets dominated, and most else receded from view. Although that shift occurred principally under a Weberian mantle, ironically it bore a striking resemblance to a less roseate view of professional behaviour earlier inscribed by the economist Milton Friedman in his volume *Capitalism and Freedom*.[2] Friedman saw professionalism as an ill-disguised monopoly, whose primary benefits flowed to professionals themselves. What were construed by professionals as noble features of self-regulation turned out, on inspection, to be ideologically camouflaged pretences for artificially cre-

---

[1] M. Sarfatti-Larson, *The Rise of Modern Professionalism: A Sociological Analysis* (Berkeley, Univ. of California Press, 1976).

[2] M. Friedman, *Capitalism and Freedom* (Chicago, Univ. of Chicago Press, 1962).

ating scarcity of supply of services, for boosting prices of services, and for thereby excluding large numbers of potential consumers from the market for professional services.

In the same vein, sociological studies converged to show that professional communities, including lawyers, could be seen as markets only modestly restrained from the unbridled competition of neo-classical economics by ethical rules and regulations. Legal education, barriers to entry, internal discipline—all served economic monopoly more than any ideal of professional disinterest or public good.[3]

This pervasively market-oriented conception of lawyers received a sophisticated recasting in Abbott's ecological account of professions, which has propagated new research agendas that look to the mobilization of professional knowledge as ways of seizing and holding 'jurisdictions' of work.[4] While the means and mechanisms may have changed, however, the ends remain remarkably similar to earlier formulations: Abbott's professions are territorial aggrandizers. The terrain is work, the weapons are knowledge, the adversaries are rival occupations, the prize—power, material, and social capital.

At the bottom of these conflicts lay contrasting views of professional actors, professional activities, and professional encounters with society. But the hidden assumptions *uniting* these theoretically conflicting schools of theory and research were as important as the lines of conflict themselves. Their shared, hidden assumptions provide the foil for this book. We find three sets of problems with the orientations-in-common held by functionalists and their interlocutors alike.

First, politics are missing. The vast preponderance of research and writing on professions proceeds as if politics do not matter, and especially politics writ large—the politics of the nation-state or of the groups and institutions that determine its policies and their implementation. In theories of economic monopoly, status attainment, and jurisdictional control, the politics of professionals appear only as levers to acquisitive ends, personal and collective.

Second, history receives short shrift. It may be bowdlerized: professions before capitalism and after; pre-modern professions and modern professions; aristocratic professions and meritocratic professions; closed

---

[3] The most vigorous expression of this point of view can be found in the works of Richard Abel on American and English lawyers. See R. L. Abel, *American Lawyers* (New York, Oxford Univ. Press, 1989).

[4] A. Abbott, *The System of Professions: An Essay on the Division of Expert Labor* (Chicago, Univ. of Chicago Press, 1988).

professions and open professions. It may be caricatured: history vindicates lawyers' commitment to 'Unequal Justice'. But for most social scientists, it is simply ignored, and this on two counts. On the one hand, sociological and economic theoretical formulations may be detached from systematic historical research that would qualify and specify their proclivities to historically dissociated generalizations. On the other hand, the generalizing dispositions of other social sciences may give less credence to specifically historical problematics—the peculiarities of the British, the German problem, the exceptionalism of American institutions, the French Revolution. As a result, sociological theorizing about lawyers too often floats free from a grounded past, from the contingent understandings forced by close encounters with the *longue durée*. Generalizing theoretical impulses inadequately are disciplined by particularizing historical moments.

Third, the cultural hegemony of Anglo-American formulations of professionalism prevails, and with them, the primacy of the market. Such a theory has great merits, for it compels scholars to take measure of a primary institution in modern societies. But it is linked to a scholarship written in the shadow of weak states and in the grip of energetic markets and it cannot survive unscarred the exposure to other nations where strong states preceded vibrant capitalist markets, and where encounters with states define much of national identity, history, and markets themselves. If this critique applies to professions generally, it is compounded for lawyers, who in every modern 'liberal' state are defined in part by their obligations as officers of the courts, servants of public order, and masters of the 'language of the state'. Thus comparisons among national 'singularities' are the only way to overcome sociocentrism and to appraise rigorously the relative importance of markets for legal and other professions.

This book asserts that politics matter. They matter to lawyers. More importantly, they matter for the viability of liberal societies. To show they matter, we have brought together sociologists and historians to look afresh at the legal profession in the rise of modern, liberal societies. More precisely, we pose a new question for ourselves and for scholarship on professions: how have lawyers affected the rise of modern political liberalism? Of course, it is a question that far exceeds what one book can manage. But the question must be asked, not only for intellectual progress, but for insight into the extraordinary task of reconstructing twentieth-century political regimes that have been anything but liberal.

We have designed this collective project on lawyers and political liberalism in such a way as to force encounters across the barriers between disciplines, across time, and among places. We seek to show that politics matter, by comparing four countries: France and Germany, and Britain and the United States. Historically, the two former have been strong states, where state formation preceded the growth of liberal markets, where the state dominated civil society, and where legal professions were defined or defined themselves substantially in relation to the state—though we shall see that the German experience contrasted radically with that of France. The two latter countries, Britain and the United States, have historically been rich civil societies, weak states, and markets that developed faster than the states that came to regulate them. Their lawyers have both been relatively autonomous of the state, yet intimately implicated in its steady growth from the late nineteenth century to the present. All four countries have experimented with liberal politics, but not without cataclysms and reversals, revolution and war, advance and retreat. These experiments span more than two centuries and they will span the turn of a millenium—but the heart of the problem remains the same: how is it possible to create a liberal political order, where rights confine states and protect citizens, and how do lawyers impede or facilitate that political transformation?

Since sociologists and historians, European and North American scholars, bring disciplinary diversity to answers of these questions, we have paired an historian and sociologist on each country. Each of the sociologists writes from within his own theoretical perspective and each of the historians advances particularly historiographical views. Yet all converge on this simple, strangely neglected, proposition: politics matter. The introductory essay by Halliday and Karpik, 'Politics Matter', places national and historical differences in lawyers' forms of action within a common theoretical framework, whose dimensions are directly linked to the building and maintaining of the liberal polity. This interpretation of lawyers' encounters with liberalism is organized along three dimensions. First, we consider, historically and sociologically, the impact of lawyers' collective action on the moderation of absolutist, authoritarian, or totalitarian states. Second, we indicate ways that lawyers' associations contribute to the creation and defence of a civil society. And, third, we point to lawyers' roles in the expansion of citizenship rights.

Chapter 1 concludes with considerations of the limits to lawyers' liberal commitments and some broad brush strokes on differing national-historical profiles of lawyers' political action. Let us anticipate three general conclusions of our analysis. First, although lawyers' political orientations are more visible or less visible from one time to another in one country or another, they are always relevant. Thus the distinctiveness of action by national legal professions is brought into bolder relief by a framework that links lawyers to the formation and continuity of political liberalism.

Second, the diversity of meanings that lawyers attribute to political liberalism, and the variety of forms in which they have engaged in liberalizing politics, can be meaningfully connected to the difference between substantive democracy and procedural democracy. Third, it is impossible to comprehend long-term historical change for legal professions without taking into account their commitment to political liberalism. As a result, such an analysis of lawyers cannot be confined to the sociology of legal professions, as is usually the case, because it belongs also to history, historical sociology, and political sociology.

The second and third chapters demonstrate how the Paris Order of Barristers became a springboard for liberalizing political sentiments in the seventeenth and eighteenth centuries. Drawing on his larger work, *Lawyers and Citizens: The Making of a Political Elite in Old Regime France*,[5] historian David Bell charts the rise of barristers as an 'independent republic', an association that did not depend on royal decree or the state for its existence. From this exclusive, self-regulating voluntary corporation, barristers emerged as 'architects of civil society'. Since the Order was one of the very few institutions to escape censorship, and the courts provided a stage on which barristers could express their unmuffled views, barristers used the expedient of publishing briefs to shape the political sentiments of an educated public. As a self-designated 'organ of the People', the Order became a springboard for religious movements, such as Jansenism, and political theories that valorized an independent judiciary, limits on executive power, and the expansion of civil society. But after the 1760s, argues Bell, the process met its limits. As the Order itself lost control over entry to the bar and powers of self-regulation, the last twenty years before the Revolution undid the image of barristers as constitutionalists. New barrister-*philosophes* used their position to support the Jacobin assault on civil society, which sought to break down the barriers between the public and private and to eliminate intermediate associations. Whereas the previous century 'had seen the development of the Order of the Barristers

5 (New York, Oxford Univ. Press, 1994).

as an independent association between the state and individual subjects, the next twenty years saw its rapid disgrace, decline and final disappearance'. Political engagement, in other words, carried peril as well as promise. By embracing such new political ideals as the general will, many barristers embraced a political culture ultimately inimical to a viable civil society and its protection from 'a strong, rational unfettered executive power'.

Based on his historical sociology of the French Bar from the thirteenth to the twentieth Century, *Les avocats*,[6] Lucien Karpik argues an even stronger case for the primacy of French lawyers as 'collective actors who fashioned the liberal state as well as the liberal society' over the *longue durée*. Against the Anglo-Saxon model of legal professions as economic agents 'aloof from politics', Karpik's essay maintains that political action was a dominant organizing principle of collective activity by the Paris Bar. Indeed, through a series of episodes briefly recounted here, he demonstrates that lawyers helped craft both a civil society and a moderate state in eighteenth-century France. Through such actions as their defence of Jansenism and through the elaboration of citizens' rights in peasant trials of the eighteenth century, in alliance with the *Parlement* and against the absolute monarchy, lawyers articulated views that sovereignty resided in the public, that citizens had property rights and rights of free expression, and that individual freedoms could exist only within a moderate state. Through attacks, setbacks and reversals up to the Revolution and into the nineteenth century, lawyers nevertheless maintained a momentum as builders of liberal political society. They did so, most remarkably, Karpik proposes, by constituting themselves as 'spokesmen for the public'. They thereby both constituted the public and claimed to be its representatives on behalf of liberal ideals. While that political logic maintained its force through the nineteenth and first half of the twentieth century, it is now under attack by the logic of the market. But this long view reminds lawyers and scholars alike that contemporary French lawyers are heirs to a spirit of independence that still manifests itself episodically despite the encroachments of a market logic.

To explain this lasting commitment to political liberalism, Karpik connects two lines of analysis. On the one hand, lawyers' politicization is linked to a theory of the spokesmen of the public as a form of collective action. On the other hand, an interpretation of the Bar's durable

---

[6] L. Karpik, *Les avocats: Entre L'État, le public et le marché, XIIIe–XXe siècle* (Paris, Gallimard, 1995); (trans. Nora Scott), (Oxford, Oxford Univ. Press, forthcoming).

oppositionalism towards the state reveals a professional identity historically constituted around a moral principle and a spirit of independence. This identity was successfully maintained so long as the national
society was dominated by a political antagonism between the state and
the public.

Despite the historical contrasts conventionally drawn between the
trajectories of French and English politics and society, the two chapters
on English barristers reveal some surprising commonalities between the
two professions and their relations to liberal politics. Michael Burrage,
an English sociologist, turns the assault by Lady Thatcher (then Mrs
Thatcher) on the professions into a searching essay about the constitutional status of professions in English political life. Since crisis frequently
brings to the surface understandings and institutional relations that may
otherwise lie out of view, Burrage takes Mrs Thatcher's effort to redefine and enlarge the powers of the state as an occasion to understand
how professions, and most notably the Bar, came to occupy a seldom-
heralded position in the unwritten English constitution. While Mrs
Thatcher's Government mounted its attack on the legal profession for
its economic inefficiencies, self-regulatory ideals and historical precedents were treated, Burrage writes, with scepticism and even contempt.
Burrage argues, however, that this cavalier disregard for history should
be held in tension with the fate of professions in the Glorious
Revolution of 1688–9. Like their French counterparts, English barristers (among others) were attacked by Charles II and James II as 'so
many little commonwealths, . . . little republics', whose continued existence 'would not be conducive to good government'. Like the French
barristers, whose autonomy also rested on custom, the English Bar
found itself threatened by a state jealous of its independence. But, says
Burrage, the accession of William and Mary restored to most chartered
bodies and the professions 'liberties and privileges,' which in fact come
to constitute what Burrage calls the 'deep structures' of English life.
From the seventeenth century to the late twentieth century, professional
self-government has remained substantially unchallenged as a pillar of
civil society, and thus as a bulwark of liberal political society. Ironies
abound, concludes Burrage, for not even Mrs Thatcher's attack on the
professions dented their appeal and deep-seated legitimacy as an
English institution. Moreover, under Mrs Thatcher's attacks, barristers
discovered their need to create public support. Indeed, government policy may have been oriented rather less to deregulation of the market
than to creation of a strong state.

Wesley Pue, a Canadian legal historian, takes a less benign view of the Bar in the eighteenth and nineteenth centuries, but he observes a strong trace of 'Frenchness' in the English Bar that shows distinct affinities with aspects of both portraits developed by Karpik and Bell for French avocats. Pue takes issue with two historical interpretations of English lawyers: their political quiescence since the Glorious Revolution; and their conservative disposition towards political stability in the face of 'the great liberating causes of the past two centuries'. At first blush, he says, English lawyers seem tame compared to the interventionist French lawyers, who challenged the state directly, and who used lawsuits to advance political causes, including concepts of legality and citizens' rights. While this may have been true of the great majority of the Bar, there are numerous instances where English barristers stepped on to the political stage and used courts, in particular, as a platform for advancing broadly liberal ideals. From the defence of Queen Caroline's divorce to the political movement of the Wilkites, from creation of procedures for criminal trials to advocacy of citizens' rights in the nineteenth century, barristers exercised political voice to inhibit state power and expand individual protections. Even if 'it is abundantly clear that English barristers have been actively involved in "liberal", "reform", or "radical" causes throughout the eighteenth and nineteenth centuries', the Benchers, a self-perpetuating oligarchy of Bar leaders, activated the regulatory powers of the Bar—admission and discipline— to muzzle the most outspoken 'spokesmen' for liberal causes. Thus, concludes Pue, 'a fully deliberate fettering of the independence of the English Bar by their own professional associations rendered English barristers a subservient profession by the standards of their French counterparts.' Like Karpik, Pue discovers English lawyer-spokesmen for the public, though never so many, nor so dominant. Like Bell, however, he finds internal professional conflicts, even repression, which substantially hobbled the impetus of the Bar's most 'liberal' leaders.

Germany represents an important comparative foil, not only because its lawyers eventually confronted liberalism's ultimate denouement, but because German lawyers were far more creatures of the state than were their English or French counterparts. Dietrich Rueschemeyer's interpretive essay embeds the historical experience of German lawyers with liberalism within two great institutional movements: the early emergence of strong states in Prussia and other German principalities and their uneven path towards the political unification of Germany; and the late capitalist development of the economy. Into these institutional changes lawyers sought to insert a liberal conception of their own profession, and of the profession and its members as advocates of a rule-governed liberal state. But the transition from 'a Bar of quasi-civil servants', which persisted into the late eighteenth century, into a private profession heavily modelled on the English pattern by the mid-nineteenth century, brought its own internal contradictions. The development of a thriving capitalist economy brought great new opportunities for legal work as it concomitantly sought stable contractual and property relations. The capitalist image of private parties contracting as equals lay 'at the heart of the new liberal ideology'. From the 1840s, German lawyers pressed for a free bar, for self-employment and self-regulation, for the creation of their own voluntary associations and the freedom of lawyers to engage in political activity. Their ideals and presence were pervasive in mid-century liberal politics. But to obtain emancipation from state control, lawyers sought open admissions to practise at significant material cost. In practice, open admissions brought larger numbers, a decline in income, and a large increase in the number and proportion of Jewish lawyers. As liberalism weakened in national politics, and 'overcrowding' led to internal fissures and the rise of anti-Semitism at the bar, the achievement of a 'free Bar' on the liberal model became vulnerable from inside and without. Ultimately, says Rueschemeyer, the historical precedence of a strong state, the complications of state-building, and the residue of a Civil Service orientation, all confounded the profession's liberal inclinations that had been stimulated by the English example and facilitated by late capitalist development. German lawyers had substantially succeeded in creating a *Rechtsstaat*, but the material and political price of their liberal ideals and accomplishments came high indeed.

It is the final episode in the fall of the German bar from its high liberalism of the 1840s to its demise as a liberal bastion in 1933 that engages Kenneth Ledford, a social historian of Germany, whose essay draws on his recently published book, *From General Estate to Special Interest: German Lawyers, 1878–1933*.[7] Ledford confronts the conundrum faced by German historians who puzzle how a profession seen as a bearer and ally of liberal political ideals, and an architect of the rule-governed state, could 'succumb so easily to the procedural irregularity and illiberalism of National Socialist co-ordination'. In face of competing theories of professional collapse, Ledford advances the ironic argu-

[7] K. Ledford, *From General Estate to Special Interest: German Lawyers, 1878–1933* (Cambridge, Cambridge Univ. Press, 1996).

ment that it was liberalism's own triumphs—the ascendancy of proceduralism in problem-solving, open admissions to the bar, and its elite-
dominated institutions—that laid the seeds of the bar's destruction.
Wed to procedural concepts of justice, the bar could not adapt to new
substantive notions of equal justice. Committed to open admissions, it
could not forestall internal conflict and forge a profession-wide consensus. Unable to resolve its own internal disputes, it found itself compelled
to turn to the state as arbiter. Divided hierarchically, in conflict over
economic and status interests—the profession could no longer sustain
any claim before the public to represent the 'general estate'. When confronted with gross substantive injustice, concludes Ledford, lawyers
remained within the framework of the paradigmatic independent profession, but thereby 'demonstrated the limits of procedural liberalism'.

The chapters on the United States display lawyers' encounter with the
three aspects of political liberalism—the moderate state, civil society,
and citizenship—principally from the vantage point of the market.
Politics matter, but inseparably from issues over supply of legal and judicial services. In the accounts of other chapters in this book, pressures for
the moderate state have come directly from lawyers and their allies.
Halliday and Carruthers demonstrate that American lawyers, not without some internal conflict, have mobilized actively, in a century-long
campaign, to differentiate American courts from party and executive
control. Yet the impulses for this moderation of the state, or division of
power, are not confined to lawyers acting through their state and federal associations. Drawing from their research on the reform of corporate bankruptcy law in the United States, Halliday and Carruthers show
that the financial industry allied with lawyers' groups to create bankruptcy courts that were efficient, neutral, and competent. The logic of
court reform was commercial: without strong courts with competent
judges, clear jurisdictions, and complete judicial impartiality, the powerful financial industry effectively threatened to 'veto' the legislation or
to search for alternative mechanisms outside the courts for effective
reorganizations of bankrupt companies. That commercial logic, however, coincided substantially with the historic push of American lawyers'
associations for formally rationalized justice. From both sides, therefore,
came a unity of purpose—the assertion of court independence and
autonomy. Commercial interests therefore emerge as potential bulwarks
of the judicial independence institutionalized in liberal political regimes.
But if strengthened, independent courts are more safe for the powerful,
it remains to explain the more fundamental question: when will courts

that are independent of political interference in commercial law extend that autonomy into the more contested areas of substantive rights around citizenship and political freedoms?

If Halliday and Carruthers show that pressures from financial institutions can complement lawyers' projects for independent courts, Grossberg, a social and legal historian of the United States, turns to the least powerful fringes of American society to explore how their needs for legal services correspond with lawyers' projects. More importantly, Grossberg demonstrates that a convergence of interests between the recipients of legal aid and their putative counsel have an institutional significance directly salient to a peculiarly American approach to state services, civil society and citizenship. Legal aid in America is a creation of the late nineteenth and early twentieth centuries. A moment of significant discontinuity occurred for American lawyers during those years and legal aid was a direct product of this professional turmoil. As the conscious creation of the American bar, legal aid reveals the particular political dynamics of the legal profession and the powerful role of lawyers in the reconstruction of the liberal state in America during that era. Purposely labelling their effort a professional reform, legal aid lawyers used their self-assumed role representing poor clients to police the profession's lower reaches and to protect its autonomy from state intervention and interference from other humanitarian efforts to aid the poor. Particularly importantly, most legal aid lawyers worked for private societies and the movement itself resisted the provision of legal services by the state. Staking out and defending the line between public and private thus became a critical and revealing role of the legal aid lawyers.

Legal aid, argues Grossberg, cannot be understood either as the singular product of changes wrought by industrial capitalism or simply as a functionalist response to swelling popular demands for representation. On the contrary, lawyers created legal aid in a conscious attempt to stake out new boundaries for legal practice in an era when the existing ones had become uncertain. They did so in part as distinctive participants in a new wave of humanitarianism, one dominated by professional interests and methods. Legal aid was, in short, a lawyers' reform that mediated the forces of change by emphasizing the liberal ideals of procedural justice and defending the legitimacy of the legal system itself. Equally important, legal aid also represented an attempt to redefine individual rights by detaching those rights from their traditional moorings to property ownership. By creating a new form of representation, legal aid participated in the era's redefinition of the relationship between individual autonomy and state authority.

Movements towards political liberalism take place in a historical canvas that extends well beyond any nation-state or particular legal profession. We would assert that professionalization cannot be detached from transnational and global movements in politics any more than in economics. However, we shall argue in the concluding essay on political liberalism and globalization that the dynamics and trajectories of economic and political globalization look substantially different, though they are not independent. 'Whereas markets universalize', we argue, 'politics particularize', and for this reason we can expect to see significantly wider variations on the theme of political than economic liberalism.

Historically, there are two contrasting models for lawyers' engagement with political liberalism: an apolitical model, represented by Britain, and a political model, represented by France. We review the conditions, mechanisms, and forces through which these models have moved about the world, sometimes as they are imposed by force, and at other times as they are adapted and reinterpreted by recipient countries. We observe how new models have been created, most notably the American model after the Second World War, which has become strongly favoured throughout the world in the train of United States' economic and political influence and the energetic entrepreneurialism of American lawyers. Within this perspective we can identify the global forces that explain, at least partially, the international similitudes and diversities in lawyers' engagements in the construction of liberal politics.

At the present time, powerful commercial forces attenuate the historic role of lawyers as agents of political liberalism. But as this book demonstrates over four countries and several centuries, it would be imprudent indeed to conclude that late twentieth-century developments have rendered lawyers' affinity for liberal politics either antiquarian or redundant. Even more imprudent would it be to assume that the production and reproduction of moderate states, civil society, or citizenship rights can be taken for granted and left without its champions.

We are grateful for the financial support received for the production of this book from several institutions. The National Science Foundation's Law and Society Program on Globalization provided substantial funding for our collective project. Together with the International Institute for the Sociology of Law, it underwrote a conference held in Oñati, Spain, in July 1993, and supported subsequent production costs. The American Bar Foundation extensively underwrote this collective project and we are indebted to its director, Bryant Garth, for his continued support for global studies of legal professions. Support was also provided by the Centre de Sociologie de L'Innovation, École des Mines, Paris.

We have received a great deal of valuable commentary and constructive criticism from colleagues at a variety of academic meetings, most especially from those organized by the Working Group on Comparative Studies of Legal Professions, from which this project initially emerged. In particular we thank our colleagues at the American Bar Foundation and at the Centre de Sociologie de L'Innovation, École des Mines, for their insights. Hannes Siegrist and David Sugarman were unable to join us in the final phase of this project, but their contributions to the Oñati conference, and subsequent critiques, have been most stimulating. We benefited also from the perceptive critiques of reviewers.

This project has been made possible by a great deal of editorial, administrative, research, and secretarial support from many colleagues. We are grateful for the early research assistance of Chan-ung Park, at the University of Chicago; for the excellent organization of our conference by the Oñati administrative staff, most notably Serena Barkham-Huxley; for the accomplished editorial guidance from Keith Hawkins and Richard Hart; for the production management of Dominic Shryane and the copy-editing of Charlotte Barrow; and not least, through the entire life of the project, for the superb administrative support and flawless competence of Brenda Smith, at the American Bar Foundation.

Finally, we wish to express our appreciation for the work and participation at earlier stages in the project of Terry Johnson. Shortly after our conference in Oñati, in which Terry participated, he suffered a debilitating illness that left him unable to continue with the project. However, readers will see our indebtedness to several of his perceptive ideas and analyses in both the first chapter and the Postscript to this book.

1 Politics Matter: a Comparative Theory of Lawyers in the Making of Political Liberalism

Terence C. Halliday and Lucien Karpik

Three theoretical systems have dominated scholarship on professions: functionalism, market control, and jurisdictional control. The first studies how a community could maintain cultural conformity in order to achieve a service relationship; the second concentrates on the monopolistic strategy of extracting market rent and thus social privilege; and the third treats the deployment of knowledge for the creation and defence of work jurisdictions as a way to define boundaries between work domains. Although significantly different from each other, these approaches have one feature in common—the neglect of politics. That politics is a marginal reality can be observed even if the scholarly frame is enlarged to include new class theories[1] and theories based on knowledge.[2] With few exceptions, lawyers were and still are considered as *homo socius* or *homo economicus*, but never as *homo politicus*.[3]

The rediscovery of politics has come recently. The main contributions have appeared almost simultaneously from scholars dispersed across different countries, several of whom are represented in this

---

[1] A. W. Gouldner, *The Future of Intellectuals and the Rise of the New Class* (New York, Seabury Press, 1979); I. Szelznyi & B. Martin, 'The Legal Profession and the Rise and Fall of the New Class', in R. Abel & P. S. C. Lewis (eds.), *Lawyers in Society*, vol. 3, *Comparative Theories* (Berkeley, Univ. of California Press, 1989).

[2] C. K. Derber, W. Schwartz, & Y. Magrass, *Power in the Highest Degree* (New York, Oxford Univ. Press, 1990); A. Abbott, *The System of Professions: An Essay on the Division of Expert Labor* (Chicago, Univ. of Chicago Press, 1988).

[3] One important exception is provided by Talcott Parsons, who sketched two relevant lines of analysis. On the one hand, he considered lawyers' action to be the result of an ambiguous but dynamic relationship with the state. Lawyers redefine political authority as well as transform their clients' relationships with political society (T. Parsons, 'A Sociologist Looks at the Legal Profession', in T. Parsons (ed.), *Essays in Sociological Theory* (Glencoe, Ill., Free Press, 1954), 370–85). On the other hand, he opened the way to the specific study of internal bar politics with the notion of a 'collegial association' that can coalesce with a 'company of equals'. See T. Parsons, *The Social System* (Glencoe, Ill., Free Press, 1951); T. Parsons & G. M. Platt, *The American University* (Cambridge, Harvard Univ. Press, 1973), 103–62, 284. See also the important recent study by R. Shamir, *Managing Legal Uncertainty* (Durham, NC, Duke Univ. Press, 1994).

volume. Together we challenge the neglect of politics and show that under specific conditions politics is systematically linked to the legal profession, that politics may become a dominant principle of lawyers' collective action, and that politics therefore demands its own theoretical frame and programme of empirical research.

The general hypothesis that orients our analysis, however, is more demanding for two reasons. On the one hand, it proposes that what matters is not politics *per se* but a specific form of politics, namely, political liberalism. This notion is necessarily imprecise since it covers several countries and several historical periods, and it reflects a complex phenomenon with numerous streams and transformations. Precise meanings can only be given within specific contexts, but provisionally we define it in terms of the liberal polity, which includes citizenship and the moderate state, and liberal political society, which includes civil society and the existence of independent publics. On the other hand, we look not only at lawyers as one part of the universe of political liberalism who are influenced by global changes, political forces and ideologies, but above all as they have been active in constructing political ideas, formulating and fighting for political goals, and transforming political reality. Moreover, posing the problems of lawyers' politics in terms of their engagement with political liberalism compels us to transcend everyday political activity, and to confront the taken-for-granted, institutional foundations of politics. Indeed, much of everyday politics can be reinterpreted, and given a wider context, with the liberal question squarely on the agenda. Our perspective argues that Western legal professions have historically been engaged in 'political projects' that constitute political liberalism. They have been among the builders of the liberal state and society.

This approach is not confined to the past. Lawyers' association with the classical centre of a nineteenth- and sometimes eighteenth-century liberalism does not render them irrelevant to the twentieth century. In point of fact, the nucleus of liberalism has been sharply contested throughout this century by war, totalitarian and authoritarian political movements, military dictatorship, conquest, and internal purges. Early nineteenth-century political liberalism, albeit in more contemporary guise, recurs in such diverse circumstances as post-Second World War democratization movements, the collapse of Communism in Eastern Europe, and the transition of South American politics from bureaucratic authoritarian and military regimes to more liberal societies. Even in societies where the liberal core seems safely protected, lawyers are periodically forced to defend or rethink the classical liberal core. One needs only to recall the position of the Parisian bar during the Algerian War, the New York City bar on non-self-incrimination during the McCarthy period, and a minority of the United States bar on free speech and rights of association during the Civil Rights era. If they are ever to take a concerted stand, it must be on lawyers' distinctive conception of liberalism, a conception much narrower than broad political definitions, and one that is closely tied specifically to the rule of law. Therefore this battle is never settled. Even in democratic societies, the question of individual liberties is still lively. Although on a different scale, the old struggle remains, often in such new contexts as the consequences of unemployment or immigration. Moreover, new forms of liberalism have appeared with the extension of rights and the transformation of the state. Their relationships with legal professions still remain to be understood.

Let us sharpen our focus at the outset. First, to consider political commitment as collective action requires attention to both corporate and individual action, whether the latter are oriented or co-ordinated by the bar, or whether individual actions are acknowledged by the bar as individual activity on its collective behalf. Second, we do not assume that lawyers across countries, or within countries over the *longue durée*, have always been centrally interested in politics. That assumption would amount to the same fallacy as those we critique, namely, that social actors are perpetually driven by material interests and are predominantly inclined to increase their profits through market control. We argue that only under certain conditions, which we begin to specify, will lawyers adopt politics as a dominant basis of collective action. Third, we do not presuppose that lawyers have always stood shoulder to shoulder with liberal reformers. Any theoretically robust account must follow lawyers not only in their commitment to political liberalism, but also in their association with anti-liberalism, or with politics outside the realm of liberalism. But we do posit that political liberalism is a useful heuristic rule to follow for describing and explaining lawyers' political action. Fourth, we do not postulate that lawyers have followed, interpreted, or defended every brand of liberalism. On the contrary, we shall show that they usually have adopted, formulated and fought for a specific form of liberalism.

Until this point we have used the notion of lawyer in a diffuse way. To define it more precisely is to meet the difficulty stemming from a great deal of international diversity that is rooted in very different forms

of the division of labour and in very different institutional arrangements. The two most contrasting cases are probably the United States
and France. In the former case, the concept of lawyer encompasses
attorneys, judges and legal professors; in the latter case, it is much more
limited, as lawyers are not only independent from judges and legal professors but also from professions such as the *notaires* or the *avoués* which
have quite specific legal functions.[4] The only way to overcome this classic difficulty in international comparison is to link the profession to a
specific activity which we will find everywhere, whatever the title. We
call 'lawyers' those professionals whose task is to represent and to
defend others, whether individuals or corporate clients. This representation may take place in or out of court, whether through representation by a solicitor or office lawyer in negotiations or contracts, or
through court appearances. In some countries, such as the United
States, representation may extend to congressional hearings, public
examinations, and the like.[5] Lawyers can be private practitioners or
public defenders. But the constant and distinct criterion, everywhere—
its definitional core—is the right to prepare and carry out a defence of
clients in court, despite the fact that those functions are sometimes
divided.

Few genuine comparative studies can be found in the burgeoning literature on lawyers,[6] although there are significant advances in national
studies on common agendas.[7] Our study is based on the analysis of four
national experiences in Western countries: France, England, Germany,
and the United States. It seeks to transcend parochialism and to
develop a general approach that has relevance to each country without
denying their singularity. Yet it is clear that the development of political liberalism in general and the implication of the legal professions in

---

[4] Public notaries (*notaires*) had the monopoly over the writing of authentic documents,
for real sales, inheritance papers, and the like. Lawyers (*avocats*) and attorneys (*avoués*) were
responsible for defence in the courts. Lawyers usually conducted the lawsuits and had a
monopoly of pleadings; attorneys dealt with the written part of the proceedings through
certification and deposition of documents. This latter division was abolished in 1972. See
E. Suleiman, *Private Power and Centralization in France: The Notaires and the State* (Princeton,
Princeton Univ. Press, 1987), 331–2.

[5] See D. Rueschemeyer's 'Comparing Legal Professions: A State-Centered Approach',
in R. Abel & P. S. C. Lewis (eds.), *Lawyers in Society* for a proposal for a functional definition that transcends national and historical particularities.

[6] Compare D. Rueschemeyer, *Lawyers and their Society: A Comparative Study of the Legal
Profession in Germany and in the United States* (Cambridge, Mass., Harvard Univ. Press, 1973).

[7] R. Abel & P. S. C. Lewis (eds.), *Lawyers in Society* (3 vols., Berkeley, Univ. of Calif.
Press, 1988–9).

Western constitutionalism belong to transnational processes. Therefore it is necessary for us to follow the evolution of professional politics in different countries, to explore the general mechanisms and forces which could explain lawyers' political action, and through them to identify convergences across countries. The priority given to national studies should be considered as a first and necessary step for the study of the process and limits of political globalization. The themes of transnational and global dynamics of lawyers and political liberalism are taken up in the Postscript. Our effort to appraise how far the 'political projects' of professions can be seen as a transnational phenomenon with national variations has been significantly advanced by the respective contributions of a historian and sociologist on each country.

This introduction proposes a general framework and demonstrates its utility. In order to accomplish this in a limited space we make several oversimplifications. Some of these choices are contingent and should not be confused with theoretical stances. First, the conflation of events, when we seek to summarize a profession's complex historical evolution in a few sentences, can suggest a tone of 'retrospective determinism', as Rueschemeyer has styled it. But we recognize that, for the actors, the present is uncertain; we only become 'sophisticated' in our interpretation of these uncertainties after history has been made. In other words, the failure of professions to achieve a liberal outcome does not mean that the actors were not convinced by the goals for which they were fighting. Second, and for the same reason of brevity, we equate the bar and collective action. But of course this relation is anything but mechanical. As our collaborators repeatedly demonstrate, national bars experience many conflicts. In fact, it is through internal divisions and battles that collective action becomes possible. But in this chapter we have chosen mostly to give more weight to the choices than to the means by which they were (and are) achieved. Third, the contributions display some variation in interpretive approaches. For the sake of an integrated analysis we have chosen to ignore this theoretical diversity.

We begin with the proposition that the collective autonomy of legal professions may be strongly linked to the development of political liberalism. We then appraise lawyers' politics against an ideal type of three central elements of political liberalism: constituting the moderate state, through judicial restraint on sovereign or executive power; constituting civil society, principally through the creation of publics; and constituting citizenship, through grants of individual rights. Societies vary in both their relative emphasis on each of these and their historical sequence. We demonstrate how the national studies display the rich dimensionality, and substantial contingency, of lawyers' political engagement over time and place. In the conclusion of this chapter we derive from the case studies several propositions that can orient future research. In the Postscript, we shall return to the dimensions of political liberalism as a transnational phenomenon. The tension between national politics and global movements adds another key dynamic to the explanation of why legal professions choose to engage politics in the manner distinctive to their national histories and yet in an often surprisingly similar way across those histories.

The Collective Autonomy of Lawyers and the Moderate State

The traditions of anti-absolutist thought can be divided into two streams, one exemplified by Locke and derived from medieval Christian thought, and the other epitomized by Montesquieu and derived from the political ideas of classical Greece, with some indebtedness to medieval politics.[8] The 'Montesquieu' stream of thought sought the foundations of modern political liberalism not in a prepolitical civil society, but in the dispersion of power throughout political society. Montesquieu elaborated on feudal frameworks of governance where a system of rights and duties bound lords and vassals, sovereigns and subjects, into a legal frame in which each had their rightful place and specific obligations. Medieval political regimes were punctuated by relatively independent cities, with jealously protected prerogatives. The estates of the Middle Ages vindicated the principle that certain alternative power centres must be accommodated by the sovereign.

Montesquieu's theory of the separation of powers distributed power not only among different branches of the state, but also in both the centre and periphery of political society. Thus, in the same tradition, Alexis de Tocqueville portrayed the strength of democracy in America as a lattice-work of political associations. These performed two functions. They were at once bulwarks against despotism, because they presented alternative centres of opinion and power outside the state; and they were classrooms for self-rule, because they taught political expression and political arts in the local community.

[8] C. Taylor, 'Invoking Civil Society', *Working Papers and Proceedings of the Center for Psychosocial Studies*, no. 31 (Chicago, Ill., 1990).

In Taylor's interpretation, this vision of the moderate state has five primary components:

(1) an emphasis on the rule of law, as it is expressed through constitutionalism or proceduralism;
(2) strong '*corps intermédiaires*' to defend the rule of law, that is, bodies in civil society that will spring to the defence of constitutionalism, the courts, legal proceduralism, and other pillars of the rule of law;
(3) strong political associations, such as political parties and interest groups, which presented the politically active face of voluntary associationalism to the exercise of power;
(4) the institutional separation of powers within the state, including an independent judicial system; and
(5) a balance of national and local political authority, as in federalism, or in the English local government/Westminster arrangement.

In this section, we focus on the connections between strong intermediate bodies, such as lawyers' associations, and the institutional structure of the state.

The autonomy of legal professions as a political project is reciprocally tied to the rise of liberal political systems. Professional self-government exists not merely as an end in itself, but as an integral element of an emerging political regime where bar autonomy becomes, potentially, an instrument to constrict the power of the state more broadly. Bar autonomy is a weapon that, in certain circumstances, can defend the interests and liberty of itself, other intermediate groups, and citizens more generally. Political autonomy is not therefore a spontaneous creation of civil society, but an artefact of social construction in response to diverse political, economic, and religious situations, and it requires constant adaptation to and reconstruction of cultural and institutional change. Moreover, as the national case studies demonstrate, bar autonomy cannot be separated from the relative autonomy of judges and the courts: indeed the autonomy of the administration of justice from the sovereign and executive agencies constitutes, for lawyers, the principal axis of political engagement over the separation of powers. The studies of Germany, France, Britain, and the United States indicate significant variety in the emphasis given to independence, in the strength of the link with judicial independence, and in the degree of professional mobilization for judicial autonomy.

A. *England: Autonomy before Statehood*

Our two studies on England reveal a creative tension between two kinds of professional politics: one, observed in Burrage's chapter, speaks directly to the constitution of the moderate state; the other, considered by Pue, relates to civil society and citizenship, to which we return in the next section.

An independent Bar, jealous of its prerogatives, long precedes the birth of the modern state in England. By the fourteenth and fifteenth centuries, the Inns of Court were firmly established as guilds without reliance for their existence or authority on either royal decree or parliamentary statute. Burrage argues in this book that the Bar's independence has been fundamentally challenged only twice since early modern times—once in the reign of James II and once again by the government of Margaret Thatcher three centuries later.

Following the English Civil War, the restoration of Charles II (who favoured tolerance of Roman Catholics) and the subsequent reign of the Roman Catholic James II, together precipitated a conflict with municipalities, universities, and associations, whose charters or historical prerogatives gave them some independence from the Crown. Without bringing these somewhat autonomous bodies to heel, 'there would be so many little commonwealths, by themselves independent of the crown, in defiance of it, little republics would spring up all over the Kingdom which would not be conducive to good government.'[9] However, the revolution that installed William and Mary on the throne defended the rights of these 'little republics' and affirmed the cross-party consensus that self-regulating professions both constitute civil society and provide a foundation of English constitutionalism.

Except in rare occasions of political crisis, therefore, the English legal profession came to occupy an invisible status in the body politic. England's unwritten constitution implicitly assigned constitutional status to bodies outside the state that keep Westminster at arm's length, in part by distributing power between the central authority in Westminster and local power in city boroughs, county councils, and local municipalities. The ancient universities and professions boasted a similar standing as time-honoured centres of power clearly outside the direct sphere of state intervention and thus, albeit invisibly, pillars of a robust civil society. The same was true for the judiciary.

---

[9] Quoted in M. Burrage, 'Mrs Thatcher Against Little Republics', chap. 4 *infra*.

The very conditions of this unwritten liberal constitutionalism can only be hidden as long as they remain unthreatened. It took Mrs Thatcher's policy of abruptly reducing the powers of professions to reopen the debate. First, the strong hostility of barristers and solicitors towards her policy revealed that Bar autonomy was still considered crucial by the lawyers. Second, and curiously enough, as Burrage provocatively demonstrates,[10] the constitutional status of English justice was thrust into political debate not when the courts were under fire, but when the solicitors and the Bar—whose members practise in the courts and selectively rise to the Bench—were under threat of reorganization from Mrs Thatcher's Conservative Government. The defence of barristers' ancient prerogatives to exclusive rights of audience and self-governance stimulated a flood of constitutional self-justification, which wrapped the organization of the Bar in the robes of the unwritten constitution. The Bar protested that an independent judiciary was integral to English democracy. And the viability of an autonomous Bench could scarcely be conceived without an autonomous Bar, whose ancient rights were entrenched in English constitutionalism from medieval times. Like the French, therefore, the English Bar owed nothing of its independence to any grant of sovereign authority. And in a similar sense, it was able to claim deep roots in civil society that provided the ballast for a judicial institution in the structurally awkward position of being in the state but not of it.

Third, although the attack by the Conservative Government was dangerous, the profession's reaction was inept. Caught by surprise, lawyers demonstrated that they had long taken for granted their collective powers as 'natural'. Public politics were not their suit, nor were they very successful at attracting popular support for their cause. Contrary to the French lawyers, who were long habituated to the opposition of the state, English lawyers could draw on no ready repertoire of arguments and actions to defend their autonomy: a depoliticized body could not easily divine what arguments would persuade the English public. Essentially they needed time to re-invent the political principles that would vindicate their independence.[11] The by-product of the Thatcherite attack was consequently a heightened sensitivity by professions towards their public. Now that their vulnerabilities were transparent, solicitors and barristers moved perceptibly to shore up their support from the public, mostly by educating

[10] Ibid.   [11] Ibid.

clients and the public-at-large about the values of constitutional autonomy for lawyers.

Mrs Thatcher's effort to legislate on the organization of legal representation therefore attempted what the seventeenth century monarchs
had failed to do—subject barristers to legislation for the first time in
their five- or six-hundred-year history. Parliamentary initiatives
assaulted the presumption that lawyers' authority lay not in a grant of
powers from the Crown or Parliament, but in civil society itself. The
autonomy of law and the 'sovereignty' of the professions, therefore,
counterbalanced state power, not on the sufferance of state largesse, but
with the time-honoured ballast of civil authority. In English constitutionalism, not the state, but the professions asserted their customary
calling to understand the public interest, and to do so according to a
principle of disinterestedness.

Burrage shows that the reform made on behalf of free markets would
have, as its main consequence, a concentration of state power. It took
strong state power to limit the traditional regulatory power of the bar
and this weakening of lawyers' autonomy permitted the state the more
easily to enlarge its intervention. Deregulation meant concomitantly,
and paradoxically, more market *and* more state power. More precisely,
the English case is a good test of the thesis that the independence lost
by the bar and the judiciary is the gain of executive authority. It took
the conflicts and disturbances of the 'deep structure' of English institutions to reveal these taken-for-granted foundations of English political
life.

B. *France: Autonomy from Statehood*

French lawyers became actively engaged in political action against the
absolutist state from the beginning of the eighteenth century. Together
with the courts, they developed a rhetoric of limited government, in
which the monarchy was subject to the rule of law and which, in turn,
was institutionalized and defended in the *parlements*.[12] The occasions,

[12] Under the Ancien Régime, the *Parlement* was a semi-judicial and semi-political institution. As a High Court, it received and decided appeals from the lower courts. It also
had a political function, which it aspired to extend, that was founded on the right of registering new laws (*droit d'enregistrement*) and the right of remonstrance (*droit de remontrance*).
The law could not be applied until it was registered and during the 18th century the
Parlement increasingly used its right of remonstrance and refused to register the king's decisions. Its opposition could only be overcome by an assembly, with the king present, called
the '*Lit de Justice*'. There were twelve *parlements*, but by far the most prestigious and influential was the *Parlement de Paris*. The Parisian *parlement* was created in the 13th century,
followed by the other *parlements* in the 15th and 16th centuries.

forms, and means of lawyers' engagement were diverse, but not their aims. In the final century before the French Revolution, lawyers joined a multiform opposition with the courts against royal absolutism.

First, lawyers took part in the numerous and tumultuous battles between the *Parlement* and the Crown on the central issue of sharing power. For a long period, until the breakdowns in the 1770s described by Bell, lawyers and the courts found common cause against arbitrary absolutism. The courts reinforced lawyers' propensity to contest royal edicts. And the bar used the courts as a protective canopy to resist the executive power of the king in his alliance with the church hierarchy. The Bar brought its own independent standing, and its means of political expression, to fortify the independent position of the *parlements*. Faithful to the *Parlement*, not only because they were part of the judicial universe, but also because they were willing to limit absolute power, again and again lawyers went on strike, sometimes for long periods. On occasion they stalled completely the judicial machine at a time when justice was still considered as the prime function of the state, thereby embarrassing the royal authorities.[13]

Second, autonomous action by the Bar appeared for the first time with the complex political and religious issue of Jansenism, an Augustinian movement within the Catholic church that challenged many ideas of the Counter-Reformation and seemed to contemporaries to veer dangerously close to Protestantism.[14] Louis XIV, deeply suspicious of the Jansenists, and aided and abetted by his allies in the church hierarchy, drove Jansenism underground with a series of repressive actions. But Jansenism had attained a substantial foothold especially in Paris and with the bar. After Louis XIV's death in 1715, lawyers began to mobilize actively against this repression, most effectively through *consultations*, or *factums*, written and signed by lawyers, which circulated audacious political–legal arguments, sometimes publicly and sometimes secretly, thereby effectively evading censorship of dissenting opinions. A complicated episode that lasted from 1728 until 1731 demonstrated most powerfully that the bar itself, under the leadership of the *bâtonnier* (the president), became a political actor. Its criticisms, such as the idea that 'laws are contracts between those who govern and those who are

---

[13] L. Karpik, *Les avocats: Entre l'État, le public et le marché, XIIIᵉ–XXᵉ siècle* (Paris, Gallimard, 1995); (trans. Nora Scott), (Oxford, Oxford Univ. Press, forthcoming).

[14] D. A. Bell, 'Barristers, Politics, and the Failure of Civil Society in Old Regime France', chap. 2 *infra*. See also D. A. Bell, *Lawyers and Citizens: The Making of a Political Elite in Old Regime France* (New York, Oxford Univ. Press, 1994).

governed', directly confronted the fundamental principles of the absolute monarchy, for the intimation of a social contract between governors and the governed displaced divine election and threatened a breach between the king and nation.[15]

Could the Bar define a strategy, mobilize people and resources, protect its members and fight such powerful adversaries as the Crown or the church without autonomy? The link between both realities is direct: collective action arose at the beginning of the eighteenth century as a way to express the reality of an independent body that had been created in the last half of the seventeenth century out of an institutional organization in which lawyers were under the direct control of the *Parlement*. Self-government developed through informal delegation of power from the *Parlement* and was reinforced during the eighteenth century by a reciprocal alliance of the bar with the *Parlement* against the king and church. This alliance was critical for lawyers as it was the condition for protecting their individual liberties and for fighting for common goals. The Revolution dissolved the Bar. Napoleon resuscitated it but with diminished powers, a policy maintained with variations till 1870. During that entire period lawyers were involved in a sustained battle to recover their integrity. After re-establishment in 1870, their autonomy has been maintained to the 1990s without interruption.[16]

Autonomy is a specifying attribute of professions, especially in Anglo-Saxon countries. But as contexts vary, it takes on different meanings. In France, autonomy did not only mean that lawyers could freely elect their representatives, govern themselves through general rules and discipline, and protect themselves from outside powers. It meant also that they had the will and capacity to mobilize for political action. Autonomy was not limited to the control of professional matters; it extended to the very possibility—rooted or not in the court-rooms—of opposing the state. It is thus a demanding notion and it raises the puzzle about how it could be maintained under royal absolutism, as well as, with minor limitations, under authoritarian regimes.

The principal basis of Bar autonomy in France during the Ancien Régime was judicial independence. From its very beginning the monarchy required a credible system of justice to act as the central instrument for creating and maintaining civil peace. And from the beginning, royal

---

[15] L. Karpik, 'French Lawyers and Politics', chap. 3 *infra*. This theme is developed more fully in L. Karpik, 'Lawyers and Politics in France, 1814–1950: The State, the Market and the Public', *Law & Social Inquiry*, 13 (1988), 707–40.

[16] Karpik, 'Lawyers and Politics in France, 1814–1950'; Karpik, *Les avocats*.

officials were obliged to permit the individual independence of lawyers in order to obtain an independent defence as the basis of independent justice. For a long time the protection of lawyers' autonomy was provided by the *Parlement*. Subsequently the bar's collective independence was strongly rooted in the fight by the *parlements* for greater independence from the Crown, in the alliance with the *parlements* and later with other political forces and the liberal opinion. For two complementary reasons the link between the independence of the justice system and the independence of the Bar prevented any radical move from a state not completely immune from the temptation of getting rid of this opposition: on one hand, the lawyers could mobilize powerful forces on their side; and on the other hand, the risk that the state might hurt the public representation of justice was too high. Therefore the state's attempts at control, whenever they existed, remained weak, limited and finally inefficient.

If Bar autonomy was a necessary condition for political involvement, it was not sufficient: internal divisions and conflicts could destroy the basis for collective action. Until the 1770s, French barristers had common purposes and maintained a strong solidarity. While they were unified, they exuded invulnerability. But in the two decades preceding the Revolution, as Bell clearly shows,[17] the Bar began to shatter internally, the *bâtonnier* lost his authority, and by the time of the Revolution, the conflict had become so acute that some lawyers asked for dissolution of the bar. For them autonomy was over. When the deluge came, both the autonomous Bar and the independent *parlements* were swept away.[18] Even though the numbers of dissenters were relatively few, and not all were lawyers, nevertheless for the first time a section of the Bar had emerged which refused to admit to the importance or necessity of belonging to the Bar. The willingness to be incorporated within the corporate actor had disappeared, and with it went one of the conditions of the Bar's collective autonomy, a circumstance that bears an eerie resemblance to the events of the German bar at the end of the Weimar Republic. Although acute, however, this crisis has remained rather exceptional: in very different contexts, the internal rules of the game and the minimal agreement of autonomy were respected. In sum, political engagement of the profession has required both collective autonomy and a relative unity.

[17] Bell, chap. 2 *infra*.
[18] For an extended account of the immediate pre-revolutionary period, in the context of the 18th cent., see Bell, *Lawyers and Citizens*, 1994.

C. *The United States: Statehood as Autonomy*

The concept of a moderate state, with a judiciary at arm's length from legislative and executive control, permeated the drafting of the American constitution, and the debates over its ratification. But the powerful defences of judicial independence in *The Federalist Papers*,[19] and elsewhere, scarcely laid the problem to rest. The independence of judges and courts became politically contested just as soon as the potential powers of the courts to strike down legislation became apparent in the early nineteenth century.

From the eighteenth century forward, autonomy of the profession was intertwined explicitly and repeatedly with the concept of the moderate state. The colonial profession inherited certain ideals and elements of the English bar, including notions of guilds, circuits, and the expectation of professional independence. The American Revolution eventually destroyed the ancient regime of private self-governing associations,[20] and they were not revived until the 1870s.

Yet the American bar differs from other countries in its centrality to constitutional construction. Bar autonomy was not only a form of organizational protection for lawyers; it was directly and perpetually linked with judicial independence and therefore with the central organization of the polity. The proximity of courts to politics—to the executive and political parties—became a central drama in the legal history and professional politics of the American republic. Since the 1870s, bar associations have been agents of a century-long campaign to formally rationalize the court system. Indeed, the *raison d'être* of bar organization in the late nineteenth century may be attributed as much to the desire to upgrade the administration of justice as to self-regulate the profession. Studies of the New York City Bar Association[21] and the Chicago Bar Association[22] reveal an extensive mobilization by lawyers to keep city 'political machines' at bay. The techniques varied from decade to decade and from one part of the country to another. But their general

---

[19] A. Hamilton, J. Madison, & J. Jay, *The Federalist Papers* (New York, The New American Library, 1788 [1961]) no. 78.

[20] See M. Burrage, 'Revolution as a Starting Point for the Comparative Analysis of the French, American, and English Legal Professions', in Abel & Lewis (eds.), *Lawyers in Society*, vol. 3.

[21] M. J. Powell, *From Patrician to Professional Elite: The Transformation of the New York City Bar Association* (New York, Russell Sage Foundation, 1988).

[22] T. C. Halliday, *Beyond Monopoly: Lawyers, State Crises and Professional Empowerment* (Chicago, Univ. of Chicago Press, 1987).

thrust was similar: to assure the merit appointment of lower court judges; to permit the judiciary to govern itself in a hierarchical, rationally-organized, state-wide system, so that individual courts could not be manipulated by local politicians.

Compared to European legal liberalism, however, the American variant was strongly judge-centred. In the liberal model of jurisprudence, lawyers were no longer satisfied to be 'orator-statesmen', but legislative reformers of the civil service, of voting, of court procedure, and of crooked judges. But this action was a specific way of moderating the state by elevating the courts and thus the profession. In his overview of lawyers' engagement in judicial politics, Halliday and Carruthers' chapter shows that a strong commitment to reform of the judiciary has been a unifying theme in the politics of elite lawyers since the 1870s. The underlying juridical assumption of this nation-wide movement rests firmly on liberal ideology, for it presumes that only neutral courts, removed from the interference of party politicians, and staffed by expert judges, can withstand the tyranny of the majority, a central conundrum in the constitutional debates and *The Federalist Papers* from the founding of the Republic.

Celebrated battles range from President Roosevelt's efforts to 'pack' the Supreme Court through the Civil Rights era and into the bitter confirmation hearings of Judges Bork and Clarence Thomas. But if it is a battle never won, the bar has achieved a number of victories, not least of which is the involvement of the American Bar Association in the selection of federal judges, and the uneven moves towards the merit selection of judges in state courts.

Lawyers have been key players on both sides of the campaign to remove courts from the orbit of partisan control. Those lawyers with strong ties to parties have historically supported elections of judges and legislative control over judicial financing and budgets. Elite lawyers in their turn have more often favoured the independence of the courts, whether in methods of appointment, financing, jurisdiction, or internal management. Their primary vehicle was bar associations, and they came very substantially to define themselves in terms of judicial independence from direct political interference in the administration of justice.

However, the impetus towards independence of the courts comes not only from constitutionally-minded bar associations. Halliday and Carruther's chapter demonstrates that a major thrust towards court independence has come from the financial and commercial communities, whose recourse to the institutions of justice has been contingent, in their view, on the ability of courts to deliver justice of high quality that is not unencumbered by any political interference or patronage consideration. In other words, economic interest in judicial neutrality has effectively come to be in consonance with the reform campaigns of the organized bar.[23] Yet lawyers, too, have been jealous of their autonomy, as Grossberg shows through the debates over the institutional location and funding of legal aid. Here lawyers fought simultaneously on two fronts, for they strongly resisted funding of legal aid from the state and they resisted entanglements with non-lawyer groups which also aspired to aid or fund the poor who were in legal difficulties. From the state they feared that financial subsidies could lead to supervision and to erosion of lawyers' prerogatives to defend clients, often against the state itself. From private groups, they feared competition from other professionals that would coincidentally diminish protection available to clients.[24]

Professional autonomy in the United States therefore rests on a dual foundation: on the one hand, professional autonomy from political intervention derives from lawyers' alliances with powerful clients who demand some guarantee of a neutral justice unalloyed with party and patronage bias; on the other hand, professional autonomy from state incursions relies upon the protection of the courts, with which lawyers have formed alliances to effect a differentiation of the substantive rationality of political purpose from the formal rationality of procedural justice. Lawyers' dual alliance with courts and factions of their clients not only provides them with degrees of freedom from either ally, but this alliance moderates the state by attenuating the fusion of judicial and executive functions.

D. Germany: Statehood before Autonomy

Formation of the German legal profession as a nation-wide, independent, collegial, self-governing entity, long post-dated the foundations of the German Civil Service and the administrative apparatus of the modern German state. Professional autonomy must therefore be understood as the result of active differentiation from the state, a path to institutional freedom, for by obtaining some measure of autonomy, lawyers

---

[23] It remains an open question, however, how far a court system that is relatively autonomous in matters of commercial adjudication can convert that independence into measures of autonomy for decisions on cases that have political implications. Research must show the conditions under which transitions will take place from courts that are independent from external influences in commercial cases to courts that will overturn any legislation or frustrate executive power.

[24] M. Grossberg, 'The Politics of Professionalism', chap. 9 *infra*.

were concomitantly moderating the power of the state, and providing courts with an ally that was independently anchored in civil society.

Rueschemeyer's chapter shows that German lawyers shared many of the European-wide, liberal ideals that infused the 1848 revolutions, where lawyers could frequently be counted in the vanguard. They aimed to break free of the civil service, and to wrench the law, courts, and the Bar away from the tight grip of the absolutist state. The liberal political parties became natural allies in their commitment to the rule of law and its presumption of an independent judiciary. And in their search for a *Rechtsstaat*, the liberal Bar intertwined its own future with that of the Bench.[25] A liberal society requires a judiciary somewhat emancipated from Civil Service control and free from patronage appointments. Such a judiciary, of course, would be repugnant, on the one side, to the Civil Service's pretensions to efficient public administration, and on the other side, to the populists' wariness of elite jurists who were beyond accountability to popular government. For the state to be subject to restraint by law, however, it was imperative for the Bar to be open, highly qualified, self-governing, and thereby 'free' of bureaucratic control, even at the price of economic interests. But the relative autonomy of German lawyers was delayed long after our other national cases, since the creation of the German Bar Association took place as late as 1879, after German unification.

But if the independence of the courts and profession grew together from the 1840s, reaching their zenith in the Imperial Justice Laws of 1877–9, the robustness of neither would prove assured enough to resist the assault on the rule of law in the first half of the twentieth century. Sullied by internal fractiousness, and assaulted by the Weimar and National Socialist attacks on their integrity, neither bench nor bar could protect a semblance of autonomy from the concentration of political power in the ultimately totalitarian one-party state.

How can we explain this complete retreat from the high liberal ideals of the 1830s? What seems clear is that the surrender of bar autonomy did not have to wait for the Nazi regime: it effectively happened before Nazism and it awaited the Third Reich only for its legal institutionalization. Several intertwined causes explain the collapse of professional autonomy.

Although the link with political liberalism was real, as real as in other advanced countries, and it justified the claims for a *Rechtsstaat*, for

[25] D. Rueschemeyer, 'State, Capitalism, and the Organization of Legal Counsel', chap. 6 *infra*.

judicial independence and for bar autonomy, the task was daunting because German lawyers could not rely on the taken-for-granted collective autonomy of the English profession, nor on the strength of an independent bench in the United States, nor on the long tradition of lawyers' opposition to the Crown or the state apparatus in France. When German lawyers were forced to assert the values of liberalism, they were compelled to do so simultaneously with everything—the transformation of the state, of the judiciary, and of the bar.

Further, German lawyers never had the prestige of their French and English counterparts, and their manifest subservience to judges sharply restricted their capacity to form an effective political alliance with judges against an encroaching state apparatus. More importantly, under certain conditions lawyers refused collective autonomy as a result of an internal disunity that found its apotheosis in the quarrels among German lawyers after 1900. As Ledford's chapter demonstrates, the noble aspirations of the mid-nineteenth-century profession dissolved by the 1920s, when the pressure of overcrowding, and the competition over jurisdiction between higher- and lower-status lawyers, led to an ignoble scramble for economic self-defence. So intense were the inner fights that the ostensibly self-governing profession was compelled to call on the state to intervene, thus symbolically surrendering its own liberty. Weakened internally, German lawyers fragmented in 1933. Residues of liberalism were extirpated in the totalitarianism of the Third Reich, where positivist jurisprudence provided a convenient shelter from pangs of doubt over abrogation of rights, limits on state power, and the autonomy of law. Although the contexts were radically different, the German bar during the Weimar Republic displayed an internal disunity similar to the Parisian bar's experience during the last two decades before the Revolution. Both professions shared the same loss of collective identity and the willingness to defend self-government. In the face of violent and hostile events, both disappeared without resistance.

E. General Formulations

Four general considerations can be formulated from these national comparisons of the moderate state and professional autonomy.

First, bar autonomy is not an instinctive social value for lawyers: it is the product of lawyers' action. The bid for autonomy may not exist or it may disappear. Moreover the loss of autonomy may occur without mobilization to obtain, enlarge, or protect it. Therefore common will and relative unity of the professional collectivity are necessary conditions of professional autonomy. Of course, collective consensus need not be complete—professionals always have issues on which to disagree—but it is necessary both that lawyers share the willingness to maintain their self-government and that the issues on which professions disagree do not permeate all potential common ground. In theory, of course, professionals could rely upon a paternalistic sponsorship of their autonomy by judges, state officials, or the Crown, but this hardly qualifies as autonomy in any robust meaning of the term. A profession's autonomy is strongest when its warrant is substantially independent of the state and when its leadership can deliver some form of collective action, from a decision on behalf of the profession to active political mobilization.

Second, timing explains at least partly the national differences in the meanings linked with bar autonomy. In France, politics were strongly connected to bar autonomy as early as the eighteenth century. This explains why, after having been dissolved during the French Revolution, it did not take long for the lawyers to recover the legal freedom to rebuild collective autonomy and to use it as a basis for obtaining more freedom to fight against authoritarian states in order to defend and enlarge individual liberties. This long-standing autonomy was a fundamental element of the pride of the profession, the basis of its action, the means to political commitment, and its reason for refusing the business market. By contrast, as the autonomy of German lawyers occurred very late, despite the authenticity of their liberal aims, they could not rely on such a powerful and lively tradition of collective will. In the face of new dangers, the profession dissolved rather easily. In England, autonomy was a given for so many centuries that it took some time for lawyers to rediscover during the period of the Thatcher Governments that autonomy was also the product of political action. The fact that autonomy in the United States was built during the revival of the bar during the second half of the nineteenth century, a period characterized by the development of the federal state and by the growth of corporations and national markets, indicates that it takes on a dual meaning.

Third, as a political reality, bar autonomy cannot be dealt with as a separate fact in any country: it belongs to the political constitution of society, and, more specifically, it is linked to the relative autonomy of judges and the courts. Although judicial independence is the product of different forces of the state itself, of struggles among political forces, of lawyers' direct intervention (when they are allied with the magistrates and judges) or their indirect intervention (when they are defending judicial independence in order to defend their own independence), in all cases the moderate state is both the condition and the result of a complex process in which the effectiveness of lawyers' projects for autonomy can exert a powerful influence. Thus the variety of professional independence in Germany, France, Britain, and the United States does not only measure the relative capacity for professional collective action; it also expresses a partial realization of liberal society.

Fourth, this political construction of lawyers' autonomy casts legal professions in an entirely different light from the quite limited notions of autonomy either of lawyers from their clients, or of a professional cartel from a market-constructing state. It conceives of the moderation of the state by the creation of small 'republics' that control human, symbolic, and material resources and which exercise the capacity of acting even against the state. Thus our perspective construes professional autonomy as an institutional pillar of modern political liberalism.

Civil Society and its Publics

Civil society complements the internal moderation of the state by forming an expansive social basis for modern political liberalism. Medieval political thought had already bequeathed early modern politics with building-blocks for civil society.[26] One was the premiss that political organization is not synonymous with society, and that royal and political authority are therefore but two of many bases of legitimacy for social ordering. Another was the related proposition that the society of medieval Christendom was 'bi-focal', one part spiritual, and the other part temporal. Both parts derived their authority from God, but they existed for different purposes.

John Locke acknowledged, too, that since all authority was derived from God, civil society thereby had a transcendent basis. For Locke, society existed as a community endowed with natural rights before the existence of government. Civil society is created to cope with the 'insufficiencies' of the state of nature. Government arises through contract with society and has a fiduciary responsibility for the social good. If this trust relationship is abused, the contract can be revoked, and government dissolved. But for Locke, political association is not differentiated from civil society: the two are synonymous.

[26] Taylor, 'Invoking Civil Society'; A. Seligman, *The Idea of Civil Society* (New York, Free Press, 1992).

Subsequent thought in the Lockean tradition modified features of this conception without ultimately challenging its central axiom—that there exists a realm of social organization separate from and prior to the state. The Scottish Enlightenment figures, wrestling, among other things, with Smith's theory of economic exchange, found the solidarity of civil society less in divine interdiction than in moral sentiments that instinctively bound men together. Thus Hume could write that the edifice of civil society arose not from any principle of natural law or transcendence, but from human conventions—and these applied as much to market exchanges as to the general fabric of social relations.[27]

The emancipation from the society of the absolute king was a major symbolic, political, and social transformation. The appearance of socially constituted publics became a new force in history. Publics took on two combined meanings. First, they were the condition and the product of a collective debate. In Kant's philosophy, the shared public arena becomes the context for working out practical reason and substantiating the working of pure reason, a view that has been adapted and extended into the contemporary period by Arendt's and Habermas's contention that the public arena guarantees man's autonomy. Through active participation in civil society, spheres of autonomy are secured against the predations of the state. And all members of the civil society, who have the capacity to participate, debate the issues with equal formal standing. Within that public space, every argument can be formulated. Reason mobilizes, without immediate recourse to violence or tradition. Civil society therefore is not simply a web of voluntary association or a market of economic exchanges. Civil society is a realm of discourse, where ideas encounter each other and inform political understandings.

Second, by its very existence, the public expresses civil society as a limitation of monarchical power. It existed mainly as the body which had responsibility for the exercise of a critical function: it was antagonistic to the state or, more precisely, antagonistic to a power that wanted to conduct secretly the public affairs of the kingdom without accountability. It is the general context defined by the conflict between the state and civil society which gave the means for a general understanding of lawyers' political action.

[27] Ibid.

A. France

In France religious conflict within the church pushed its internal camps to make alliances with sympathetic allies outside the church and this enabled French barristers to craft civil society by cultivating a public sphere in which they were active publicists.[28] The moves of the profession can be analysed in terms of what Habermas has called the formation of the 'political public sphere': it springs from the literary public space and may be conceived as the sphere of private persons coming together as a public that exercises a critical counter-weight against public authority.[29] The political public sphere thereby expresses the separation between civil society and the state. Within this public sphere, in the salons, academies, coffee houses or the Bar, public debate around the general issues of the kingdom was conducted in a manner that emancipated the merits of the arguments from the social status of the speaker. Reason subordinated the authority of tradition.

Two different meanings can be given to the notion of public in France and elsewhere. On one hand, the French public was real—readers, listeners, and literate classes who consumed and discussed the titillating ideas packaged in *consultations, memoires judiciaires*, or *factums*. Its pre-revolutionary form as an 'enlightened public' was later replaced by the 'public-at-large'. But, on the other hand, central to lawyers' action was the public as an imaginary social construction, lawyers vested with the political legitimacy of the 'sovereign authority'. Symbolically constituted, this invisible entity was crafted by self-proclaimed prophets— like the lawyers—who seized upon a powerful counter-weight to the massive force of the Crown and state. This symbolic public became the new source of legitimation, the new last court of appeal. By acting on behalf of the public, the Bar as spokesman not only found legitimacy measured by popularity, but also attracted followers and allies who reinforced lawyers' influence and power. Lawyers participated in public debate on the most sensitive public issues, they opposed the absolute state by acting on behalf of the new sovereign authority of the public, and their influence and prestige became a yardstick of their legitimacy as spokesmen for the public. Such an outcome could not develop without a carefully elaborated strategy largely built around a disinterested-

---

[28] Bell, chap. 2 *infra*.

[29] J. Habermas, *The Structural Transformation of the Public Sphere: An Inquiry into a Category of Bourgeois Society*, T. Burger & F. Lawrence (trans.) (Cambridge, Mass., MIT Press, 1989).

ness that demonstrated again and again the Bar's dedication to the public.[30] It worked well.

B. England

In England, Pue argues that publics were also being created by the active agency of liberal barristers, who were, however, not at the centre but at the margins of the Bar. Like their French counterparts (whom English barristers were disposed to think they were quite unlike), courtrooms provided a platform for rhetoric and persuasion, not only to the immediate audience, but through extensive coverage and debate in the press. For instance, during the repression that accompanied the Napoleonic Wars, 'radical' lawyers exploited the 'educative potential' of trials to defend rights, expose corrupt government, and publicize causes. The practice of going on circuit, and travelling with England's assize courts to large county towns outside London, gave barristers regional publics far removed from Westminster. The assizes were at once occasions when judges could convey the government's views to localities and when localities could express their convictions back to Westminster.[31]

Consequently, the circuit permitted travelling barristers to create and extend networks of association between radical or dissenting barristers from London and provincial leaders sympathetic to their views. Argument frequently elided the distinction between legal and political spheres. The courtroom might be used, defensively, to keep the state at bay, or progressively, to extend rights or social visions. 'It simultaneously provided opportunity for crucial defences of dissident politics, assertion of individual right, articulation of radically democratic political visions, and moments of significant class formation.'[32]

But the courtroom was not the only stage, nor political liberty the only cause, for English lawyers, too, often sought 'to speak to (and constitute) a public considerably larger than that actually in the courtroom' through pamphleteering, publication of books, and public lectures. And of course powerful rhetoric stimulated not only public debate, but the publicity fuelled political careers. A number of the radical barristers of nineteenth-century England also served as Members of Parliament, though Pue shows that this political status scarcely guaranteed immunity from the long disciplinary arm of the

[30] Karpik, *Les avocats*; Karpik, chap. 3 *infra*.
[31] W. W, Pue, 'Lawyers in C18th and C19th England', chap. 5 *infra*.
[32] Ibid.

authorities who stood at the apex of the Bar, and who looked askance at radical politics.

Hence the profession was a 'sleeping' political actor, or more precisely, an apolitical actor since its political choices had been quasi-permanently institutionalized. For that reason, Mrs Thatcher's policy not only against lawyers, but against professions in general, was a significant move, transforming the previous balance of powers, putting under state control what previously belonged to civil society, and creating a new situation in which the legal profession had to deploy political weapons against the state. The only means for the profession to counteract this assault was, as Burrage clearly shows, to invoke the public good by arguing for the independence of the bar. In other words, to mobilize publics requires, through civic discourse and forms of action, the constitution of a certain conception of the public.

While for Burrage, the profession, long institutionalized in English civil society, exemplifies an apolitical model, for Pue, radical barristers were actively political in their liberal politics. Like their French counterparts, radical barristers of the nineteenth century could also be found in Parliament. However, the two views are less contradictory than first appears. Although they used their rhetoric in courtrooms and public forums, although they invoked the public, although they were flamboyant and popular, liberal barristers were few in number and were under the strict control of the long arm of disciplinary authority exercised by a Bar elite that looked askance at radical politics. Sanctions were not unusual. Thus the radicals did not represent the collective orientations of the Bar; on the contrary, they were outsiders and dissenters, a vulnerable segment of the profession, a number of individuals, facing an organized bar devoted to the political status quo.

In England, as elsewhere, therefore, it is possible to recognize the existence of these liberal barristers and nevertheless to maintain that the Bar as a collective actor 'slept' for several centuries, only to be awoken by Mrs Thatcher's policies. By transforming the previous balance of power, and by seeking to put under state control what previously belonged to civil society, Mrs Thatcher created a new situation in which legal professions, as collectivities, needed to deploy political weapons against the state and to mobilize the public in its defence.

C. Germany

The sense of professional agency is more strongly represented in Germany, by contrast, where lawyers were cast in a prominent role by the writings of mid-nineteenth-century liberals, who were eager to establish a rule-based state, complete with a vital civil society.[33] But by the revolutionary 1830s, Rudolf Gneist charged that the private legal profession should conceive of itself as 'the Archimedean point' for the growth of self-government in German society. By spearheading the education of the middle class in the ways of political civility, lawyers would teach the 'art of citizenship'. Ledford concurs with O'Boyle's judgement that 'an improvement in the lawyers' status was seen as inseparable from the extension of political liberty.'[34] The formation of a yet unrealized independent lawyers' association would symbolize the autonomy of the public sphere, and act as its standard-bearer before an overweening state. Thus the political action of German lawyers came late, at a time when the constitution of an autonomous civil society was problematic, when public debate was limited in the number of its participants and in freedom of discussion, and when the coalition of the forces wanting the change remained fragile. As a force which linked self-government and the *Rechtsstaat*, they could only parallel the forces emancipating civil society from the absolutist state and invoke a general interest whose definition independently of the state remained ambiguous and fragile.

D. United States

From before the Revolution, public space in the United States was saturated with voluntary, political, and social organizations. Indeed, Madison's defence of the draft federal constitution of 1779 was premised on a civil society marked by the pervasive proliferation of interests, expressed through political associations. Fifty years later, Tocqueville marvelled at the profusion of civil associations of every kind, and the dense mosaic of political expression outside the state. Lawyers featured in both these accounts as a new aristocracy of sorts, who could exercise public leadership in Ciceronian style. And indeed there is a lawyers' rhetoric that uses the courtroom as a stage for the expression of public values, though it reaches none of the histrionic proportions visible in France.

Although lawyers have always been major players on the political stage, and the legal profession has been the prime occupational route

---

[33] Ledford, 'The German Bar in the Weimar Republic', chap. 7 *infra*. More generally see K. F. Ledford, *From General Estate to Special Interest: German Lawyers, 1878–1933* (New York, Cambridge Univ. Press, 1996).

[34] Ledford, chap. 7 *infra* and *From General Estate to Special Interest*.

to political office, the American profession has continued to be distinguished by its complex mosaic of voluntary associations. Bar associations parallel every level of government—federal, state, metropolitan, county—and they express every major ascriptive attribute of American lawyers—gender, race, and ethnic origins, not excluding religious and political associations as well. The more politically active of these associations forge some continuing and many episodic political relationships with government. Whether these take pluralist or neo-corporatist forms, the American profession has expressed itself collectively through alliances and negotiations with other interest groups. The century-long bid for the political independence of state judiciaries, for instance, has demanded that lawyers' groups negotiate with political parties and build alliances with other civic groups, such as the League of Women Voters, in order to push reform through the legislature. Halliday and Carruthers demonstrate how the reform of bankruptcy law brought lawyers' groups into conflict and alliance with each other and with commercial and financial interest groups.[35] In short, the political activism of the American profession has increasingly shifted from a Ciceronian model of civic oration to a Madisonian model of interest group politics, sometimes expressed in corporatist concertation.

Grossberg's history of legal aid in the first part of the twentieth century demonstrates that the organized bar in the United States served concomitantly to limit the scope of state incursion into civil society and to solidify civil society's own institutions.[36] American legal aid lawyers emerged in a wider wave of middle class humanitarianism at the beginning of the twentieth century. Committed to legal representation as a form of equality before the law, legal aid lawyers sought to carve out a niche to secure rights for poor clients. Struggles over where that representation would be located—inside the state or in civil society—turned into negotiations of two sorts.

On the one hand, lawyers engaged in boundary disputes with state agencies, such as municipal public legal aid bureaux, on the grounds that 'state expansion threatened to shrink the American public sphere'. Clients liked the idea of public agencies as a public service. Moreover agencies had the additional benefit that they had resources not available to private charities. But many lawyers in the private bar saw the municipal employment of lawyers as a threat to their independence for

---

[35] T. C. Halliday & B. G. Carruthers, chap. 8 *infra*.
[36] Grossberg, chap. 9 *infra*.

they owed their income and jobs to government authorities. Not only could legal aid be subverted by bureaucratic inefficiency, but the corruption pervasive in urban politics would politicize law, and thereby subvert law's 'neutrality'.

On the other hand, lawyers in the private bar pushed their claim that legal aid, while firmly lodged in civil society, should not be seen as a charity. If legal aid were a charity, then it was something less than a right. Furthermore, the field of charity had been colonized by social workers, and lawyers resisted the assimilation of their activities into the jurisdictional aspirations of another professionalization project. Ironically enough, the struggle of private lawyers with charity, on the one side, and social workers on the other, had the effect of strengthening civil society for while the three groups may have been in conflict over who should control legal aid, they all agreed that it should not be the state. At once, therefore, the jurisdictional conflict over work modestly reinforced a certain concept of the allocation of power in liberal political society. Moreover, to win jurisdictional conflicts placed lawyers on a political stage, to talk on behalf of the poor, and to champion the good society. As lawyers were consolidating their own position as private advocates for the poor, they were articulating to diverse publics a concept of the good society, where certain rights were institutionalized outside the state.

E. Commonalities and Variations on the Theme of Civil Society

Across societies, therefore, the public space evidences itself in two connected, but analytically discrete, forms: as a public, which may be either symbolically constructed or a realm of public discourse; and as a civil society organized through voluntary associations and intermediate groups outside the state. The relative emphasis on these alternative ways of constituting the public space varies significantly and the politics of legal professions follow suit. At one extreme, lawyers can avail themselves of a rich civil society and dense associational life; at another extreme, the absence of such a civil society will impel lawyers towards constituting publics as symbolic and social allies. In the former, lawyers construct political alliances; in the latter, lawyers act as spokesmen for publics they themselves help create.

The variations on the theme of civil society are reflected in the permutations of the case studies. French lawyers were active in expressing and constituting civil society: they reacted against an absolutist state and were part of a powerful coalition of forces anchored by the *parlements*. But since associational life was not so highly developed in France, French lawyers principally oriented themselves towards the creation and education of publics. Like their American colleagues, individual *avocats* also used the bar as a springboard to political leadership, but this was analytically separable from the collective action of the bar. By the mid-nineteenth century, the American profession, by contrast, had traded in its role as a public spokesman for collective activism through the political market-place. Its political orientations have historically ranged from classic interest group politics, at which they have not always been very successful, through to the effective 'inside' politics of corporatist, expert consultation. The English case, once again, looks exceptional not because the separation between the state and civil society did not exist, but because it was so well accepted that it could not become the basis of political action. German lawyers began with aspirations both to build civil society and to educate publics in the mores of democratic citizenship. In practice, however, their politics were directed through political parties. And when the liberal parties began their retreat from prominence, lawyers found they had no independent basis for political action, either as spokesmen for the public, for they had never earned that role, or as coalition builders, for they had limited capacity themselves to forge links with a relatively sparse population of political associations.

Citizenship

That citizenship should be universal within the nation-state became widely accepted by the late nineteenth century. But that success should not hide the long and conflictual path through which it was achieved and the ways lawyers were enmeshed in it. In fact, the actors and the contours of political battle changed with the contents of citizenship. Thomas H. Marshall's three-fold paradigm of citizenship, which remains the classic formulation of the alternative rights that attach to the status of citizen, and their historical unfolding, can help make the necessary distinctions.[37] The civil element of citizenship grants citizens legal rights and personality. Civil rights protect individual freedoms— freedom of speech, thought, and faith; the right to own property; freedom to travel; the right to make contracts; and the right to justice and due process of law. The political aspect of citizenship grants individu-

[37] T. H. Marshall, *Citizenship and Social Class* (Cambridge, Cambridge Univ. Press, 1950).

als the right to participate in the exercise of political authority as voters or representatives in parliamentary bodies. Social citizenship endows individuals with rights to economic welfare and security and lies at the heart of the welfare state.

The independent development of these citizenship rights is a relatively late development. Civil, political, and social rights in medieval Europe were intertwined and enmeshed in feudal orders. Only after 'the institutions on which the three elements of citizenship depended parted company', and they were detached from the estates, did 'it become possible for each to go its own separate way, travelling at its own speed under the direction of its own peculiar principles'.[38] The attachment of rights to individuals presupposed their emancipation from the residue of feudal societies. Old World societies in which feudal remnants, estates, and status groups persisted, 'precluded the full institutionalization of a civil society of autonomous, moral, and economic individual agents'.[39] The doctrine of individualism thus underwrites all three kinds of citizenship and the institutions that support them.

For lawyers, representation, or the right of access to the judicial system, is a central component of citizenship. As counsel for plaintiffs seeking to establish property rights, as public advocates of freedom of expression, as champions of the rights of defendants to the protections afforded by legal counsel, as advocates of legal advice and assistance to the weakest members of society, and as sponsors of courts as forums for business conflicts and disputes, lawyers insistently push at the frontiers of representation, ever widening both the scope of their own domain of work and the protections afforded individuals, real and fictive, from each other and the state.

A. France

Lawyers' role in the extension of civil rights can be observed from the eighteenth century in France. Karpik finds early evidence for creation of property rights for legally marginalized Burgundy peasants during the Ancien Régime.[40] On the one hand, Burgundy peasants took their overlords to court to get rid of the feudal custom of seigneurial dues, thereby stimulating plaintiffs' lawyers to develop new legal arguments

---

[38] Marshall, *Citizenship and Social Class*, 73.

[39] J. Barbelet, *Citizenship: Rights, Struggle and Class Inequality* (Minneapolis, Univ. of Minnesota Press, 1988), 107.

[40] Halliday & Carruthers, chap. 8 *infra*.

to demonstrate the illegality of seigneurial rights. By invoking the notion of contract, and relying on superior general laws, the plaintiffs' counsel claimed for the peasants the autonomy of consciousness and rights to property which amounted to an equality of rights, a claim deeply antagonistic to traditional and personal relations of domination.

On the other hand, in order to defend their clients, lawyers in the second part of the eighteenth century followed Voltaire's strategy for fighting the miscarriage of justice and played the public against the judges in cases like the *Calas* case. Through letters and pamphlets, and with the help of some lawyers of high reputation, Voltaire mobilized his friends, great personnages of the royal court, and the enlightened public against *l'erreur judiciare* and defeated the powerful *Parlement* of Toulouse. That capacity to mobilize people in order to influence judges (and to build their reputation) became a model for lawyers. In a flourishing production of judicial briefs, which they wrote and circulated widely, especially during famous trials (*causes celèbres*), lawyers aroused the passions of readers by presenting them with a combination of legal arguments and political criticism directed especially toward the judiciary and the fragile freedom of the Ancien Régime. The profession rose so sharply in status, according to Bell, that the career of barrister began to look highly appealing to would-be *philosophes*.

Throughout the nineteenth century until the Second World War lawyers continued their advocacy of free expression. Lawyers fought against emergency laws, special courts, limits on personal freedoms, and the silencing of the Press. In the so-called 'Lawyers' Revolution' of 1830, they sprang to the defence of the Constitution, parliamentary power, and the Press. They were in the opposition before the 1848 Revolution and in Louis Napoleon's Empire, consistently advocating a 'radical moderation' in resistance to state incursions on individual freedoms and the autonomy of the individual. In fact, their commitment took two main expressions. They transformed the courtroom into a political forum—disputation over the great questions of rights and freedoms before packed court-rooms enlarged by an expanding press—and their visibility as defenders of liberal ideals propelled them increasingly into political office. The growing valorization of lawyers in the mid-nineteenth century cast them as the collective 'champions of the individual and his liberties'.[41] With the Third Republic, established in

---

[41] Karpik, 'Lawyers and Politics in France, 1814–1950', 730.

1875, they crowded the executive and legislative branches of the state, becoming a ruling elite.

B. Great Britain

Advocating meaningful rights through representation similarly characterized Pue's radical lawyers in nineteenth-century Britain. The Wilkites, a political movement which attracted numbers of barristers, insisted on equality before the law for all citizens. In lawyers' own domain, criminal defence and prosecution, they 'attacked the legality of general warrants, . . . prosecuted state officials for illegal conduct', defended individuals from prosecution for 'seditious libel', pressed for a stronger procedural justice, demanded that legal proceedings be open and public, and resisted summary proceedings. Representation played an important part in the transition from criminal trials in Tudor and Stuart England that were 'nasty, brutish and short', where defendants were seldom represented by counsel, rules of evidence were exceedingly relaxed and favoured the prosecution, and judges acted in a prosecutorial manner, to criminal trials in the nineteenth century, where adversarial proceedings were substantially institutionalized, procedural rules governed proceedings, and judges acted less as prosecutors and more as adjudicators.

Emergence of the right to counsel, therefore, was a critical step in this evolution to a rule-of-law judicial regime. Evidence was tested and witnesses cross-examined. Pue cites the case of Thomas Paine, on trial for seditious libel following publication of *The Rights of Man*, who was defended by Thomas Erskine's ringing assertion that 'I will forever, at all hazards, assert the dignity, independence and integrity of the English bar, without which impartial justice, the valuable part of the English constitution, can have no evidence'. That independence could not be detached from the widespread concern expressed by several English lawyers, at the time of the American and French Revolutions, 'over the apparent corruption in the government, its unconstitutional behaviour', and a sense that 'England was threatened by a tyrannical and oppressive regime'. Representation offered lawyers' resistance to the encroachments of an immoderate state.[42]

C. The United States

Legal liberalism came to ascendancy in the fifty years from 1870 to 1920 and it firmly committed American legal science to classical

---

[42] W. W. Pue, chap. 5 *infra*.

European liberal ideals.[43] At the core of liberal jurisprudence lay three principal tenets. First, all adult males should be formally equal before the law. Second, the individual or the state should have primacy over custom in the determination of legal obligation, with the result that contract should pre-empt status as a basis of legal relations. And, third, the justice system itself should be formally rational in order to ensure predictable legal relations. Underlying all three tenets was the presumption that freedom demands zones of activity that are protected from state incursion. 'By the "rule of law", advocates of liberal legal science meant the subjection of all social actors to a regime of general rules that were to specify in advance the limits of autonomous conduct, within which the state was to abstain totally from regulating conduct.'[44] It was a classic form of negative freedom.

Nevertheless there is substantial evidence that the main body of the elite bar, as it was represented in major national and local associations, did not seize opportunities from the late nineteenth century through the Civil Rights era of the 1960s to redress civil wrongs with emphatic endorsements of civil rights.[45] If anything American lawyers have been distinctly dilatory in their advocacy of racial equality before the law, and not merely in the extension of political and social rights. In fact, lawyers have not consistently acted to extend substantive rights of political participation and racial justice. In practice, charges Jerold Auerbach, they have been purveyors of 'unequal justice'. That fringe of the profession that has been actively engaged in broader substantive civil rights has frequently been marginalized by professional elites, and during the McCarthy era, its leading association, the National Lawyers' Guild, was itself a butt of Congressional investigation. Moreover the commitment of professional associations to civil rights operates within narrow parameters—the rule of law, the rights of privacy, and proceduralism in the administration of justice are paramount. During the McCarthy period of anti-Communist purges during the late 1940s and early 1950s, the New York City Bar and the Chicago Bar Association, among others, adopted a strong procedural defence of individual rights, demanding that Congressional committees follow rules of due process,

---

[43] R. W. Gordon, 'Legal Thought and Legal Practice in the Age of Enterprise', in G. L. Geison (ed.), *Professions and Professional Ideologies in America* (Chapel Hill, Univ. of North Carolina Press, 1983), 70–110.

[44] Ibid. 94.

[45] J. S. Auerbach, *Unequal Justice: Lawyers and Social Change in America* (Oxford, Oxford Univ. Press, 1976); Halliday, *Beyond Monopoly*, chap. 8.

including the right to legal representation.[46] In both federal and state governments, lawyers promulgated codes that would limit state intrusion into the private lives of citizens, and would give them some protection before investigative bodies. This negative defence of liberty had a natural affinity with lawyers' juridical liberalism. But the evidence indicates that these protective stances were the exception rather than the rule.

Yet Grossberg shows that legal aid is one site where the organized bar, at least earlier in the century, did mobilize on the cause of representation. For legal aid lawyers in Grossberg's study, representation was a crucial right of citizenship: it provided the right of access to the judicial system in which rights could be enforced. Concomitantly legal aid lawyers rejected any notion that representation or the right of the poor to counsel was charity, for that eroded its status as a fundamental procedural right, and at the same time it effectively reduced lawyers to the status of social workers, which undermined their professional project.[47]

Grossberg maintains that legal aid signifies a significant shift in citizenship rights, which previously had been tightly linked to property. Attaching the right of counsel to citizenship expanded the notion of citizenship from property to civil rights, and that shift, coupled with lawyers' own initiatives to actively ensure universal representation, raised the prospect that formal civil rights would be realized in practice. Thus legal representation lay at the heart of the profession's initiatives as lawyers strove to detach representation from the ability to pay (which essentially linked it to property rights) and fixed it to the civil component of citizenship.

By adopting the function of representation, lawyers effectively created a new citizen, but with strict limitations. Legal aid lawyers restricted representation to the respectable, deserving poor. They only accepted cases from legal aid clients that were within their definition of morality. They refused to accept cases of personal injury, criminal, or divorce law—areas that impinged on middle class morality, management–worker relations, public order, and the stability of the family. But for normal clients they would accept all cases, irrespective of morality. Thus the undeserving poor, who did not share middle class morality, were effectively deprived of this new less-than-universal right. Within

---

[46] Powell, *From Patrician to Professional Elite*; T. C. Halliday, 'The Idiom of Legalism in Bar Politics: Lawyers, McCarthyism, and the Civil Rights Era', *Amer. Bar Found. Res. Jrnl* (Fall 1982), 911–89.

[47] Grossberg, chap. 9 *infra*.

political society, therefore, the rights to representation rested on two foundations: on the one hand, those who had property rights, who could pay, could avail themselves of the full panoply of legal protections; on the other hand, those who evinced middle-class morality, even without adequate financial means, could obtain representation through legal aid. Thus the civil rights of the citizen were constituted, but in a very particular way.

In the face of extraordinary variegation and heterogeneity within the profession, therefore, American lawyers can be characterized as a whole only with the risk of caricature. But that should not prohibit a few general observations. First, it is difficult to make a global connection between civil rights and the organized bar universally. It is necessary to talk about minorities, groups and so on. But this consideration should be related to the type of profession. One cannot directly compare the French or the European professions, which have been centred for so long around tribunals, with a profession whose work centres on individual and corporate markets. Diversity is what was supposed to exist; it already existed in France. Therefore one should put the theory in history and compare what is comparable and distinguish between historical forms of the legal profession. In that case, the commitment of minorities to civil rights is what would be expected. Second, civil rights issues periodically become hotly contested within a large part of the bar. They represent one of its limiting grounds of consensus.

D. Germany

In contrast to the United States and especially to France, German lawyers in neither the nineteenth nor twentieth centuries appear to have framed their encounter with liberalism principally in terms of the rights that are adduced to citizenship. Ledford views the 'modernization' of the nineteenth-century bar to be of a piece with the establishment of a liberal polity, in which lawyers were anticipated to champion liberty through advocacy of free speech, trial by jury, and others of the core civil rights. He joins Siegrist[48] in arguing that lawyers saw their own fortunes to be intertwined with those of political liberalism: 'Lawyers in Germany had long been allied with political liberalism conceiving of themselves, and being perceived by liberals, as the particular bearers of the main achievement of German liberalism, the *Rechtsstaat*,

---

[48] H. Siegrist, 'Public Office or Free Profession? German Attorneys in the Nineteenth and Early Twentieth Centuries', in G. Cocks & K. H. Jarausch (eds.), *German Professions, 1800–1950* (New York, Oxford Univ. Press, 1990), 46–65.

the state ruled by law.'[49] In fact, individual rights were pursued through proceduralism.

It is around the state and more globally around the transformation of society that lawyers mobilized. During the decades of the 1830s and 1840s, the liberal vision of leading German lawyers was inextricably bound with the formation of a German *Rechtsstaat* and a liberal political system.[50] Lawyers' campaign for a 'free Bar', released from the tutelage of official state control, was directed to independent representation of clients. But its import far exceeded the structuring of legal services. It was inseparable from the institutional transformation of legal institutions towards the liberal ideals of independence of the judiciary, the separation of judicial and administrative authority, and the autonomy of law through adherence to judicial precedent. Furthermore, establishment of a 'free Bar' released lawyers from the civil servant rule against political activities, thus permitting lawyers for the first time to support political parties and engage in liberal politics, releasing their energies to stimulate and even lead the liberal political movement. From their position in the vanguard of the 1848 Revolution, lawyers were prominently represented in the National Liberal and Progressive Parties, the two principal liberal parties prior to the First World War.

German liberalism took a special shape as it was defined not by substance but by procedure. Passage of the 'Imperial Justice Laws' in the late 1870s marked the high point of legal liberalism, as modified versions of lawyers' liberal ideals were institutionalized as part of Bismarck's programme for German unification. But the Imperial Justice Laws were heavily committed to a procedural conception of political liberalism. Ledford concludes that 'in compromising to assure the procedural unification of Germany, the National Liberals believed that they were . . . securing the *Rechtsstaat* and with it an important foundation for the protection of individual rights and *burgerliche* identity. In so doing, they also acted within the broader framework of modern liberal doctrine.' It was this approach that defined political liberalism and that explained the centrality of the *Rechtsstaat* which 'signifies above all not the aim and content of the state, but only the method and nature of their realization'.[51] The procedural doctrine of German liberalism meshed with lawyers' emphasis on the primacy of procedure. It

---

[49] K. Ledford, 'Alien, Arbiter, Adversary: German Lawyers and the State, 1918–1933', paper presented to Conf. on Lawyers and Political Liberalism, Oñati, Spain, 1993, 4.

[50] Rueschemeyer, chap. 6 *infra*.   [51] Ledford, chap. 7 *infra*.

explained a form of mobilization and the primacy of the state reform over the citizenship claims.

Proceduralism, autonomy, and political leadership characterized the political liberalism of German lawyers and defined an action which claimed to be conducted on behalf of the 'general estate' representing the 'universal interests of the community', and which after some successes became a failure long before the Nazis seized the power of the bar. After 1879, lawyers' liberal programme was successively eroded and during the Weimar Republic it faced external and internal issues it could not solve. On the one hand, bar leaders failed to convince people that lawyers represented the general interest, and on the other hand, they could not agree among themselves. Although the events were specific, the profession's evolution shared the general fate of political liberalism in Germany.[52]

E. Limits to Liberalism

We have postulated that lawyers have their own distinctive contribution to political liberalism. Their definition can be identified not only by their positive choices but also by negation or indifference—by what they refuse to fight for or engage in.

The limits of lawyers' liberalism are more precisely defined on the dimension of citizenship rights than on the dimensions of the moderate state or the constitution of civil society. Lawyers' liberal core centres on proceduralism—the commitment to procedural justice via representation of American legal aid lawyers, the procedural reforms of criminal justice championed by nineteenth-century English Wilkites—on an equality of rule-boundedness that incorporates all citizens, despite wealth, power, or status. But even here their advocacy of expansive civil rights meets formidable barriers. Some are financial: those with property and wealth can afford access to justice while those without are effectively deprived of their rights to representation. Some are moral: those who are 'undeserving poor', whose behaviour runs afoul of middle-class norms, may not be eligible for representation in areas of criminal or family or employment law. Some are political: when civil rights demand the incorporation of races or genders or religions in the workplace or neighbourhood, lawyers themselves divide and professions stumble. In other words, substantive values intrude frequently to limit the scope of the rights attached to civil citizenship.

[52] Ledford, 'Alien, Arbiter, Adversary', 17.

If lawyers' general tendency may be to protect a certain liberal core, they often neglect and even resist its extension. On the one hand, lawyers have often been reluctant to fight for the expansion of universal suffrage. They fought neither on behalf of men in Great Britain nor of women in France. On the other hand, for the most part they have tended to resist the welfare state. We find this limit to their liberalism in France, Great Britain and Germany. It is not general in the United States with the New Deal, but even there it is necessary to distinguish between the resistance to installing a paternalist state and the creation of an administrative apparatus that offered enormous new markets for American lawyers. Like doctors in nationalized medicine, lawyers in the United States came to see their opportunity almost against their will. Consequently, we can conclude that the massive centre of the twentieth century profession protects the core of liberal institutions without venturing too far out into the uncharted waters of social and economic substantive rights. Lawyers' political liberalism should not be confused with political democracy or social democracy: it is a classic or restricted liberalism.

These choices could be explained by different interpretations, ranging from the most specific to the most general. First, the oldest legal professions—the French, the English, and partially the American—had constructed themselves around struggles for civil rights and some political rights, such as freedom of the press. Thus classical liberalism became an integral part of lawyers' professional culture. Second, modern lawyers can find substantial internal consensus on the rule-governed state, particularly over the grand design of legal institutions and the merits of proceduralism. But political party differences divide the profession and inhibit its collective action on the insatiable expansion of rights' discourse, since the expansion—or constriction—of rights divides society.

Thus there are two kinds of politics that have radically different consequences for lawyers. When lawyers adhere to a politics of proceduralism on which they can obtain unity, they can act collectively and effectively. However, the more lawyers' politics approach the issues that orient differences in party politics, the more difficult it is to mobilize and the less unquestionably legitimate are their positions. Those limits are constantly being tested within national professions because vanguard groups on the periphery of professions seek to push them beyond their conventional limits. Faced with vociferous dissenters, or potential insurgents, bar elites can then exercise the levers of power they control through admissions, unauthorized practice, and legal ethics to quash dissent and insurgency. Just as the regulatory apparatus of professions can be deployed to ensure economic monopoly, so too they are available for a politics of conformity.

Third, political and social conservatism might result from lawyers' location within a bourgeoisie that is indifferent or hostile to the extension of the suffrage to other classes and to women, and is reluctant to see a broadening of economic and social rights. More precisely, it is through the very strong adherence of lawyers to a 'pure', autonomous political outlook which is strictly limited to the protection of individual freedoms, that lawyers have made an indirect and often hidden powerful social choice. For all these reasons, and despite the fact that it sprang from a society where the central conflict was between the state and civil society, 'limited' political liberalism was forcefully maintained in a society where priorities changed and new cleavages appeared. That represented at once a limit—it separated lawyers from new political and social issues, and from new political and social forces—but also a strength as this *grundnorm* permitted lawyers to maintain collective unity and, though in a weakened form, to keep a vigorous link with the defence of individual liberties.

Profiles of Lawyers' Political Action

We have proposed that the political action of lawyers can be meaningfully analysed within a theoretical framework that contains the aims, means, and conditions of political liberal action. We have shown that the political meanings attached to bar autonomy, to the fight for civil and political rights, as well as to the moderation of the state, varied in different countries and in different periods. It is clear therefore that this political reality is not a marginal phenomenon and that international diversity does not preclude a common political model of action. Thus, and before reviewing our findings, it is necessary to show the bounds beyond which our approach loses its relevance and to consider lawyers' relevance to new forms of liberalism.

A. Boundaries of Liberal Action

Although we have concentrated on the politics of the bar, it should be clear that we do not make the claim that politics is always the dominant logic of professional action. Thus anti-liberal politics, well exemplified by the totalitarian states, seems to invalidate completely the approach advanced by this book, since anti-liberal politics are defined by loss of bar autonomy, by fusion between the state (or the party) and civil society, and by restrictions on political freedom. But up to a certain point, to be at the opposite extreme is to remain in the same universe. That explains why the approach taken in this volume becomes especially relevant in periods of transition, since these are the questions that surface in public consciousness. But for theoretical reasons, we will insist more on the varying relative importance of politics and economics in professional histories.

Politics versus economics

Three different situations can be identified that vary according to the relative emphasis that is placed on the political actions of lawyers versus their economic orientations. A strong emphasis on the market hinders collective political action. The best example is, of course, the United States. This results not only from the intense pursuit of material interests, but also from the fact that the strong commitment to corporate markets largely prevents the pursuit of other goals. Both also undermine the credibility of those who would seek to link political goals and the public good. Moreover, intense competition and a strong internal hierarchy divide the bar and inhibit its capacity to reach some sort of substantive consensus. These conditions do not prevent political action, but they explain why it is usually limited to minorities, such as elites, or bar interest groups, which are trying to act on behalf of their colleagues. For the opposite reasons, a strong emphasis on politics prevents commitment to the economic project. That was clearly the case in France until the middle of the twentieth century. But this opposition should not be overstated. Even when political aims are replaced by economic interests, when the market becomes the dominant concern, the political perspective should not be eclipsed by the economic perspective because even in a profession dominated by fierce competition between megafirms it is a matter of degree more than of kind: politics does not completely disappear. An adequate comparative and historical theory requires elements of both political and economic accounts of professionalization. Professions' theory must identify the conditions under which one or another will be more salient to the profession. For instance, Karpik's account of French lawyers charts the shifting relationships of the profession to the state, market, and public respectively, over several centuries, and thereby demonstrates that the salience of one orientation changes with shifting political and economic circumstances.[53]

The new liberalism: technocracy and politics

Eighteenth- and nineteenth-century liberalism rested on the dualism between the state and civil society, and its basis was national. The twentieth century has witnessed the rise of progressively more ambitious states confronted with highly complex social and economic problems that are compounded by the international movements of populations and trade. The modern state defines its mandate expansively—from the delivery of social services to the cultivation of the arts and the regulation of the economy. Concomitant with complex, bureaucratic management of the ambitious state is government by expert or technocratic administration. Moreover new forms of authority are appearing on a supra-national basis and without the necessary safeguards that have been long elaborated and put to use. Liberal politics therefore confronts a new challenge—rule by professionals, high civil servants, public managers, and technocratic elites, all out of view, and often out of reach, of mass politics, and sometimes alongside poorly defined citizens' rights.

Two forms of the new politics are exemplified by the policies of economic organization in the United States and the European Community. Halliday and Carruthers show that the politics of bankruptcy reform in the United States display a contradiction.[54] As bankruptcy law is counted among the most arcane and inaccessible areas of legal practice, even to non-specialist lawyers, its sheer technical complexity permitted the momentum and substance of policy changes to be heavily influenced by a very small circle of expert lawyers. Legal experts joined forces with bankers to produce a piece of legislation that had unexpected repercussions for the institutional structure of the polity. The American banking elite formed an alliance with a fragment of the legal elite to reinforce the independence and authority of the courts, most notably for major corporations, whose willingness to fall back on judicial solutions to corporate reorganization depended on guarantees of competence, integrity, and independence of the judiciary. Indirectly, therefore, powerful commercial institutions underwrote the autonomy of the courts, and in so doing reinforced the institutional foundations of the moderate state. Nevertheless, this was primarily an elite settlement lead by lawyer-experts and only moderately altered by legislators.

---

[53] Karpik, *Les avocats*.   [54] Halliday & Carruthers, chap. 8 *infra*.

If the United States' case represents an elitism with a liberal cast, Johnson portrays the construction of the European super-state by technocrats without a commensurate protection for individual rights. Brussels' Euro-civil servants promulgate rules and advance the cause of legal homogeneity, but this elitism with a liberal deficit occurs precisely because no European 'citizen-subject' has ever been properly constituted. While it is the case that the nation-states of the EC provide a national counterbalance to the growing power of Brussels, the European Court has not yet emerged as an effective judicial counterweight to either Strasbourg or Brussels. No European bar exists that could help create the European 'public space' through which individual liberties might be defined and defended. Thus, legal rights and responsibilities, and their institutional foundations, remain poorly specified, and present an unresolved task for the constitution of the emerging European super-state.[55]

The new challenge to liberalism places lawyers on both sides of proto-corporatist politics. As insiders, their professional associations lend technical advice to law-makers. As outsiders, they represent interests of clients fearful of being excluded from closed-door decision-making. In either case, their technical facility in law-making and law-interpretation provides them unusual access to political decision-making across the entire agenda of the modern state. The corporatist state combines authority and civil society and therefore professions, at the same time, participate both in the exercise of authority and in interventions to defend individual rights. Moreover, multinational corporations are using increasingly sophisticated legal machinery that is created by public and private experts like lawyers in order to impose specific forms of economic regulation.

These developments create new complex relations between the profession, civil society, and the state. On the one hand, the corporatist regime integrates professions into the state decision-making apparatus and thereby mitigates the conflict that characteristically can arise between autonomous groups in civil society and the state. On the other hand, while much of the profession is assimilated into state policy-making and implementation, nevertheless some segments of the profession will continue to fight on behalf of individual rights against the state, with the consequence that 'classical' politics of professionalism

---

[55] T. Johnson, 'Professions and State Formation: Some Notes on the Relationships between Expertise and the European Single Community', paper presented to Conf. on Lawyers and Political Liberalism, Oñati, Spain, 1993.

liberalism may remain alive in one segment of the profession but at the cost of conflict with the body of the profession that is aligned with state interests.

B. The Dimensions of Lawyers' Political Action

From the national cases, we can derive three propositions on *bar autonomy and the moderate state*. First, bar autonomy, which may be defined as self-government and emancipation from direct control by the state, can be considered by lawyers as a goal in itself since it implies the protection of lawyers' individual freedom, and concomitantly serves as a means for collective action. A profession's autonomy is strongest when its warrant is substantially independent of the state and when its leadership can deliver some form of collective action, from a decision on behalf of the profession to active political mobilization.To attain that goal, two conditions must be satisfied. On the one hand, bar autonomy cannot be achieved without a political system in which the judiciary has obtained (relative) independence from executive authority. On the other hand, bar autonomy depends at a minimum on lawyers' readiness to fight against external adversaries in order to obtain and protect it. Collective autonomy is not a spontaneous social value for lawyers. Under certain conditions the bid for autonomy may not exist or it may disappear. Moreover the loss of autonomy may occur without automatic mobilization to obtain, enlarge, or protect it.

Moreover, bar action is both an expression of the autonomy of *civil society* and the means of opposition to the state, as well as a force that reinforces this dualism. Bar action constitutes (with others) civil society. This commitment is not only a matter of intensity, but also of strategy. Lawyers gain influence and legitimacy through two alternative forms of action—a strategy of leadership on behalf of the general interest they call the public; and a strategy of interest groups in alliance with political parties and political associations. The two dimensions will combine in varying proportions according to time and place. For instance, French lawyers were active in expressing civil society, while, in contrast, the bar in the United States followed an interest group strategy. Germany, like France, reacted against an absolutist state and shared the battle for emancipation from it. But as it was weak in its representative function, it joined in alliance with political parties. The English case, once again, looks exceptional, not because the separation between the state and civil society did not exist, but because it was so well accepted that it could not become the basis of political action.

Lawyers' commitments to *citizenship*, even in its narrowest denotation, must be viewed historically and comparatively as quite uncertain, sometimes springing to the fore, as in nineteenth-century France, sometimes taking a muted and inconsistent form, as in the United States and Britain over the past two centuries, and sometimes withdrawing altogether, as in inter-war Germany. But these reservations notwithstanding, on the whole lawyers in these four countries have over long historical periods displayed a strong tendency to defend civil and political citizenship whenever it has been severely threatened.

Besides these characteristics in common, the national case studies indicate a major cleavage between action oriented towards substance and action oriented towards procedure, between specific rights (whether civil, political or social) that are linked to the person and rules of procedure through which these rights can be obtained and protected—to which also should be added institutional arrangements such as the *Rechtsstaat* or the prominent position given to the Supreme Court in the United States. The difference does not create a pure separation between substance and procedure, because lawyers as legal experts nowhere separate rights completely from procedure: as political actors they cannot mobilize procedures without at least some reference to specific rights. Yet the differences can be great. France was deeply involved during the eighteenth and nineteenth centuries in the fight for specific rights, while German lawyers sought to build the *Rechtsstaat*. American lawyers, who combined substantive rights and procedure, represent another configuration, which is also true for the English bar since the consensus of reliance upon the unwritten constitution, as well as precedent, gives emphasis to the enforcement of the rules of functioning already existing.

Thus, lawyers' political forms of action can be characterized by the cross-cutting of two general dimensions: on the one hand, the alternative between the representative and the interest group functions, and on the other hand, the primacy given to substance of rights versus proceduralism.

	Proceduralism	Substantive Rights
Representative Interest Groups	Germany England, USA	France —

Forms of lawyers' political action

Historically, each legal profession is defined by a specific configuration of action. At the two extremes are eighteenth- and nineteenth-century French lawyers, with their emphasis on citizenship and their neglect of institutional construction, in contrast to German lawyers (during the second half of the nineteenth century and the beginning of the twentieth century), with their emphasis on the *Rechtsstaat* and their limited interest in citizen rights. The United States, from the last third of the nineteenth century, distinguished itself by an intermediate position on both dimensions and though its action on citizenship was partial, it was systematic and tenacious in the building of the courts, which amounts to an effort to bound the state. English lawyers once again, and until Mrs Thatcher' Government, were more distinctively organized around the relationships with centres of power, and thus the moderate state, than around the conquest of rights.

Our collective comparative analysis reveals that although a core of professional politics was widely present in the biography of quite diverse national professions, nevertheless those professions evince quite distinctive patterns of political action. In the voluminous literature on legal professions, it is lawyers in the United States who have most clearly been valorized for an autonomy from the state that is rooted in the market. It is not surprising, therefore, that scholarly theories of professions that emerge from the United States heavily invest the professionalization of American lawyers with a collective project of market control. Even the recent jurisdictional theory of professions advanced by Abbott has a premiss of ecological struggle in a market substantially unconstrained by political intervention.[56]

This collection of studies suggests a counterpoint to the American model, for it is in France that lawyers have defined themselves most categorically in terms of politics. This is not to say that politics are absent from any of the other nations: we have shown the contrary. Nor is it the case that the market has been irrelevant to French lawyers. But in France professional identity itself has historically been defined in terms of an explicit rejection of market transactions in favour of a political definition of the collective self. The account of the French profession shows a two-fold dominance of political action. On the one hand, professionals engaged in a sustained fight against the absolutist state, and later against the illegality and the excesses of authoritarian states. On

---

[56] Abbott, *System of Professions.*

the other hand, lawyers led a fight for civil equality, stronger property rights, freedom of expression, personal security, and, subsequently, the creation and extension of individual and public liberties.

Karpik's historical sociology of French lawyers over the *longue durée* demonstrates that politics has not been a contingent involvement for French lawyers but a durable and a dominant engagement.[57] Two necessary conditions were required: on the one hand, self-government and the emergence of a 'public' as an orienting pole for the framing of lawyers' collective action; and on the other hand, a specific organization distinguished by the continuity of the craft and of legal knowledge, by a market made up of individual clients and stubbornly maintained by the refusal of the business market until the middle of the twentieth century. Once institutionalized as a predominantly political actor, the profession had a tendency to reproduce itself and therefore to reproduce the priority given to political action. In short, in the theory of professions, and in the collective orientations of professionals, France may be to politics what the United States is to the market.

Juxtaposing these two professions as respective exemplars of market and politics has much more than antiquarian interest. Just as the German case demonstrates that professions, and law among them, can surrender in the aftermath of a weak tradition of independence, so the French case suggests that in the wholesale reconstruction of political regimes in South America and Eastern Europe, some reformations of professional identities may repudiate a market model of professional power in favour of a political model of professional influence. Indeed, insofar as professions under authoritarian and totalitarian rule have been forced to accommodate themselves to 'absolutist' authorities, or have defined themselves as one of the few remaining centres of political autonomy, the political model exemplified by France may be a more immediate and more compelling alternative than a radical transformation into an Anglo-American type of commercially viable profession. Here then are historically generative axes of professional action that might frame future collective behaviour: the *liberal political* definition of professional self is modelled most dramatically by eighteenth-century France; the *liberal market* definition is exemplified by nineteenth-century America; and the *conservative communalist* reaction is represented at the totalitarian extreme by Nazi Germany.

These historical and comparative cases put the lie to any assumption

[57] Karpik, *Les avocats*.

that either the elaboration of rights, or their defence, can be laid to rest. Whether their extension takes the form of controlling major corporations, or their defence requires mobilization of lawyers on behalf of unpopular minorities, lawyers cannot be gainsaid either as liberal actors-in-waiting or as perpetual creators of rule-of-law regimes. Often enough, indeed, we have observed lawyers as complicitous subverters of rule-of-law regimes. Nevertheless the theoretical and pragmatic problem flagged by the German case also remains: when lawyers will stand and effectively defend the classical core of liberalism must count as a problem entirely as critical in its magnitude, and far more consequential in its human cost, as when they will struggle to obtain market monopolies.

Selective Bibliography

As every contribution in this book includes its own references, this general bibliography has limited purposes. First, it is very selective: it intends to help readers with a few papers and books to give them a general background. For practical reasons, references are presented by countries. Second, it is oriented towards lawyers and politics and, when possible, towards lawyers and political liberalism. Therefore important writings solely on lawyers are not mentioned. Third, it does not distinguish between historical and sociological studies. Fourth, the general section presents on the one hand some of the first works that have attempted to deal with the political dimension of lawyers and on the other, some important writings that belong to other theoretical perspectives.

General Section

A. Early Political Analysis of Lawyers

Bertilsson, M., 'The Formation of Professions: Knowledge, State and Strategy', in R. Torstendahl & M. Burrage (eds.), *Professions in Theory and History: Rethinking the Study of Professions* (London, Sage Publications, 1990).

Burrage, M., 'Revolution as a Starting Point for the Comparative Analysis of the French, American, and English Legal Professions', in R. L. Abel & P. S. C. Lewis (eds.), *Lawyers in Society*, vol. 3, *Comparative Theories* (Berkeley, Univ. of California Press, 1989).

Burrage, M., Jarausch, K., & Siegrist, H., 'An Actor-Based Framework for the Study of the Professions', in R. Torstendahl & M. Burrage (eds.), *Professions in Theory and History: Rethinking the Study of Professions* (London, Sage Publications, 1990).

Halliday, T. C., *Beyond Monopoly: Lawyers, State Crises and Professional Empowerment* (Chicago, Univ. of Chicago Press, 1987).

——'Lawyers and the State: Neo-Corporatist Variations on the Pluralist Theme of Liberal Democracies', in R. L. Abel & P. S. C. Lewis (eds.), *Lawyers in Society*, vol. 3, *Comparative Theories* (Berkeley, Univ. of California Press, 1989), 375–426.

Karpik, L., 'Lawyers and Politics in France, 1814–1950: the State, the Market, and the Public', *Law and Social Inquiry*, 13: 4, 1988, 707–36.

——'Technical and Political Knowledge: The Relationship of Lawyers and other Legal Professions to the Market and the State', in R. Torstendahl & M. Burrage (eds.), *The Formation of Professions: Knowledge, State and Strategy* (London, Sage Publications, 1990), 186–97.

Parsons, T., 'A Sociologist Looks at the Legal Profession', in T. Parsons (ed.), *Essays in Sociological Theory* (Glencoe, Ill., Free Press, 1954), 370–85.

Rueschemeyer, D., 'Comparing Legal Professions: A State-Centered Approach', in R. L. Abel & P. S. C. Lewis (eds.), *Lawyers in Society*, vol. 3, *Comparative Theories* (Berkeley, Univ. of California Press, 1989).

Sarfatti-Larson, M., 'The Changing Functions of Lawyers in the Liberal State: Reflections for a Comparative Analysis', in R. L. Abel & P. S. C. Lewis (eds.), *Lawyers in Society*, vol. 3, *Comparative Theories* (Berkeley, Univ. of California Press, 1989).

B. Other Frameworks

Abbott, A., *The System of Professions: An Essay on the Division of Expert Labor* (Chicago, Univ. of Chicago Press, 1988).

Abel, R. L., *American Lawyers* (New York, Oxford Univ. Press, 1988).

——*The Legal Profession in England and Wales* (Oxford, Basil Blackwell, 1988).

Bourdieu, P., 'La force du droit. Elements pour une sociologie du champ juridique', *Actes de la Recherche en Sciences Sociales* 64 (1986) 3–19.

Brint, S., *In the Age of Experts* (Princeton, Princeton Univ. Press, 1994).

Derber, C., Schwartz, W. A., & Magrass Y. (eds.), *Power in the Highest Degree: Professionals and the Rise of the New Mandarin Order* (New York: Oxford Univ. Press, 1990).

Osiel, M., 'Lawyers as Monopolists, Aristocrats and Entrepreneurs' (Review of R. L. Abel and P. S. C. Lewis (eds.), *Lawyers in Society*), *Harvard Law Rev.* 103: 8 (June 1990).

Torstendahl, R. & Burrage, M. (eds.), *Professions in Theory and History: Rethinking the Study of Professions* (London, Sage Publications, 1990).

France

A. Before the Revolution

Bell, D. A., *Lawyers and Citizens: The Making of a Political Elite in Old Regime France* (New York, Oxford Univ. Press, 1994).

Berlanstein, L., *The Barristers of Toulouse in the Eighteenth Century, 1740–1793* (Baltimore, Johns Hopkins Univ. Press, 1975).

Bluche, J. F., *Les magistrats du Parlement de Paris au XVIIIe siècle* (Paris, Economica, 1960).

Delbke F., *L'action politique et sociale des avocats au XVIIème siècle* (Louvain, Uystpruyst, 1927).

Egret, J., *Louis XV et l'opposition parlementaire* (Paris, A. Colin, 1970).

Fitzsimmons, M. P., *The Parisian Order of Barristers and the French Revolution* (Cambridge, Mass., Harvard Univ. Press, 1987).

Fournel, J. F., *Histoire des Avocats au Parlement et du Barreau de Paris depuis St. Louis jusqu'au 15 octobre 1790* (2 vols., Paris, Maradan, 1813).

Gaudry J.-A., *Histoire du barreau de Paris, depuis ses origines jusqu'a nos jours* (2 vols., Paris, 1864).

Gresset, M., *Gens de Justice à Besancon de la conquête par Louis XIV à la Révolution française (1674–1789)* (2 vols., Paris, Bibliothèque Nationale, 1978).

Karpik, L., *Les avocats: Entre l'État, le public, et le marché, XIIIe–XXe siècle* (Paris, Gallimard, 1995); (trans. Nora Scott), (Oxford, Oxford Univ. Press, forthcoming).

Kelley, D., *The Beginnings of Ideology: Consciousness and Society in the French Reformation* (Cambridge, Cambridge Univ. Press, 1981).

Levy, D. G., *The Ideas and Careers of S. N. H. Linguet. A Study in Eighteenth-Century French Politics* (Urbana, Ill., Univ. of Illinois Press, 1980).

Maza, S. S., *Private Lives and Public Affairs: the* Causes Celèbres *of Prerevolutionary France* (Berkeley, Univ. of California Press, 1993).

Poirot, A. A., Le milieu socio-professionel des avocats au Parlement de Paris à la veille de la Révolution (1760–90), unpub. Thèse de l'École Nationale de Chartres (1977).

Seligman, E., *La justice en France pendant la Revolution* (Paris, 1901).

B. After the French Revolution

Charles, C., 'Le déclin de la République des avocats', in P. Birnbaum (ed.), *La France de l'Affaire Dreyfus* (Paris, Gallimard, 1994), 56–86.

Debré, J.-L., *La République des avocats* (Paris, Librarie Académique Perrin, 1984).

Fabre, J., *Le Barreau de Paris, 1810–1870* (Paris, J. Delamotte, 1895).

Halperin, J.-L., *Les professions judiciares et juridiques dans l'histoire contemporaine. Modes d'organisation dans divers pays européens* (Paris, Centre Lyonnais d'histoire du Droit, 1992).

Karpik, L., *Les avocats: Entre l'État, le public, et le marché, XIIIe–XXe siècle* (Paris, Gallimard, 1955); (trans. Nora Scott), (Oxford, Oxford Univ. Press, 1998).

Le Beguec, M. G. (ed.), *Avocats et barreaux en France 1910–1930* (Nancy, Presses Universitaires de Nancy, 1994).

Germany

Jarausch, K. H., 'The Decline of Liberal Professionalism. Reflections on the Social Erosion of German Liberalism, 1867–1933', in K. H. Jarausch &

L. E. Jones (eds.), *In Search of a Liberal Germany: Studies in the History of German Liberalism from 1789 to the Present* (New York, Berg Publishers, 1990), 261–86.

—— 'The German Professions in History and Theory', in G. Cocks & K. H. Jarausch (eds.), *German Professions: 1800–1950* (New York, Oxford Univ. Press, 1990), 3–24.

—— 'The Crisis of German Professions, 1918–33', *J. Contemp. Hist.* 20 (1985) 379–98.

—— 'The Perils of Professionalism: Lawyers, Teachers, and Engineers in Nazi Germany', *German Studies Rev.* 9 (1986) 107–37.

——(ed.), *The Unfree Professions: German Lawyers, Teachers, and Engineers between Democracy and National Socialism, 1900–1950* (New York, Oxford Univ. Press, 1990).

—— & Jones, L. E., 'German Liberalism Reconsidered: Inevitable Decline, Bourgeois Hegemony, or Partial Achievement?', in K. H. Jarausch & L. E. Jones (eds.), *In Search of a Liberal Germany: Studies in the History of German Liberalism from 1789 to the Present* (New York, Berg Publishers, 1990), 1–23.

John, M., 'Between Estate and Profession: Lawyers and the Development of the Legal Profession in Nineteenth-Century Germany', in D. Blackbourn & R. J. Evans (eds.), *The German Bourgeoisie: Essays on the Social History of the German Middle Class from the Late Eighteenth to the Early Twentieth Century* (New York, Routledge, Chapman & Hall, 1991), 162–97.

Krach, T., *Jüdische Rechtsanwäelte in Preußen. Bedeutung und Zerstörung der freien Advokatur* (Munich, Beck, 1991).

Ledford, K., 'Conflict within the Legal Profession: Simultaneous Admission and the German Bar', in G. Cocks & K. H. Jarausch (eds.), *German Professions: 1800–1950* (New York, Oxford Univ. Press, 1990), 252–69.

—— *From General Estate to Special Interest: German Lawyers 1878–1933* (Cambridge, Cambridge Univ. Press, 1996).

Rueschemeyer, D., *Lawyers and Their Society: A Comparative Study of the Legal Profession in Germany and the United States* (Cambridge, Mass., Harvard Univ. Press, 1973).

Siegrist, H., 'Professionalization with the Brakes on: the Legal Profession in Switzerland, France, and Germany in the Nineteenth and early Twentieth Centuries', *Compar. Social Res.* 9 (1986) 267–98.

—— *Advokat, Bürger, und Staat. Sozialgeschichte der Rechtsanwälte in Deutschland, Italien und der Schweiz (18.–20. Jahrhundert)* (Frankfurt, Vittorio Klostermann, 1996).

Great Britain

Abel-Smith, B. & Stevens, R. B., *Lawyers and the Courts: A Sociological Study of the English Legal System: 1750–1965* (Cambridge, Mass., Harvard Univ. Press, 1967; London, Heinemann, 1967).

Baker, J. H., 'The English Legal Profession, 1450–1550', in W. Prest (ed.), *The English Bar, 1550–1770* (London, Croom Helm, 1981).

Duman, D., 'The English Bar in the Georgian Era', in W. Prest (ed.), *The English Bar, 1550–1770* (London, Croom Helm, 1981).

—— 'Pathway to Professionalism: The English Bar in the 18th and 19th Centuries', *Jrnl. Social Hist.* 13 (1980) 615–28.

Johnson, T., 'The State and the Professions: Peculiarities of the British', in A. Giddens & G. McKenzie (eds.), *Social Class and the Division of Labour* (Cambridge, Cambridge Univ. Press, 1982).

—— 'Mrs Thatcher's Professions: Law, Medicine, and the English State', Paper presented to XIIth World Congress of Sociology, Madrid, 1990.

Prest, W. (ed.), *The Rise of Barristers: A Social History of the English Bar, 1590–1640* (Oxford, Clarendon Press, 1986).

—— 'The English Bar, 1550–1770', in W. Prest (ed.), *The Rise of Barristers: A Social History of the English Bar, 1590–1640* (London, Croom Helm, 1981).

—— (ed.), *The Inns of Court under Elizabeth and the Early Stuarts, 1590–1640* (London, Longman, 1972).

—— (ed.), *Lawyers in Early Modern Europe and America* (London, Croom Helm, 1981).

The United States[58]

Burrage, M., 'Revolution and the Collective Action of the French, American, and English Legal Professions', *Law and Social Inquiry* (1988) 225–77.

Carruthers, B. G. & Halliday, T. C., *Rescuing Business: The Making of Corporate Bankruptcy Law in England and the United States* (Oxford, Oxford Univ. Press, expected 1998).

Freidson, E., *Professional Powers: A Study in the Institutionalization of Formal Knowledge* (Chicago, Univ. of Chicago Press, 1986).

Halliday, T. C., *Beyond Monopoly: Lawyers, State Crises and Professional Empowerment* (Chicago, Univ. of Chicago Press, 1987).

Rueschemeyer, D., *Lawyers and Their Society: A Comparative Study of the Legal Profession in Germany and the United States* (Cambridge, Mass., Harvard Univ. Press, 1973).

Watson, R. A. & Downing, R. G., *The Politics of the Bench and the Bar: Judicial Selection Under the Missouri Nonpartisan Court Plan* (New York, John Wiley, 1969).

[58] While there is a quite substantial literature on the role of individual lawyers in American legislatures, very little research or theory attends either to the collective action of legal professions towards substantive politics (as opposed to the control of markets via politics) or, even less, to the constitution of political society in the terms in which it is defined in this volume. For a recent review of the earlier literature, and a revisionist account of lawyers in politics, see M. C. Miller, *The High Priests of American Politics: The Role of Lawyers in American Political Institutions* (Knoxville, Univ. of Tennessee Press, 1995). A sophisticated structural analysis of lawyers among other lobbyists in federal politics can be found in J. P. Heinz, E. O. Laumann, R. L. Nelson, & R. Salisbury, *The Hollow Core: Private Interests in National Policy-making* (Cambridge, Mass., Harvard Univ. Press, 1993).

2 Barristers, Politics, and the Failure of Civil Society in Old Regime France

David A. Bell (Johns Hopkins University)

> I resolved to write only on matters of the sort that belonged par-
> ticularly to the *philosophe* or literary jurist; to lift these cases, as
> much as I could, to their true dignity, and when they bore on a
> possible reform of the laws, to examine the law itself along with
> the case, and to amass the materials for improved legislation . . .
> In point of fact, I was hardly a barrister except in name.—Pierre-
> Louis de Lacretelle, *Un Barreau Extérieur à la fin du XVIIIe siècle*
> (1823).

The close relationship between lawyers and politics in France, obvious
even to casual modern observers, has a long and complex genealogy.
Before François Mitterrand, long listed as a member of the Paris Bar,
before the voluble advocates who made the Third Republic a veritable
république des avocats, there were the men Edmund Burke derided as
'obscure provincial advocates . . . the fomenters and conductors of the
petty war of village vexation', men named Vergniaud, Barnave,
Danton, Billaud-Varenne and Robespierre, all leaders of the French
Revolution. And before *them*, there were further generations, stretching
far back into the Renaissance. As early as 1559, the jurist François de
Baudouin remarked concisely: '*Jurisconsultus hoc est homo politicus.*'[1]

The relationship may have a conspicuous history, but understanding
it is not necessarily easy. Generally speaking, the problem has been
approached from two different angles. The first, and most commonly
used by sociologists, begins with the lawyers themselves. It involves first
examining the collective interests of members of the Bar (whether oriented towards material gain, status or power), and then explaining patterns of political action in terms of these interests. Alexis de Tocqueville

---

This essay derives from a longer work entitled *Lawyers and Citizens: The Making of a
Political Elite in Old Regime France* (New York, Oxford Univ. Press, 1994). A complete guide
to source material may be found in D. A. Bell, 'Les avocats parisiens d'ancien régime:
Un guide de recherches', *Revue de la société internationale d'histoire de la profession d'avocat* 5
(1993) 213–54.

[1] 'The jurist is a political man', F. Baudouin, *Commentarius de jurisprudentia Muciana*
(1559), quoted in D. Kelley, *The Beginnings of Ideology: Consciousness and Society in the French
Reformation* (Cambridge, Cambridge Univ. Press, 1981), 203.

himself provided a classic example of this approach in *Democracy in America*. 'There are societies', he wrote, 'in which men of law cannot take a position in the world of politics analogous to that which they hold in private life; one can be sure that in such a society lawyers will be very active agents of revolution . . . Lawyers played a prominent part in overthrowing the French monarchy in 1789.'[2] More recently, Lucien Karpik's work has emphasized the 'strategy' of going into politics by which French barristers acquired esteem and influence in the modern period. Studies of English and American lawyers have taken this approach as well.[3]

The second way of conceiving of the relationship begins not with the lawyers but with the political culture of the country in question. It treats the legal profession not as a collection of actors concerned with pursuing collective interests, but as a vehicle that can be used by different political groups. It looks less at the way the social position of the profession determines the political activities of its members than at the way its position within the polity serves the pre-existing political agendas of those who choose to enter it. This way of looking at things, which highlights the services lawyers perform rather than the rewards they can gain, of course dovetails with the way lawyers themselves tend to present their profession, particularly in the sort of bar association oratory that hails lawyers as the selfless servants of the commonwealth. Perhaps for this reason, scholars are hesitant to adopt this perspective. Yet from the very origins of the profession down to the days of Bill Clinton, countless practitioners have in fact treated the law principally as a springboard to political power, to the point of willingly sacrificing the collective interests of their colleagues to their own political goals. Bar association oratory need not be dismissed just because it is self-serving.

These two approaches to the subject of lawyers and politics are, of course, complementary, not competing. One can hardly doubt that lawyers have collective interests, and that these interests affect their political comportment. Yet lawyers also claim a special right, based on their professional capacities, to help *define* the common weal.[4] In 1774,

---

[2] A. Tocqueville, *Democracy in America*, J. P. Mayer (ed.), G. Lawrence (trans.), (New York, Harper & Row, 1988), 264–5.

[3] See most recently L. Karpik, *Les avocats: Entre l'État, le public et le marché, XIIIᵉ–XXᵉ siècle* (Paris, Gallimard, 1995); (trans. Nora Scott), (Oxford, Oxford Univ. Press, forthcoming). Also L. Karpik, 'La profession libérale: Un cas, le barreau', in P. Nora (ed.), *Les lieux de mémoire*, part III: *Les France* (3 vols., Paris, Gallimard, 1993), vol. II, 284–321.

[4] Do lawyers differ in this respect from other professions? Probably mostly in the fact that their own special expertise has a direct and explicit relationship to the legislative

the Parisian barrister Jean-Baptiste Darigrand declared, 'The profession of barrister gives me the priceless right to be the organ of the People.'[5] Countless professional colleagues sitting in English parliaments, American congresses, and French assemblies have since echoed his sentiments. In effect, the legal profession in modern societies has become a common channel for political action. The precise shape of this channel depends, though, on a great deal more than formal political structures. Even while the constitutional nature of the state remains constant, broad-reaching changes in political culture can drastically affect the way the bar functions as a vehicle for political goals.

The purpose of this essay is to explore the relationship between lawyers and politics through a discussion of Parisian *avocats* (barristers) under the Old Regime, and also to take a new approach to the relationship, by considering lawyers not merely as defenders of collective interests, or as politicians-in-training, but as potential architects of civil society. I will first trace the creation of a distinct professional organization under Louis XIV, its transformation into a political *organisation de combat* under Louis XV, and its virtual collapse under Louis XVI, leading directly to the temporary abolition of the profession during the Revolution. I will suggest that until the 1760s the development of the legal profession contributed to the development of an autonomous civil society in France. But I will also argue that in the following decades, the changes in French political culture unleashed by the unravelling of the absolute monarchy, which opened up new possibilities for barristers and gave ambitious men new incentives to take up the law, not only reversed this process, but turned the Bar into the spearhead of a wide-ranging assault on the very idea of civil society. The Jacobin desire to eliminate distinctions between public and private, and to subsume all social activity within the ambit of the state, grew directly out of the late eighteenth-century legal milieu. Throughout, my emphasis will be particularly on the most influential members of the Paris Bar.

---

aspects of government. See J. Kocka's definition of the professions, as quoted in M. Burrage, K. Jarausch & H. Siegrist, 'An Actor-Based Framework for the Study of the Professions', in R. Torstendahl & M. Burrage (eds.), *Professions in Theory and History: Rethinking the Study of Professions* (London, Sage Publications, 1990), 205.

[5] J.-B. Darigrand, *Discours prononcé à la Cour des Aydes le 13 décembre 1774, par Me. Darigrand, Avocat* (Paris, 1775), 3–4 (in Bibliothèque de la Société de Port-Royal, Collection Le Paige (BSPR LP), vol. 573, no. 135).

A la Recherche de Noblesse Perdue

It is well known that over the centuries, French barristers have gone through many different professional incarnations. Time and again, from the Renaissance to the present day, the French state has stepped in to redistribute the functions of legal representation between them and other groups (including notaries and solicitors). Thus while the requirements for entering the profession have remained relatively stable (a law degree, the taking of an oath, a brief apprenticeship, no *numerus clausus*), its professional territory has alternately advanced and receded.[6] What is less well known is that the barristers have also gone through many different political incarnations, even before the French Revolution. Men seeking to use the legal profession as a means of gaining political influence proceeded in very different ways in the Renaissance and in the last century of the Old Regime.

During the Renaissance, French lawyers were rapidly gaining wealth and visibility. As the monarchy struggled to impose order on the fractious kingdom, great noble houses and ecclesiastical institutions increasingly chose to settle their differences in royal courts, leading to an explosion of litigation, and in the number of lawyers. By 1573, in his treatise *Francogallia*, the French Protestant spokesman François Hotman could write, 'Everywhere in France today a class of men predominates whom some call lawyers; others, pleaders . . . in every town where a seat of this kingdom [i.e. a court] is located, nearly a third of the citizens and residents, attracted by the great rewards, have applied themselves to the practice and study of the art of verbal brawling.'[7] Paris alone provided employment for some four hundred barristers, representing a far greater proportion of the capital's total population than their professional descendants do today.[8] Furthermore, thanks to their literacy and legal skills, barristers not only aided their clients in lawsuits,

---

[6] For a brief overview, see L. Karpik, 'Technical and Political Knowledge: The Relationship of Lawyers and Other Legal Professions to the Market and the State', in R. Torstendahl & M. Burrage (eds.), *The Formation of Professions* (London, Sage Publications, 1990), 186–97. The most important social histories of the legal profession in early modern France are L. Berlanstein, *The Barristers of Toulouse in the Eighteenth Century (1740–1793)* (Baltimore, Johns Hopkins Univ. Press, 1975), and M. Gresset, *Gens de justice à Besançon de la conquête par Louis XIV à la Révolution française (1674–1789)* (2 vols., Paris, Bibliothèque Nationale, IV, 1978, Thèse II).

[7] F. Hotman, *Francogallia*, repr. in J. H. Franklin (trans. & ed.), *Constitutionalism and Resistance in the Sixteenth Century: Three Treatises by Hotman, Beza & Mornay* (New York, Pegasus, 1969), 88.

[8] R. Delachenal, *Histoire des avocats au parlement de Paris* (Paris, 1885), 23.

but also served served as their principal agents and counsellors in dealings with each other and with the Crown.

Beyond these functions, barristers also claimed an explicitly political role for themselves, as the master technicians of royal state-building. In a series of letters and treatises written in the late sixteenth and early seventeenth centuries, a series of prominent jurists sketched out their vision of the French polity, and the barrister's place in it.[9] In this vision, the king's authority as lawgiver and executive stood absolute and unchallenged, even over the Catholic Church. However, the lawyers argued that the king did not properly rule as a supreme administrator (as later theorists of absolutism would have it), issuing orders and passing laws to deal with every contentious issue that arose. Rather, he ruled as a supreme judge, acting as the vessel through which divine justice flowed into his kingdom, arbitrating between contending interests and thereby maintaining a proper balance in the land. As far as the jurists were concerned, the king's proper agents outside the capital were not the governors or *maître des requêtes* who sometimes claimed to rule as miniature monarchs in their provinces, but rather the magistrates of law courts, particularly the fifteen or so sovereign courts called *parlements* (which had no relation to the English parliament, although they did claim a consultative role in the legislative process). As the historian Michel Antoine has emphasized, the French monarchy did indeed 'have in its origins an intimately judicial essence and structure' (the absolutist regime described by Tocqueville was a relatively late development).[10] These Renaissance authors wished to endorse and solidify this tradition, and also to emphasize the courts' double-edged role as both the principal agent of, but also the principal restraint upon, royal authority.

---

[9] Among the most important works are: A. Loisel, 'Pasquier, ou Dialogue des Advocats du Parlement de Paris' (1602), in A. Dupin (ed.), *Profession d'avocat. Recueil de pièces concernant l'exercice de cette profession* (Paris, 1844); Guy du Faur de Pibrac, *Recueil des poincts principaux de la première et seconde remonstrance faicte en la Cour de parlement de Paris, à l'ouverture des plaidoiries après les festes de Pasques & la Sainct Martin* (Paris, 1573); A. Arnauld, *La justice aux pieds du roy, pour les parlements de France* (1608); C. Loyseau, *Traité des ordres et simples dignitez*, in *Les oeuvres de maistre Charles Loyseau, avocat en parlement* (Paris, 1678); É. Pasquier, 'Lettre à Théodore Pasquier', reprinted in Loisel, *Pasquier*, 204–11. On these men, see D. Kelley, *Foundations of Modern Historical Scholarship: Language, Law and History in the French Renaissance* (New York, Columbia Univ. Press, 1970).

[10] M. Antoine, 'La monarchie absolue', in K. M. Baker (ed.), *The French Revolution and the Creation of Modern Political Culture* (3 vols., Oxford, Pergamon, 1987), vol. I, 3–24 at 10.

This vision of the polity obviously gave pride of place to magistrates, but it did not overlook barristers, whose supreme legal expertise, moderation, and experience in counselling the great made them an integral part of the system. As Antoine Loisel asserted in the early years of the seventeenth century, 'A state cannot exist without justice, and justice cannot be done without the help and advice of its ministers, above all barristers.'[11] His colleague Étienne Pasquier even likened barristers to priests, suggesting that they performed something of the same function for seekers after justice, that priests performed for seekers after salvation.[12] The jurists endlessly praised the 'noble' aspects of legal practice, although they refrained from claiming full noble status for barristers (who hailed mostly from the upper bourgeoisie). They also emphasized that the Bar was not so much a career goal in and of itself, as an 'order' from which members could be called to greater positions in the state. It was, to quote one much-repeated phrase, the 'nursery of dignities'.[13]

To be sure, one can hardly expect the careers of ordinary lawyers to correspond with much exactitude to the ideal portraits sketched out in these panegyrics. Yet the portraits do have some relevance to the achievements of the elite of the Bar, and they represented the goal towards which others strove. Barristers such as Étienne Pasquier and Antoine Loisel stood high in the ranks of the *politique* party, which supported Henri IV (reigned 1589–1610) in the French Wars of Religion, and they helped in the efforts to reconstruct a strong central government after his victory. They produced much of the period's notable political theory (for instance the work of Jean Bodin and Charles Loyseau), and nearly all of its notable works of history (Pasquier has particular importance here). They naturally directed the great efforts of codification and unification that characterize Renaissance French jurisprudence.[14]

Unfortunately for French barristers, however, this ideal portrait was steadily *losing* relevance in the sixteenth and seventeenth centuries, even as the great project of French state-building to which the Bar hoped to contribute was progressing. Most immediately, this change had its origins in the practice called 'venality of offices', whereby a monarchy perenially strapped for funds openly sold off high judicial and financial offices (and also the titles of nobility which they had the power to confer). By the time of Henri IV's assassination in 1610, judgeships in the

---

[11] Loisel, *Pasquier*, 14.   [12] Pasquier, 'Lettre à Théodore Pasquier', esp. 205–6.
[13] Loisel, *Pasquier*, 14; du Fair, *Recueil*, fo. 12.
[14] For an introduction to these issues, see Kelley, *Beginning of Ideology*.

parlements, as well as the other principal 'dignities' to which barristers had once aspired, had become fully-inheritable pieces of property whose cost put them well beyond the reach of most legal practitioners.[15] The same jurists who praised the barrister's role in the polity harshly criticized venality, and called for a return to a supposed golden age (in fact, much exaggerated) in which men had advanced freely from Bar to Bench. Loisel wrote bitterly, 'The day is past when men were sought for their merit and value.'[16] Even as the Crown confirmed the full membership of magistrates in the nobility, barristers seemed to slip ever more firmly into the ranks of the Third Estate, where they risked being confused with solicitors, recorders, bailiffs, and other despised legal 'mechanicals'.[17] During the seventeenth century, matters got steadily worse. Barristers found their access to judicial positions almost entirely blocked, lost much of their standing in French intellectual life, and although they contributed to Louis XIV's great legal ordinances (for which opportunity they displayed a lavish and somewhat pathetic gratitude), they failed to exercise their former influence on the development of French law.[18]

Barristers reacted to this loss of status in a predictable 'corporate' manner, and struggled collectively to rectify matters. As early as 1602, a quarrel over honorariums (which barristers saw as simple gifts from their clients, but which the Crown and the high courts wanted to treat as taxable fees) led to a successful two-week work stoppage.[19] This incident seems to mark the first time that barristers acted together as an independent unit, for until then they had left all matters of recruitment, discipline and organization at the Bar entirely to the magistrates.[20] Over the next few decades, leading barristers continued to consult

[15] See R. Mousnier, *Le vénalité des offices sous Henri IV et Louis XIII* (Paris, Presses Universitaires de France, 1945), and M. Marion, *Dictionnaire des Institutions de la France aux XVIIe et XVIIIe siècles* (Paris, Picard, 1923, repr. 1984), 431.

[16] Loisel, *Pasquier*, 60. See also du Faur, *Recueil*, fo. 12; Loyseau, *Traité des Ordres*, 50.

[17] Du Faur, *Recueil*, fo. 7.

[18] See A. M. Hamscher, *The Parlement of Paris after the Fronde, 1653–1673* (Pittsburgh, Univ. of Pittsburgh Press, 1976), 45–6; W. F Church, 'The Decline of French Jurists as Political Theorists, 1660–1789', *Fr. Hist. Stud.* 5: 1 (1967), 1–40. On the bar and Louis XIV's ordinances, see Barthélémy Auzanet, 'Lettre de Maître Barthelemy Auzanet, écrire à un de ses amis, Touchant les Propositions arrêtées chez Monsieur le premier Président' (unpag.), in *Oeuvres de M. Barthelemy Auzanet, ancien avocat au Parlement* (Paris, 1708).

[19] M. Yardeni, 'L'ordre des avocats et la grève du barreau parisien en 1602', *Revue d'histoire économique et sociale*, 44 (1966) 481–507.

[20] Delachenal, *Histoire des avocats*, 23–34, 122. The barristers did belong, along with the solicitors (*procureurs*) to a 'community' descended from a medieval confraternity, but by 1600 they had entirely ceased to patronize it.

informally with each other about possible threats to their standing in the courts, and in 1660, they decided to formalize these arrangements by forming an independent body—in effect, the first French bar association. Wary of being compared with artisans or tradesmen, they eschewed the title of 'corporation' and did not request a formal charter from the crown, preferring to endow the new body with the traditional name of 'order', which had agreeable monastic and chivalric connotations. None the less, the organization, which featured regular '*conférences*' between 'deputies' chosen from the membership as a whole, and which claimed the right to act as the bar's spokesman, clearly represented a new departure.[21] The minutes for 14 December 1661 include what amounts to a quiet declaration of independence: 'Resolved . . . That those affairs which depend on the barristers alone and which can be settled by amicable agreement [*une bonne intelligence*] will be dealt with by them alone.'[22] Over the next fifty years the Paris 'Order of Barristers,' generally numbering about 500 men, gained accoutrements such as a library and meeting-place, a training programme for new recruits (to supplement the scandalously lax university programmes) and an annual printed list of the membership (the *Tableau*). More importantly it also gained a complete monopoly on a firmly-defined range of legal functions in the Parisian courts (essentially pleading and consultation), and full control over recruitment and disbarment (subject, extraordinarily, to no oversight whatsoever). It had, in other words, become a recognizably modern professional body.[23]

Although the 'Order of Barristers' would later achieve political notoriety, its early leaders had little concern for affairs of state. They sought, rather, to reverse by simple and direct means what they considered a dangerous decline in the social status of the profession.[24] The Order's

---

[21] The full evidence for these assertions can be found in Bell, *Lawyers and Citizens*, 41–66. The most important documents are the registers of the barristers' *conférences de discipline*, preserved in mss. 368 and 362 of the Bibliothèque de la Cour de Cassation (BCC), on permanent loan to the Bibliothèque des Avocats à la Cour d'Appel de Paris. In later years, barristers eager to demonstrate the immemorial nature of their 'order' sought to play down the importance of these changes, but other commentators recognized their importance. See for instance Voltaire's comments, in his *Histoire du Parlement de Paris* (Paris, 1835), 316.

[22] BCC 362, fo. 33.   [23] See Bell, *Lawyers and Citizens*, 41–66.

[24] Indications of the sense of crisis felt by the barristers can be found in the 1697 oration by *bâtonnier* François Levesque in BCC 360, no. 5, fo. 7; in the testament of Étienne Gabriau de Riparfonds, reprinted in Alfred Franklin, *Les anciennes bibliothèques de Paris*, (3 vols., Paris, 1873), vol. III, 177–80; and H.-F. d'Aguesseau, 'La décadence du barreau' (1698), in *Discours de Monsieur le Chancelier d'Aguesseau* (Paris, 1773), 99–121.

very first public action in the 1660s was to request that its leaders, the *bâtonniers*, receive grants of hereditary nobility (the Crown refused).[25] Thereafter, it exerted itself most forcefully to insist that its members receive the proper marks of ceremonial respect from magistrates. On at least fifteen occasions between 1660 and 1730, when magistrates failed to use the appropriate etiquette (on one notorious occasion, insisting that a barrister uncover his head while reading from a statute), the Order threatened to stop working *en masse* and occasionally did so. In general, their actions produced the desired results.[26] Such behaviour may seem absurd in twentieth-century eyes, but Norbert Elias has reminded us that early modern France was a society that tended to value social status above monetary wealth, and measured this 'commodity' in terms of strict codes of protocol.[27] His generalizations apply to the *Palais de Justice* just as well as they do to the court of Versailles.

Given that barristers could no longer aspire to high offices in the state, or hope to influence royal policy, the late seventeenth century also saw the publication of a flurry of works aimed at providing the Bar with new professional ideals. The critical idea of professional 'disinterestedness' first took hold at this time, particularly in an oration by the magistrate and future Lord Chancellor, Henri-François d'Aguesseau, entitled 'The Independence of the Barrister'.[28] Interestingly, d'Aguesseau made frequent use of terms that would later grow fraught with political meaning in France, such as 'citizen' and 'the public'. Moreover, his repetition of the words *vertu*, *liberté*, *indépendance* and *patrie*, along with his call for barristers to dedicate themselves to the interests of the commonwealth while guarding against luxury and corruption, can hardly fail to recall the classical republican tradition revived in the Italian Renaissance, and further developed in seventeenth-century England. But d'Aguesseau was a fervent monarchist, Gallican, and faithful follower of Bossuet's writings on divine-right monarchy. His was a wholly depoliticized republicanism, a call for barristers to live by the code of Roman citizens within the limits of a Christian absolute monarchy, and to satisfy their craving for status not by seeking to steer the

---

[25] BCC 362, fos. 27, 35, 42, 45.

[26] For one example, see BCC 360, no. 61, and M. Duchemin, *Journal des principales audiences du Parlement*, vol. VII, (7 vols., Paris, 1754), 484. For a more general treatment, see Bell, *Lawyers and Citizens*, 50–62.

[27] N. Elias, *The Court Society*, E. Jephcott (trans.), (New York, Pantheon Books, 1983).

[28] H.-F. d'Aguesseau, *L'indépendance de l'avocat* (1698), in *Discours*, 122–43. See also P.-F. Biaroy de Merville, *Règles pour former un avocat* (Paris, 1711). Cf. L. Karpik, 'Le désintéressement', *Annales: Économies, sociétés, civilisations*, XLIV 3 (1989) 733–51.

ship of state but rather by selflessly defending the private interests of their fellow subjects and reaping their reward in the form of 'glory'.[29] Following the death of Louis XIV in 1715, the French Bar would indeed become politicized, but this change occurred less because barristers wanted to heighten their social status further, than because certain religious dissenters found in the newly-autonomous Order a perfect platform from which to defend themselves against persecution by the French church and state.

Jesus's Lawyers

If the royal court represented one pole of French cultural and religious life in the sixteenth and seventeenth centuries, to a certain extent the Paris *Palais de Justice* represented the opposite one. The court bore the stamp of baroque art, mannerist painting, *salonnière* sensuality, and a theology heavily influenced by the Jesuit Order, all of it bound up in one overriding project: the glorification of a semi-divine monarch. By contrast, the *Palais* stood for a stern classicism, an austere, almost puritanical morality, and a pessimistic Augustinian theology that veered dangerously close to Calvinism. Politically, the men who served there tended to see themselves as necessary restraints on an all-too-human, and therefore all-too-fallible, monarch. Thus it is no surprise that the *Palais* provided exceptionally fertile soil for the development of the Catholic movement called Jansenism, an Augustinian reaction against certain aspects of the Counter-Reformation stressing the relationship between individuals and God, and also the need for wholly corrupt humans to receive God's efficacious grace if they were to have any hope of salvation.[30] To a certain extent, it can even be said that French Jansenism was born in the *Palais*, since many of its leading figures came from the family of the *politique* barrister Antoine Arnauld.

---

[29] For the best treatment of republicanism in the French context, see F. Venturi, 'From Montesquieu to the Revolution', in *Utopia and Reform in the Enlightenment* (Cambridge, Cambridge Univ. Press, 1971), 70–94. On republicanism in general, the key work is J. G. A. Pocock, *The Machiavellian Moment: Florentine Political Thought and the Atlantic Republican Tradition* (Princeton, Princeton Univ. Press, 1975).

[30] On the *Palais de Justice* as a cultural and religious centre, see M. Fumaroli, *L'âge de l'éloquence: Rhétorique et 'res literaria' de la Révolution au seuil de l'époque classique* (Geneva: Droz, 1980), esp. 427–92 and 585–660. On the relationship between Jansenism and the *Palais*, a flawed but still classic work is L. Goldmann, *Le dieu caché: Étude sur la vision tragique dans les Pensées de Pascal et dans le théâtre de Racine* (Paris, Gallimard, 1955).

Despite this heritage, the influence of Jansenism on the history of the French legal profession was hardly predetermined. Jansenists never made up more than a minority of the Order of Barristers, even if the movement did enjoy widespread sympathy in its ranks. Furthermore, many of the Jansenists who did practise law had come to their calling unwillingly. According to the eighteenth-century magistrate Pierre-Augustin Robert de Saint-Vincent, would-be Jansenist priests often balked at the requirement that seminary students sign an anti-Jansenist 'formulary', and ended up in the more relaxed Faculty of Law by default.[31] Yet in the early eighteenth century, Jansenist barristers saw an opportunity to use the Order as a weapon for their cause, and did so very effectively. They ended up transforming the nature of French legal practice.

The ascendancy of the Jansenists in the Order came about because of an odd series of events. Towards the end of his life, Louis XIV, who had always feared and mistrusted Jansenists, conceived a desire to rid France of them at all costs. In 1709, supported by the hierarchy of the French Catholic Church, he sent dragoons to disperse the Jansenist nuns and priests at the movement's stronghold, the convent of Port-Royal, and then had the buildings razed and the graves of prominent Jansenists desecrated. In 1713 he solicited from the pope the Bull *Unigenitus*, which condemned a popular work of French Jansenist exegesis as heretical. He and his tame bishops threatened dire penalties against all clerics who did not subscribe to its terms. Two years later, however, the king died, and the regent for his infant successor unleashed something of a mild revolution in French political life. Gone were the harsh restraints Louis had imposed on the nobility. Gone was the muzzle he had put on the *parlements*. Gone was his insistence on draconian censorship.[32] Thus the Jansenists had both motive and opportunity to launch a campaign against their tormentors in church and state. It was a campaign that would rely heavily on the printing press, and on the nascent force of 'public opinion'.[33]

---

[31] Archives de la Famille Vinot Préfontaine: P.-A. Robert de Saint-Vincent, *Mémoires du conseiller Pierre-Augustin Robert de St. Vincent* (typescript copy), 10.

[32] On the political history of the Regency, see most concisely J. Egret, *Louis XV et l'opposition parlementaire* (Paris, Armand Colin, 1970), 9–25.

[33] On the birth of 'public opinion' in France, and the growth of the literary marketplace in the century before the French Revolution, see R. Chartier, *The Cultural Origins of the French Revolution*, L. G. Cochrane (trans.), (Durham, NC, Duke Univ. Press, 1991), 20–66.

Much of this campaign, which lasted for fifty years and occupied the forefront of the French political stage, was waged directly by the large Jansenist minority within the French clergy. They published hundreds of clandestine pamphlets and issued an 'appeal' for a general council of the Catholic Church to be held in the hope it would revoke the Papal Bull.[34] But Jansenists also hoped to fight their battles through the court system. In the Renaissance, the same jurists who had celebrated the bar as the 'nursery of dignities' had also won acceptance of an important legal principle, namely that the judgments of church courts could be appealed to secular tribunals. They had aimed to strengthen the power of the king and the 'liberties' of the Gallican church, but now the same principle proved highly useful to Jansenist clerics in danger of suspension or unfrocking, who could move their trials from the kangaroo courts set up by their bishops to the more favourable precincts of the *parlements*.[35] By doing so they could also transform individual cases of persecution into *causes célèbres* that would highlight the plight of Jansenists for readers throughout the kingdom. In the decade following the promulgation of the Bull *Unigenitus*, scores of these cases found their way to trial.[36]

Barristers naturally had an extremely important role in these trials, and one privilege they enjoyed made their position even more crucial. Under the Old Regime, barristers presented most of their evidence and arguments to courts in the form of written briefs, called *factums* or *mémoires judiciaires*. By the late sixteenth century it had become common for barristers in important cases to have their *factums* printed (usually in a few hundred copies) and distributed free of charge to interested readers. Since *factums* were official court documents, bore a barrister's signature as a gage of responsibility, and had to be run off quickly during a trial, the royal administration had agreed early on to exempt them from preliminary censorship—a very rare privilege indeed under the monarchy.[37] This freedom made *factums* an obvious vehicle for opposi-

[34] See C. Maire, 'L'Église et la nation: du dépôt de la vérité au dépôt les lois, la trajéctoire janséniste au xviiie siècle', *Annales: Économies, sociétés, civilisations*, xlvi 5 (1991), 1177–1205, and also E. Préclin's *Les jansénistes du 18e siècle et la constitution civile du clergé* (Paris, Sorbonne, 1929).

[35] See M. Cagnac, *De l'appel comme d'abus dans l'ancien droit français* (Paris, Champion, 1906).

[36] See Préclin, *Les jansénistes du 18e siècle*, 54–61.

[37] On *factums*, see S. Maza, 'Le tribunal de la nation: les mémoires judiciaires et l'opinion publique à la fin de l'ancien régime', *Annales: Économies, sociétés, civilisations*, xlii, 1 (1987), 73–90, and L. Lavoir, 'Factums et mémoires d'avocats aux xviième et xviiième siècles', *Histoire, économie et société*, vii, 2 (1988), 221–42.

tion propaganda, and the perfect medium to make the case for persecuted Jansenists.

Hardly had the Bull *Unigenitus* arrived in France than Jansenist barristers seized upon this opportunity with relish. In one particularly sensational case that lasted from 1715 to 1717, involving six clerics from
Reims who had run afoul of their bishop, the barristers Louis
Chevallier and Claude-Joseph Prévost concentrated less on the facts of
the case than on the threat posed to Gallican 'liberties' by the alien
hand of the papacy. Taking for granted a favourable verdict from the
magistrates of the *parlement* of Paris, they used their speeches and *factums* principally to generate opposition to the Papal Bull (the principal
Jansenist history of the events, published in 1723, as much as admitted
that the case had been fought with the educated public's reaction in
mind).[38] They also expounded theories that would radically restrict the
secular authority of the Church at the expense of the state (as represented by the royal courts), and even flirted with ideas about restricting
royal power that had first been proposed in the sixteenth century by
radical Protestants. Within the space of a year, they produced twelve
separate, incendiary, pamphlet-sized publications, many rushed hastily
off the presses but all perfectly legal, thanks to the barristers' printing
privileges.[39]

From this beginning, Jansenist barristers fought what soon became
known as the anti-Jansenist 'inquisition' in scores of cases over the next
two decades, and in the process they gained a tremendous degree of
public attention. Indeed, the Jansenists came to overshadow their more
orthodox colleagues, whose less sensational cases could not compete
with the Jansenist *causes célèbres*. In one particularly important case from
1728, the barrister Jacques-Charles Aubry collaborated with a Jansenist
theologian on a *factum*, co-signed by forty-nine other barristers, that
challenged the church's ability to suspend one of the last remaining
Jansenist bishops, Jean Soanen of Senez.[40] Despite belated, illegal
attempts by the royal authorities to block its publication, Aubry's

[38] J. Cadry and J. Jouail, *Histoire du livre des Réflexions morales et de la Constitution Unigenitus*,
vol. I, (4 vols., Amsterdam, 1723), 685–92 at 692.

[39] The *factums* and speeches may be found in Bibliothèque Nationale (BN), Fonds Joly
de Fleury (JF), vol. 2298; and in its general collection under the *cote* Ld⁴, nos. 773, 800,
801, 802, 812, 913, 933, 934, 935 & 936. See also the material in BSPR LP, vol. 19, nos.
407–8, & vol. 414. For more details on the case see Bell, *Lawyers and Citizens*, 73–81.

[40] *Consultation de MM. les Avocats du Parlement de Paris au sujet du jugement rendu à Ambrun
contre M. l'Evêque de Senez* (Paris, [1728]). In general, on this period, see G. Hardy, *Le
Cardinal de Fleury et le mouvement janséniste* (Paris, Champion, 1923) and Maire, 'L'Église et
la nation'.

blistering and tightly-argued attack went through four editions, and was loudly hailed as a triumph by the clandestine Jansenist newspaper, the *Nouvelles Ecclésiastiques*. According to the journal of one disapproving, non-Jansenist barrister, 'the paving-stones are crawling with copies'.[41] In some ways, the prestige of the Bar had not stood so high for more than a century. The Crown eventually issued a formal condemnation of the *factum*, but it balked at prosecuting the signatories themselves, thanks to the institutional strength the Order had acquired since the 1660s. According to a diary kept by the barrister Edmond Barbier, leading magistrates told the Prime Minister 'that there were no concrete measures to take against members of this corps, who would immediately cease all their activity in the bar and even in their offices'. He later added that the signatories 'believed that they were the only ones who had the right, thanks to their independence, to proclaim the great truths of the Church'.[42]

Yet for all the crown's forbearance in this case, the Jansenists' activity did involve real dangers for the Order. In 1729 and 1730 the royal ministry sponsored a series of pamphlets attacking the barristers for exceeding their professional 'competence'.[43] Then, in 1731, a somewhat unbalanced Jansenist named François de Maraimberg put the Order into real jeopardy with a *factum* for three Orléans priests that seemed to launch a direct attack not simply on the church, but on the state as well. Its most incendiary line read, 'all laws are contracts between those who govern and those who are governed'.[44] The king's council immediately insisted that Maraimberg and his thirty-nine co-signatories either retract or disavow the *factum* on pain of disbarment—an action that represented a clear challenge to the Order's hard-won

---

[41] M. Marais, *Journal et mémoires et Mathieu Marais, Avocat au Parlement de Paris, sur la Régence et le règne de Louis XV (1715–1737)*, M. de Lescure (ed.), (4 vols., Paris, 1863–8), vol. III, 527. In general on the story of the brief, see Bell, *Lawyers and Citizens*, 81–8.

[42] E.-J.-F. Barbier, *Journal historique et anecdotique du règne de Louis XV*, A. de la Villegille (ed.), (4 vols., Paris, 1847), vol. I, 265, 270.

[43] The most important, written by a *cordelier* named Poisson, was called *Avertissement donné aux vingt avocats sur leurs consultation du 1er juillet 1727 par la cause de M. de Senez, ou Prelude de l'Avertissement qui sera donné aux cinquante avocats sur leur Consultation du 30 october 1727 au sujet du jugement rendu à Embrun contre M. de Senez* (Brussels, 1728). On these pamphlets, see Bell, *Lawyers and Citizens*, 88–91.

[44] *Mémoire pour les Sieurs Samson Curé d'Olivet, Coüet Curé de Darvoi, Gaucher Chanoine de Jargeau, Diocèse d'Orleans, & autres Ecclésiastiques de différens Diocèses, Appellans comme d'abus; Contre Monsieur l'Evêque d'Orleans & autres Archevêques et Evêques de différens Diocèses, Intimés. Sur l'effet des Arrests des Parlements, tant provisoires Que Définitifs en matiere d'Appel comme d'Abus des Censures Ecclesiastiques* (Paris, 1730), 3. The name 'Samson' in the title is a misprint for 'Sanson'.

autonomy, and therefore succeeded like nothing else in rallying the majority of the barristers behind the Jansenists. Thus the stage was set for a standoff that lasted for more than a year, featuring lengthy negotiations between the Order of Barristers and the ministry, and that culminated in a three-month work stoppage by the Order in the autumn of 1731. At one point during the crisis, a frustrated counsellor to Prime Minister Fleury denounced the Order as 'a sort of absolutely independent little republic at the heart of the state'.[45] In the end, unwilling to disrupt the Parisian courts by dismissing the barristers, the Crown essentially backed off, leading Voltaire to write later, in his history of the *Parlement*, that 'simple citizens triumphed, having no arms but reason'.[46] However, the loss of income during the strike, and the danger that the crown might take severe steps against the Order (at one point, Fleury contemplated abolishing it altogether) produced a great deal of resentment among the rank and file of the bar, who increasingly came to see their Jansenist colleagues as dangerous 'zealots'.[47]

This resentment did not take long to boil over, particularly since, as an adviser to the ministry put it, 'the haughtiness of this order has now reached an extreme degree'.[48] In 1735 the *Parlement* itself, although generally sympathetic to their cause, ran afoul of the Jansenists by suppressing an open letter they had published (in the name of the Order) to yet another persecuted Jansenist. In this letter, not only had they congratulated themselves on their piety in extravagant terms, they had also attacked the French episcopate as corrupt and unworthy, and the *Parlement* feared another dangerous confrontation with the Crown.[49] The letter had scandalized most barristers, who quietly applauded the *Parlement*'s prudence, but the most zealous Jansenists were of course outraged. In fact, the incident left them so anxious to upbraid the magistrates that they seized upon an apparently minor quarrel over protocol in order to call for another strike, this time against the *Parlement* itself. On this occasion, however, they could not rally the non-Jansenists

---

[45] Archives des Affaires Étrangères, Mémoires et Documents: France (AAE MDF), vol. 1271, fo. 279.

[46] Voltaire, *Histoire du Parlement de Paris*, 315.

[47] See D. A. Bell, 'Des stratégies d'opposition sous Louis XV: L'affaire des avocats, 1730–31', *Histoire, économie et société*, vol. IX, no. 4 (1990), 567–90. The most important document of the crisis, which testifies to the resentment felt against the Jansenists, is a private account written by one of the chief negotiators with the ministry, Jean-Louis Julien de Prunay, in Archives Nationales (AN) AB[xix]3947. Only part of the account has survived.

[48] Marquis d'Argenson, in AAE MDF, vol. 1297, fo. 58.

[49] *Lettre de MM. les Avocats au Parlement de Paris à M. l'Evêque de St. Papoul au sujet de son Mandement* (Paris, 1735).

behind them, and even Aubry, the hero of 1728, expressed his doubts about their actions. After a week, more than seventy barristers decided to return to work. The strike thus collapsed, and the Jansenist leaders, including Claude-Joseph Prévost, became public laughing-stocks, the butt of the songsters who haunted the Pont-Neuf and of young law clerks who published satirical pamphlets about the episode.[50]

The events of 1735 showed that the politicization of the Bar under the Old Regime had limits. Clearly, the rank and file of the Order did not entirely approve of their organization being used as a vehicle for the ambitions of a religious minority, particularly when it threatened their own basic material interests. Following this date, the Jansenists never again dared try to lead the Order into fully-fledged confrontation with the Crown or with the high courts. Yet the incident did not halt the process of politicization altogether. Over the next twenty years, the Jansenists continued to publish *factums* on behalf of persecuted Jansenist clerics on a regular basis, taking advantage of their printing privileges to keep the issues before the eyes of the growing French reading public.[51] In defence of their actions, they came close to claiming free speech for themselves, arguing that barristers had a right to issue written opinions on all matters that might conceivably come before a court ('where the judge can rule, the barrister can consult').[52] Furthermore, as long as they avoided provoking open conflicts with the authorities, they enjoyed widespread support among their colleagues. Young barristers saw participation in these *causes célèbres* as a quick way to make names for themselves. In the single case of a priest suspended by the bishop of Cambrai in 1740–1, 126 (out of 699 then practising) affixed their signatures to at least one brief.[53] One Jansenist author, who dedicated a theological treatise to the barristers, went so far as to tell them that God 'has put the Church of Jesus Christ itself among your clients'.[54]

---

[50] The incident is described most thoroughly in the private journal of L.-A. Le Paige, BSPR LP, vol. 460, no. 23, and in Barbier, *Journal historique et anecdotique*, vol. II, 107–22. For more details, see Bell, *Lawyers and Citizens*, 106–12.

[51] See Bell, *Lawyers and Citizens*, 112–22.

[52] [J. Besoigne], *Question nouvelle. A-t-on droit d'accuser Mrs les Avocats du Parlement de Paris, d'avoir passé leur Pouvoir; & d'avoir traité des matières qui ne sont pas de leur Compétence, dans leur célèbre Consultation sur le Jugement rendu à Ambrun, contre M. de Senez?* [1728], 9.

[53] *Recueil des Consultations de MM. les Avocats du Parlement de Paris au sujet de la procédure extraordinaire instruite à l'Officialité de Cambrai, contre le Sieur Bardon, Chanoine de Leuze; sur son refis de souscrire aux Bulles contre Baïus et Jansénius, & à la Bulle Unigenitus* (Paris, 1740).

[54] *De la nature de la Grace, Où l'on fait voir ce que c'est que la Grace de JÉSUS-CHRIST, considérée en général, & indépendamment du sujet: c'est-à-dire de l'être particulier où elle consiste, dédié à Messieurs les Avocats du Parlement de Paris* (1739), 13.

The Nursery of Publicists

The Jansenists' activity ended up transforming the nature of the French legal profession, because it showed that the Order of Barristers offered an excellent platform from which to appeal to the nascent force of 'public opinion'. Recent works of history have emphasized the extent to which, as the notion of the divine right of kings lost its hold over an increasingly secularized population, and as the market for printed matter exploded, the ability to speak for a somewhat abstract and undefined 'public' became a mark of political legitimacy in France.[55] Yet speaking for the public in a society that lacked a free press and representative institutions was not an obvious proposition. The Old Regime was not so repressive as to crush all unofficial expressions of opinion, but authors could not count on staying out of the Bastille unless they enjoyed a degree of institutional protection. Certain *philosophes* gained this protection for a time in the 1750s, when the liberal magistrate Malesherbes served as Director of the Book Trade, but at other points Voltaire, Diderot and many others found themselves in trouble with the law. The magistrates of the *parlements*, by contrast, had a much firmer institutional footing (although the king did send them into internal exile on five separate occasions in the eighteenth century). They turned their 'remonstrances' to the king into a potent form of propaganda. Yet entry to the Bench was impossible for those without a heavy purse or a careful taste in parents. To educated bourgeois, and even to low-ranking nobles, the Bar thus offered an attractive alternative.

In the 1750s, a long-standing conflict between the *parlements* and the king (over both financial questions and the fate of the Jansenists) degenerated into a full-scale constitutional conflict. The magistrates, advised by Jansenist barristers, demanded a greater role in the legislative process as representatives of the 'nation' while the king tried to restrict them to purely judicial functions. Having no wish and no ability to start an armed rebellion, and no obvious legal recourse against a theoretically absolute monarch except for work stoppages, the high courts increasingly relied on the support of 'public opinion' in order to intimidate

[55] See Chartier, *Cultural Origins*, 20–37; K. M. Baker, *Inventing the French Revolution: Essays on French Political Culture in the Eighteenth Century* (Cambridge, Cambridge Univ. Press, 1990), 167–99; M. Ozouf, ' "Public Opinion" at the End of the Old Regime', *Jrnl Mod. Hist.*, 60, Supp. (Sept. 1988), S1–S21.

Louis XV and his ministers.[56] To this end, they published and distributed their *remontrances*, but they also put together a large stable of pamphlet writers to do the bulk of the work. Thanks to their long experience
in these matters, and their familiarity with the legal issues, the Jansenist
members of the Order of Barristers provided nearly all the recruits in
this stable. Of sixty-four key works cited in a recent dissertation on the
crisis, fully forty-three came from the pens of Parisian barristers, particularly the prolific Jansenist trio of Louis-Adrien Le Paige, Gabriel-
Nicolas Maultrot, and Claude Mey.[57] The barrister Jacob-Nicolas
Moreau, who later abandoned the *parlementaire* cause, captured the
atmosphere in his memoirs, recalling that after he published one short
diatribe, 'many of the magistrates at the head of the party sounded me
out about writing for them, since they were then distributing brochures
with unparalleled prodigality'.[58] Some of these ephemera, and particularly Le Paige's attempt to justify the *parlements'* claims historically by
linking them (spuriously) to fifth-century gatherings of the Frankish
nation, sold extremely well. Indeed, for a brief time they outshadowed
other, more lasting works published at the same time, such as *The Spirit
of the Laws* and Rousseau's *First Discourse*.[59]

For a time, it was the Jansenists who dominated the ranks of the bar-
rister-pamphleteers. Yet their very success eventually drew imitations
from men who did not share their political and religious beliefs. The
first great example was Jacob-Nicolas Moreau himself, who soon abandoned the *parlementaire* cause to write propaganda for the Crown.[60]
Given the plentiful funds available from the ministry for able hack writers willing to plead the cause of absolute monarchy, he soon had many
followers.[61] Then, in 1762, another set of possibilities opened up. In
that year, Voltaire took up the cause of a Toulouse Protestant, Jean
Calas, who had been executed on trumped-up charges after a trial

---

[56] See Baker, *Inventing the French Revolution*, Egret, *Louis XV* and D. Van Kley, *The
Damiens Affair and the Unravelling of the Old Regime, 1750–1775* (Princeton, Princeton Univ.
Press, 1984).

[57] D. C. Joynes, 'Jansenists and Ideologues: Opposition Theory in the Parlement of
Paris (1750–1775)', unpub. Ph.D. diss., Univ. of Chicago (1981). In general on this phenomenon, see Bell, *Lawyers and Citizens*, 115–22.

[58] J.-N. Moreau, *Mes souvenirs*, (2 vols., Paris, 1898–1901), vol. I, 49.

[59] L.-A. Le Paige, *Lettres historiques sur les fonctions essentielles du Parlement, sur le droit des
pairs, et sur les Loix fondamentales du Royaume*, (2 vols., Amsterdam, 1753–54). See also Bell,
Lawyers and Citizens, 115–22.

[60] Moreau, *Mémoires*, vol. I, 50; cf. [J.-N. Moreau], *Lettre du chevalier *** à Monsieur ***,
Conseiller au Parlement; ou, Reflexions sur l'arrest du Parlement du 18 Mars 1755* [1755].

[61] See Bell, *Lawyers and Citizens*, 122–8.

marked by wild outbursts of religious prejudice. The *philosophe* was determined not merely to turn Calas into a martyr of bigotry and a saint of Enlightenment, but to obtain a posthumous vindication from the *parlement* that had condemned him, and for this he needed the help of barristers. Helped first by a stalwart of the Toulouse Bar, Théodore Sudre, and then by the Parisian Jean-Baptiste-Jacques Élie de Beaumont, he initiated legal motions and also collaborated in the writing of *factums*.[62] The old publishing strategy used for so long by Jansenists was thus being taken up by a very different group. Although Voltaire in general had little respect for lawyers, he recognized that *factums* 'take the place of judicial rulings, and direct those of the judges'.[63] He also admitted, on one occasion, that 'if barristers lose their right to make arguments then there will be no law or justice in France'.[64]

To many barristers, it was as if Voltaire, with his European stature and royal acquaintances, had opened up a new horizon, far beyond the minor squabbles and pettyfogging of the Parisian courts. For Élie de Beaumont, thirty years old at the start of the Calas case and barely known beyond the precincts of the *Palais de Justice*, the *philosophe* conjured up visions of European glory: 'I will send your *factum* to all the princes of Germany who are not bigots . . . I wish to be the first trumpet of your glory in Saint Petersburg and Moscow.'[65] Voltaire's eventual victory in the case not only confirmed Élie's reputation, it also paved the way for the French legal system to become a major battleground of the Enlightenment, the site of dozens of spectacular *causes célèbres* in which the theoretical foundations of the regime were placed in the dock. Thus the career of barrister suddenly began to seem attractive not only to upwardly-mobile bourgeois and would-be Jansenist priests, but also to would-be *philosophes*, to men who wanted to battle *l'infâme* from a secure institutional position while earning enough of a living to keep them out of the gutters of Grub Street.[66] Typical of this

---

[62] See E. Nixon, *Voltaire and the Calas Case* (New York, Vanguard, 1959), and F. Delbeke, *L'action politique et sociale des avocats au XVIIIᵉ siècle* (Louvain, Presses de l'Université de Louvain, 1927).

[63] Voltaire, *Les oeuvres complètes de Voltaire*, T. Besterman (ed.), 134 vols. (Oxford, The Voltaire Foundation, 1970–6), vol. CIX, 203 (Voltaire to Charles-Augustin Feriol and Jeanne-Grâce Bosc Du Bouchet, 6 Sept. 1762).

[64] Ibid., vol. CX, 22 (Voltaire to Damilaville, 4 Feb. 1763).

[65] Ibid., vol. CXIV, 73 (Voltaire to É. de Beaumont, 1 Feb. 1766).

[66] See Bell, *Lawyers and Citizens*, 129–36; cf. R. Darnton, 'The High Enlightenment and Low-Life of Literature', in R. Darnton (ed.), *The Literary Underground of the Old Regime* (Cambridge, Mass., Harvard Univ. Press, 1982), 1–40.

new breed of lawyer was the eccentric Simon-Nicolas-Henri Linguet, who had failed in a literary career, and had previously written about his contempt for the bar. 'I have never respected the profession of barrister', he wrote to a friend in 1764, 'but I am going to enter it. That is because one must do something in life. One must make money, and it is better to be a rich cook than a poor and unknown savant.'[67] Linguet was too cynical. By the end of the decade, after taking on the case of the Chevalier de la Barre, a libertine nobleman eventually executed for having desecrated a religious shrine, Linguet had established himself as one of the most brilliant—and most outrageous—legal orators of his generation, numbering dukes and peers among his clientele.[68]

Neither the Jansenists at the Bar, nor the traditional leaders of the Order, had much taste for these new trends in advocacy. Still imbued with a reverence for traditional French jurisprudence, they blanched at the new men's angry *factums*, which attacked judges as bigots and even held up the law itself for excoriation ('our criminal laws, more worthy of Draco's Code than of the Code of a gentle and polite nation, will terrify the most virtuous man' read one typical brief produced in the early 1770s).[69] In reaction, the Parisian Order imposed an increasingly harsh discipline on its members, meting out the so-called 'civil death' of disbarment for all manner of minor offences (even keeping a mistress—this in the France of Louis XV!), and frequently expelling those it deemed overly 'literary', hostile to Jansenism, or disrespectful of the magistrates in their court appearances. When François-Charles Huerne de la Mothe defended a woman whom the Church had excommunicated for becoming an actress in the Comédie-Française, composing his brief in the idiom of the *philosophes*, the *bâtonnier* himself denounced the man to the *parlement*, which suppressed his *factum* and confirmed his disbarment.[70] Élie de Beaumont and Linguet both flirted with disbarment as well.[71]

---

[67] Quoted in J. Cruppi, *Linguet: Un avocat-journaliste au XVIIIᵉ siècle* (Paris, 1895), 46.

[68] In general on Linguet see the meticulous biography by D. G. Levy, *The Ideas and Careers of Simon-Nicolas-Henri Linguet* (Urbana, Univ. of Illinois Press, 1980).

[69] P. Firmin de Lacroix, *Mémoire pour le sieur Pierre-Paul Sirven, Feudiste, Habitant de Castres, Appellant, Contre les Consuls & Communauté de Mazamet, Seigneurs-Justiciers de Mazamet, Hautpoul & Hautpouloi, prenant le fait & cause de leur Procureur Jurisdictionnel, Intimés* (1771), 127.

[70] F.-C. Huerne de la Mothe, *Liberté de la France contre le pouvoir arbitraire d'excommunication* (Paris, 1761). The records of the case are in BN JF 575, fos. 64–94. See also Barbier, *Journal historique et anecdotique*, vol. IV, 391.

[71] See Bell, *Lawyers and Citizens*, 130–6.

Yet these traditionalists were fighting a dubious and somewhat futile fight. It was they themselves who had raised the battle cry 'where the judge can rule, the barrister can consult', and addressed themselves explicitly to the tribunal of public opinion, all of which amounted to a cry for free speech and a more democratic political life. To attempt to limit the speech of other barristers therefore appeared more than a little contradictory. Moreover, given that the Order continued to reject the status of a guild, and the rigid structure of offices that went with it, the leadership of the Order had no easy means of dictating to the membership, if opposed by a majority. It would ultimately have little choice but to heed that majority's desires.

Thus by the early 1770s, a new vision of the barrister's place in the polity was coming to supersede the one first elaborated by the jurists of the late sixteenth century. In this new vision, the barrister was less a 'priest of the law' and counsellor to the architects of absolute monarchy, than a spokesman for 'public opinion'. Furthermore, proving important cases to the public now seemed to matter as much as proving them before a court of law: the king had lost his semi-divine position as the font of all justice. Linguet regularly gave the following advice to his more notorious clients: 'your judges will be, even without realizing the fact, compelled or restrained by the Public, by the most widely spread opinion. It is thus the Public we must instruct, convince, and win over.'[72] By 1774, the liberal magistrate Malesherbes was arguing in an unpublished essay that the freedom to publish *factums* was the single most important part of the barrister's vocation, and indeed represented the last vestiges of French liberty: 'the sole salvation of citizens, the sole resource of the weak and oppressed against audacity and violence, the sole rampart which we have to guard our proprieties'.[73] We should remember, however, that this transformation was coming about despite the resistance of a large segment of the Order of Barristers. It was due less to the longing of established barristers for European glory than to the fact that in a political culture, rapidly changing thanks to the waning of the absolute monarchy and the beginning of the Enlightenment, the law now appeared an attractive career to literary-minded men who would never have considered it earlier in the century.

---

[72] S.-N.-H. Linguet, *Aiguilloniana; ou, anecdotes utiles pour l'histoire de France au dix-huitième siècle, depuis l'année 1770* (London, 1777), 20–1.

[73] Chrétien-Guillaume de Lamoignon de Malesherbes, 'Mémoires sur les avocats', in Malesherbes papers, AN 263 AP 10, dossier 1, no. 2, fo. 59.

Building-Blocks of Civil Society?

In *The Old Regime and the French Revolution*, Alexis de Tocqueville observed that 'it was our judicial system that, above all, enabled the oppressed to make known their grievances. For though as far as administration and political institutions were concerned France had succumbed to absolutism, our judicial institutions were still those of a free people.' He had particular praise for 'the leading members of the Bar', who had stood ready to sacrifice everything for the ideal of liberty.[74] In these remarks, Tocqueville echoed Malesherbes, his great-grandfather, in seeing the French bar as the last vestige of a lost, medieval liberty. Yet Tocqueville was a far more sophisticated thinker, and just as he had earlier turned conventional wisdom on its head to detect Europe's future, not its past, in the American experience, so he could also see the future as well as the past in the practices of the Bar:

> The practices of the law courts had entered in many ways into the pattern of French life. Thus the courts were largely responsible for the notion that every matter of public or private interest was subject to debate and every decision could be appealed from; as also for the opinion that such affairs should be conducted in public and certain formalities observed. Obviously incompatible with the concept of a servile state, such ideas were the only part of a free people's education furnished by the old regime.[75]

Clearly, Tocqueville saw in the activities of eighteenth-century barristers possible building-blocks for the construction of a free, democratic society.

Following from this lead, I would like to argue that the history of the French Bar before 1770, as I have described it, can be understood as part of the process by which an independent civil society was beginning to emerge in Old Regime France. As defined by thinkers such as Victor Pérez-Diaz and John Keane, the essence of modern 'civil society' lies in social institutions (including markets, voluntary organizations, and professional organizations) and a public sphere (in which 'autonomous agents' debate freely over matters of public interest) that lie outside the direct control of the state.[76] Pérez-Diaz has emphasized that while civil

---

[74] A. Tocqueville, *The Old Regime and the French Revolution*, Stuart Gilbert (trans.), (New York, Anchor Books, 1955), 115–17.

[75] Ibid., 117.

[76] See J. Keane, 'Introduction', in J. Keane (ed.), *Civil Society and the State: New European Perspectives* (London, Verso, 1988), 1–31, esp. 19; and V. Pérez-Diaz, 'Civil Society and the State: Rise and Fall of the State as the Bearer of a Moral Project', *The Tocqueville*

society can only exist in a 'full' way in conjunction with a limited state that observes the rule of law, none the less it can emerge in a 'mitigated' way under authoritarian regimes.[77] Although historians of civil society generally point to England, Scotland and the Netherlands as the model cases for its development in early modern times, the story of the French Bar indicates that parallel processes took place, at least for some time, in France as well.[78]

To begin with, the Bar (both the Parisian one, and also its imitators throughout the kingdom) was an example of an independent, voluntary association. To be sure, the Old Regime was a 'corporate' society *par excellence*, peppered with thousands of guilds, *corps*, communities, and other such 'intermediary' bodies. But these organizations differed from the Order of Barristers in several important ways. First, they were hardly independent of the state: most of them had been *created* by the state (particularly thanks to the efforts of Colbert in the seventeenth century) and the state kept them under close surveillance.[79] The barristers, who had always refused the status of a chartered corporation, emphasized this point themselves in a 1782 pamphlet: 'All the *corps* are subject to a superior authority which bends them to its will . . . By contrast, the constitution of the Order of Barristers follows a different model . . . This association that the Barristers form is nothing other than an agreement to exchange information [*communiquer ensemble*] . . . What authority could possibly wield force over such a society?'[80] Furthermore, the *corps* were privileged bodies which generally maintained a *numerus clausus* and admitted members on the basis of heredity, a payment, or other essentially arbitrary factors. Once again, the barristers took pains to emphasize their difference. D'Aguesseau proclaimed in his oft-cited 1698 oration, 'In entering this famous body, men abandon the rank which prejudice attributed to them in the world, to resume the rank that reason has given them in the order of nature

Review/ La revue Tocqueville, xiii, 2 (1992), 5–30, esp. 7. Obviously, these works are just the tip of the iceberg of a vast literature on the concept of civil society.

[77] Pérez-Diaz, 'Civil Society and the State', 7. Pérez-Diaz has been particularly interested in the case of Spain under Franco, the subject of a forthcoming book, but many of his observations apply well to pre-modern States as well.

[78] Particularly influential in this regard has been the work of J. Habermas, *The Structural Transformation of the Public Sphere: An Inquiry into a Category of Bourgeois Society*, T. Burger & F. Lawrence (trans.), (Cambridge, Mass., MIT Press, 1989).

[79] See most recently J. Revel, 'Les corps et communautés', in Baker (ed.), *French Revolution*, vol. I, 225–42.

[80] *Exposition abrégé de la Constitution de l'Ordre des Avocats au Parlement de Paris* (Geneva, 1782), 12.

and truth.'[81] In fact, in the Old Regime, the Order of Barristers offered one of the very few examples of a professional organization *not* organized on the basis of privilege.[82]

In addition to the simple fact of its existence, the Order of Barristers also contributed to the development of civil society through its role in the opening up of a sphere of public debate—a factor that Pérez-Diaz argues is crucial to civil society as a whole.[83] Not only did the barristers encourage debate through their own contributions to it, both in *factums* and illicit pamphlets, they also helped establish its legitimacy through their repeated invocations of the notion of 'public opinion'. In addition, through their maxim 'where the judge can rule, the barrister can consult', they set forth a theoretical claim to the single most important element of any sphere of public debate: free speech. They did not demand this free speech for everyone, of course, only for themselves. Yet the ease of entry into their profession made it into a unique channel of public expression in a society lacking a free press or regular representative institutions. Malesherbes, as usual, recognized this fact most eloquently in his 1774 essay on the barristers: 'If we examine what this highly praised, but also highly-criticized barristers' liberty consists of, we will find that it is simply the natural liberty of all men, which all other men have been deprived of, and which the barristers alone have conserved.'[84]

Finally, it can be argued that the dominant political strain in the bar before 1770—what one historian has called 'Jansenist-*parlementaire* constitutionalism'—itself contributed to the development of civil society under the Old Regime.[85] Obviously, this set of ideas, which originally turned around the claim of hereditary office-holders to represent the 'nation' thanks to a spurious link with the fifth-century Frankish assemblies, are a far cry from any reasonable conception of liberal democracy. None the less, they did have one crucial element in common with theories of civil society: the idea of the limited state. Le Paige and his fellow Jansenist barristers were writing with the principal aim of imposing restraints on the executive power of the monarchy and subjecting it to the impartial force of the law as safeguarded in the legal 'reposi-

---

[81] D'Aguesseau, 'L'indépendance de l'avocat', *Discours*, 127.

[82] For the complicated situation of the medical profession, see M. Ramsey, *Professional and Popular Medicine in France, 1770–1830: The Social World of Medical Practice* (Cambridge, Cambridge Univ. Press, 1988), esp. 39–42.

[83] Pérez-Diaz, 'Civil Society and the State', 8.

[84] Malesherbes, 'Mémoire sur les avocats', AN 263 AP 10, dossier 1, no. 2, fo. 20.

[85] See Van Kley, *The Damiens Affair*, 166–225.

tories' of the *parlements*. To this end they gladly accepted the notion that the state itself has a limited sphere of operations. The *summum* of Jansenist-*parlementaire* constitutionalism, written by Jansenist barristers in the early 1770s and entitled *Maximes du droit public français*, was for this reason surprisingly receptive to British republican authors, including Locke and Harrington, as well as to continental natural law theorists. In a long paraphrase of Christian Wolff's *Jus Naturae*, the book distinguished between the 'public power' and the 'domain of property', and emphasized that the former 'can only affect the free actions of citizens insofar as these actions concern the public order.'[86] Interestingly, this book also marks a turn by the Jansenist barristers away from a dogmatic support of the *parlements* towards the notion that the nation should choose its representatives by election.

To conclude this argument, let me propose a counter-factual question. If the French Revolution had begun in the 1760s instead of in 1789, what vision of the French polity would have been pursued by barristers elected to the National Assembly? (The question is not an idle one: in the 1750s the political philosopher Mably wrote that France was already on the brink of revolution, and sketched out the way events would later unfold in a remarkably prescient manner.)[87] Conceivably, these barristers would have called for a constitutional monarchy, with severe limits on the executive power of the king enforced by a strong, independent judiciary. They would have called for the right to free expression. They would have been encouraging of voluntary, non-corporate professional organizations such as the Order of Barristers. In short, they would have tried to advance the development of civil society, building on the foundations already laid down over the course of the century by their own Order.

Yet the French Revolution did not begin in the 1760s, and over the next twenty years, as the absolute monarchy crumbled further, a sea change took place in French political culture, wrecking whatever chances had existed for the development of civil society and a stable liberal democracy. The real National Assembly of 1789, numbering more members from the legal profession than from any other walk of life, proved intensely hostile to two of the building blocks of civil

---

[86] G.-N. Maultrot, C. Mey, G.-C. Aubry, A. Blonde *et al.*, *Maximes du droit public françois*, (2 vols., Amsterdam, 1775), vol. I, 123. On the influence of this work, see D. Van Kley, 'The Jansenist Constitutional Legacy in the French Prerevolution', in Baker (ed.), *French Revolution*, vol. I, 169–201.

[87] Baker, *Inventing the French Revolution*, 86–106.

society discussed above, namely voluntary associations and the idea of the limited state.[88] The reasons for this change go far beyond the scope of this essay.[89] None the less, it is instructive to note that, once again, the legal profession was at the heart of the developments, and that as the political culture changed, the relationship of lawyers to politics took a new and radical turn.

The School for Scandal

Among the men who joined the Order of Barristers in the 1760s in the hope of discovering the next Jean Calas, there were many who disliked the very idea of an organized legal profession. Simon Linguet, in a blistering attack on French law published in 1764, asserted that in ancient Rome, men had needed no special privilege to speak on legal matters in public, but only 'genius', a good voice, and the 'art of touching hearts'. Did they need more in modern France? He expressed the hope that in a 'regenerated' legal system, the law would possess such clarity and simplicity that there would be no need for professional lawyers to interpret it.[90] His colleagues Ambroise Falconnet and Pierre-Louis-Claude Gin, while not going to such extremes, likewise minimized the importance of formal legal training and expertise for courtroom advocates, preferring to underline the importance of sympathy and sentiment.[91]

These opinions, while not what one would generally expect from practising lawyers, derived quite naturally from the intellectual climate that prevailed at the end of the Old Regime. Most immediately, they arose out of a movement for legal reform, inspired partly by the writings of Beccaria, which gained extraordinary momentum in the two decades before the French Revolution. The adherents of this movement argued for a radically simplified law code, and great restrictions on the power of judges, who, they argued should behave as much as possible

[88] On the composition of the National Assembly, see E. H. Lemay, 'La composition de l'assemblée nationale-constituante', *Revue d'histoire moderne et contemporaine*, xxiv (1977), 345.

[89] Two crucial works for the understanding of these issues are Baker, *Inventing the French Revolution*, and F. Furet, *Interpreting the French Revolution*, E. Foster (trans.), (Cambridge, Cambridge Univ. Press, 1981).

[90] S.-N.-H. Linguet, *Nécessité d'une réforme dans l'administration de la justice et dans les loix civiles en France* (Amsterdam, 1764), esp. 93–4.

[91] [Ambroise Falconnet], *Essai sur le barreau grec, romain et français, et sur les moyens de donner de lustre a ce dernier* (Paris, 1773); P.-L.-C. Gin, *De l'éloquence du barreau* (Paris, 1767).

like automata rigidly applying a set of standardized rules.[92] More broadly, though, these opinions reflected a growing distaste among educated Frenchmen for any sort of intermediary body coming between individual citizens and central public authority—whether bodies as grand and ancient as a *parlement*, as petty as a guild of coopers, or as benign as a scientific academy. François Furet and Keith Baker have suggested that this distaste itself had two powerful sources in French political culture. On the one hand there was the legacy of the absolute monarchy, which had long desired to clear out the corporate brushwood limiting its own freedom of action, and whose goals had recently gained a set of new, 'enlightened' rationalizations in the writings of the school of writers called the physiocrats (they promoted the ideal of an impartial, rational, all-powerful sovereign managing society in its own best interests). While absolutism itself was crumbling, the mental habits it had inculcated proved more durable, leading writers to endow the abstract, collective body of the 'nation' with much the same powers once claimed by the monarch. On the other hand, there was the influence of Jean-Jacques Rousseau, whose *Social Contract* insisted that only by surrendering wholly to the General Will could human beings overcome the alienation and inequality that inevitably accompanied the birth of complex societies.[93] Whereas Montesquieu (like the pessimistic Jansenist barristers, and also like the authors of the American Constitution) had seen the principal danger to the commonwealth coming from the abuse of executive power, Rousseauians and the heirs of absolutism alike tended to have more fear of the machinations of selfish, privileged, exploitative minorities, and thus looked askance at any voluntary association not explicitly sanctioned by the state.

Before 1770, despite the best efforts of Linguet, Falconnet, and Gin, these ideas had only limited currency in the Order of Barristers, thanks to the continuing clout of the Jansenists, and the membership's predictable concern for their own material interest. In 1771, however, a larger political crisis unexpectedly changed the entire shape of legal practice in France. In this year, after two decades of constitutional strife with the *parlements*, Louis XV and his Lord Chancellor, Maupeou, finally lost their patience. Facing yet another prolonged work stoppage,

[92] See J. A. Carey, *Judicial Reform in France before the Revolution of 1789* (Cambridge, Mass., Harvard Univ. Press, 1981) and D. Y. Jacobson, 'The Politics of Criminal Law Reform in Pre-Revolutionary France', unpub. Ph.D. diss., Brown Univ. (1976).

[93] See Furet, *Interpreting the French Revolution*, esp. 28–46; Baker, *Inventing the French Revolution*, 121–3.

they had the recalcitrant magistrates arrested and sent to remote villages. By the end of the year they had effectively abolished the old *parlements* and created new ones, staffed not by venal officers, but by trusted royal appointees.[94] With one stroke, the judicial system that had endured with few changes for centuries, was turned upside down.

The barristers responded to this expression of royal despotism in varying ways. The Jansenists, of course, immediately girded themselves for battle: they refused to practise before the new courts, cajoled the rest of the membership into joining their strike, and unleashed a massive propaganda campaign against Maupeou and the king. Louis-Adrien Le Paige, who had the support of the king's disaffected cousin, the Prince de Conti, supervised the pamphleteering operations from his position as Bailiff of the Temple, the gloomy fortress in northern Paris where Louis XVI would later reside as a prisoner. Similar strategies had worked very well during Louis XV's more limited attempts to bring the *parlements* into line in the 1750s, but this time the Jansenists faced greater odds. For one thing, they now had to reckon with the existence of strong ideological opposition within the Bar from figures such as Linguet and Gin, who enthusiastically supported the Lord Chancellor's actions. Furthermore, Maupeou himself, recognizing the importance of the barristers' co-operation for the success of his new court system, assiduously courted them, naming nine members of the Bar—including Gin—to judgeships, and appealing to the non-Jansenists in a slew of pamphlets. Given these pressures, and the economic pressures that resulted from any long work stoppage, the strike collapsed in November 1771, and half of the 540 barristers then belonging to the Order, including several of the most prominent orators, returned to work.[95]

Maupeou's experiment lasted for only three years. In 1774, Louis XV died, and his successor Louis XVI recalled the old *parlements* as a gesture of goodwill. During these three years, however, much had changed in the courts. In one of the decrees creating the new judiciary, Maupeou had opened the profession of barrister to any law graduate who took a perfunctory oath, thereby abolishing the Order's monopoly

---

[94] On the 'Maupeou Crisis', see most recently D. Echeverria, *The Maupeou Revolution: A Study in the History of Libertarianism* (Baton Rouge, Louisiana State Univ. Press, 1985), and D. Van Kley, 'The Religious Origins of the Patriot and Ministerial Parties in Pre-Revolutionary France', in T. Kselman (ed.), *Belief in History: Innovative Approaches to European and American Religion* (South Bend, Univ. of Notre Dame Press, 1991), 173–236.

[95] See Bell, *Lawyers and Citizens*, 138–44, and also D. A. Bell, 'Lawyers into Demagogues: Chancellor Maupeou and the Transformation of Legal Practice in France, 1771–1789', *Past and Present*, no. 130 (1991), 108–141.

on advocacy. Furthermore, although half the membership eventually returned to work, the leadership of the Order remained on strike, and so the Order itself remained in suspension. Thus pleading in the Parisian courts was no longer limited to those who had its imprimatur, and the barristers' conduct was no longer supervised by a leadership ready to impose the 'civil death' of disbarment for the slightest impropriety. Given the freedom of expression already available to barristers, these developments amounted to the complete end of censorship for those men who did return to practice—the equivalent of the general freeing of the presses in 1789.[96]

It did not take long for the effects of this liberation to make themselves felt. By early 1772, observers of the Parisian courts were noting a sudden surge in 'sensational' and 'scandalous' trials in which barristers, no longer restrained by the Order's unwritten code of conduct, eclipsed their own clients and frequently turned their summations into assaults on the character of the opposing counsel. Led by the pale, skeletal, intense figure of Linguet, many adopted an increasingly self-conscious literary style, crafting their speeches and *factums* in imitation of the fashionable, melancholic *drames bourgeois* then appearing on French stages. In one particularly sensational trial, in which a family of bourgeois money-lenders sued an aristocratic client, Linguet, appearing for the defendant, employed a claque of three hundred noblemen to hiss and jeer the opposing counsel, and strode through the *Palais* with a bodyguard of sixty nobles.[97] One typical comment on the new trends in advocacy came from the pen of a former solicitor, Louis Groustel: 'At present several [barristers], who are more Novelists than Jurists, recognize no leader and no discipline. In a sort of stupor, driven by avarice, with their eyes closed, they strike out at every object they come across.'[98] Clearly, this new generation of barristers saw themselves less as 'priests of the law' than as the citizens of some classical city-state, debating in the *agora*.

The accession of Louis XVI and the return of the old *parlements* did little to arrest this trend. Although the Jansenists and the leadership of the Order duly returned to the *Palais de Justice*, their attempts to re-establish their former dominance ended in almost complete failure. Quite simply, during the years of the Order's suspension, those barristers who did practise had realized the advantages to be reaped from a

---

[96] See n. 95.   [97] Cruppi, *Linguet*, 287, 327.
[98] L. Groustel, *Mémoire relatif à l'affaire du comte de Morangiès* (Paris, 1773), 3.

more open, loosely organized legal profession. Thus while for the most part they welcomed the re-establishment of the Order's monopoly, they refused to accept the reimposition of its disciplinary powers, or its unwritten code of conduct. The leadership barely managed to disbar Linguet for his behaviour during the crisis, and failed to expel any of his allies. During the last fifteen years before the Revolution, they managed to disbar only five men, in contrast to the hundreds who had suffered this fate in the fifty years before 1770.[99] Despite indignant protests from some older members, the sensational *causes célèbres* that had flourished under Maupeou continued with barely an interruption. Furthermore, lawyers increasingly used these cases to launch withering attacks on France's archaic system of criminal justice, on its lack of religious toleration, and on 'abuses of power' such as the arbitrary arrest orders called *lettres de cachet*. The leading members of the Bar also achieved unprecedented fame, with their court appearences celebrated in engravings and in verse (most of it execrable), their speeches reported in full in news-sheets, their *factums* selling tens of thousands of copies.[100] When, in 1785, the city of New Haven, Connecticut chose to honour eleven Frenchmen by making them honorary citizens, two of them— Guy-Jean-Baptiste Target and Pierre-Louis de Lacretelle—were Parisian barristers.[101]

During this same period, however, the Order of Barristers as an organization rapidly sank into decrepitude. Dissenters within its own ranks attacked it for purveying a useless and pedantic legal education, for promoting a stultifying and unworthy style in oratory and legal writing, and for stifling the careers of the most promising advocates.[102] Following on Linguet's example these critics in fact denounced the very existence of the Order as illegal, a blatant attempt to create the most cramped and bigoted sort of guild without submitting it to the oversight normally exercised over guilds by the Crown. One of the critics, the future revolutionary leader Jacques-Pierre Brissot, declared, in language worthy of Louis XV, 'the state should not tolerate the existence of a

[99] On Linguet's disbarment see the accounts in Levy, *Ideas and Careers of Linguet*, 155–65, Cruppi, *Linguet*, 326–91, and H. Carré, *Le barreau de Paris et la radiation de Linguet* (Poitiers, 1892). On the disbarments in general, see Bell, *Lawyers and Citizens*, 165–74.

[100] On these developments, see S. Maza's 'Le tribunal de la nation', and also S. Maza, *Private Lives and Public Affairs: the* Causes Célèbres *of Prerevolutionary France* (Berkeley, Univ. of California Press, 1993).

[101] [Louis Petit de Bachaumont, M.-F. Pidansat de Mairobert, *et al.*], *Mémoires secrets pour servir à l'histoire de la république des lettres*, (36 vols., London, 1777–89), vol. XXIX, 135.

[102] See Bell, *Lawyers and Citizens*, 165–74.

corps which can cause and which has caused dangerous troubles'.[103]
Another asked indignantly, 'Shall there exist a democracy within a
monarchical state? . . . [The Order] eclipses even royal authority, since
it is freed from all authority.'[104] These attacks found a resounding echo
within France's growing network of 'enlightened' publicists, and in the
thunderstorm of pamphlets and newspapers published in the pre-
revolutionary crisis of 1787–9.[105] Thus the Order, which had previously prided itself on its reputation as a guardian of the public interest,
now found itself held up as the very model of unjustifiable, arbitrary
privilege. By 1789, its authority had grown so weak that law graduates
who had never registered as members were appearing regularly in the
Parisian courts.[106] Given this background, it is not surprising that a revolutionary National Assembly dominated by barristers would soon
abolish French Orders of Barristers altogether, and that unlike members of most other guilds, the profession as a whole—humble work-
horses of the Bar as well as the elite, provincials as well as
Parisians—accepted this decision with barely a murmur of protest.[107]

The Triumph of Sparta

In the early 1790s the aged magistrate Pierre-Augustin Robert de
Saint-Vincent, writing his memoirs in lonely German exile, confessed
his inability to understand how the barristers he had known as loyal
auxiliaries to the *Parlement* had helped overturn the entire edifice of
French jurisprudence.

Who would not be confounded by the capriciousness of the human spirit upon
seeing that men who enjoyed public esteem in the profession of barrister . . .
put themselves at the head of the Revolution of 1789? Here the human mind
is seized with stupor . . . For how can the feelings of respect for religious

---

[103] [J.-P. Brissot], *Un indépendant à l'ordre des avocats* (Berlin, 1781), 46.

[104] *Thémis dévoilée, dédiée aux Etats-Généraux* (Paris, 1788), 34.

[105] See Bell, *Lawyers and Citizens*, 165–74, 181–9.

[106] See Beaumarchais, *Avertissement de M. de Beaumarchais* (Paris, 1787), 1. The great
playwright, involved in one of his many lawsuits, is here denouncing barristers who have
taken on cases and won recognition from the courts without belonging to the Order. See
also N. Bergasse, *Mémoire pour le Sr. Bergasse dans la cause du Sr. Kornmann contre le Sr. de
Beaumarchais, et contre le prince de Nassau* (Paris, 1788), 139.

[107] On the abolition of the Order, see M. Fitzsimmons, *The Parisian Order of Barristers
and the French Revolution* (Cambridge, Mass.: Harvard Univ. Press, 1987), 33–64.
Fitzsimmons claims that the Order *did* protest its abolition, but he bases this claim largely
on a series of 'pseudonymous pamphlets, which almost certainly emanated from the
Order' (at 62). In fact, they did not. See Bell, *Lawyers and Citizens*, 189–94.

principles and for monarchical authority, of which the older barristers were always the principal defenders and buttresses, be reconciled with this sudden effervescence which caused an entire order of citizens, known for their wisdom, prudence, learning, experience and maturity, to fly off the handle [*sortir de ses gonds*]?[108]

Given the sea-change in French political culture traced out by recent historians of the Old Regime, this 'effervescence' now seems more comprehensible. Yet the fundamental shift in the relationship between lawyers and politics in this period was no less momentous, and its consequences for the development of civil society were no less severe.

In every way, the changes in French legal practice between 1770 and 1789 marked a reversal of the trends that had prevailed in the previous century. Most obviously, whereas that century had seen the development of the Order of Barristers as an independent, voluntary association between the state and individual subjects, the next twenty years saw its rapid disgrace, decline, and final disappearance. It may seem odd that barristers would willingly abandon an organization that had doggedly upheld the profession's social status and protected the material interests of the membership. Yet barristers' careers were hardly suffering during this period: indeed, they reached new peaks as a result of the public's endless taste for sensational *causes célèbres*. Furthermore, the generation of barrister-*philosophes* who now dominated the Bar in fact cared just as much about using their cases as vehicles for advancing a programme of radical social and political change. That programme itself had no place for intermediary bodies such as bar associations, and since it called for the complete restructuring of France's legal system along classical Roman lines, with a blurring of the boundary between judicial and political advocacy, its adherents naturally supported the replacement of lawyers by simple 'eloquent citizens'. Instead of posing as privileged *defenders* of the public interest, the barrister-*philosophes* were now dubbing themselves the simple *representatives* of the public, and that concept left no place for institutional divisions between barristers and others. Nor was their hostility to the Order assuaged by the fact that the remnants of the leadership continued to rail against their activities, and to call for their expulsion from the Bar.

The period between 1770 and 1789 also saw the dramatic decline of Jansenist-*parlementaire* constitutionalism within the Bar and, more broadly, of support for a strong, autonomous judiciary and a limited

---

[108] P. A. Robert de Saint-Vincent, *Mémoires*, 7–8.

executive. This shift reflected partly the success of Beccaria's ideas, partly the broad shift in French political culture away from the idea of the division of power. More immediately, however, it accompanied the triumph of the barrister-*philosophes* and their conception of the profession's place in the polity. Earlier, as 'priests of the law' and political auxiliaries to the magistrates, barristers had naturally been dependent on the survival of a judiciary possessing considerable latitude with regard to the interpretation of statute. They therefore shared the magistrates' strong distrust of executive power. Now, as 'voices of the nation' (to quote Ambroise Falconnet's 1785 definition of barristers), as publicists more concerned with the exposure of injustice than with strict legal standards of proof, their dependence on the courts was gone.[109] Furthermore, in the 1780s the most prominent barristers, far from remaining in opposition to the Crown, began working hand in hand with several of Louis XVI's reforming ministers. These ministers—including, yet again, Malesherbes—had realized that *causes célèbres* could serve not simply to denounce 'abuses' in general, but to direct attention to the particular abuses they wished to reform. They thus cultivated the friendship of the barristers, and steered them in the direction of certain cases in the hopes of paving the way for new legislation. For instance, before proceeding with the emancipation of French Protestants in 1788, the ministry collaborated with the barristers Élie de Beaumont and Target on a case designed to highlight the iniquities of the existing anti-Protestant laws.[110] Given that the principal opposition to such initiatives came in large part from the ranks of the magistrates, the collaboration naturally strengthened both the barristers' turn away from the *parlements*, and also their belief in the need for a strong, rational unfettered executive power.

To be sure, there was one basic continuity in the barristers' politics in the last two decades of the Old Regime: their dedication to the sovereign power of 'public opinion'. Yet even here, one can perhaps trace a shift in emphasis from their earlier treatment of the 'public' as a final court of appeal, and their newer vision of it as the bearer of the general will. In general, the development of legal rhetoric during this period supports Keith Baker's idea that at the end of the Old Regime

---

[109] A. Falconnet, 'Essai sur les mémoires', in *Le Barreau français: partie moderne*, (2 vols., Paris, 1806–8), vol. I, p. xxxi.

[110] A. Lods, 'L'avocat Target défenseur des Protestants', *Bulletin de la société de l'histoire du protestantisme français*, XLIII (1883), esp. 606. In general on this collaboration, see Bell, *Lawyers and Citizens*, 174–81.

the French concept of 'public opinion', as opposed to the English one, carried few connotations of free debate among competing parties. Instead it signified a single, indivisible voice making definitive judgements.[111] Needlesss to say, this later conception of the 'public' was hardly conducive to the idea of a separation between the state and civil society.

Beyond the fact that barristers turned against their earlier contributions to the development of civil society in this period, it can also be argued that, through their participation in the most sensational *causes célèbres*, they participated in an assault on the very notion of civil society. Sarah Maza, who has studied these cases in detail, suggests that the barristers' strategies commonly involved the imposition of political meanings on private, domestic disputes. In the case of the moneylenders and the aristocrat mentioned above, for instance, the moneylenders' counsel portrayed the aristocrat's alleged reneging on a loan as symptomatic of the oppression of the common people by the privileged orders.[112] In the case of a nobleman imprisoned at his family's request, the barrister Pierre-Louis de Lacretelle (who generally sought to 'elevate cases to their true dignity' and considered himself a 'barrister only in name') not only turned the trial into an assault on the legal instruments that had allowed such imprisonment in the first place, but used his eloquent *factum* as a thinly-veiled attack on all forms of 'arbitrary' and 'despotic' power, particularly when wielded by women.[113] In the spectacular scandal called the Diamond Necklace affair, in which two adventurers gulled a Cardinal into giving them a necklace he thought destined for the Queen, favouritism and sexual dalliance at the court of Louis XVI and Marie-Antoinette were stigmatized as inherently corrupting.[114] Implicitly following Rousseau's dictum that 'everything depends fundamentally on politics', the barristers sought to conflate the private and public aspects of their cases, reading the state of the com-

---

[111] Bell, *Lawyers and Citizens*, 165–74; cf. Baker, *Inventing the French Revolution*, 167–99.

[112] S. Maza, 'The Véron-Morangiès Affair, 1771–1773: The Social Imagery of Political Crisis', *Hist. Reflections/Réflexions historiques*, XVIII, 2 (1992).

[113] S. Maza, 'Domestic Melodrama as Political Ideology: The Case of the Comte de Sanois', *Amer. Hist. Rev.*, XCIV 5 (1989), 1249–64. Lacretelle's remarks, quoted more fully in the epigraph to this essay, can be found in *Oeuvres de P. L. Lacretelle ainé*, vol. I (5 vols., Paris, 1823–4), 123.

[114] S. Maza, 'The Diamond Necklace Affair Revisited (1785–1786): The Case of the Missing Queen', in L. Hunt (ed.), *Eroticism and the Body Politic* (Baltimore, Johns Hopkins Univ. Press, 1991), 63–89.

monwealth in the state of individual families, and vice versa.[115] It is hard not to see in this conflation a foreshadowing of the Jacobin republic, and its ambition (wholly impractical in the eighteenth century) to subject all social activity to standards of Spartan 'virtue' set by the state.[116] Given that civil society, to exist, requries a private sphere separate from the state, the success of the barrister-*philosophe* illustrates the failure of civil society to take hold under the Old Regime. It marks the triumph of an illusion that would bewitch the French revolutionaries, the illusion of France as a regenerated classical *polis*, where private and public blended together.[117]

To be sure, this illusion did not last for long, and neither did the radical vision of a France free of lawyers. The judicial system of perfect transparency that Linguet had longed for never came into being, and the attempts to carry on without lawyers in the ruins of the old system pleased no one. By late 1794, after the fall of the Jacobins, the former barristers of the *parlements* had already begun to regroup, and to plan for a restoration of their former status. In 1811 Napoleon granted their wish.[118] Yet the Order did not immediately recover its former autonomy, for the legislation governing it now stipulated that barristers could only practise upon taking an oath not to 'say or publish anything contrary to laws, to rulings, to morals, to the security of the State or to public tranquility'. It banned unauthorized assemblies of barristers, and assured government control over disciplinary matters and the choice of *bâtonniers*.[119] This legislation fitted in well with the Emperor's reluctance (shared by many of his successors) to aid in the post-Revolutionary re-emergence of civil society. The Order only fully recovered its earlier liberty with the coming of a stable liberal democracy to France in the 1870s.[120]

Despite the Napoleonic restrictions, and indeed throughout the rest of the nineteenth and much of the twentieth century, the legal profession retained the heavily political colouration it had developed in the eighteenth. Barristers continued to turn their cases into trials of the

---

[115] J.-J. Rousseau, *Les confessions*, in *Oeuvres complètes* (Paris, Gallimard, 1959), vol. I, 404. See the discussion in L. Hunt, *Politics, Culture and Class in the French Revolution* (Berkeley, Univ. of California Press, 1984).

[116] This is Chartier's argument in *Cultural Origins*, 195–7.

[117] See Pérez-Diaz, 'Civil Society and the State', 13, for a discussion of the private sphere and civil society.

[118] See Fitzsimmons, *Parisian Order*, 111–92. [119] Ibid., 178, 181–2.

[120] L. Karpik, 'Lawyers and Politics in France, 1814–1950: The State, the Market, and the Public', *Law and Social Inquiry*, 13: 4 (1988), 707–36, esp. 716–17.

regime and to define their calling by its special relationship to the 'public'. They reaped many rewards in terms of status and occasionally income for doing so.[121] Yet this brief survey of the Old Regime shows that the first steps taken by French barristers towards an engagement in the politics of public opinion had little to do with the advantage of the profession as a whole. Barristers under the Old Regime tended to pursue their collective advantage in more mundane ways, such as in the quarrels over protocol that obsessed the Order in its first seventy-five years of existence. Indeed, both in the cases of the Jansenists who flirted with royal censure, and of the barrister-*philosophes* who prepared the way for the Order's abolition, political engagement worked to the profession's considerable collective *disadvantage*. The engagement came about initially because the law offered a useful means of political expression for men who found all other avenues blocked off. To conclude, then, one cannot simply say that lawyers turned to politics in Old Regime France. It would be more accurate to say that lawyers and politics turned to each other.

[121] Karpik, 'Lawyers and Politics in France'; and see also Karpik, 'La profession libérale'.

3   Builders of Liberal Society: French Lawyers and Politics

Lucien Karpik (École des Mines, Paris)
(translated by Nora Scott)

The sociology of lawyers, which has long been built on Anglo-Saxon reality, or rather on a particular representation of this reality, has conceived the profession as a community whose organization and privileges revolved around service relations or as an economic agent seeking to control the market while remaining aloof from politics.[1] The last ten years, however, have seen the active rehabilitation of the political orientation.[2] From this perspective, French lawyers occupy a crucial position. Over the long term—from the beginning of the eighteenth to the mid-twentieth century—their relationship with politics has been so fundamental that the professional actor and the political actor have become one, in other words the relationship has become so close-knit that the 'profession' has come to designate both a craft and a political movement.

Three questions guide our examination of the significance and the scope of the singularity of French lawyers. What was the nature of their

---

[1] With a few exceptions, in particular that of T. Parsons, 'A Sociologist Looks at the Legal Profession', in T. Parsons (ed.), *Essays in Sociological Theory* (Glencoe, Ill., Free Press, 1954), 370–85.

[2] M. Burrage, 'Revolution as a Starting Point for the Comparative Analysis of the Legal Profession, in R. L. Abel & P. S. C. Lewis (eds.), *Lawyers in Society*, vol. 3, *Comparative Theories* (Berkeley, Univ. of California Press, 1989), 322–74; M. Bertilsson, 'The Welfare State, the Professions and Citizens', in R. Torstendahl & M. Burrage (eds.), *The Formation of Professions: Knowledge, State and Strategy* (London, Sage Publications, 1990); K. H. Jarausch, 'The Decline of Liberal Professionalism. Reflections on the Social Erosion of German Liberalism, 1867–1933', in K. H. Jarausch & L. E. Jones (eds.), *In Search of a Liberal Germany: Studies in the History of German Liberalism from 1789 to the Present* (New York, Berg Publishers, 1990), 261–86; T. C. Halliday, *Beyond Monopoly: Lawyers, State Crises and Professional Empowerment* (Chicago, Univ. of Chicago Press, 1987); T. J. Johnson, 'The State and the Professions: Peculiarities of the British', in A. Giddens & G. McKenzie (eds.), *Social Class and the Division of Labour* (Cambridge, Cambridge Univ. Press, 1982), 186–208; D. Rueschemeyer, 'Comparing Legal Professions Cross-nationally: From a Profession-centered to a State-centered Approach', in Abel & Lewis (eds.), *Lawyers in Society*, 289–321; R. Shamir, *Managing Legal Uncertainty: Elite Lawyers in the New Deal* (Durham, NC, Duke Univ. Press, 1995); H. Siegrist, 'Professionalization with the Brakes on: the Legal Profession in Switzerland, France and Germany in the Nineteenth and Early Twentieth Centuries', *Compar. Social Res.*, 9 (1986) 267–98.

political commitment? Can this collective action be considered to have had an effect on political society? Has it transformed the profession itself? First of all, despite their diversity, I intend to establish that all of the lawyers' commitments share one common feature: political liberalism, if, in this introductory phase, the term—of necessity vague, since its meanings have varied over time—can be taken to mean a concern with defending individual and public liberties as well as moderate government. However unlikely such a prospect may seem, in view of the duration and the changing circumstances of this history, the analysis nevertheless attempts to show that the multiple orientations of lawyers' actions ultimately fall within a unitary political framework.

Next, far from considering that lawyers have acted in a context that lay beyond their purview, that they mobilized their energies in a society that was a given in which they had no choice but to submit to social determinations, I intend to show that, as a collective actor, their orientations, their struggles, their failures and their successes transformed reality and played a sometimes eminent role in shaping and developing liberal society in France. Lastly, instead of regarding political action as being alien to the profession, as something added to the normal line of business, to the organization of the collective body, to market relations or to professional knowledge, I maintain that, during the period under study, political action was the dominant organizing principle and as such affected all components of the collectivity.[3]

Far from considering that the profession's relations with political liberalism were merely episodic and that they had no substantial effect on either the profession or on the state and society, I propose to examine the following general hypothesis: *French lawyers are among those collective actors who fashioned the liberal state as well as the liberal society, and in so doing constructed themselves as a judicial and political actor dedicated to liberal action.*

Such a perspective implies two tasks: one historical, the other analytical. The first part of this essay presents some examples of political action undertaken by lawyers drawn from the rich and turbulent history of the French eighteenth and nineteenth centuries; all attest the reference to political liberalism and show the nature of the bond that grew up between the professional body and political society. In the second part, analytical tools are presented and used to explain the orien-

---

[3] Over the very long term, three principles of organization dominated the profession, or, if one prefers, the profession took three distinct historical forms, see L. Karpik, *Les avocats: Entre l'État, le public et le marché XIIIe–XXe siècle* (Paris, Gallimard, 1995); (trans. Nora Scott), (Oxford, Oxford Univ. Press, forthcoming).

tations and effects of collective action. The multiplicity and persistence of lawyers' interventions in political life, and the ensuing consequences—change of magnitude, popularity, conquest of the state—are linked to the construction and implementation of a theory of public spokesmen, while their consistent 'choice' of political liberalism is explained by both a spirit of freedom rooted in a legal tradition and by a collective identity all the more relevant to the political society for having fostered its construction.

Lawyers and Political Action

For over two centuries, lawyers distinguished themselves by their intense and constant relations with politics. In the eighteenth century they were involved principally in defending the Jansenists, aiding *Parlement*[4] in its struggle against monarchical power, in representing the peasants in their legal suits against the *seigneurs*, or, following Voltaire's struggle against judicial error, in the proliferation of *factums* (legal briefs) in the 1770s and 1780s. The nineteenth century was marked by an upsurge in the number of court cases and the sudden appearance of a new figure, the political lawyer; at the same time it saw many lawyers playing a role in the liberal and republican movements and parties which would gradually lead to their conquest of the state.[5]

Should these forms of action be considered as signs of very different preoccupations and situations or, from a certain perspective and despite the long span of time covered, can they all be considered part of a unitary political model? This is the question I would like to answer by examining three episodes, briefly presented below: lawyers' assistance to the Jansenists persecuted by the official church and by royal power, their pleadings on behalf of the peasants in the courtroom, and the judicial defence action during the nineteenth century.[6]

---

[4] The *Parlement* was not only the High Court which received and decided appeals from the lower courts of the kingdom, it also had a political function which it aspired to extend, founded on the right of registering new laws (*droit d'enregistrement*) and the right of remonstrance (*droit de remontrance*).

[5] The central actor of this story was the Order of Paris, which throughout the period (and today) represented the largest, most powerful and most prestigious bar association in the country, the politics of which often provided the guideline for the other French Bars.

[6] For a general presentation and analysis of this tumultuous history, see L. Karpik, *Les avocats*, 29–227. For lawyers under the Ancien Régime, see also, D. A. Bell, *Lawyers and Citizens: The Making of a Political Elite in Old Regime France* (Oxford, Oxford Univ. Press, 1994).

A. The Ancien Régime: Defending the Jansenists

In 1728, two priests and a canon from the diocese of Orléans were suspended by their bishop for being in violation of the Papal Bull,*Unigenitus*; they appealed to the *Parlement*, but the bishop had the question brought before the King's Council. The three Jansenist clergymen engaged a lawyer, who drew up in their defence a *consultation* (legal brief) which was eventually signed by forty lawyers. A violent piece of writing, it went well beyond the judicial and religious problems in point to deal with general principles of the monarchical state. Three thousand copies of the *consultation* were printed and distributed; it was a huge success. The opposition was up in arms and lost no time in obtaining the suppression of the *consultation* and an injunction against the signatories stipulating that they recant or they would be 'forbidden to exercise their functions'.

The Order convened to prepare its response. The general assembly of lawyers decided that there would be no recanting or retracting, and set about elaborating a common defence. Presented to the General Assembly, it was again signed by 'the Forty', as well as by the *Bâtonnier* (President of the Order) and 250 lawyers, half of the body. By dint of solicitation, the defence was read before the Prime Minister: the effect was all they had hoped, and it led to a joint negotiated declaration which favoured the lawyers.

Reaction was violent: the bishops were furious, the State Council displeased, while the largely Gallican and Jansenist Parisians applauded the lawyers and ridiculed their enemies. At this point the church officials pronounced against the lawyers, and the case was further aggravated when the Archbishop of Paris obtained permission to condemn the *consultation* with a Pastoral Letter and declared those responsible to be heretics.

More incidents and several General Assemblies later, discontent led the lawyers to strike. *Lettres de cachet* were delivered against the ten lawyers judged the most recalcitrant; the strike continued, while the Prime Minister considered suppressing the Order altogether. The courts went into recess, and when they reconvened, both sides sought a compromise: the negotiations ultimately concluded in the lawyers' favour.[7]

---

[7] Concerning the lawyers' role in this political–religious quarrel see also D. A. Bell, chap. 2 *supra*.

Without going any further, five observations can be made:

1. Far from representing a force subordinated to the *Parlement*, far from
   being the modest allies, dependent on and respectful of the aristocratic caste of parliamentarians, as they have so often been depicted,
   from the time they first appeared on the public scene, lawyers
   showed themselves to be an independent force, driven by their own
   aims and goals, capable of mobilizing their own resources and conducting their own action.
2. This was a collective action, as is clearly shown by the *consultation* of
   the Forty, the *Bâtonnier*'s interventions, the General Assemblies, the
   votes, etc. The fight was not led by a few isolated minorities, but by
   the Order itself, committed by its official representatives, who did
   not hesitate to go to extreme lengths to keep members in line. It was
   through common action that the profession's self-government
   proved its effectiveness.
3. The professional commitment cannot be separated from the political commitment. The profession was defending individual judicial
   cases, but in order to do so, it had to mobilize general arguments,
   and this double-edged reality found expression in the invention of a
   new language which was a blend of law and politics, combining the
   rationality of the first with the passion of the second, and therefore
   capable of swaying widely divergent publics.
4. The *consultation* of the Forty contained a political reflection which
   basically revolved around two general propositions: the first states
   that '*Parlements* are the Senate of the Nation'; and the second, that
   'All laws are contracts between those who govern and those who are
   governed'. In the first case, the Bar was defending the shift of legislative power towards the *Parlement*; in the second it was claiming that
   law was no longer a simple matter of the king's will, it also required
   the consent of the governed; therefore the bar association considered
   that the king should treat his subjects as equals and that evoked the
   civil equality of all those who were part of the kingdom. In short,
   the rather blunt criticism, even though it was at times denied by the
   lawyers, strikes a blow at the very foundations of monarchical absolutism.
5. This consultation won the Bar popular acclaim. Applauded and
   praised for a pamphlet in which they demanded tolerance on behalf
   of the public, lawyers discovered to their surprise that the rest of the
   population recognized themselves in their persons and that, when

this convergence occurred, it produced esteem and sometimes even public glory.

The growing number of these *consultations* clearly shows the right of conscience to contest the authorities, thereby sharing in a veritable construction of individual expression. This construction was all the less restrained as, on an issue mobilizing royal power, the clergy, sovereign courts and a growing portion of the Paris population, the lawyers were acting as an autonomous agent defining its own action, having allies and dealing directly with the powers at hand, and thus demonstrating its growing influence.[8]

B. *The Ancien Régime: Peasant Trials*

The eighteenth century was marked, in many French provinces, by an increase in the number of lawsuits brought by peasant communities seeking to obtain a reduction, if not the repeal, of seigneurial dues.[9] These dues were a fundamental bone of contention. Varying widely in nature and amount from one seigneury to the next, they were not merely a material exaction imposed by landowners on the peasantry, they also defined in concrete terms the status of persons and goods, since they created sharp inequalities of condition and harsh restrictions on the use and free disposal of property.[10] In the 1730s and 1740s, peasant communities began organizing their resistance, even if this meant going deeply into debt in order to bring their case before the courts of justice; and despite a high rate of failure, they persisted in this course until the French Revolution. More and more lawyers rallied to

[8] 'What is most honourable here is that the lawyers dealt personally with the Prime Minister and with the Chancellor without calling upon either the *Parlement* or the public prosecutors [*avocats généraux*]. And I am fundamentally convinced, as are many others, that *Parlement* is jealous of their success in this affair; for, since lawyers already enjoyed an elevated position in society, it is to be feared that this may increase because of this event, which may be regarded for them as a *felix culpa*.' (E. J. F. Barbier, *Chronique de la Règence et du règne de Louis XV (1718–1763) ou Journal de Barbier*, 8 vol. II (Paris, Charpentier, 1857), 137.) (Author's translation.)

[9] A. Cobban, *Le Sens de la Révolution Française* (Paris, Juilliard, 1984), 54; M. Gresset, *Gens de Justice à Besançon de la conquète par Louis XIV à la Révolution française (1674–1789)*, (2 vols., Paris, Bibliothèque Nationale) IV, Thèse, 1978, II, 730–4; O. H Hufton, 'Le paysan et la loi en France au xviiième siècle', *Annales*, 3 (1983) 679–700; R. L. Kagan, 'Law Students and Legal Careers in 18th Century France', *Past and Present*, no. 68 (1975), 54 and 66–7.

[10] *Corvées* were free services rendered to the landlords; *banalités* required the villagers to pay for the mandatory use of the landlord's flour mills, wine presses and bread ovens; the *triage* authorized the landlord who had granted a wood to his peasants to take back one-third, etc.

these new causes and developed previously unknown legal notions and arguments to make their case, as illustrated by the example of Burgundy.[11]

The widespread rejection of manorial rights led lawyers to take two distinct lines of argument in both their case statements and their pleadings. In the first place, a continuity of payments from the earliest times was no longer regarded as validating these dues and, inasmuch as tradition was thus annulled, landlords were invited to 'produce' the original legal titles. Soon, however, the violence and barbarity of the early times were invoked as grounds for voiding agreements that were not a product of consent freely given by the contracting parties. In the second place, lawyers abandoned the discussion of legal claims and turned to another type of argument altogether: seigneurial rights, which were defined and collected in a wide variety of ways, should be *extinguished* when inconsistent with custom or royal laws. All privileges that exceeded the territorial norm, and regardless of other legal considerations, should thus be annulled. This twin-pronged line of reasoning was to throw the whole seigneurial system into question.

The two arguments were tantamount to a redefinition of the individual's rights. In the first instance, the transformation of the seigneurial bond into an agreement altered the nature of the actors involved: in lieu of the arbitrariness of history, it restored the formal requirements for a valid contract, namely the autonomy of the contracting parties and the agreement of their wills. The landlord thereby found himself despoiled of the advantages associated with a form of social domination, while villagers became defined by the independent exercise of their conscience and their power of decision. This change of register replaced the weight of tradition and relations of power with an individualistic and egalitarian principle which applied to all parties to the contract. The innovation was more striking in the second instance, since the diversity of seigneurial rights, which was simply the expression of the particularism inherent in the form of personal relations that arose in the Middle Ages, was limited by the uniformity imposed by provincial or national collectivities. In this way the effect of the seigneurial regime depended entirely on an external principle the all-pervasiveness of which indicates the presence of a common condition in the eyes of the Law, a form of equality that governed all intermediate powers.

[11] The following paragraph closely follows H. L. Root, 'Challenging the seigneurie: Community and contention on the eve of the French Revolution', *Jrnl Mod. Hist.*, (Dec. 1985), 652–81.

What was the effect of such a change in legal thinking? This repertory of concepts and reasonings can be seen as the direct precursor of the language used by the Constituent Assembly to bring down the seigneurial system, for the revolutionary assembly[12] was replete with lawyers; but such a viewpoint does not seem to provide a satisfying explanation for a legal construction which had an active role in building a society suited to absolute monarchy, since the newly defined legal status of the individual simultaneously weakened the intermediate power of the landlord and reinforced the ongoing transformation of subjects into individuals equal and interchangeable in the eyes of royal authority. Lawyers were therefore responsible for the construction of an ambiguous reality: the subject of the Crown became an autonomous individual, but his rights, far from being incorporated into a human nature that would make them intangible, were grounded in and circumscribed by the monarch's sovereignty; this was the bond that would be dissolved by the Revolution.

C. The Nineteenth-Century 'Liberal Experience': Political Trials

The end of the Napoleonic era ushered in a half century that saw three monarchs, two revolutions, one republic and an emperor. The 'liberal experience'[13] testifies to the difficulty of stabilizing French society before consent founded the continuity of the Third Republic. As a defence against its many and dangerous political adversaries, the constitutional monarchy made broad use of prosecution, particularly against the press: this was the era of trials. It was also the era of lawyers. Early in the Restoration period, lawyers began crossing over to the opposition. And under the next two monarchies, the shift continued, each time for similar reasons: the rejection of extraordinary laws and measures ('*lois d'exception*'), and the struggle against attempts to stifle freedoms. This action on the part of the lawyers, of which only the broad outlines can be indicated here, was pursued in two areas: the courts and the national political arena.[14]

Notwithstanding the diversity of the cases tried, the defence adopted a common strategy, readily evident from a comparison of the pleadings,

---

[12] 'The records of the court cases . . . suggest that changes in legal thought during the late eighteenth century foreshadowed the position taken during the Revolution by the Constituent Assembly.' (Root, 'Challenging the seigneurie', 669.)

[13] R. Rémond, *La Vie politique en France depuis 1789*, vol. 2 (Paris, A. Colin, 1969), 267.

[14] For a more detailed presentation, see Karpik, *Les avocats*, 92–131, & Karpik, 'Lawyers and Politics in France, 1814–1950: The State, the Market, and the Public', *Law and Social Inquiry*, 13: 4 (1988), 707–36.

which was based on two principal methods. On the one hand, lawyers defending freedoms constantly appealed to the Constitution, which incorporated the ideals of the 1789 Revolution: they thereby played on the contradiction between the basic laws guaranteeing civil equality, individual liberties, freedom of expression, and religious tolerance, and the emergency laws that constantly overrode these principles. Their repeated public demonstration thus made the arbitrary conduct of the Government tangible. On the other hand, far from being restricted to 'pure' judicial reality, their pleadings addressed the most fraught questions of the day: freedoms, tolerance, church–state relations, the electoral question, constitutionality, etc. Everything was exposed, defended, combated. Everything was translated into a language that established a close link between law and politics.

Not only was this strategy to prove effective in the face of an accusation in disarray, but it had two additional overall consequences. The courts became a political-judicial forum, an effect exacerbated by the presence of a third party: the spectators. Trials were momentous events: the courtrooms were packed, daily Press accounts were avidly read, the pleadings were printed and sold: public passions crystallized around legal questions. Independently of any capacity to win cases or guarantee freedoms, the defence presented itself as the instrument of a veritable political pedagogy, which, in its colourful and dramatic way, handed liberal forces and public opinion the arguments with which to consolidate and extend true civil and political citizenship.[15]

At the same time, the Bar, as a collective person whose concrete expression was multifaceted, gradually came to be seen as embodying the defence of freedoms. Nothing could have favoured this public assessment more than the repeated crossovers to the opposition and the spontaneous convergence of lawyers from varied political sensibilities. Monarchists, liberals, republicans, none hesitated to take up the defence of a political adversary, nor did they cease to pool their talents

---

[15] While the Jansenist quarrel provided an example of a collective action based on the process internal to the bar, lawyers' activities in the 19th cent. represent a second type of collective action: when the members of a group identify with the representatives the validity of whose actions they ratify in so doing. At the time, not all lawyers were politically active, but all identified—all the more strongly for the powers of the Order being under threat from the authorities—with those who expressed, in the courts as in the public arena, a set of widely shared convictions (adhesion to the achievements of the Revolution and defence of freedoms), and all benefited from an action which drew public esteem and heightened the grandeur of the Bar.

for the same causes.[16] In so doing, they publicly demonstrated the unity of a group that passionately devoted itself to the defence of the law and of liberties. The wide interest aroused by the trials and the prestige of the title were reflected in electoral successes: increasingly lawyers took up political careers and rose to the highest state positions.[17]

D. A Model of Liberal Action?

The principles unifying the forms of action adopted by the profession under the Ancien Régime were by no means obvious, and all the less for the adversaries being so different: lawyers were hostile to the absolute monarchy, but favoured it in their defence of peasant communities; they sided with the *Parlement* in its fight against a centralized state and the disappearance of particularistic collective liberties, but opposed it when criticizing the seigneurial system and criminal justice, etc. This relative heterogeneity stems, to a large extent, from the many roles lawyers played (defence in and out of the courts, spokesmen or militants), and from the different periods under consideration. Over time, however, the ambiguities and contradictions tend to blur, and two converging lines emerge. In the conflict over the foundations of power that shook society, lawyers, whether defending the *Parlement* or intervening independently, consistently opposed absolute monarchy; they even developed, fairly early in the day, the principle that, far from having an external divine origin, sovereignty resided in the body politic: the public. And concerning the rights and freedoms of the subjects of the realm, there can be detected, perhaps more confusedly through a tangle of peasant trials, religious quarrels and *factums*, a growing emphasis on the autonomy of the individual and on the rights that guarantee it. Innovators in the field of law, propagators of ideas, lawyers defined themselves by claims and practices which were a first step towards citizenship: civil equality, stronger property rights, freedom of conscience and expression, personal security, etc. In short, the central orientations tended to coalesce around individual freedoms and a moderate state (and more of the first than the second); these orientations defined a proto-liberalism which was part of the 'first cycle of liberalism' that preceded the Revolution.[18]

[16] The collective defence of the same cause, which was a common practice, often brings together lawyers of different political sensibilities: monarchists, moderate and advanced liberals, and republicans.

[17] By 'State positions' is meant positions in Parliament or Government.

[18] P. Manent, *Histoire intellectuelle du libèralisme. Dix leçons* (Paris, Calmann-Levy, 1987), 173.

In the nineteenth century, with the advent of the liberal state, and once human rights and individual freedoms were guaranteed by the constitutions, the drive for liberalism came into the open and changed quarters. Lawyers set about denouncing a largely counter-revolutionary clergy, but the strongest and most insistent demands were reserved for the freedoms of assembly, of the press, and of expression in general; these demands completed civil and political citizenship. It was this tradition, carried forward by the 'radical' movement, that recruited so many lawyers under the Third Republic and which was dedicated to the creation of a liberal, parliamentary, and anti-clerical republic.[19]

What can such actions, so diverse and covering such a long period of time, have in common? Politics, of course, but what else? Eighteenth-century lawyers tried to limit the absolute monarchy and to bring in individual freedoms; their nineteenth-century heirs never ceased defending a legal order capable of protecting the basic freedoms. Over the long term, these commitments became part of the *political liberal model*; lawyers were among the builders of the liberal political society.

However the lawyers' political universe is determined not only by what it takes in, but also by what it leaves out: the Dreyfus affair and the 'social question' help trace these limits. The Dreyfus affair could have been a new 'cause' for lawyers. After all, was it not a miscarriage of justice that needed righting, a 'cause' that had all the outward appearances of others they had espoused in the past? And yet lawyers were missing from the debate, replaced by intellectuals, who mobilized in the name of law, morality, and justice, and who would occupy a long-lasting position on the French political scene.[20] How can this absence be explained? True, the anti-Dreyfus bourgeoisie comprised a large portion of lawyers' clientele, but perhaps another, more basic, explanation may be advanced. Anti-Dreyfusards—the Army, the clergy, a fraction of the petty bourgeoisie and a large portion of the Press, all driven by anti-Semitism and nationalistic ideology—expressed an altogether different dividing line running through society than that to which lawyers had been accustomed, one that did not simply oppose the state and the public, but one which made it impossible as a

---

[19] 'Until 1914, "radicalism" was simply a movement, the obstinate pursuit of revolutionary truths that had grown out of the eighteenth-century tradition of legal and political thought.' (Y.-H. Gaudemet, *Les Juristes et la vie politique de la IIIᵉ République* (Paris, PUF, 1970), 39.)

[20] 'The professors lived the Dreyfus affair, that intellectual uproar, while the "political lawyers" passed through without even getting their togas wet.' (A. Thibaudet, *La République des professeurs* (Paris, Ressources, 1927), 33–4.)

consequence to confuse the quest for freedom or justice with a sovereign will external to the state.[21]

The 'social question' set another limit. From the mid-nineteenth century onwards, there were few lawyers who supported the aspirations of the working class and, once in power, they tended to adopt a socially conservative position on popular demands, combining the often violent repression of labour strikes with timid social legislation,[22] which explains their wariness and even their hostility to the developing welfare state. Here, too, as the intellectuals had done, new representatives—professionals from the unions and from the Socialist and Communist parties—took up the function of expression that lawyers had refused. With this twofold restriction, the lawyers' political liberalism revealed its specific nature: it presented itself as a 'pure', 'rigorous' conception whose principle of action lay exclusively in the uncompromising defence of civil and political rights against the arbitrariness and violence of the state.

Despite its ups and downs, this form of collective action ultimately strengthened the profession's social position. In the eighteenth century, lawyers rose to popularity and gained influence, as is shown by their ability sometimes to engage the powers of the realm in single-handed combat; the public esteem they enjoyed is reflected in the large number elected to the Estates General that opened the French Revolution. In the nineteenth century, their popularity weighed heavily in the electoral balance, opening the way to state positions, and, under the Third Republic, transforming them into a ruling elite.

An Interpretative Framework

Nothing in their functions seems to have predisposed lawyers to such persistent political action, nothing seems to explain why this professional body so resolutely and continually engaged in a direction that led it to accumulate conflicts with the state, the church and numerous political forces, but which also enabled it twice to achieve outstanding collective success. Compared with the evolution of lawyers in other countries, this history exhibits a singularity that is the best embodiment

---

[21] On lawyers and the Dreyfus affair, see C. Charles, 'Le Déclin de la République des avocats', in P. Birnbaum (ed.), *La France de l'Affaire Dreyfus* (Paris, Gallimard, 1994) 56–86.

[22] 'Radical discourse supports progress within the limits implied by attachment to private property and ultimately respect for the social order.' (M. Reberioux, *La République radicale? 1898–1914* (Paris, Le Seuil, 1975), 50.)

of the 'French exception'. These paradoxes and this originality are at the root of three interrelated questions: why this passion for politics? Why the connection with political liberalism? How could a body with so few members, and so little wealth and power rise so irresistibly to state power? The answers are to be sought in two directions: on the one hand, in the formulation of a theory of the lawyer as spokesman for the public and, on the other, in the interpretation of the influence of a specific form of professional tradition and identity.

A. The Lawyer as Spokesman for the Public

The interpretation that explains such exceptional features rests basically on lawyers' long-term strategy as spokesmen for the public. A sequence of five fundamental arguments underpins this interpretation:

1. Lawyers claim to speak for the public.
2. The public is merely a figure of political speech.
3. Political action, spokesman, and the public are intimately linked.
4. For the spokesman, credibility is central.
5. Popularity, influence, and power are the yardsticks of the success of the public's spokesman.

Lawyers claim to exercise the function of spokesmen for the public

The strategy pursued by lawyers appeared explicitly for the first time in d'Aguesseau's famous speech on the 'Independence of the Lawyer'.[23] To explain why, of all the professions, lawyers alone managed to maintain their independence, and avoid the authority of the state as well as the dynamic of capitalist accumulation of wealth, d'Aguesseau suggested the 'virtue' which, for him, set lawyers apart and which later would be called disinterestedness, in other words, a passion for the *public good*. Taking a complex line of reasoning, the *Discours* argued that, faced with apparently superior hostile forces, the profession could maintain its independence only by allying itself with the 'public'.

From this conclusion, d'Aguesseau deduced two principles that were supposed to guide collective practice: if lawyers wanted to enjoy 'glory', they had to prove their dedication to the public, and since the public had no direct means of expressing itself, lawyers should be the ones to

---

[23] H. F. d'Aguesseau, 'L'Indépendance de l'avocat', in d'Aguesseau (ed.), *Oeuvres complètes du chancelier d'Aguesseau. Nouvelle édition . . . par M. Pardessus* (Paris, 1693), 1–13. At the time of his *Discours*, d'Aguesseau was a senior magistrate whose analysis reflected the lawyers' state of mind, as he was close to these professional circles.

ensure such expression. *In a single movement, lawyers both constituted the public and claimed to be its representatives.* This inaugural text set out a strategy, but its scope was still limited to judicial matters; it was rapidly to extend to political concerns: by the turn of the eighteenth century, lawyers would constantly invoke the authority of the public to justify their involvement in politics.

The public is merely a figure of political speech

What does the term 'public' designate? Whereas in the seventeenth century, *le public* still meant the reading audience and theatre-goers, for d'Aguesseau and those who followed, the term no longer admitted of material attributes. It was an impersonal mechanism which distributed esteem and glory in exchange for merit and virtue. Comparison between what the public demanded—merit and virtue—and what it handed out in return—social approbation, dignity—reveals an asymmetry inherent in the relationship: the public is the master who rewards those who serve it. Since the term also designates an authority that admits of no obstacle, one which is beyond the purview of both Crown and church, the public becomes none other than the *Sovereign*.

Habermas was the first to assign a central position to public opinion, in his theory of the public sphere, but he included it in a realistic approach which was widely followed and which led to studying the variations in the intellectual and social composition of this public.[24] It would seem more useful to consider the public simply as a 'fictional person', a category of collective representation, an imaginary being who comes with the action and provides its justification.[25] From this perspective, the term 'the public' does not designate a concrete entity; it cannot be circumscribed by any objectivist description that would list its attributes or study its social composition.

Which does not mean that the term designates a hollow or arbitrary entity, but that *the public can be defined only by the properties attributed to it by*

[24] See J. Habermas, *The Structural Transformation of the Public Sphere*, T. Burger & F. Lawrence (trans.), (Cambridge, Mass., MIT Press, 1989).

[25] K. M. Baker stressed the conceptual approach without actually separating it from the sociological conception: 'the "public" was much more an abstract political category than it was a sociological one.' (K. M. Baker, 'Defining the Public Sphere in Eighteenth-Century France: Variations on a Theme by Habermas', in C. Calhoun (ed.), *Habermas and the Public Sphere* (Cambridge, Mass., MIT Press, 1992), 192.) See also K. M. Baker, *Inventing the French Revolution: Essays on French Political Culture in the Eighteenth Century*, (Cambridge, Cambridge Univ. Press, 1990), chap. 6. The same ambiguity can be found in R. Chartier, *The Cultural Origins of the French Revolution* L. G. Cochrane (trans), (Durham, NC, Duke Univ. Press, 1991).

those who speak on its behalf. For the lawyers of the time, who were not the only ones claiming to speak for the public, the latter became a sovereign authority, independent and critical of the state's power. Through their battles, lawyers actively contributed to a breach which they time and again reopened and enlarged and which, under different but far from equivalent dichotomies—the state and the public, state and nation, state and civil society—would constantly provide the antagonistic terms around which French political dynamics revolved.

Political action, spokesman and the public are intimately linked

The political involvement is inseparable from the ongoing crisis that marked the end of the first Bar. Having sided with the state, after their fourteenth- and fifteenth-century heyday, the profession entered a period of crisis and decline which was felt to be inevitable. Loisel's *Dialogue*, the first document reporting lawyers' actual words, is a melancholy, bleak meditation on a collectivity threatened with 'social nothingness'.[26]

In a matter of a few decades, between the second half of the century and the turn of the eighteenth, everything changed. The principal institutional mechanisms of the Order had been put in place and the profession gradually began to govern itself. At the same time, reflection on professional action was channelled by three requirements: independence affirmed by refusing the logic of the state and the logic of the market, the claim to speak for the public, and the will to recover past grandeur and influence. The solution lay in taking up public issues, the only way of circumventing professional finitude.

But such a solution is obvious only in retrospect. It first had to be invented. The lawyers' active and independent participation in the Jansenist quarrel was the opening move. For the first time, three terms appeared together which thereafter were to be systematically associated: political action, spokesman for the public, and popularity. For many reasons, and having to do in particular with the composition of the Order, which contained many high-powered Jansenist intellectuals who did not hesitate to resort to action, lawyers took an active stand on the religious question of the time as part of that France which opposed both the king and the official church: the mandate the lawyers claimed for themselves and which, for d'Aguesseau, was still limited to

---

[26] A. Loisel, 'Pasquier, ou Dialogue des Avocats du Parlement de Paris' (1602), in A. Dupin (ed.), *Profession d'avocat. Recueil de pièces concernant l'exercice de cette profession* (Paris, 1844), 147–258.

the courts, now extended to the whole of the political sphere: in their words as well as in their deeds, they constantly made reference to the public and, to their surprise, their criticism earned them vast popularity in the strongly Jansenist Paris of the time. In short, in the 1730s, lawyers discovered, from the attacks they drew and the support they received, from the forces they were dealing with—the king, the church hierarchy, the people of Paris—the effectiveness of speech, the popularity and influence to be gained from winning recognition as spokesman for the public. Such a choice was not irreversible; it turned out to be too fortunate to be renounced.

For the spokesman, credibility is the central issue

The notion of spokesman for the public is the result of displacing and extending the mandate governing relations between lawyer and client.[27] And for those unaware of the broad discretionary powers enjoyed by lawyers, the notion seems to reproduce a legal relationship which assumes that the mandatory respects the intentions and decisions of the mandator. In this case, the function of the spokesman would be merely to express the opinions and aims of those he represents; this would even be the condition of his success and continued existence.

Such a perspective corresponds, however, neither to their writings nor to their practices; it assumes a pre-existent reality, a history already largely accomplished. However, far from assuming that the mandator's aims preceded the mandatory's action, the fact is that, for the first half of the eighteenth century as for the beginning of the liberal era, the *representative constituted those he represented by the very fact of representing.* Together with the other spokesmen, lawyers employed in their speeches and writings, the devices of designation, argumentation, identification, and denunciation, which enabled their fellow citizens to recognize themselves in their representatives; success depended not on faithfulness, but on credibility. Which raises two questions: who was it that took the lawyers' claim to speak for the public seriously? And why did they take this claim seriously?

Who? The credibility of the spokesman for the public depended on the judgements formulated by others who also claimed to speak for the public and who are spontaneously confused with public opinion. It is

---

[27] For an overview of lawyers and their mandate, see M. Sarfatti-Larson, 'The Changing Functions of Lawyers in the Liberal State: Reflections for a Comparative Analysis', in R. L. Abel & P. S. C. Lewis (eds.), *Lawyers in Society*, 427–77.

through representatives (the Press in particular) that an 'opinion' attributed to the public comes to be heard, and the world of these delegates is not easy to circumscribe, as their opinions circulate in writing as well as spoken form.

Why? As a general rule this credibility has been linked with the demonstration of dedication to the public by a strategy of *disinterestedness*. But just what is meant by disinterestedness? It designates not merely a value, but a complex symbolic and material configuration of discourses, rules, disciplinary authorities, forms of training, and mechanisms of social control like networks and sociability, etc., whose influence can be felt in the exercise of professional authority, in the economic relations with clients, and in the relationships with society at large. What do these concrete expressions have in common? Restriction of self-interest on behalf of the public good.

Disinterestedness is not an everlasting reality: it sprang up and gained ground in the eighteenth century, took root in the nineteenth century, and entered a state of crisis in the second half of the twentieth century. In the nineteenth century, among other examples, its effects can be seen, a few individual defections notwithstanding, in lawyers' systematic opposition to authoritarian regimes, despite offers of positions and material advantages, or in lawyers' explicit refusal to enter the business market. The latter was all the more remarkable and remarked for having been particularly strongly voiced during the rise of modern industrial and banking capitalism between 1860 and 1880, at the very time American lawyers were moving in the opposite direction.

This configuration has long been central to lawyers' political action for two basic reasons: first of all, morality is the weapon of the weak who appeal to the universal in order to form an alliance with the other; and second, repression of material self-interest justifies the credibility of the public spokesman. Of course it is perfectly possible to invoke an ideal and then, wittingly or unwittingly, do the opposite. But the study of lawyers' practices indicates, first that their moral failings, which indeed existed, were (let us say with more than due caution) never so severe that they vouchsafed behaviours that would have existed had there been no rules and, second, that lawyers were often seized with a passion for politics for its own sake.[28]

Indeed by associating political action and disinterestedness, lawyers could only reinforce the trust in the words and the deeds of those who

---

[28] R. Rémond, *La Vie politique en France depuis 1789*, vol. 2 (Paris, A. Colin, 1969), 267.

claimed to represent the public. And public opinion recognized the 'sufficient' *authenticity* of this collective practice by underwriting both the figure of the protector of liberties and the profession worthy of impersonal global trust.

Influence and power are the products of an active transformation of popularity

What changes does the spokesman function trigger when it is credible? A change of magnitude. The representative takes on an entirely different dimension as does his action. The weight he carries is the weight of all those who see themselves in him, together with that of those who might identify with him. Especially, as was the case of the nineteenth-century Bar, when he is assimilated to a collective person whose presence merges with such central values as the defence of individual freedoms. When this is the case, the representative can equal apparently more powerful social and political forces. And he attracts the esteem of the public.

This popularity was the fundamental source of lawyers' political success. To which must nevertheless be added some specific advantages; in the competition between the various spokesmen, these made the difference: nineteenth-century lawyers had the benefit of the prestige enjoyed by law in French society, of the respect for eloquence and of the efficacy of the networks embedded in local society; it was only after the First World War that these began to wane in the face of political-party and union representatives. Public esteem, which had been slowly crystallizing over the eighteenth century, exhibited, in the nineteenth century, a dazzling trajectory, based on the electoral value of the professional title that culminated under the Third Republic when lawyers came to form a veritable ruling elite.[29]

B. *Tradition and Identity*

While the spokesman-for-the-public theory may explain the politicization, the subordination of personal interests to the public good and the success, it is not enough to account for the emergence and continuity of a collective action that belongs to the liberal political model. If the explanation is to be completed, we must include the active influence of

---

[29] Between 1881 and 1920, one out of every 4 representatives to the Assembly was a lawyer. The proportion of lawyers who were *Presidents du Conseil* was even higher; to which must be added several Presidents of the Republic and a large number of ministers.

a tradition and the constitution of an identity whose permanence was favoured by the situation it helped shape.

A tradition: the spirit of freedom

Lawyers' proclivity for contention is rooted, paradoxically, in the formation of the French modern state. As Kosselleck has so remarkably shown, absolute monarchy sprang from the separation between a *Raison d'État* that drew its justification from itself and a morality that was relegated to the realm of private conscience; by fostering the split between private and public persons, it managed to quell the generalization of anarchy and ensure civil peace. But as absolutism endured into the long term, it was in the name of morality that those excluded from political power would confront the state and that the exigency of external freedom would be added to the possession of internal freedom.[30] This is illustrated by lawyers. For this profession, morality came in the form of a collective virtue—disinterestedness—which stood somewhere between public space (outside the state sphere) and private space, but which unified the entire personal experience. This was the resource, reinforced by the resistance to royal absolutism, which had long been the driving force of the *parlements*, which lay behind the lawyers' opposition to the absolute state; it was this force that instigated their rejection of intolerance and made it possible to conceive of and to defend individual rights in the face of state power.[31]

While morality fostered opposition to the absolute state, it cannot wholly explain the public stance; for this, lawyers needed a spirit of independence, which they drew from their participation in the *Parlement*. Not only did this institutional belonging provide them with an orientation, it also created a remarkable penchant for action, which Tocqueville praised in hyperbolic terms,[32] while seeking to discover its

---

[30] R. Koselleck, *Le Règne de la Critique* (Paris, Editions de Minuit, 1959 [1979], 9; trans. as *Critique and Crisis: Enlightenment and the genesis of Modern Society* (Cambridge, Mass., MIT Press, 1988.

[31] Lawyers' defence of personal rights in the 18th cent. seems to have undergone little direct influence from the philosophical movement, but the possibility cannot be excluded that it was affected by a two-fold experience: that of court debates, with the rule that both parties and the defence had the right to express themselves freely, which opposed an antithetical reality to an absolute state dominated by secrecy; and that of the Order itself, with its moderate power, judicial equality, and a veritable collective organization for the protection of personal freedoms.

[32] 'When in 1770 the *parlement* of Paris was dissolved and the magistrates belonging to it were deprived of their authority and status, not one of them truckled to the royal will. Yet more conspicuous was the stand made by the leading members of the Bar practising

origins. Having listed the major drawbacks of the judicial system under the Ancien Régime, he remarks that 'not one of them truckled to the royal will', and he goes on to say that the freedom that was a part of earlier mores was still there in the eighteenth century, 'within these judicial bodies and all about them'. This spirit of independence proved its strength in the many conflicts which, over the eighteenth century, punctuated relations between lawyers and royal power, and also in lawyers' promptness to act, which impressed observers of the time.[33]

The action in favour of a more moderate state and the defence of individual rights stood at the intersection of two causes: a moral law that presented itself as a higher principle enabling the social actor to oppose monarchical absolutism and a form of independence rooted in a remote past which helped turn a critical stance into an active commitment.

The secret of a continuity: the central position of the antagonism between the state and the public

It is difficult not to be struck by the persistence, over such a long period of time and in such varied situations, of lawyers' active attachment to the liberal model of action. It is difficult not to be surprised that the diversity of the conflicts cannot conceal the monotony of the stance. No decision freely taken by the actor, no economic, social or political cause seems to account for this phenomenon. Two mutually complementary explanations can be advanced. One should not underestimate the influence of the first moment, the impact of lawyers' involvement in the politico-religious quarrel of the 1730s—which combined rejection of a decline of past grandeur, opposition to the arbitrariness of royal power, the strategy of spokesman for the public, defence of individual rights in the name of a long-standing passion for freedom—which met with a success that was as dazzling as it was unexpected. The event fascinated lawyers; it was a model of exemplary action which fed their imaginations and their practices. Of course the cause itself could only die away with time: but it was gradually replaced by a reciprocal construction of the profession's identity and situation.

before the *parlement*; of their own will they shared its fate, relinquished all that had assured their prestige and prosperity, and, rather than appear before judges for whom they had no respect, condemned themselves to silence. In the history of free nations I know of no nobler gesture than this; yet it was made in the eighteenth century and in the shadow of the court of Louis XV.' A. Tocqueville, *The Old Regime and the French Revolution* S. Gilbert (trans.), (Gloucester, Mass., P. Smith, 1955 [1978]), 117.

[33] In his *Journal*, Barbier notes the ease with which lawyers decided to strike, often for long periods, in opposition to royal power.

The liberal political model is inseparable from the formation of a collective subject acting within a historical context and which, through its commitments fashions a world favouring the reproduction of the positions it has taken. Political identity, as a guiding principle for action, is inseparable from a political universe which is at once the product and the condition of action, and which is characterized, for lawyers in the first instance but soon for the whole of society, by the eminent simplicity of its architecture: on one side, the public, on the other the state; on one side Justice, on the other arbitrariness; on one side freedom, on the other despotism. Very early on, from the beginning of the eighteenth century, lawyers took part in forming the simple-because-simplified *representation* of the opposition between the two camps. Within this archetypal conflict, their identity constructed itself around an initial position, the reproduction of which was all the more certain for its being constitutive of a representation that became generalized to a variety of political forces conspiring at its reproduction; everything then weighed on the side of lawyers continuing in the same direction.

To be sure, decisions were taken, but aside from moments of bifurcation, crises, and reassessments (all of which were finally rare) explicit choices were not indispensable: the continuing existence of a certain representation of political society and of lawyers' consent to the policy of the Order could not help but foster the continuation of standing preferences and commitments. As long as the self-government of the profession did not meet with serious opposition from either outside or inside, it could rely on the mechanisms that had ensured the reproduction of past commitments without excluding, either *de jure* or *de facto*, a decision that at any moment might throw everything into question.

Explanation therefore involves a realistic conception of the actor, neither a prisoner of structures or culture nor constantly given to exercising his sovereignty. There is no need to choose between the social process whereby the social actor fits into society and the deliberate choices of the Order, for the first is never so powerful that the subjects of history do not manage to retain their autonomy, while the second are never so unrealistic as to neglect the weight of the past and the constraints of action. In short, the liberal model was indeed the product of a long-lasting strategy that was only intermittently explicit and conscious because it was in accord with a certain collective identity and a certain political society.

Conclusion

Over the very long term, lawyers' collective action fostered the formation and consolidation of civil and political citizenship as well as the constitution of a moderate state based on law. The refusal to commit themselves on social questions and their opposition to the welfare state delimited *a contrario* a 'strict' version of political liberalism which was for lawyers the ultimate horizon. In the course of these struggles the profession fashioned itself. Although no one decision stands out as more crucial than the rest—with the exception of the wager, at the end of the seventeenth century, of entering into an alliance with the public—their relationship with the political sphere had become *the dominant organizing principle of the profession*. Without this link it would be impossible to account for the formation and development of the *classical* profession, one of the three historical forms which marked the seven-centuries-long history of French lawyers. It is the priority given to political action together with the distance the collectivity maintained with respect to capitalist accumulation of wealth—thus providing a market compatible with its political aims—which enables us to understand the presence of a profession that has come down nearly unchanged to the mid-twentieth century and which is now slowly breaking up; a profession characterized by self-government, a rigorous code of ethics, a moderate economics, primacy of the courts and the pleadings, a preponderance of individual clients, etc.

In conclusion, this analysis leads to three theoretical comments. First of all, only by taking a long-term approach could a historical sociology bring out the scope and the singularity of the political phenomenon; a study limited to the contemporary profession, even in France, would certainly have failed to recognize it. Next, above and beyond proposing an interpretation of the omnipresence of the liberal political model for lawyers, we must emphasize the strategic value of a spirit of independence rooted in the distant past; without this legacy, there is no assurance that French lawyers would have embarked so determinedly on the course they did. And last, and more generally, this interpretation of lawyers' political activity has made it possible to elaborate the theory of spokesman for the public. To be sure the mandate theory is present in the social sciences, if often disjointedly—it turns up in the study of legal relations, in the analysis of political life, especially concerning relations between the elected and their electors, and in the agency theory used to explain economic relations—but it is more rarely used to account for all the modalities and occasions which lead certain persons to claim to speak and act on behalf of others. In this sense, the analysis of the French lawyers' collective action has made it possible to integrate the variability of the mandator, the diverse ways of constituting representative and represented as well as the modalities governing the mandatory's credibility.

Since the 1950s, the political logic of the profession has been in decline, progressively replaced by the logic of the market: the profession has become a composite body. With this evolution has come a crisis of the spokesman function; at the same time the alliance with the public is breaking down, at least in its general form. Another story is unfolding.[34] And yet, in a sometimes unexpected way, an implicit predisposition, embedded in the craft, passed on from one generation to the next, remains alive and manifests itself from time to time by a collective action resistant to the power of the state and favourable to personal liberties. In 1993, for instance, a law was passed which, for the first time in France, gave a person the possibility of calling in a lawyer when held by the police for questioning. In the face of the open hostility of magistrates, the police and imposing political forces, lawyers not only officially supported the law, but went even further and spontaneously organized volunteer, free (for a time at least) day-and-night help aimed at ensuring that the reform was actually applied; their tenacity won them victory. How could such a movement, in which there was apparently nothing of financial interest to be gained, but which, on the contrary, was regarded by some as an embarrassment and a threat to the new image of business lawyers, have gathered so much momentum with the altogether official backing of certain Orders? The riddle would remain unsolved were it not for the liberal movement, which, even in decline and in often hard-to-recognize ways, has never ceased to be an active influence.

---

[34] Which is to say, coming back to our initial idea, that the 'profession' cannot be defined in general since the organization and the action of French lawyers were successively dominated, in specific historical conditions, by the logics of the state, the public, and the market.

4 Mrs Thatcher Against the 'Little Republics': Ideology, Precedents, and Reactions

Michael Burrage (London School of Economics)

Neglected Members of Civil Society

Political scientists have not paid much attention to the professions as lesser forms of government. Professions might have been expected to figure in their discussions of pluralism and corporatism, two major themes of the subject in recent times, but attention has usually focused on capital and labour, the two actors in the class theory that they hoped to supersede or discredit. Similarly, in the discussion of the relationship between states and civil society, evidence has seldom been drawn from the professions even though they were probably the first, and have usually been the most durable, expression of civil society's attempt to organize itself. And in the vast literature on states, the mini-governments of the professions have rarely been used as means of understanding the larger state formations on which they depend.

This relationship between states and professions is most exposed and visible at moments of crisis and open conflict, notably during revolutions, when it is contested, debated, and in most cases forcibly redefined.[1] The Thatcher era fell some way short of a revolutionary crisis. Nevertheless, it provides a lesser, but still illuminating, opportunity to understand this relationship for in their attempts to create an enterprise culture, her Governments redefined and enlarged the powers of the state, and in so doing inevitably came into conflict with the formal and informal regulatory powers of many professions.

Post-mortems on the Thatcher era have not paid a great deal of attention to these conflicts. They have portrayed the reform of the Civil Service, of education, health care, and legal services, as merely confrontations with so many 'vested interests' and 'institutions' and therefore tended to overlook the underlying professional formation on which

---

[1] As I have argued in 'Revolution as a Starting Point for the Comparative Analysis of the French, American, and English Legal Professions', in R. Abel & P. S. C. Lewis, *Lawyers in Society*, vol. 3, *Comparative Theories* (Berkeley, Univ. of California Press, 1989).

they all depended.[2] However, with just a slight change of angle, we may bring the state–profession relationship to the foreground and by so doing better understand both the nature of the reforms, and of the ideology which inspired them.

In this essay I outline the attacks on six professions, before describing that on the legal professions, the last, the most vehement, the most explicit, and also the least successful. I then consider what all these attacks may tell us about the still-puzzling phenomenon of 'Thatcherism'. I next look for historical precedents for the kind of relationship between the state and civil society that Mrs Thatcher (as she then was) sought to create, a search which leads back to the attacks by Charles II and James II on all the 'lesser governments' in the kingdom and uncovers the foundations of the distinctive English form of professional organization. I conclude by examining the corporate responses of the legal and other professions to the Thatcher attacks and speculate briefly about their future behaviour.

An Outline of the Earlier Attacks on Six Professions 1979–1991

In most countries civil servants are considered bureaucrats rather than professionals and in their campaign rhetoric the Conservatives often found it useful to portray them as such.[3] However, in the century after the implementation of the Northcote–Trevelyan reforms in 1870, the higher Civil Service in Britain absorbed, and adapted to its own very different work conditions, ideas of practice-based training, of unwritten ethics, of an autonomous work jurisdiction, and of corporate self-government which had long been institutionalized among barristers, physicians and, to a lesser degree, the dons of the two ancient universities. While the elite of the Service subsequently changed their name, (from

---

[2] See for example D. Kavanagh, *Thatcherism and British Politics: The End of Consensus* (Oxford, Oxford Univ. Press, 1987), 286–8; H. Young, *One of Us: A Biography of Margaret Thatcher* (London, Macmillan, 1989), P. Jenkins, *Mrs Thatcher's Revolution: The Ending of the Socialist Era* (Cambridge, Mass., Harvard Univ. Press, 1987). The exception is the most recent, S. Jenkins, *Accountable to None: The Tory Nationalization of Britain* (London, Hamish Hamilton, 1995). Though this contains much valuable information about the professions, the main focus is the expansion of central state control.

[3] The Fulton Commission was beset and befuddled with this confusion of terms. It in fact recommended the extension of managerial controls and techniques but it insisted on calling these 'professional' and castigated civil servants for their 'amateurism' and lack of professionalism. *The Civil Service: Vol. 1, Report of the Committee 1966–68*, Chmn Lord Fulton, Cmnd. 3638 (1968).

'first division clerks' to the 'administrative class' in 1921, and to the 'unified grades' or 'open structure' after the Fulton Report of 1968), it retained these corporate, professional characteristics and their own exclusive, collective association—the First Division Association.

No doubt, the subordinate classes of civil servants came rather closer to the bureaucratic model but since the 'first division clerks' and their successors had little interest in directing and managing their work, the Service as a whole is best conceived as a hierarchically co-ordinated cluster of professional and semi-professional occupations rather than as a bureaucracy. Most of the inferior occupations were also trained on the job, also established their own distinct work jurisdictions, also had their own separate career ladders, and were typically organized in their own exclusive professional associations.[4] It was the enduring appeal of professional ideals and professional forms of organization that gave the British Civil Service its distinctive structure and culture.

Before her election Mrs Thatcher ominously threatened to 'deprivilege' the Civil Service but her efforts to reform it opened innocently enough with the importation of a senior manager from Marks & Spencer, Derek Rayner, to head a small 'efficiency unit'. This Unit conducted 'scrutinies' of the administrative work of Civil Service departments with the main aim of cutting costs and manpower. In itself it was a rather modest intrusion into professional prerogatives of Civil Servants but it developed into something more because of the importance Mrs Thatcher personally attached to the work of Rayner's Unit. By 1988 it had extended its aspirations beyond cost-cutting scrutinies and proposed a radical structural change to 'release managerial energy' and apply 'real and sustained pressure . . . for continuous improvement in the value for money obtained in the delivery of policies and services' by spinning off the work of departments into independent, executive agencies which were to be run like business enterprises.[5]

By the time of her resignation, about 80,000 or 14 per cent of civil servants were employed in these executive agencies but their psychological or ideological effect was far greater than this suggests since they challenged the long-standing assumption that, subject to periodic accountability to Royal Commissions, senior civil servants alone had the right, the skill, and the experience to decide how the public service

---

[4] These professional associations are all listed as witnesses to the Fulton Commission, ibid., 185–90.

[5] Efficiency Unit, *Improving Management in Government: The Next Steps* (London, HMSO, 1988).

should be run on a day-to-day basis. The agencies had, in short, broken a professional monopoly and badly bruised the self-esteem of civil servants by continuously denigrating or dismissing their expertise and ethics. Mrs Thatcher herself did little to disguise her contempt for civil servants. 'She doesn't think that clever chaps like us should be here at all,' said one of Hennessy's informants. 'We should be outside, making profits.' Another complained of being 'told by politicians that they don't want whingeing, analysis or integrity', that we must simply 'do as we are told.'[6] Civil Service methods were 'repeatedly compared unfavourably with the superior methods of private business.' Ministers constantly reminded them that 'they have several friends in the private sector who could do the job in the morning with one hand tied behind their back.'[7]

Like the Civil Service, the National Health Service (the NHS) was often mistaken for a bureaucracy but ever since its formation it too had provided a very high degree of autonomy for the professionals and semi-professionals within it. In 1983 Roy Griffiths, a director of a food supermarket chain, was asked to examine its internal organization. By the time he and his team arrived, the NHS had developed its own unique form of 'consensus management' which rested on the deliberations of elected representatives of every significant professional or semi-professional group in the Service, each of which constituted a sort of self-governing 'soviet', and each management team a sort of supreme soviet, though this analogy does not quite convey the extent of professional prerogatives since every representative held a right of veto.[8] The Griffiths team derided this 'consensus management' and compared it to 'a "mobile": designed to move with any breath of air, but which in fact never changes its position, and gives no clear indication of direction.'[9]

Their Report recommended that it be replaced by a conventional system of line management, directed by an NHS board chaired by the Secretary of State for Health, with a 'chief executive of the NHS' reporting to it; the chief executive would head a hierarchy of regional, district, and unit managers down to every last unit delivering medical care within the Service. These managers were encouraged to devise measures of output and efficiency, and to be given appropriate finan-

---

[6] P. Hennessy, *Whitehall* (London, Fontana, 1989), 633.

[7] P. Cosgrave, *Thatcher: The First Term* (London, Bodley Head, 1985), 169–73.

[8] P. Hennessy, P. Strong, & J. Robinson, *The NHS—Under New Management* (Milton Keynes, Open Univ. Press, 1990), 16–19.

[9] *NHS Management Inquiry*, Team Leader Roy Griffiths, Oct. 1983.

cial responsibility to enable them to reward or punish those under their control. Since the Griffiths Report did not require or propose legislation, implementation began almost immediately and continued over the next few years. In due course, it entailed a redefinition of the responsibilities and conditions of employment of both general practitioners and consultants and some means of measuring their output and efficiency.

The new 'contracts' imposed unilaterally on general practitioners by the Secretary of State for Health in 1988 were intended to give patients more information and more choice, to simplify the complaints procedure, to promote competition between doctors, and to make their remuneration system performance-related. It included mandatory hours of consultation (26 per week) and other rules with regard to their place of residence, staff employed by them, and other commitments, and also required annual returns on their prescriptions and hospital referrals. It offered incentive or 'target' payments for immunizations, cervical smears, and other kinds of screening and preventive tests.[10] In 1990 consultants were also required to negotiate a 'job plan with their general managers', which would be the basis of their contracts which, for the first time, set out their main duties and responsibilities, and included 'a work programme for a typical week'. The day-to-day management of these contracts was devolved from the regional health authorities, where they had been lodged since the founding of the NHS to prevent any interference with consultants' clinical autonomy, to their direct managerial supervisers in the district health authorities.[11]

An analogous line-managerial logic was applied to nurses, who constituted about half of the NHS workforce. Nurses were an extraordinarily diverse collection of near-professions and semi-professions, differentiated and stratified by their training, their qualifications, their specialties, and their places of work, but they nevertheless shared many of the characteristics of their professional seniors. They were, for instance, usually trained on the job, had a strong sense of their own jurisdiction and responsibilities, and had high rates of associational membership which indicated their high degree of corporate solidarity, even though the more 'professional' Royal Colleges of Nurses and Midwives were often at odds with the two major trade unions for nurses, the Confederation of Health Service Employees and the

[10] *General Practice in the National Health Service: The 1990 Contract: The Government's Programme for Changes to GPs' terms of service and remuneration system*, issued by the Health Depts of Great Britain, Aug. 1989, 5–7.

[11] *Health Circular HC(90)16*, Dept of Health, May 1990.

National Union of Public Employees. 'Consensus management' had, in fact, marked something of a triumph for nurses, the successful culmination of a long struggle for professional recognition.

In October 1988, as part of an attractive pay package, nurses were 'regraded'. Every kind of nurse, from aides and auxiliaries, State Enrolled and State Registered Nurses, hospital and district nurses, ward sisters, midwives, and teaching staff, each of which had previously developed their own grades and career paths were assigned to one of nine letter grades of a uniform national scale. This new grading system struck at the very heart of their collegial relationships. Ward sisters, for instance, who had previously been jointly responsible for the running of a ward, had to compete for the only grade G permitted for each ward since only one of them could be a 'ward manager' and satisfy the requirements of being in charge with 'continuing responsibility'.[12]

Rational bureaucratic pyramids of control and accountability were therefore superimposed on the host of professional and semi-professional enclaves and communities of the NHS. Whether they in fact controlled their professional subordinates (or improved efficiency) is uncertain, but a second wave of reform sought to bring market discipline to bear on both hospital consultants and general practitioners and in so doing provided them with escape routes.[13] In 1990, hospitals, by the majority vote of their consultants, were allowed to 'opt out' of Health Authority control and become independently-financed NHS Trust Hospitals, which enabled them to conduct their affairs as they wished, subject to guidelines from the Department of Health. Similarly, general practitioners (GPs), with more than 9,000 patients on their list, were allowed to 'opt out' of the control of the Family Practitioner Committee and become independent 'fund-holding' practices. This allowed them to act as independent business enterprises, to purchase services from any hospital that they chose and to compete with other general practitioners in an 'internal' NHS market. The medical professions were therefore offered a choice between the discipline of line management under the

[12] Government spokesmen sometimes defended regrading on the grounds that it provided a career structure for clinical nurses. Nurses evidently saw it differently. In its 'election manifesto' of 1992 the Royal College called for 'a clinical career structure' so that nurses who go into management retain 'a clear responsibility for clinical work with patients'. *A Manifesto for Nursing and Health*, Royal College of Nursing, 1992.

[13] 'Managers rapidly saw that their interest lay in establishing local alliances with doctors rather than in confronting them, . . . that a quiet life depended on re-establishing the old consensus,' Jenkins reported. He went on to describe the rather frantic search for some way of controlling the still escalating costs, S. Jenkins, *Accountable to None*, 70–7.

Department of Health and Social Security (DHSS) or the discipline of an internal market subject to the overall control of the DHSS.

A somewhat similar choice was eventually offered to schools. Teachers, like civil servants and nurses, were less a single profession than a cluster of kindred professions, linked by overlapping areas of expertise, of concern, and of jurisdictions and by interconnected career paths. Along with pre-school, elementary and secondary-school teachers, the cluster included educational administrators in local authorities and, rather more distantly, teachers at schools of education. Of them all, only pre-school teachers emerged unscathed from the Thatcher years.

During the first and second Thatcher Governments, policy signals were not all in the same direction though a number clearly threatened the autonomy of the profession.[14] The 1980 Education Act, for instance, included provisions to increase the market choice of parents in the state sector.[15] In 1983, a White Paper proposed a system of teacher appraisal which would be linked to merit payments and dismissal. It was also decided to publish the previously confidential reports of Her Majesty's Inspectors of Schools.[16] In the same year, the Government also decided to exclude teachers' representatives from national educational policy by abolishing the Schools Council which, though without formal powers, had been much the most influential national body on curriculum and assessment issues. It was replaced by two bodies, the National Curriculum Council and the School Examinations and Assessment Council, whose members were to be appointed in a personal rather than representative capacity by the Secretary of State.[17]

In November 1986, the Government not only rejected the agreement reached by the Burnham Committee, the national negotiating body which brought together representatives of employers, the 104 local education authorities, and six teaching unions, but subsequently decided to abolish the Committee itself and to impose a new contract

---

[14] The internal party debates and disputes behind these mixed signals have been carefully dissected in C. Knight, *The Making of Tory Education Policy in Post-War Britain* (London, Falmer, 1990), 135–84.

[15] K. Jones, *Right Turn, The Conservative Revolution in Education* (London, Hutchinson Radins, 1989).

[16] *Teaching Quality*, DES, 1983.

[17] For the historical context of these reforms see J. Maw, 'National Curriculum Policy' in D. Lawton and C. Chitty (eds.), *The National Curriculum* (Bedford Way Papers, Inst. of Education, Univ. of London, 1988).

on the teachers.[18] In so doing, it indicated that it wished to abolish uniform national pay and conditions, which teachers' unions and associations, like other professional bodies, had long considered a fundamental precondition of their professional status. Instead, the Government required school governing bodies and head teachers to behave like other employers and to fix pay and conditions according to conditions in their local labour market. The newly imposed contract set out more precisely than ever before the powers of headmasters and mistresses over their colleagues, the days and hours teachers were required to work, their obligations to cover for absent colleagues and to participate in further training and in performance appraisal.

After their election victory in the spring of 1987, the tempo of educational reform accelerated. In July 1987 a consultation document on the national curriculum was issued and in August an educational reform bill was published which allowed teachers' associations the rest of the summer vacation to respond to a series of far-reaching proposals which were to be introduced in the House of Commons in the autumn. This bill included three measures which had a decisive impact on most segments of the profession: open enrolment, opting out, and the national curriculum.[19]

Open enrolment increased the power of parents as consumers over what Sir Keith Joseph (as he then was) had called the 'agents for the delivery of the curriculum',[20] meaning teachers, by enabling parents to choose the school that their children could attend. It thereby sought to create something approximating market competition between schools since money would flow to the 'good' schools that attracted large numbers of pupils, while the others might go the wall. Apart from its effects on teachers in the schools, this measure also undermined the powers of educational administrators who had previously been responsible for the allocation of children to particular schools.

Opting out allowed a majority of parents to vote to remove the school their children attended from local authority control. Since edu-

[18] For a full account see R. Saran, 'Schoolteachers' pay and conditions of employment in England and Wales', in R. Saran & J. Sheldrake (eds.), *Public Sector Bargaining in the 1980s* (Aldershot, Avebury, 1988), 7–26; P. Leighton, 'Codification, Classification and Prescription in Teachers' Contracts', 129–34 in R. Saran & V. Trafford, *Research Education Management and Policy: Retrospect and Prospect* (London, Falmer, 1990).

[19] For a full analysis of the consultation papers and all the provisions of the bill see B. Simon, *Bending the Rules: The Baker 'Reform' of Education* (London, Lawrence & Wishart, 1988) 47–135.

[20] Ibid., 91.

cational administrators and teachers, as well as the rest of the community, had no vote, this measure emphasized in the most emphatic manner the power of consumers at the expense of professionals. The imposition of a national curriculum for five to sixteen year-olds had a similar effect since it drastically reduced the scope of teachers' professional judgement about how and what pupils should be taught and imposed a large proportion of compulsory core subjects, though less than the 90 per cent originally planned. Moreover, by linking this to national tests of all children at the ages of seven, eleven, and fourteen, whose results were to be published, it enabled parents to act as informed consumers and judge how well 'their' school and 'their' teachers were doing.[21]

In the view of many of those who helped to form Government policy, those mainly responsible for the deplorable state of English education were to be found not in the classroom at all, but in the teacher training colleges, since it was they who had failed to provide teachers with basic teaching skills and subject knowledge and had instead filled their heads with fashionable theories of education and the sociology of educational inequality. Throughout the era of educational reform, therefore, a variety of measures were designed to control this segment of the profession.

In 1984 Sir Keith Joseph had established a Council for the Accreditation of Teacher Education to set criteria for, and accredit the courses of, schools of education. In the following year the Government again showed its distaste of voluntary, representative bodies by abandoning the Advisory Committee for the Supply of Teachers and allowing the Department of Education and Science (DES) to assume direct control of in-service teacher training. Seven years later, in March 1991, it invented the state-licensed teacher, a seemingly modest adaptation of in-service training which enabled university graduates or other qualified persons to become 'licensed' teachers mainly by on-the-job training, with only part-time attendance at a school of education for one day a fortnight. Though innocently presented as a means of meeting shortages of teachers in mathematics and science subjects, this scheme also broke the monopoly of teacher training colleges over admission to the

---

[21] For a brilliant comparison of the 'professional' orientation of earlier proposals by Her Majesty's Inspectors (HMI) for a national curriculum versus the 'bureaucratic' assumptions of that introduced in the Act see C. Chitty, 'Two Models of a National Curriculum: Origins and Interpretation', in Lawton & Chitty (eds.), *National Curriculum*, 34–48.

profession. Its expansion after the fall of Mrs Thatcher suggests that it was primarily intended for precisely this purpose, to inaugurate a new kind of profession over which schools of education had little influence.[22]

The Educational Reform Act of July 1988 also marked the culmination of a long campaign to check and control the autonomy of university teachers. This had begun as a by-product of the attempt to limit public expenditure and differed from the attacks on other professions in that two bodies, the University Grants Committee (UGC) and the Committee of Vice-Chancellors and Principals (CVCP), which academics had long considered immovable defenders of academic independence, had decided in the early 1980s to increase their managerial control over the universities. The UGC, which had hitherto allocated public funds in quinquennial block grants to eliminate any suspicion of state interference in academic decisions, decided to be more 'selective' and to support the use of various productivity measures to discriminate between universities, subject areas, and departments.[23] The CVCP, after an inquiry chaired by Alex Jarratt, a director of a paper company, recommended line management replace the traditional, academic version of 'consensus management', that vice-chancellors should become more like chief executives, that there should be more precise corporate plans, greater departmental accountability, and more public indicators of academic performance.

At the time these measures were widely defended as attempts to forestall or pre-empt direct state intervention and control of the universities but their effect seems to have been exactly the opposite, encouraging the Government in the view that the universities needed, and would accept, still more direct state intervention. The Educational Reform Act 1988 considerably reduced academic self-government. The UGC itself was abolished and along with it lingering notions that the Government would be reluctant to use its funding as a means of controlling the universities. Henceforth, they were to be directly controlled by the central government by means of a University Funding Council (UFC) which was to be a 'non-departmental' public body of academics and such non-academics who appeared to the Secretary of State 'to have experience of and to have shown capacity in industrial, commer-

[22] See *Independent*, 18 Mar. 1991 & 6 Jan. 1992. *The Sunday Times*, 24 May 1992: 'Patten to stamp out "trendy" Teaching.'

[23] For further details of, and references to, this and all the preceding cases see M. Burrage, 'Mrs Thatcher Versus Deep Structures: Ideology, Impact and Ironies of an Eleven-year Confrontation', *Inst. of Governmental Studies Working Papers* (Berkeley, Inst. of Governmental Studies, June 1992).

cial or financial matters or the practice of any profession.' The UFC was to have none of the representative or protective functions of the UGC and, despite its 'non-departmental' status, was made a creature of the DES and was not, therefore, to report to Parliament. Its deliberations and views were to be confidential and in contrast to the UGC, it was not to be advised by disciplinary sub-committees.[24]

Line management, as recommended by Jarratt, was extended from the Secretary of State via the chief executive officer of the new UFC who, unlike his UGC predecessor, was to be a full member of council and serve indefinitely. The managerial powers of the Secretary of State were unambiguous. He was not only authorized to present 'strategic guidance' about the size and balance of the university system, and about the Government's own funding and policy intentions but, lest the UFC ignore this guidance, he had a 'reserve power' to issue directions to it. The only remnant of the buffer principle was that the Government could not issue directions relating to any specific institution, a rather empty gesture since the Chief Executive could. The Act also strengthened the powers of management within the universities by authorizing the appointment of University Commissioners who would visit universities to amend their statutes unilaterally so that universities could dismiss, for redundancy or other good cause, staff appointed or promoted after 30 November 1987. By this means, tenure was abolished. The Commissioners were also to ensure that universities had established effective disciplinary procedures to deal with complaints against academic staff.

Just as the Government had attempted to create a market for secondary-school places, so the Act also empowered the Secretary of State to create something like a market for university students through his powers to determine the conditions under which funds were distributed to the universities. This was done not by legislation but in subsequent memoranda between the Secretary of State and the funding bodies to determine the financial relations between them. In 1989 the UFC announced a 'system of contracting' under which universities would competitively tender to provide for certain kinds of educational services for specific groups of students at a certain price. The UFC could attach 'such terms and conditions as it thought fit to the bids it accepted and would monitor performance in accordance with the contracts'. The

---

[24] In its final year the UGC consisted of 16 academic members and 3 senior industrial executives. Its 15 subject sub-committees were entirely composed of academics.

accepted bids were to be re-negotiated on a 'rolling', apparently annual, basis, 'taking account of institutions' relative performance'.[25]

These new bidding procedures necessarily removed the subsidy of university research via funds for teaching on which British universities, like those everywhere else, have historically depended. The funding of research was thereafter to be precisely identified and distributed by a comparable system of 'contracting' via the existing research councils. Although the UFC and the research councils were to determine the criteria by which they distributed funds, the Government nevertheless declared its continuing interest in how they distributed their funds and specifically its support for the use of criteria 'which will lead to greater selectivity in the allocation of funding . . . in the interests of sustaining and enhancing quality and cost effectiveness'.[26]

Analogous measures were taken to remove the so-called 'public sector' of higher education, of polytechnics and colleges of further education from local government control and bring them under that of the central government. The National Advisory Body, on which local government was strongly represented, was replaced by the Polytechnics and Colleges Funding Council, in many respects parallel to the UFC, though under still firmer DES control. The Act included specific requirements about the composition of polytechnics' governing bodies. At least half of their members were to represent business, industrial, professional, and other employment interests including trade unions. Only one-fifth could be drawn from local authorities, two from their own academic staff and one from their students.

A New Vision of Legal Practice

Before the attack on the two branches of the legal profession was launched, therefore, a number of professions had experienced the reforming zeal of the Thatcher Governments. In the early years, it looked as though barristers and solicitors would escape altogether. Shortly after she was first elected, a Royal Commission had completed a three-year examination of legal services and, though it had recommended a considerable number of reforms, it declared itself generally satisfied with the organization of the two branches of the profession and recommended that they be left alone to implement its recommenda-

---

[25] The procedures are outlined in UFC circular 39/89.
[26] J. Griffith, *The Attack on Higher Education* (London, Council for Academic Freedom & Democracy, *c.* 1987), 14.

tions.[27] By past precedents this ought to have ensured the two branches a decade or more of tranquillity. The Commission itself suggested as much.

The issue of the reform of the two branches of the profession surfaced, however, rather unexpectedly, in 1983, when a Labour Private Members' Bill to abolish solicitors' monopoly of conveyancing, somewhat surprisingly, received the support of the Commons on its second reading. Initially, the Government had not supported the bill, but it then decided to bring forward its own measure to similar effect, if the Member agreed to withdraw his bill. He did so and the Government bill which eventually became law created a new profession or semiprofession of 'licensed conveyancers'. This threat to their monopoly prompted the solicitors to look frantically for other markets for their services, and in particular to question the bar's monopoly of audience in the High Court and the crown courts. The two branches of the profession then embarked on increasingly bitter public disputes about their respective jurisdictions, which are sometimes referred to as the 'Bar wars'.[28]

While the two branches were squabbling with each other, the Government introduced a number of other reforms which demonstrated a distinctively new vision of the legal system. Since its introduction in 1948 public funds for legal aid had been administered by the solicitors' professional association, the Law Society, a rather remarkable example of professional self-government. In 1985 the Government decided that legal aid should be removed from the profession and brought under the control of a central, state agency, the Legal Aid Board: the Board was to be responsible to the Lord Chancellor, himself a judge but a political appointee and member of the Cabinet.

In the following year, it also decided that it would create a centralized Crown Prosecution Service. In England and Wales prosecutions had previously been brought by the police, either through solicitors that they themselves employed, or through private solicitors, whom they retained just as any ordinary citizen might.[29] The only central office of public prosecutions was the Director of Public Prosecutions (DPP). This had been established in 1879 and was therefore a fairly recent

---

[27] *The Royal Commission on Legal Services*, Chmn Sir Henry Benson, Cmnd. 7648 (1979) (2 vols.).

[28] M. Zander, *A Matter of Justice: the Legal System in Ferment* (London, Tauris, 1988).

[29] J. Rozenberg, *The Case for the Crown: The Inside Story of the Director of Public Prosecutions* (Wellingborough, Equation, 1987), 86–7.

innovation in the English legal system. Earlier attempts had all failed because of the fear of the excessive power it might place in the hands of the central government. When the office was eventually created in 1879 its powers were strictly limited to cases of 'importance and diffi-culty' and subsequent DPPs followed this rule in a self-effacing manner, declining cases which they thought a police or private solicitor could handle satisfactorily. The office of the DPP therefore grew very slowly. In 1986 it employed about eighty lawyers, and retained private barris-ters like any private person to represent the Crown in court.

In 1978, just before the election of the first Thatcher Government, a Royal Commission had found much that might be improved in these arrangements, but emphatically recommended that the independence of the prosecuting function would be best served by the continuation of a decentralized service accountable to the same body as the police. Nevertheless, one year later, the Government suddenly announced that it intended to centralize the prosecuting powers of the police in a newly-created Crown Prosecution Service under the Director of Public Prosecutions, on the grounds that a centralized prosecution would be more independent of the police than a local one. This decision led to the rapid creation of a new central state legal bureaucracy which by 1990 employed 1,700 lawyers and a total staff of some 4,000.

This determination of Thatcher Governments to centralize powers previously delegated and dispersed rather untidily and vaguely in soci-ety itself was further demonstrated in the 1989 plan to reform the mag-istrates' courts. These lower courts had previously been jointly funded by central government and local authorities, and though loosely under the supervision of the Lord Chancellor, both the magistrates and their professional clerks had enjoyed considerable discretion in the limbo between central and local government. The plan, inevitably, was that they both be brought under the clearly-defined control of a central gov-ernment agency.[30]

Finally, the attention of the government turned to the two branches of legal profession themselves, and in a Green Paper entitled *The Work and Organization of the Legal Profession* published in 1989, it proposed to continue the process of state centralization at the expense of their self-

---

[30] The Justices' Clerks' Society responded angrily to what they saw as a threat to the independent advice their members gave to magistrates and insisted that 'There must not be the remotest hint that legal advisers to lay benches might be subject to any direction whatever from the government policy makers.' See *The Times*, 27 Nov. 1989.

governing bodies.[31] A committee appointed by the Lord Chancellor, a majority of whose members would not be lawyers, was to determine the admission and training requirements as well as the rules of practice of what the Green Paper called 'licensed advocates'. Both the Bar Council and the Law Society were invited to submit applications to be recognized as suitable training institutions and to submit their codes of ethics for similar approval, so that the Lord Chancellor's Committee could determine whether they had 'sufficient control' over their members to ensure that satisfactory standards of conduct and behaviour were maintained and enforced. They were, however, warned that the Lord Chancellor's Committee, rather than the two branches, would first determine 'what should be the principles embodied in these codes'. They were also advised that they would be treated 'like any other industry' and that 'historical precedents would count for nought'.

In a formal sense this Green Paper, and two companion papers issued at the same time, anticipated, even celebrated, the end of sovereign, self-governing professions.[32] It was sceptical, at times contemptuous, of the ethical rules of the two branches which it viewed as self-serving arguments to insulate them both from competitive forces. Most of them might, it suggested, be abolished. The profession should no longer be divided. Barristers should be able to employ, or to form partnerships with, other barristers, or with solicitors, or other professionals. They should be able to practise wherever they wished, to receive clients directly without referral by solicitors, to advertise, and perhaps to negotiate contingency fees. In short, 'the legal professions should be as free as possible, consistent with safeguarding of clients' interests, to offer their services in ways that they find best meet their clients' demands.' The final arbiter to determine whether they were serving the interests of their clients would be the state, rather than the professions. Thus, their advertising, would 'like any other business' be subject to the principles of the Advertising Standards Authority which, the Green Paper claimed, provided 'strong safeguards' for the protection of their clients. The complaints and disciplinary procedures of both professions should in future be supervised by a state official, a Legal Services Ombudsman.

---

[31] Lord Chancellor's Dept, *The Work and Organization of the Legal Profession*, Cm. 1979, No. 570.

[32] It was published along with two other papers, *Contingency Fees*, Cm. 1979, No. 571 and *Conveyancing by Authorized Practitioners*, Cm. 1979, No. 572.

To appreciate the nature of this attack on the legal profession, one must recall that in seven hundred years as an organized profession, the bar had never been subject to legislation and had rarely even been mentioned in law. Thus the very idea of legislative regulation was itself without precedent, while their substantive proposals anticipated a wholly different relationship with the state. Green Papers, however, are discussion documents, often revealing about the Government's intentions but not necessarily indicating the outlines of the legislation which eventually ensues. So it proved in this case. Reaction to these Green Papers evidently prompted the Government to drop many of their proposals from the White Paper that appeared three months later, preceding the introduction of the bill. The prospect of open access to the courts for 'licensed advocates' who might be former barristers, solicitors or members of other professions in place of the Bar was universally condemned and forgotten.[33] The Lord Chancellor's Advisory Committee appeared in the White Paper as a less imperative and more advisory body, whose more important decisions would have to secure the agreement of a panel of senior judges. The Inns of Court and the Law Society were also rehabilitated and left to decide a number of contentious issues, such as partnerships for barristers, multidisciplinary partnerships and direct access to the bar, for themselves. While the Green Papers had dismissed the idea that there might be a conflict of interest for solicitors or licensed conveyancers employed by lending institutions who undertook conveyancing work on behalf of their employers, and that a statutory code would provide ample safeguards, the White Paper acknowledged that there might indeed be conflicts of interest. It therefore included a number of requirements that limited the opportunities for mass conveyancing by banks and building societies.[34] In the passage of the bill through Parliament, one crucial amendment, moved by a past Chairman of the Bar, limited still further the chances of solicitors competing freely with barristers as advocates in the higher courts. The last attack on the professions of the Thatcher era, more perhaps than any of the others, ended therefore with 'a fairly massive retreat'.[35]

---

[33] The only exception being the Consumer's Association magazine *Which?*

[34] The provisions of the Green and White Papers are compared in detail in M. Zander, 'The Thatcher Government's Onslaught on the Lawyers: Who Won?', *The International Lawyer*, 24: 3 (1990) 776–81.

[35] Ibid., 784.

Unravelling the Ideology of the Reforms

These brief summaries of the reforms, or attempted reforms, of the professions make them sound rather more original, and more coherent, than they actually were. There were precedents for many of them.[36] And they often seemed, at the time, to have had a serendipitous, almost accidental, character as though the Government had just thought of them while dealing with some other problem. The Health Service reforms, for instance, were not planned as two stages, the second 'opting out' phase was rather frantically cobbled together after the failure of the managerial reforms following Griffiths.[37] The first Thatcher Government had rejected the whole idea of a legislated national curriculum.[38] The idea of abolishing the UGC and having a single funding agency for both universities and polytechnics was not even raised during the first two Thatcher Governments. The reforms of the legal profession were perhaps the most accidental of all, since they were triggered by the unexpected success of the private member's bill to abolish the solicitors' conveyancing monopoly.[39]

For all their accidental and serendipitous quality the reforms were remarkably consistent. They were pursued through three Governments, numerous ministerial changes, and in a variety of institutional settings, and they repeatedly struck at exactly the same target—the discretion

---

[36] Rayner, for instance, had previously served as a Civil Service consultant during the Heath Government, and the idea of executive agencies is foreshadowed in Heath's 'new style of government' which proposed that executive blocks of work should be delegated to accountable units of government. A number of these units, known as 'departmental agencies', were created in the 1970s including the Defence Procurement Executive and the Property Services Agency. Rayner had served as Chief Executive of the Defence Procurement Executive—see G. Drewry & T. Butcher, *The Civil Service Today* (Oxford, Blackwell, 1988), 196. The national curriculum had been discussed for several years before Mrs Thatcher came to power, and could be said to have been put on the political agenda by the previous Prime Minister, James Callaghan, in a much-cited speech of 1976. Earlier changes in the 'buffer' role of the UGC are described in R. O. Berdahl, G. C. Moodie, & I. J. Spitzberg Jnr., *Quality and Access to Higher Education: Comparing Britain and the United States* (Buckingham, Soc. for Research into Higher Educ. & Open Univ. Press, 1991) at 16–25.

[37] S. Jenkins, *Accountable to None*, 70–7.

[38] In 1981 the Sec. of State observed that the Government 'did not think it would be right for secretaries of state to determine syllabuses and the government did not propose to introduce legislation . . . in relation to the curriculum'. Quoted R. Aldrich, 'The National Curriculum: An Historical Perspective', in Lawton & Chitty (eds.), *National Curriculum*, 21–33.

[39] Mrs Thatcher had earlier defended the Bar's monopoly.

and autonomy of professionals.[40] For that reason, we are entitled, I think, to describe them as principled and ideological, even though neither Mrs Thatcher nor her Ministers articulated this ideology as a party programme. With the exception of the teachers, professions were rarely mentioned in their election manifestos.[41] An implicit ideology, I suppose one should call it, or a set of assumptions but in any event, it is difficult to accept them as no more than 'a bundle of nostrums and prejudices'.[42] Nor would it would be plausible to suggest that all these professions merely happened to be in the way of a government that was singularly resolute in its determination to cut public expenditure. Jenkins observed that it was the 'bureaucratic reaction' to the International Monetary Fund (IMF) crisis in 1975–6 'that gave Thatcherism its forward drive. The Treasury's need to control public spending was the engine, the car and the fuel.' But if that was the entire explanation we have to suppose that this pressure on public expenditure was of an entirely different order from that of other European democracies for many of them, as Jenkins himself points out, were at the time moving in an entirely opposite direction, and really doing what the Thatcher governments always claimed to be doing, namely increasing local democracy and participation.[43] In any case, some of the reforms go far beyond what was required for the purpose of limiting public expenditure.[44] And it would be even less plausible to search

[40] 'Thatcherism was never an ideology. It was not a coherent set of principles to be used as a guide to policy.' S. Jenkins, *Accountable to None*, 2.

[41] Teachers are the exception to this proposition. The Government seems to have considered teachers a rather unpopular profession and fair electoral game, no doubt because the recent industrial action of some of them had infuriated parents. Many educational reforms which affected them, such as national standards in reading, writing, and arithmetic, open enrolment, and the reform of teacher education, were mentioned in both the 1979 and 1983 manifestos. The latter, under the heading 'How to defend Britain's traditional liberties and distinctive way of life', spoke of reducing the cost of administering the Health Service and commended the Rayner investigations. School, university, Civil Service and Health Service reforms are all mentioned in the 1987 manifesto, but the implications for the professions concerned not made explicit.

[42] Young, *One of Us*, 532.

[43] S. Jenkins, *Accountable to None*, 243, 255–7. For evidence that these selfsame pressures on public expenditure were affecting public expenditure in all European societies, albeit without recourse to the IMF, see the country by country surveys in P. Flora (ed.), *Growth to Limits—The Western Welfare States Since World War II* (vol. 2, Berlin, Walter de Gruyter, 1986).

[44] The President of the Society of Education Officers, referring to the city technology colleges, observed that it was 'a criminal waste of public money to be investing in new school places when there is already apparently a surplus' (*The Times*, 26 Jan. 1990); for other examples see Simon, *Bending the Rules*, 57–79, 162.

for the cause of these reforms in the internal dynamics of these professions, or in wider changes in the economy, for then we would have to
suppose that such dynamics, or such changes, simultaneously affected
seven different professions.[45]

Pinpointing the principles and ideology that inspired the Thatcher
policies, however, is not so easy. Ministers tended to justify their
reforms by referring to 'value for money', or 'accountability', occasionally to the virtues of free markets and competition, and even to local
participation. None of these terms, however, is particularly illuminating
or an accurate description of their policies and at times they seem
grossly misleading. It would be difficult to believe, for instance, that the
limitation of public expenditure, or 'getting value for money', somehow
entailed the abolition of the Schools Council or the imposition of commissioners on the universities. In 1983 the universities were all but
forced to take a one per cent increase in their 1984 grants to cover academic salaries and introduce merit and incentive payments in which
none of them had expressed any interest. Other reforms were pursued
in complete disregard of their impact on public expenditure. No evidence whatever was collected about the cost of open enrolment, or the
opting out of schools, or city technology colleges. Indeed, they were
pursued over widespread objections from the Government's own supporters that they would be an extremely wasteful use of educational
resources.[46]

Market competition is also not much of a guide to Government
actions. On occasion, it was explicitly rejected, most notably in the case
of the educational vouchers, long touted by the right-wing of the party
and by the mid-eighties attracting support elsewhere. In response to the
proposal for higher education vouchers, a Department of Education
discussion paper in 1992 declared that 'student demand alone' was an
insufficient basis for planning' since it 'may not coincide with what

---

[45] Just prior to the Thatcher attack, the solicitors' branch of the legal profession was,
as it happens, finally accepting the administrative logic of the large multi-partner multi-
national firm but this appears to have been an entirely coincidental development.

[46] This is not to deny that the pressure of public expenditure was an important consideration in many of the reforms, though one is bound to observe that the understanding of the role of the professions in public expenditure seems to have been rather crude,
simply that the increased efficiency brought about by its reforms would lessen expenditure. In all likelihood, the English professions have reduced demand for their services,
and weakening professional control and reinforcing market pressures might therefore be
expected to *increase* the demand for professional services and therefore *increase* public
expenditure.

employers and government consider desirable'.[47] Having dismissed the claims of the apparent 'consumers', the students, it then used its powers to promote the claims of other 'consumers', namely 'business, industrial, professional and other employment interests' who for more than a century had shown little interest in the education universities provided, and put them in positions, on the UFC and polytechnic governing bodies, where they might, with ministers and civil servants, control higher education decision-making.

On other occasions, the Government decided that a free market solution was politically or administratively impractical, and invented quasi-markets, such as open enrolment and opting out of secondary schools, 'fund-holding' GPs in an 'internal' NHS market, NHS Hospital Trusts, and university 'bidding' for students. Whatever their resemblance to real markets may be, these fabricated markets had one thing in common: they all increased the power of central government. Schools might, for instance, 'opt out' of local government control but they did not then enter the market-place as independent schools, but became 'grant maintained', under the direct control of the DES. NHS Trust Hospitals might 'opt out' of the control of the regional health authorities but they then became directly responsible to the Department of Health. General practitioners might become 'fund-holding' but they likewise became dependent on the funds provided for their services by the Department of Health. The market fabricated for the universities in 1989 had in fact only one buyer, a state agency, the UFC. These quasi-markets were clearly not offering either market competition or freedom from state control. On the contrary, since their rewards and sanctions, the rules under which they operated, were all determined by departments of state, they were merely transferring power to the central government.

The one thing that the Thatcher Governments manifestly did not do, despite Mrs Thatcher's repeated claims, was to get the 'state off our backs'—at least in the services in which these professions were engaged.[48] Since her Governments also increased market choice by pri-

---

[47] It went on to say that it would itself determine the prospective needs for new graduates by means of an interdepartmental review and, in the discussion paper of 1992, that it wished to 'steer' the system.

[48] Out of office, Mrs Thatcher continued to claim that she had reduced state controls: 'Don't Undo My Work' (*Newsweek*, 27 Apr. 1992, 26–7). E.g. 'So much was controlled by what had almost become a corporate state . . . I cut back the powers of government. Now they've got to be jolly careful they don't give government too many extra powers and undo what I've done.'

vatization, by the sale of council homes and tendering for local government services, it is clear that to understand Thatcherism we must first abandon the view that market competition and state control are opposites, zero-sum alternative policy options. Her Governments frequently moved in both directions simultaneously, increasing both market choice and state control. This dichotomy must, therefore, be false and misleading. There is, as the preceding narratives indicate, a third form of market regulation, that of corporate self-government, created and enforced by the professions. And there is reason to think that this third form of market regulation has always been peculiarly important in Britain, since in practice state employment and state control, as we have already noted with respect to civil servants, doctors, and teachers, usually depended on a high degree of professional self-regulation, what in the NHS was called 'consensus management'. In the past, state services, and even nationalized industries, had therefore relied, not on bureaucratic or managerial oversight or public accountability, but on the discretion of those who ran them to determine proper standards of service and output.

Thatcherism may therefore be described as a preference for market competition and state control at the expense of professional or corporate self-regulation. Their aversion to corporate self-regulation was repeatedly revealed when they came to create a new profession or reconstruct an old one as in the cases of 'licensed conveyancers', 'licensed teachers', 'licensed receivers' and the putative 'licensed advocate'.[49] On the ground, the effect of all the Thatcher reforms was to construct managerial hierarchies in work settings previously largely self-regulated and to elevate the power, incomes and status of their previously self-effacing managers, so that they could organize, measure, monitor, assess, reward, or punish practising professionals. Professional rules and conventions, and their internalized collegial controls, were invariably discredited or denigrated. The idea that professionals were disinterested guardians of the public interest, who could be trusted to try and improve the service in which they were employed, was dismissed as a sham, a cover for professionals' own self-interest. Like everyone else, professionals would, unless checked by the state or their

---

[49] 'Licensed receivers' were created in 1985 though they had originally been proposed under the Labour Government. They were immediately absorbed by the 'big six' accountancy firms and their professional association is dominated by employees of these firms; see T. C. Halliday & B. G. Carruthers, *Rescuing Business*, chap. 10.

managerial superiors, exploit both the service they were supposed to run, and the people they were supposed to serve.

The reforms also rejected the idea that the motivations and ambitions of professionals were in any way different from those of other employees and worked on the assumption that incentive and bonus payments, and performance-related pay, would increase professional productivity, just as it increased the productivity of other workers. And aiming an arrow at the very heart of the professional ethic, they assumed that their performance and merit could be measured and demonstrated in terms that any lay person or manager could readily understand and judge. Professions were built on the very opposite assumption, that lay persons cannot judge the merit or success of their work and for that very reason they disparage public or market assessments of their worth in favour of those of their colleagues. The Thatcher reforms paid no attention to such notions and imposed regular audits and productivity measures on them all and was indifferent to the implied corollary that work that didn't register on such standardized public measures was of no significance.

It would be difficult to imagine a more offensive notion to a conscientious professional. To a considerable degree the success of the reforms hinged in fact on the displacement of professional goals amongst professionals themselves and the restructuring their ambitions and careers, so that the more successful were not those who actually cared for patients, taught children, or tutored students but those who advanced up the new managerial ladders and controlled their former colleagues who continued to do these things. Thus, consultants, GPs, and nurses were encouraged to apply for NHS management positions. General practitioners were encouraged to become 'fund-holding practices' or little businesses, who would of necessity devote part of their time to the management of the practice. Headmasters of opted-out schools were to become managers responsible to something very like a board of directors. University department heads were no longer just senior colleagues but expected to exercise a full range of managerial rewards and sanctions under vice-chancellors who were in turn expected to have long abandoned teaching or research and become the divisional managers of those still engaged in it. Solicitors were discouraged from handling legal aid clients as part of their general practice, and encouraged to become managers of firms franchised by the Legal Aid Board.

One can be more certain that this interpretation catches something of the essence of the Thatcher reforms by noting those professions, or segments of professions, that were immune from her reforming zeal—accountants and engineers are the most striking cases—were precisely those whose members were for the most part employed in large enterprises and therefore already subject to managerial control. Large firms of solicitors also seem to have had little or nothing to lose from any of the Thatcher reforms. The special targets of the reforms were invariably the original, independent fee-for-service professionals (such as barristers, solo or small partnership solicitors, and general practitioners) or those (such as hospital doctors, academics, and teachers) who were formally subject to some administrative authority, but had, *de facto*, established considerable areas of autonomy and discretion and were controlled primarily by their professional ethics.

The second characteristic of Thatcherism that emerges from these attacks on the professions was its indifference to the representative functions of intermediate bodies, even to representative democracy and civil society itself, as her celebrated remark that 'there is no such thing as society' suggested. Representative bodies of all kinds fared badly during her terms of office. They were altogether excluded from the policy-making process. Royal Commissions and departmental committees which had been broadly representative of articulate public opinion, and typically invited anyone and everyone to submit evidence, were abandoned as a means of public policy formation. Local government was excluded from the reforms in the NHS, and subsequently from further and higher education. The Schools Council and the UGC both, in their different ways, representative institutions, were, as noted earlier, abolished. Teachers and academics were allowed part of the summer vacation to respond to the Educational Reform Bill and the legal professions just three months to reply to the most radical series of reforms in their history. The Thatcher Governments frequently acted on the assumption that, like the trade unions, professional associations did not really represent their members, so that the Government might always appeal over their heads to their individual members at the ballot box.

At bottom, therefore, the Thatcherite view of democracy was plebiscitary rather than representative. Her Governments assumed, for instance, that the state, meaning a group of ministers and their advisers, alone and unaided (except by a handful of business executives and management consultants) were able to determine the public interest, that her Governments needed no legitimation other than a bare electoral majority, that the ballot box was the supreme and even the only form of representation, that there was nothing that the state need hesitate to touch, no limit on the powers it might accumulate, and no need to worry about the way its powers might subsequently be exercised. Historically, it has been the French state that has been indifferent to the constitution of civil society, and preferred to exercise public power directly rather than dispersing and distributing it to intermediary bodies. Given the contemporaneous decentralization in France, the two countries might be said to have changed places over the Thatcher years.

Placing the Reforms in their Historical Context: the Glorious Revolution and the Unwritten Constitution

Observers and victims of the Thatcher reforms occasionally claimed that they were, in some sense, 'unconstitutional'. Since Britain does not have a written constitution, they could not, of course, cite any supporting precedents nor find an institutionalized means to vindicate their views.[50] The Lord Chief Justice considered the proposed reforms of the legal profession 'sinister' but, even with the help of an unusual assembly of all judges of England, could not say exactly what part of the constitution was being broken. It is therefore something of a challenge to put these reforms in their historical context, to see how far they were unprecedented and in so doing try to account for the feeling that they were 'unconstitutional' or 'sinister'. The legal profession is the best case for this kind of investigation since its history is both longer and better documented than any of the other professions.

When the Green Papers on the legal profession were published in 1989, commentators airily observed that it was the biggest shake-up of the legal profession in 100 years. It is difficult, however, to discover anything in 1889 or thereabouts to which they might usefully be compared. Presumably, those for whom a hundred years was more than a figure of speech were referring to the work of the Judicature Commission

---

[50] J. White, 'An Unconstitutional National Curriculum', in Lawton & Chitty (eds.), *National Curriculum*, 137–51; Simon, *Bending the Rules*, 113–22; Zander, 'Thatcher Government's Onslaught', 766–9. The only Government acknowledgement that any of their reforms involved constitutional questions was in the appointment of the Crohan Committee on its powers with respect to the UGC. Shortly afterwards the Government apparently decided that it did not need its advice and abolished the UGC. For similar charges that the reforms of the police were 'unconstitutional', see S. Jenkins, *Accountable to None*, 105.

which sat from 1869 to 1874. Although this Commission abolished the declining order of serjeants, and eliminated the lay jurisdiction of the ecclesiastical courts—which meant the end of their doctors (barristers) and proctors (solicitors)—it had rather little impact on the other members of the legal profession. In any case, it is not much of a precedent because it was mainly concerned with the structure and jurisdiction of courts. It did not set out to reform the legal profession at all, and did not of course, refer to other professions.[51] The earlier, mid-nineteenth-century campaign to reform legal education is perhaps a slightly better precedent since it was explicitly hostile towards the two branches of the professions and eventually raised questions about their corporate powers.[52] However, since it too was not concerned with other professions and since, over three decades, it achieved very little, it hardly bears comparison with the reforms of the Thatcher Governments.

To find a close historical parallel to the policies of the Thatcher Governments we have to go still further back, not one hundred but three hundred years, and specifically to the Glorious Revolution of 1688–9 which laid the foundations of the English professions in their modern, distinctive form. In the late 1670s and early 1680s, Charles II had begun to challenge, with writs of *quo warranto*, the legality of the charters of the municipal boroughs, the City of London, and its companies and other chartered bodies. Charles II's initial intention was to control the chartered municipal boroughs and ensure that royal nominees effectively controlled their governing bodies, and thereby to control the nomination of their members of parliament. However, the campaign soon moved beyond these electoral or parliamentary concerns and sought to change the relationship between state and civil society in its entirety.

The major confrontation took place in the King's Bench in 1683 and pitted the Crown against the most powerful chartered body of them all, the City of London. Counsel for the City rested his argument on precedent and argued that the Crown could not take action against chartered bodies because they are 'invisible, immortal, cannot be outlawed, cannot commit Treason or Felony, cannot be excommunicate, hath no Soul, cannot do Fealty, cannot be imprisoned, are not subject to Imbecility or Death.' Counsel for the King replied that 'if charters be not forfeit, there would be so many little commonwealths, by themselves independent of

---

[51] B. Abel-Smith & R. B. Stevens, *Lawyers and the Courts: A Sociological Study of the English Legal System* (London, Heinemann, 1967), 80–7.
[52] Ibid., 63–76.

the Crown, in defiance of it, little republics would spring up all over the Kingdom which would not be conducive to good government.'[53] When the verdict went against the City, a large number of bodies surrendered their charters in the hope that might receive better treatment at the hands of the Crown.

When his brother James II succeeded, he vigorously prosecuted this same policy against all the lesser governments in the kingdom, including the three medical professions (the Royal College of Physicians, the London Society of Apothecaries, and the Company of Barber-Surgeons), and even beyond the seas, to the chartered American colonies.[54] The Inns of Court could not be challenged by writs of *quo warranto* since their autonomy rested on custom rather than a charter but both Charles II and James II sought to obtain some means of controlling the Benches, the governing bodies of the Inns, by appointing increasing numbers of King's Counsel, and by insisting that they sit *ex officio* on their Benches.[55] Charles and James, it seems clear, intended to restore something resembling the 'thorough government' for which their father had lost his head.

The rewriting and re-issuing of charters was still continuing when news of preparations for William of Orange's invasion of England reached James. In a vain attempt to rally support, he hurriedly returned the surrendered charters, many of them in their original form. The Inns meanwhile decided to contest the precedence of King's Counsel on their Benches. The return of the charters, however, did little to save James his crown and the autonomy of the chartered bodies was finally established and legitimized by the Glorious Revolution and the promise of William and Mary to defend 'the liberties, privileges and the protestant religion of the English people.'[56] Amongst those 'liberties and priv-

---

[53] The trial, the circumstances leading to it and the legal merits of the arguments and its consequences are discussed in detail in J. Levin, *The Charter Controversy in the City of London 1660–1688* (London, Athlone, 1969), 28–54.

[54] For the consequences of this policy in the colonies, see M. Kammen, *The Glorious Revolution in America*; in the professions, see Sir George Clark, *A History of the Royal College of Physicians of London*, vol. I (Oxford, Clarendon Press, 1964), 353–8; H. C. Wall, C. Cameron, & E. A. Underwood, *A History of the Worshipful Society of Apothecaries of London, Vol. 1: 1617–1815* (London, Oxford Univ. Press, 1963), 105–9; J. Dobson & R. M. Walker, *The Barkers and Barber-Surgeons of London* (Oxford, Blackwell, 1979), 96.

[55] W. C. Richardson, *A History of the Inns of Court* (Baton Rouge, Claitors, 1975), 47–8. For analogous moves by James II against the universities by means of a special commission to exercise visitorial jurisdiction, see D. Ogg, *England in the Reigns of James II and William III* (Oxford, Clarendon Press, 1955), 183–203.

[56] The King's Bench decision of 1683 against the City of London was disinterred, reviled, and comprehensively overturned by statute in 1689 (2 W & M c. 8) which

ileges' were the rights of chartered bodies, including those of the professions, most of which were restored to the *status quo ante.*

In the subsequent three centuries, dozens of occupations followed, or sought to follow, the barristers and physicians and establish comparable institutions of corporate self-government that would enable them to control the admission, training, and certification of future members, to defend and regulate their work jurisdictions, and to enhance their status. Surgeons were the first to do so, and made a spectacularly rapid ascent, by professional standards, to join the physicians as a chartered Royal College in 1745. Attorneys and solicitors had a longer struggle. Although their voluntary efforts to regulate admission and conduct of members received some statutory support in the second quarter of the eighteenth century, they were not delegated formal charter powers as a self-governing body until 1821. Civil engineers first formed a voluntary association in the 1780s and became a chartered institute in 1828. In the late nineteenth and early twentieth century a host of new occupations followed suit, about fourteen per decade by Millerson's count.[57]

The process has continued in modern times. The Royal College of Nursing was incorporated in 1928 and received a charter as a Royal College in 1939, while that of midwives was incorporated in 1941 and became a Royal College in 1947. In 1987, after a long campaign to obtain recognition 'for the professional side of computing' and credentials and status comparable to those of lawyers and doctors, the British Computer Society was awarded a Royal Charter. This defined the profession of 'information systems engineering' and allowed the Society to accredit members and fellows and to monitor ethical standards. It currently claims 32,000 members.[58]

As we have already had occasion to observe when considering civil servants, nurses, and teachers, few of these occupations could hope to emulate the original fee-for-service professions. For the most part, they consisted of salaried employees who could not collectively control their admission, training, and jurisdiction as effectively as barristers and

---

'reversed and annulled . . . all charter, Grants, Letters Patent and Commissions touching or concerning any of their Liberties or Franchises or the Liberties, Privileges, Franchises, Immunities, Lands, Tenements, Hereditaments, Rights Title or Estates . . . ' and extended the same annulment to all the City's companies. *The Statutes of the Realm,* vol. VI (London, 1819), 171–3.

[57] G. Millerson, *The Qualifying Associations* (London, Routledge, 1964).

[58] *The Times,* 28 Sept. 1989. In 1986 the de Ville Committee identified that there were 76 chartered professions: *Review of Vocational Qualifications: a report by the working group for the Manpower Services Commission* (London, HMSO, 1986).

physicians. They therefore had to adapt and amend the two original models to fit their own particular circumstances. They have done so to varying degrees, in a great variety of partial and hybrid forms. In the present context, however, the important fact is not the failure to replicate the original models, but the enduring appeal of their institutions and ideals, the ever-renewed efforts of a host of occupations to emulate their credentialling and training functions, their forms of government, and their status.

Mrs Thatcher once characterized Victorian values in terms of self-help and entrepreneurship but in numerical terms, the educational, ethical, and status ideals of the professions seem to have been a far more important expression of Victorian values. And it seems safe to say that their cultural impact was also far greater since, as we have seen, professionals had a decisive and lasting influence on so many British institutions: the Civil Service, the universities, schools, the courts, hospitals and medical care. Indirectly, via accountants, engineers, solicitors, and personnel managers, they even helped to reshape the organizations that self-helping entrepreneurs had themselves created.

Moreover, professional values and institutions, unlike those of entrepreneurs, never generated an organized opposition or a counter-ideology, and were never, until the Thatcher era, subject to legislative intervention and regulation. Right through the eighteenth, nineteenth, and twentieth centuries, attempts to organize, represent, and regulate professions had the support of governments of whatever party and whatever hue. They advanced unchallenged and unobserved. The rise of the Labour Party threatened them not a bit. On the contrary, the Labour Party's foremost ideologue, R. H. Tawney, extolled the virtues of professionalism. His vision of socialism was not of class war and class victory but the professionalization of everyone. Labour Governments were, if anything, even more sympathetic than the Conservatives to professional aspirations.[59] It was the Attlee Government that created the National Health Service in a form that was peculiarly supportive of professional self-government and laid the foundations for the 'consensus management' introduced by the Wilson Government. It was also the Attlee Government that gave the Law Society, the solicitors' professional association, responsibility for administering and disbursing public funds under legal aid. And there are reasons for thinking that the appeal of the original distinctive 'public corporation' form of

---

[59] R. H. Tawney, *The Acquisitive Society* (London, Bell, 1921).

nationalization in Britain was precisely because it offered the best prospect of professionalizing the industries taken into public ownership.[60]

The fact that the professions were never the subject of political debate in England suggests that they embodied widely shared ideals and aspirations, that they were the 'deep structures' of English life. Better than anything else, they explain a number of the cultural and institutional peculiarities of English society to this day. The preference for practice-based training and practice-based knowledge rather than theoretical, formally-acquired knowledge is, for instance, deeply embedded in the admission and training requirements of both the Bar and the medical professions.[61] The assumption that it is right and proper for practitioners of an occupation to exercise sovereignty over their work jurisdictions has been documented among both the professions and trade unions in Britain, and may reasonably explain the development of rigid, institutionalized divisions of labour in both industry and the professions and, correspondingly, the rather restricted scope for managerial intervention.[62] In all probability, occupational loyalties also explain the so-called 'class' system of Britain which has little in common with Marxist notions of a bourgeoisie and proletariat, but seems to owe much to the collective efforts of professions and trade unions to instill and uphold notions of their proper status.

[60] I argued, and sought to document, this point in M. Burrage, 'Nationalization and the Professional Ideal', *Sociology* 7 (1972), 253–72. The professions are, of course, only one example of spontaneous voluntary, lay, representative associations in Britain who have come to exercise public power and fulfil public responsibilities. They might reasonably be seen as members of an extended kin network of institutions which included the jury, the inquest, the main instruments of British colonial expansion such as the chartered trading and colonial companies, the municipal boroughs, the universities and Royal Commissions, the UGC in its original form, the public corporations (especially the BBC) and a variety of other bodies which have been delegated public powers, such as the Stock Exchange, the pre-1948 Bank of England, the Football Association, and the Jockey Club.

[61] Two examples: a DES survey in 1980 found that British employers gave a very low priority to vocational training; see *Education Policy and Industry's Needs in the 1980s*, Dept of Education and Science, London, 1980. P. Whalley later reported that only 23% of his sample of university-trained engineers considered a university training 'essential' for a successful engineering career. Most of them (68%) thought that experience was an adequate substitute: P. Whalley, *The Social Production of Technical Work: The Sociology of British Engineers* (New York, State Univ., 1986), 55–6. For further historical evidence see M. Burrage, 'School Versus Practice-based Education: A Comparison of Three Modern Societies', in S. Rothblatt & B. Wittrock (eds.), *The European and American University since 1800* (Cambridge, Cambridge Univ. Press, 1992).

[62] For an empirical study in a variety of industrial settings, see P. Dubois, 'Workers' Control Over the Organization of Work: French and English Maintenance Workers in Mass Production Industry', *Organisation Stud.* 2: 4 (1981).

In any event, it is clear that the English developed a quite distinctive form of professional government and to explain and understand it we have to return to the Glorious Revolution and to the unwritten constitution which it initiated and legitimized. Conventionally, the unwritten constitution is thought to govern the relationships between the Crown, Parliament, and the courts but it evidently extended deep into civil society and protected lesser forms of government such as the professions. The repeated acquisition of charters by professional bodies through the nineteenth and twentieth centuries, and the behaviour of other parties such as the universities and neighbouring professions, is barely comprehensible without reference to it.[63] Moreover the near-constant form of these charters enables us to identify three cardinal principles which were evidently thought to govern the relationship between the state and the professions. First, whenever a group of leading practitioners of a hitherto unorganized occupation gives reasonable evidence that they represent that occupation, they should be granted appropriate powers, by charter, to govern it. Second, professions should thereafter be left to define the public interest in all matters that fall within their jurisdiction. Third, unless they could demonstrate an overriding public interest, governments should thereafter only interfere in their affairs with the express consent of their governing bodies.

All governments from the Glorious Revolution until the election of Mrs Thatcher abided by these principles and it was for this reason that the Lord Chief Justice and others considered her reforms to be 'sinister' or 'unconstitutional'. Mrs Thatcher's Governments ignored them and extended the powers of the state in ways for which there were no precedents other than those of the later Stuarts. They, in pursuit of 'thorough government', and she in the name of 'firm government', turned the power of the state against the voluntary, self-governing bodies of civil society. There is an unmistakable historical parallel between the Stuart writs of *quo warranto* which had challenged the authority of the municipal boroughs and chartered bodies and the 'writs' presented by the director of Marks & Spencer against the civil service, of Reed Paper against the universities and of Sainsbury's against the NHS. There was nothing remotely comparable in between.

---

[63] I have dealt with this point in more detail in 'School Versus Practice-based Education'.

Politics, Micro-politics, and Trade Unions

There have been no extended field studies of professional work settings that would enable us to clearly assess the effects of any of these reforms on workplace relationships and culture.[64] Some years later therefore, we can still only wonder about their effects and their success in this sense. Evidence is, however, readily available about the immediate corporate responses of the professions and we may speculate on what these suggest for the future.

They were predictably, and almost uniformly, hostile but the first notable thing about their reaction was that they did not attempt any kind of joint or collaborative action and did not even recognize their common plight.[65] There was no sign whatever of the 'service class', to which some sociologists have supposed the professions belong, acting collectively to defend their interests. The ancient professions had met the threat from Charles II and James II without seeking help from each other, and their successors responded to the Thatcher threat in exactly the same manner. The second notable thing is that it did not prompt them to abandon their traditional inhibitions towards partisan politics. A Doctors' Party was formed to oppose the NHS reforms, and soon disappeared, but there were no explicit party alignments. The professions with substantial segments organized in trade unions retained their links to the Labour Party of course but there was no discernible shift among the others towards either the Labour Party or Liberal Democrats. If there was a fundamental shift of political alignments, a not unreasonable expectation, then it is one that the pollsters still have to document. There were no public declarations by professional bodies to this effect. Still more surprisingly perhaps, there was no explicit move by these

---

[64] See Hennessy, Strong, & Robinson, *The NHS—Under New Management.* See also J. Atkins, 'Experience in Schools: Case Study 1, Kemnal Manor School for Boys', in H. Tomlinson (ed.), *Performance-related Pay in Education* (London, Routledge, 1992), 164–76; A. J. Phillimore, 'University Research Performance Indicators in Practice: The University Grants Committee's Evaluation of British Universities, 1985–86', *Research Policy*, no. 18, 1989, 255–71; T. Packwood *et al., Hospitals in Transition: The Resource Management Experiment* (Milton Keynes, Open Univ. Press, 1991); and personal responses by doctors in Sir Reginald Murley (ed.), *Patients or Customers: Are the NHS Reforms Working?* (London, IEA Health and Welfare Unit, 1995).

[65] Not, of course, in every single particular. The Law Society welcomed the extension of the rights of audience for solicitors promised in the Courts and Legal Services Bill. While opposing the reforms as a whole, the medical profession did not oppose the idea of audit, and indeed claimed that 'reference to it can be found in the Charter of the Royal College of Physicians of 1518'.

parties towards them, apart from the Labour Party's overtures to the medical profession in the 1992 election campaign mentioned below.

Reactions of the professional bodies fell into three categories. The first was to try and mobilize public opinion to have the reforms amended or abandoned, which we may designate the public political response. The second was to negotiate amendments during the passage of legislation or the implementation of the reforms to try and limit their original intent, which is the traditional, private, continuous, micro-politics of the professions. The third was to take up a defensive, adversarial stance at the workplace, and resist, undermine or sabotage the introduction of the reforms 'on the shop-floor', in the manner of trade unions.

Apart from civil servants, all the professions initially made some kind of public political response. In 1986 the Royal College of Nursing ran a mass advertising campaign against the implementation of the Griffiths Report and their grading, a campaign which, incidentally, made a direct appeal to the unwritten constitution with the slogan 'nursing should be run by nurses'.[66] Nurses also organized demonstrations and lobbied their MPs at Westminster, and their trade unions organized sporadic industrial action. During their contract dispute, the British Medical Association also sought to mobilize public support by mass advertising, though a small group hastily formed their 'Doctors' Party' which promised to field forty candidates in the forthcoming election, including in the constituencies of Mrs Thatcher and leading members of her Government.[67] After the publication of the Green Papers, the Bar similarly launched an extensive and expensive advertising campaign, which urged members of the public to write to their MPs. They also organized protest meetings of their members and held Press conferences to voice their concerns, for them a rather bold innovation.

It is difficult to assess the impact of such campaigns. Those of the doctors and nurses were probably the most persuasive since they at least provoked parliamentary discussion and polls showed consistent and overwhelming public support for the doctors' and nurses' stand.[68]

---

[66] Under a large picture of a nurse, the copy read 'She has great faith in the NHS (Which is more than the NHS has in her) . . . In more and more health areas, professional managers have taken it upon themselves to decide that nurses cannot run nursing'; see *The Times*, 16 & 20 Jan. 1986.

[67] For a retrospective account see 'Election 1992: GPs Party Disappears into Political Oblivion' (*Independent*, 23 Mar. 1992).

[68] Polls taken during the 1992 election campaign showed that 56% of the electorate, and 33% of Conservative voters, wanted the health service reforms to be scrapped while

However, even in their case, they could not stop the reforms and it is difficult to identify any single amendment of the reforms that might be attributed to them. The Bar's campaign was widely considered to be counter-productive, and provoked not the least indication of public sympathy or even interest. The other professions also seem to have been unable to stir public opinion. They never caused the Government much discomfort or embarrassment during the passage of the legislation and never made their concerns a political issue.[69] In Britain, public politics does not appear to be the professions' strong suit. Apart from doctors and nurses, there was no public or Press interest in the autonomy of the individual professions. Most of the Press joined in the criticism of individual professions and were indifferent to the wider constitutional issue of the steady, cumulative concentration of state power.

The failure of the professions to enlist public support is hardly to be wondered at. In the past they had rarely, if ever, had to mobilize popular support in defence of their prerogatives. Academics were perhaps the most supine of them all and had long entrusted the defence of academic freedom to the Treasury, the UGC and the CVCP. Intermittently, the professions had to defend their interests publicly—in the measured, decorous proceedings of Royal Commissions—but they required only tacit public approval and respect, or more accurately, the absence of public disquiet. Obviously, therefore, they were going to be at a disadvantage when the Thatcher Government, at a moment of its choosing, pitchforked them into the public arena, and required them to defend themselves against a government with a clear parliamentary majority which was also, in most cases, their employer.

During the 1992 election campaign the medical reforms became a public political issue when the Labour Party recognized that there was considerable public support for the medical professions and presented a platform distinctively sympathetic towards them.[70] It pledged to

30% wanted them to continue. 'Poll Shows Major's Popularity on the Wane' (*Independent*, 26 Mar. 1992).

[69] Academics held a rally in the Albert Hall, lobbied Parliament and briefed MPs. This may perhaps have helped to secure a number of minor amendments in the Lords. These are described in 'Chalking up the Victories', *AUT Bulletin*, Oct. 1988, 8. However, this review candidly concluded that 'While universities may have emerged victorious from some battles they, in common with other sectors of education, have lost the war.'

[70] They enjoy a public esteem far greater than that of any other profession: J. Jenkins, E. Skordaki & C. F. Willis, *Public Use and Perception of Solicitors' Services*, Research Study No. 1, Research & Policy Planning Unit, Law Soc., 1989. This survey found that doctors were 'easier to talk to', 'easier to understand', more 'efficient' and far more 'hard-working, dependable', 'up to date', and 'honest' than other professions.

create a 'GP-driven' health service which would enable GPs to veto health authorities' plans, to renegotiate their contracts, and to develop their own health promotion work in their own way. Labour also promised to abolish fund-holding general practices, NHS Trust hospitals, and the internal market, and to bring back local authority representation within the NHS.[71] However, Mrs Thatcher's successors sensed the political danger and backed away from any further confrontation with the NHS professions, or anything that might be construed as such.[72] Their victory in the 1987 election gave the reforms added legitimation and ended the professions' hopes of transforming their concerns into public political issues.[73] Shortly after the election, the major teaching and health professional associations abandoned their outright opposition to the reforms and indicated that they wanted to negotiate with the Government about how the reforms might best be implemented—that is, they abandoned public, in favour of private, politics.

It would be premature, however, to conclude that these reforms will never again become part of public political debate. The trauma of the Thatcher era seems to have made all the professions more concerned about their public image and public support. By ignoring the unwritten constitution, by refusing to acknowledge any special relationship with the professions, the Government taught the older professions that they could no longer rely exclusively on private politics. It alerted them to the dangers of being without the support of the publics they served and to the impossibility of trying to mobilize that support overnight. In the future, it seems reasonable to suppose, they will be rather better prepared so that a government will not be able to claim that it speaks on behalf of sleeping constituencies of patients, parents or litigants.[74]

[71] Labour's election manifesto, *It's Time to Get Britain Working Again*, Apr. 1992, 16. 'Labour Pledges to Scrap NHS Internal Market' (*Independent*, 21 Feb. 1992).

[72] *Independent*, 26 Mar. 1992.

[73] See e.g. 'Teachers Reject Call to Boycott Appraisals' (*Independent*, 20 Apr. 1992); 'Teachers Turn from Battle' (*The Times*, 21 Apr. 1992); 'Teachers Reject Fight over Work Appraisal' (*Independent*, 25 Apr. 1992, in which the General Secretary of the National Association of Schoolmasters and Union of Women Teachers is quoted as saying 'We tried to stop appraisal but we have failed. Now all we can do is limit the damage. Things are frankly unchangeable for the next five years'). The doctors were obviously less willing to accept that the election gave the Government a mandate to implement the health service reforms and passed a vote of no confidence at a special BMA conference some 2 months later. However, by that time the GPs remained the 'only big group of medical staff . . . trying to reverse the reforms' (*The Times*, 25 June 1992).

[74] In 1992 a National Union of Teachers official proposed that teachers form an alliance with parents and governors against the state: M. Barber, 'A Union of Interests', *Managing Schools Today*, 1: 7 (May 1992).

The professions' expensive advertising campaigns were an indication of their determination to address a wider public, if not of their skill in doing so. Their associations have been undergoing fundamental organizational changes during and since the Thatcher era, so that they will probably be more pro-active in the future, and more willing to lead their members rather than waiting for members' concerns to register and accumulate through their inevitably protracted representative procedures.[75]

Nevertheless, the immediate response after the failure of their public campaigns was to fall back on their traditional 'private' politics, on negotiations with individual members of the Commons and Lords, with fellow professionals in government departments, and such traditional private channels of persuasion. The legal profession provides the best examples of the way in which such private politics were able to limit the scope of the reforms, or seem to, since we can document only the results rather than the process itself. But as we have already observed, few of the ideas raised in the three Green Papers remained in the White Paper that preceded the introduction of the Courts and Legal Services Bill, which was in turn amended before it became the Courts and Legal Services Act 1990. Both branches of the profession continued to push for further concessions after its passage. Thus the requirements that prevented 'assembly line' conveyancing by banks and building societies were initially only temporary. However, the Law Society's persistence on this issue was rewarded. In March 1992 the Lord Chancellor announced that he would no longer attempt to find a way around this problem.[76] Solicitors could therefore rest secure facing only the competition of licensed conveyancers, which had by this time been shown to be very modest indeed. The issue that most concerned the bar, rights

[75] These changes were often piecemeal, extended over the decade, and have yet to be documented. One instance was the radical reorganization of the government of the Bar in 1986. Having ignored public opinion through its entire history, it then sought, almost overnight, to create a governing body which would represent and speak for the whole bar to government and public opinion. See the arguments and proposals in Senate of the Inns of Court and the bar, *Report of the Committee on the Constitution of the Senate*, Chmn the Rt. Hon. Lord Rawlinson, London, 1986. Another example is the creation of a Research & Policy Planning Unit by the Law Society in 1987. This Unit has continuously published reports and surveys about the profession and its work. However, to document this point properly would require an analysis of the staffing, income, and organizational structure of several professions over the decade.

[76] There were other factors. The recession had tempered the enthusiasm of building societies and banks to embark on new activities and a general election was imminent (*Independent*, 12 Mar. 1992).

of audience for solicitors, was settled by the ruling of the Lord Chancellor's Advisory Committee in 1993, which granted rights of audience to solicitors in private practice who were qualified by experience and further training, but denied them to employed solicitors, including those working for the Crown Prosecution Service. Instead of the threatened stampede a small side-door has been made for advocate-solicitors.[77]

In the hospitals there appears to have been a real shift of power over beds, equipment, and other resources in favour of managers, which no amount of private politics could prevent. However, the medical professions appear to have excluded the newly-empowered managers from critical personnel decisions of selection, promotion, evaluation, and disciplining of consultants and general practitioners. Most observers in the late 1980s agreed that clinical behaviour was 'still regarded as professional territory', that 'management stops at the consulting-room door' and that the impact of the reforms was 'outside the medical domain'.[78] Moreover, medical audits were to be conducted by the professions themselves and though they agreed that managers were to have access to them, the Joint Consultants Committee engaged in long negotiations with the Government 'about how much and what information should be passed to managers, district health authorities and the public'.[79] Health service managers must, therefore, do without some of the infor-

[77] In 1994 a mere 155 solicitors had rights of audience in the higher courts. *Trends in the Solicitors' Profession, Annual Statistical Report 1994* (London, Law Soc., 1994), 78.

[78] A. Pettigrew, I. McKee, & E. Ferlie, 'Managing Strategic Service Change in the NHS', and S. Harrison *et al.*, 'General Management and Medical Autonomy in the NHS', both in *Health Service Management Research*, 2 (1) 1989; C. J. Pollitt, 'General Management in the NHS: the Initial Impact 1983–88', *Public Administration*, vol. 69, 1991, cited in G. Wistow, 'The National Health Service' in D. Marsh & R. A. W. Rhodes (eds.), *Implementing Thatcherite Policies: Audit of an Era* (Buckingham, Open Univ. Press, 1992), 106–8, 114–16.

[79] Their representatives have insisted that 'the technical competence to assess the quality of medical care belongs to doctors and that they feel very strongly that the newly organized procedures . . . should be kept within the professional body'. They have ensured that the committees actually carrying out the audits are composed exclusively of doctors, that their proceedings are confidential, that their reports are written in a form that makes it impossible to identify either patients or doctors, and they have insisted that their work is for educational rather than disciplinary purposes. For further details see Dept of Health, *The Quality of Medical Care: Report of the Standing Medical Advisory Committee for the Secretaries of State for Health and Wales* (London, HMSO, 1990), 3, 15–16; *Health Circular HC(FP)(90)8*, Dept. of Health. HC(90)15, *Health Service Developments—Working for Patients: Medical Audit in the Family Practitioner Services*; 'Doctors to monitor each other to improve standards of medical care' (*The Times*, 20 Dec. 1991). A joint steering committee is still (June 1992) deliberating on these matters.

mation, and sanctions, that sustain managerial power elsewhere. Presumably, therefore, they will adopt a more collaborative, or dare one say it, 'consensus' style of management.

The response of higher civil servants to the reforms has remained the most private of all, but they appear to have rejected the ideology behind the reforms and strongly reaffirmed their traditional values and ethics. While admitting that 'over an enormous range of things we are like the private sector', the Head of the Civil Service appointed by Mrs Thatcher herself went on to argue that 'people do expect a certain standard of equity and ethics from the Civil Service so we have certainly got things to hang on to'. In direct contradiction of Thatcherite assumptions, he defended 'a commitment and conscientiousness to the public service which will not require personal gain or personal advantage to generate high motivation or sustained performance'. Comments of this kind led Hennessy to conclude that 'the Northcote–Trevelyan settlement would endure'.[80]

The longer-term impact of executive agencies is extremely difficult to identify. Since the administrative class never displayed much interest in managing their subordinates, it may be that they will be seen less as a threat than as providing more opportunity to concentrate on their core professional task as policy advisers, more autonomy for the elite and that other professional specialists within the Service will similarly increase their autonomy.[81] Initially, the majority of new agencies were granted a rather qualified form of independence.[82] A survey in March 1991 reported a continuing 'hands on' attitude by both their 'parent' departments and the Treasury. 'Relations with parent departments' were the second most important preoccupation of chief executives, virtually all of whom reported weekly contact with departmental officials, while a quarter had weekly contact with ministers. 'Most', the authors concluded, 'do not yet fully think and operate as businesses'.[83] After Mrs Thatcher's departure, however, the policy was continued and even

[80] Hennessy, *Whitehall*, 673–5, 681–2.

[81] Jenkins observed that there was little resistance from within the Civil Service. 'Able officials wanted to exercise their managerial skills. Social security administrators, hospital managers, school inspectors, roads engineers responded with enthusiasm. They wanted performance pay and incentive bonuses . . . Reform promised more responsibility, more career flexibility and more money . . . There are few public servants who would like to go back to the habits and indisciplines of government before 1979.' He gives no evidence, however, to support these claims. S. Jenkins, *Accountable to None*, 236, 243.

[82] Civil and Public Services Association, *op. cit.*

[83] *Executive Agencies: Facts and Trends*, Survey Report, Ed. 3 (London, Price Waterhouse, Mar. 1991).

accelerated, so that by 1995 some two-thirds of civil servants were working in executive agencies. As independent agencies they are more visible and accountable than as sections within mammoth departments but whether they have created, as Rayner hoped, an entirely different Civil Service culture, still remains to be seen.

A priori, one would expect that the third, 'trade union', response would become far more appealing to all these professions and semi-professions. There is a striking resemblance between the ideology and techniques of the Thatcher reforms and 'scientific management' introduced into American industry at the turn of the century. Both elevated the managerial role. Both imposed detailed rules on hitherto discretionary tasks. Both put great faith in measures of individual productivity and payment by results.[84] F. W. Taylor, the father of scientific management, ought perhaps to be recognized as one of the intellectual antecedents of Thatcherism.[85] For generations British trade unions responded to managerial initiatives of this kind by a host of defensive measures to resist or manipulate the incentives offered by management, to defend their notions of a just rate, and to contest the legitimacy of managerial intervention in matters that concerned the performance of their own work.[86] The distinctive British pattern of labour relations was a response to this confrontation: tranquil and tolerant as long as management accepted worker prerogatives but continuous warfare when it did not.[87] Mrs Thatcher sought, of course, to change this traditional

[84] In the US, Taylorism, with the impetus of the Progressive Movement behind it, quickly spread to the public service. In the 1920s between 40% and 50% of American school districts had performance-related pay for teachers. Subsequently, these all but disappeared until the launching of the Soviet Sputnik. In 1968 some 11% of school districts had merit pay systems. By 1978 the number had again shrunk to 4% and by 1985 to under 1%. Jacobson concluded that 'there is little to encourage the belief that performance-related pay plans can effectively improve teacher performance'. S. L. Jacobson, 'Performance-related Pay for Teachers: The American Experience', in Tomlinson, *Performance-related Pay*, 41–2. The common Taylorist influence helps to explain the resemblances between Thatcherism and American Progressivism.

[85] The other major antecedent being those who had expressed their disillusionment with over-active representative bodies in civil society such as S. Beer, *Britain Against Itself: The Political Contradictions of Collectivism* (New York, Norton, 1982); M. Olson, *The Rise and Decline of Nations* (New Haven, Yale Univ. Press, 1982); C. Barnett, *The Audit of War: the Illusion and Reality of Britain as a Great Nation* (London, Macmillan, 1986).

[86] For some striking contrasts with French workers see E. H. Lorenz, 'Two Patterns of Development: The Labour process in the British and French Shipbuilding Industries 1880–1930', (1984) *Jrnl. Econ. Hist.* 599–630.

[87] The automobile industry is the best example of the latter, and oil refining of the former, for which see D. Gallie, *In Search of the New Working Class: Automation and social integration within the capitalist enterprise* (Cambridge, Cambridge Univ. Press, 1978) 120–48.

pattern but it seems likely that in the professional work settings we have considered she may well have reproduced exactly the conditions that gave rise to it in the first place, leaving the professions to fight the kind of battles for workplace autonomy that manual workers had so frequently fought in the past.

At certain times some of the professions certainly seemed to be more willing to behave like trade unions. In response to the Lord Chancellor's decisions in 1993 about legal aid payments, the Bar Council took legal proceedings against him for his refusal to bargain in good faith. During the so-called 'reign of terror' of the early Thatcher years in the Civil Service, some observers thought civil servants were retaliating by leaking confidential documents to the Press to discredit the Government and by abandoning their lifetime careers to escape to the City, industry, local government, and the universities. General practitioners evidently decided that if they were to be treated like employees, then they would behave like them. In a BMA poll in January 1992 an overwhelming majority declared their unwillingness to continue to accept 24-hour responsibility for all their patients, a commitment that goes back to the origins of the NHS.[88] As industrial sociologists have repeatedly discovered, increased managerial pressure often generates new managerial tasks—in this instance the not inconsiderable one of providing night-time and holiday cover, with a shared responsibility, for the entire population.

Nurses were always more inclined to use trade union tactics and they used them to the full, via an appeal procedure, to resist the new grading. By February 1990 well over 137,623 nurses, which is over a quarter of the nursing workforce, had lodged appeals against their grade, more than a quarter of which were still outstanding and just under 20 per cent of which had been successful.[89] Eventually, this strategy will be exhausted but some nurses also indicated that they, like the doctors, will respond in kind and henceforth 'work to grade' that is, work exactly according to what the grade criteria specify and therefore refuse to cover, as they did in the past, for nurses in another grade.[90]

[88] *Independent*, 3 Jan. & 24 June 1992.
[89] H. Gaze, 'Fair Deal on Appeal: The Forgotten Fifty Thousand', *Nursing Times*, 7 Feb. 1990, 28–31. By June 1992, the figure had been reduced to 30,000 though at the present rate of handling them, they will not be finally settled until after the year 2000. Pers. comm., J. Fleming, Royal College of Nursing.
[90] A strategy supported by the two unions but opposed by the two colleges; T. Rice, 'Torn between Grades', *Nursing Standard*, 12 Nov. 1988, 18–19.

The educational professions also had more experience of trade union methods and they initially responded to the reforms with various kinds of resistance and sabotage commonly associated with industrial trade unions. Officers of a number of local education authorities, for instance, tried to undermine open enrolment by setting very low enrolment limits for their schools to leave themselves free to allocate the vast majority of students in the normal way. The Government closed this loophole by requiring that these limits be no lower than those set in 1979.[91] In a few cases, education officers and teachers raided schools that had opted out to recover property they deemed belonged to the Local Education Authority and the local community. To arbitrate such disputes and prevent 'asset-stripping', the Government established an Education Assets Board.[92] Similarly, in 1991 the universities responded to the attempt to establish a quasi-market for higher education by all bidding at or near the UFC's 'guide price', and the scheme was abandoned shortly thereafter.

Overall, the effect of the reforms may be to blur still further the divide between professional and trade union tactics. Just as the older professions seem rather more willing to use trade union tactics, trade unions with professional members seem more inclined to look for public support and respect. The campaign conducted by the three largest teachers' trade unions in the spring of 1993, against the national testing of schoolchildren, illustrates the adroit use of professional strategies. These tests, as noted earlier, were linked to the national curriculum and supposed to provide a means of evaluating the performance of both schools and their teachers. The teachers boycotted them but avoided any action which would have interfered with children's education. By so doing, they retained the support of both the parents and public, and completely outmanoeuvred and discredited the Secretary of State for Education, John Patten, who had committed himself to the immediate implementation of these tests. In the end, it was the teachers who emerged as having the best interests of schoolchildren at heart, and the Minister and his civil servants who were thought to be politically-motivated and alienated from the supposed beneficiaries of the reforms—the parents. The campaign led to the hasty appointment of a committee which drastically amended both the national curriculum and the testing procedures but this was not enough to save the reputation and career of Patten who was later dismissed.

[91] Simon, *Bending the Rules*, 59–60.   [92] See *The Times*, 26 Jan. 1990.

One may finally observe that despite the continuous legislative and ideological assault, there is not the least indication that professional institutions lost their appeal during the Thatcher years. The professional associations of both nurses and teachers reported substantial gains in membership during her period of office.[93] The charter granted to the British Computer Society in 1987 is one indication that horizontal, occupational loyalties, independent of the employment relationship, and often designed to obtain some autonomy from it, retain their appeal in Britain, even in industries which supposedly epitomize new trends of global capitalism. More curious still, the main beneficiaries of the reforms, those who were to inherit the powers previously shared amongst members of the professions, the managers, were themselves invited in 1988 to support a so-called Charter Management Initiative. This was conceived as the 'first step towards giving all managers the opportunity to achieve professional status' by enabling them to obtain part-time, practice-based, cumulative, nationally recognized, and transferable qualifications. It was also supposed to develop a code of management practice and in due course to lead to the creation of a Chartered Institute of Management.[94] This initiative owed more to the state and to large corporations than to grassroots support from individual managers so it has whiffs of the Thatcherite 'licensed' specialist rather than of a profession of management in the traditional accepted English or British sense. None the less, it demonstrates the deeply-embedded legitimacy of professional forms of organization and government and an unconscious acknowledgement of the continuing strength of the professional aspirations in Britain. Even as the Green Papers debunking the ethics and concerns of the legal profession were being written, the Department of Trade and Industry was encouraging managers to organize themselves in the same form for the same ends.

[93] In 1971 the Professional Association of Teachers formed in reaction to the union-led teacher militancy of 1969–70 had 2,000 members. It aimed to organize the teachers in the manner of the medical profession with a General Teachers' Council, like the General Medical Council, to enforce a professional code of ethics. By July 1988 it claimed 43,000 members.

[94] See *The Times*, 20 Sept. 1989.

5 Lawyers and Political Liberalism in Eighteenth- and Nineteenth-Century England

W. Wesley Pue (University of British Columbia)

> It is a most important subject for the consideration of this House, whether any body of men, in their own private chamber, should have the power of determining whether any person shall be excluded for life from the practice of the higher branch of the Law.—A. Baring, Address to the United Kingdom House of Commons.[1]
>
> The bar is public property.—D. W. Harvey.[2]

English Barristers—Pillars of Stability?

Daniel Duman concluded his intriguing study of the English and Colonial Bars in the nineteenth century with the observation that despite rapid increases in admissions to the four Inns of Court between 1835 and 1885 'severe overcrowding at the English bar' was avoided by the fortuitous 'emergence of new employment opportunities in the public service and in the law itself'. Opportunities relating to 'directing the economy and society', legal advice, colonial service, and business helped to stave off the 'threat of unemployment'. According to Duman this, in turn, had a significant political consequence in that the rosy career prospects for lawyers helped to produce relative political stability in nineteenth-century England.

I am grateful for the intellectual leadership, challenge, and generous collegiality provided by Terry Halliday and Lucien Karpik. The research from which this paper is derived has been assisted by research grants from the Social Sciences and Humanities Research Council of Canada. Barry Wright's encouragement and advice with respect to this project and Wilfrid Prest's generosity in sharing his work-in-progress on eighteenth-century English barristers (now published as 'Law, lawyers and rational dissent', in K. Haakonssen (ed.), *Enlightenment and Religion: Rational Dissent in Eighteenth-century Britain* (Cambridge, Cambridge Univ. Press, 1996), 169–92) is much appreciated.

[1] As quoted in D. W. Harvey, *A Letter to Lord John Russell, M.P. on the Benchers and the Bar* (London, Butterworth, 1852), frontispiece.

[2] D. W. Harvey, as quoted by C. Fell Smith, 'Daniel Whittle Harvey, 1786–1863', 24 (1915), *Essex Review* 24–30, 63–70, 132–8 at 29.

These employment opportunities prevented the emergence of a militant and powerful group of briefless barristers who could have posed a major problem for Britain and may even have become a focus for social and political discontent, as had other lawyers in the not-so-distant past. In fact their role was just the opposite; the barristers were pillars of nineteenth-century stability.[3]

Lest anyone miss its unmistakable intent, the reference to 'other lawyers in the not-so-distant past' is clarified in a footnote: the 'English Civil War and the American and French Revolutions'[4] show the sorts of problems likely to flow from leaving too many lawyers underemployed for too long.[5]

Duman's observations reflect two important, common, assumptions about England, Englishness, and English lawyers: first, there is a commonly-held belief that English barristers have been a politically quiescent lot since the troubled days of the English Civil War, the interregnum and the Glorious Revolution. Second, a powerful assumption persists that this in turn has contributed immensely to English political stability, incrementalism, and to progressive political, economic, and social development all uninterrupted by demagoguery, revolt, beheadings, or the disruptive actions of unruly mobs. Duman's passing reference to France is no gratuitous slight: that nation stands in English 'common sense' as a dreadful warning of all that can go wrong, a sort of conceptual opposite to England's altogether more sensible ways.

Similar assumptions about the political conservatism of English barristers have been expressed by others. Historians and historical figures alike have not infrequently accused the English legal profession of being singularly uninvolved in the great liberating causes of the past two centuries. Caroline Robbins, for example, described lawyers of George II's reign as 'protectors of tradition' who 'contributed little to the development of liberalism in any way'.[6] William Cobbett thought the lawyers

---

[3] D. Duman, *The English and Colonial Bars in the Nineteenth Century* (London, Croom Helm, 1983), 206–7.   [4] Ibid., 209, n. 29.

[5] According to D. A. Bell, *Lawyers and Citizens: The Making of a Political Elite in Old Regime France* (New York, Oxford Univ. Press, 1994), 62. French *avocats* in the 18th cent., by contrast, 'could no longer expect many tangible rewards for their services to this monarchy. The idea of the bar as *pépinière des dignités*, leading to high office, had lost all relevance by the end of the seventeenth century. Nor did barristers still serve as the most visible advisers to the great noble households.'

[6] C. Robbins, *Eighteenth-Century Commonwealth*, 294–5. See also P. Lucas, 'Collective Biography of Students and Barristers of Lincoln's Inn, 1680–1804: A Study in the "Aristocratic Resurgence" of the Eighteenth Century', *Jrnl. Mod. Hist.* 46 (1974), 242. I am grateful to Wilfrid Prest for bringing these sources to my attention.

of his time to be a reactionary force of 'ruffians . . . whose *business* it is to do injustice'! He told Daniel Whittle Harvey in 1834 that the Benchers of the English Inns of Court were simply 'corruption No. 2, doing the work of No. 1'.[7] An early nineteenth-century radical squib lumped 'THE LAWYERS' in with other enemies of the people including THE DANDY (George IV), THE IRISH RAT CATCHER (Castlereagh), THE DOCTOR (Sidmouth), and THE PERJURERS.[8] The identification of English lawyers with the forces of conservatism is pervasive.

Advocates and Liberalism—the European Standard

Questions relating to the role of English lawyers in the development of the liberal state have recently been given heightened importance by a blossoming of research relating to the history of lawyers and politics on the European continent and in the USA. This work has raised fundamental questions regarding the role advocates have played in the construction of a liberal polity in a number of countries.[9] Halliday and Karpik's introductory chapter to this volume draws together the theoretical implications of such research by sketching out the general dimensions of the relationship between lawyers and liberalism. Though they concede the necessary imprecision of any notion of political liberalism covering 'several countries and several historical periods', and reflecting 'a complex phenomenon with numerous streams and transformations', they none the less posit a necessary relationship between advocacy and the creation of 'the liberal polity, which includes citizenship and the moderate state, and liberal political society, which includes civil society and the existence of independent publics'.[10] Professional advocates, they say, have played a central—perhaps even indispensable—role in relation to three essential components of political liberalism:

(1) judicial constraint on executive or sovereign power,[11]

---

[7] As quoted in Harvey, *Letter to Lord John Russell*, at 7–8, note.

[8] J. A. Hone, *For the Cause of Truth: Radicalism in London, 1796–1821* (Oxford, Clarendon Press, 1982), 346.

[9] T. C. Halliday & L. Karpik, 'Politics Matter', chap. 1 *supra*; L. Karpik, 'French Lawyers and Politics'; L. Karpik, 'Lawyers and Politics in France, 1814–1950: The State, the Market, and the Public', *Law and Social Inquiry* 13: 4 (1988) 707–36; L. Karpik, *Les avocats: Entre l'État, le public et le marché, XIIIᵉ–XXᵉ siècle* (Paris, Gallimard, 1995); (trans.), (Oxford, Oxford Univ. Press, forthcoming); Bell, *Lawyers and Citizens*; D. A. Bell, chap. 2 *supra*.

[10] Halliday & Karpik, chap. 1 *supra*.

[11] Including, presumably, the sovereign people as represented in democratically constituted legislatures.

(2) the creation of 'publics', and
(3) the enhancement of individual rights.

Conceptually lawyers' activities within these areas relate respectively to the constitution of the moderate state, civil society, and citizenship.[12] The creation of 'publics' apart, each is familiar to common lawyers and students of British constitutionalism in the United Kingdom, Canada, the USA, and other former British colonies. Sophisticated scholarly research confirms, in effect, what less thoughtful professional apologists have asserted with monotonous regularity: lawyers emerge, apparently, as heroes in historical struggles for freedom, liberty and democracy.[13]

This paper demonstrates that eighteenth- and nineteenth-century English advocates, like their counterparts in other countries, were drawn with some frequency to political action. My range of reference is deliberately limited to barristers and to that portion of the attorneys' profession which specialized in advocacy. Notaries, solicitors, attorneys, and others whose work-a-day world involved large doses of bureaucratic work should not be confused with advocates. These latter are and have been culturally, socially, legally and politically quite different sorts of professionals. A further limitation should be noted. Although Paris *avocats* and English barristers (and, later, solicitors who specialized in litigation) engaged in analagous work, the *professional* context within which they operated was markedly different. It is arguable that this resulted in the activities of English barristers showing less dramatic results than their cross-Channel peers.

Historical Trajectories of Lawyers' Liberalism in France

Questions relating to the role of advocates in the creation of a liberal society raise questions which cannot be resolved at the level of theory. The thoroughly historical issues raised for consideration within this problematic can only be addressed in particular contexts and in light of careful consideration of the best available historical evidence. The essays in this collection from Europe and the United States of America provide powerful historical evidence that some strong, apparently causal, relationship has existed in some countries at some times. The French case is particularly intriguing. Well researched, it presents the

[12] Halliday & Karpik, chap. 1 *supra*.
[13] I have reviewed a substantial body of professional apologetics in W. W. Pue, 'In Pursuit of Better Myth: Lawyers' Histories and Histories of Lawyers', *Alberta Law Rev.* 33: 4 (1955), 730–67.

paradigm case of advocates working to create a liberal society. It is also of special interest precisely because of striking similarities—and at least one notable difference—between the conduct of Paris *avocats* and English barristers in a similar time period.

Paris *avocats* were actively engaged in most of France's great political battles throughout the eighteenth and nineteenth centuries, advancing the cause of political liberalism with remarkable consistency.[14] Despite immense transformations of French politics and society during the period, important features of the work of *avocats* seem to hold relatively constant. To put it crudely, lawyers intervened on the side of political liberalism in two modes. First, they sometimes challenged the state and ecclesiastical authority directly, unambiguously, and collectively. Second, *avocats* individually seized upon lawsuits to promote particular political causes and, *by the very process of representation*, advanced liberal notions of legality and citizens' rights.

The collective actions of Paris *avocats* in this period are noteworthy for they were both able and willing to stand together in defence of political rights. The Paris *Ordre des avocats* (significantly, neither conceived of as, nor styled, a corporate body)[15] engaged in extraordinary collective action on a number of occasions. This included a dramatic August 1731 work stoppage in opposition to the Crown, which emerged from the political and religious difficulties surrounding Jansenism.[16] On that occasion, *avocats* paralysed the courts, inconvenienced litigants,[17] and caused 'grave material and symbolic difficulties for a state, the primary function of which, from time immemorial, had been to administer justice'.[18] The success of this action simultaneously carved out a new role for the *Ordre des avocats* and chipped away at both royal and ecclesiastical power. Though work stoppages by and large gave way to other types of collective action in the 1730s, the strike remained a powerful reserve weapon which could, and did, reappear as occasion demanded. A failed strike a few years later gave the *Ordre des avocats* reason to pause but did not bring an end to their

efforts on behalf of Jansenist-*parlementaire* constitutionalism . . . the Order remained an *organisation de combat*. It simply functioned, so to speak, in a different key. It no longer expressed itself through collective action, but it still remained a tightly run, well-protected refuge from which [*avocats*] . . . could

---

[14] Bell, *Lawyers and Citizens*; Karpik, *Les avocats*; Bell, chap. 2 *supra*; Karpik, 'Lawyers and Politics'; Karpik, chap. 3 *supra*.

[15] Bell, *Lawyers and Citizens*, 51–2.

[16] Ibid., 98 ff.; Karpik, chap. 3 *supra*.

[17] Bell, *Lawyers and Citizens*, 98.

[18] Karpik, chap. 3 *supra*.

produce pamphlets and *mémoires*, and formulate *parlementaire* strategy with impunity.[19]

Collective action by *avocats*, most dramatically made manifest in strikes against state or church authority, is certainly remarkable and without parallel in eighteenth- or nineteenth-century England. Equally important to the great political causes of the eighteenth and nineteenth centuries in France, however, was the accretion of a series of more modest actions by individual *avocats* in defence of individual clients. Paris *avocats* more or less routinely used their privileged location in the realms of public discourse to develop and promote political arguments. They developed a 'no-holds-barred' strategy which employed courtroom rhetoric and forensic skill only as one component amongst many in a multi-faceted political strategy. *Avocats* transformed themselves, as necessity required, into constitutionalists, public speakers, authors of widely-read political pamphlets, public figures, and demagogues. They 'seized upon law suits, threats or decisions which they felt to be arbitrary',[20] using the issues in litigation as raw material from which to develop multi-dimensioned juridical political argumentation. Moreover, they used the courtroom politically: it provided a crucial, rare, forum of uncensored free expression from which *avocats* could speak to a larger public, disseminating their political views far beyond the parties involved in litigation. Knowing this, they spoke through and beyond the causes in which they acted. As representatives for litigants they engaged in a form of 'political pedagogy',[21] which effectively turned 'the public into a supreme court and thereby rival of the magistrates'.[22] Individual accused were made to transcend localized reality as their cases entered the courtroom. Through the agency of lawyers they were transmuted into 'the site where superior forces came to terms: religion versus tolerance, order versus liberty, monarchy versus the republic'.[23] Trials became 'momentous' events: 'avid crowds packed the courtroom, judicial chronicles sold out, pleadings were printed and sold: public passions crystallized around legal questions'.[24] From the Restoration to the middle of the July Monarchy, 'there was a succession of . . . "great trials"' which

were often events of considerable importance. Among the thronging crowds, political and social celebrities mixed with youths and courthouse personalities. The public took sides, passions flared. And the audience was infinitely larger

---

[19] Bell, *Lawyers and Citizens*, 112.　　[20] Karpik, chap. 3 *supra*.　　[21] Ibid.
[22] Ibid.　　[23] Karpik, 'Lawyers and Politics' at 724.
[24] Karpik, chap. 3 *supra*.

than the crowd in the courtroom; readers of the legal columns of newspapers, with their reports, commentaries, and portraits, passed on the accounts, some of which were to give rise to long-lived legends. A public passion had crystallized around judicial matters.[25]

In Old Regime France *avocats* enjoyed a unique privilege in that their legal briefs could be published uncensored. As a result, 'these documents—in theory, internal court memoranda—became an important means of appealing to, and speaking for, the new and nebulous creature called the "public".'[26] According to David Bell, 'the written arguments, or legal briefs (called either *mémoires judiciaires* or *factums* in French)' were important public documents for the barrister did not simply submit them to the judges, but often had them printed and distributed to the public, sometimes along with auxiliary briefs called *consultations*, co-signed by a number of colleagues. Briefs could run from as little as three printed pages to as many as five hundred, and complicated cases produced scores of them, drafted by teams of barristers. Even the most inconsequential trial might easily generate three or four. In the course of the eighteenth century, barristers produced at least a hundred thousand, making legal briefs one of the most common forms of printed matter in early modern France. Jurists justified the practice by arguing that publicizing the facts of cases protected their clients from courtroom intrigue. In fact, however, the briefs had other uses as well. Because of their technical status as internal court documents, and the need to print them rapidly, royal legislation exempted them from preliminary censorship as long as they bore a barrister's signature. They were practically the only document published under the Old Regime that did not require preliminary censorship to circulate legally. They thus often served political as well as strictly legal purposes.[27] During the eighteenth century the *avocats*' brief developed into 'a legal form of opposition journalism, and one of the most effective examples of it yet seen in France'.[28]

Several key elements of liberalism were reproduced as a product of the cumulative effect of representation in individual cases: regardless of the significant political differences which separated them, monarchist, republican, and liberal *avocats* alike advanced notions concerning the rule of law and the protection of certain core liberties. By publishing *mémoires judiciaires* and *consultations* to a wide readership they invoked a rational discourse of public life, and implicitly asserted the sovereignty

---

[25] Karpik, 'Lawyers and Politics' at 715. [26] Bell, *Lawyers and Citizens*, 15.
[27] Ibid., 31. [28] Ibid., 199.

of nation, not monarch. Notions of civil and political citizenship advanced by *avocats* in their professional work involved civil equality, property, personal security, freedom of assembly, the Press, and expression. In the years following the Revolution, *avocats* recurrently invoked the constitution in legal discourse.[29] On either side of the Revolution they appealed to and purported to speak for the 'public'—an entity which they simultaneously derived their strength from, empowered, *and* constituted.[30]

All things considered, Paris *avocats* appear to have been actively engaged, important, and dramatic political actors over two centuries of tremendous change in French social, economic, and political life. Indeed, liberal politics has historically been so central to the profession as to lead Karpik to the conclusion that '[lawyers'] relationship with the political sphere had become *the dominant organizing principle of the profession*'.[31]

The Political Agency of English Barristers

Looking across the Channel, English barristers of the eighteenth and nineteenth centuries seem, at first blush, a rather tame lot in comparison—merely a professional body concerned with bricks and mortar, wine cellars, dining, status, and jurisdiction, rather than with the pursuit of any coherent or even mildly significant political objectives.[32]

Neither the political quiessence of barristers nor the political stability of England in the period should be overstated, however. The relative paucity of research into the history of the English Bar in this period renders any comparison with the political activities of French *avocats* necessarily tentative. It is clear none the less that on a number of occa-

---

[29] Karpik, chap 3. *supra.*

[30] 'Central to lawyers' action was the public as an imaginary social construction, lawyers vested with the political legitimacy of the "sovereign authority". Symbolically constituted, this invisible entity was crafted by self-proclaimed prophets—like the lawyers—who seized upon a powerful counter-weight to the massive force of the Crown and state. This symbolic public became the new source of legitimation, the new last court of appeal . . . a carefully elaborated strategy largely built around a disinterestedness that demonstrated again and again the Bar's dedication to the public.' (Halliday & Karpik, chap. 1 *supra*). See also Karpik, chap. 3 *supra* (identifying the public as mandator of lawyers and noting that the 'public' was constituted by lawyers in the act of representing).

[31] Karpik, chap. 3 *supra.*

[32] M. Burrage, 'Revolution as a Starting Point for the Comparative Analysis of the French, American and English Legal Professions' in R. L. Abel & P. S. C. Lewis (eds.), *Lawyers in Society*, vol. 3, *Comparative Theories* (Berkeley, Univ. of California Press, 1989), 322–74 esp. at 356–60.

sions throughout the eighteenth and nineteenth centuries English advocates (usually barristers but, also, albeit less visibly, attorneys or solicitors) stepped on to the political stage in ways closely analagous to *avocats*
on the other side of the Channel. At least some English lawyers were
willing to use the courtroom, the printing press, the public meeting, and
even the 'mob' politically as occasion demanded. Often the political
visions they articulated were, broadly-speaking, 'liberal'. From the
sophisticated and multi-faceted politico-legal strategies of the Wilkites,
through late-eighteenth-century moves toward the creation of a 'liberal'
(or at least a rationalist) mode of criminal trial, the various legal strategies invoked in response to the repressions of the 1790s, the defence of
Queen Caroline's divorce, the working class advocacy of
W. P. Roberts (a solicitor), and mid- to late nineteenth-century efforts
by a number of barristers to expand 'citizenship' in new directions,
English advocates, like their French counterparts, used lawsuits instrumentally in order to make much larger political points.

The especial skill of the barrister was in rhetoric and persuasion:
courtroom argument frequently traversed boundaries which have subsequently been erected between legal and political spheres. Barristers
employed their rhetorical powers in a highly public forum. Their words
and actions were widely commented on, discussed, *and* reported (often
nearly verbatim) in the Press. Further, they not uncommonly published
pamphlets or books arising from their cases, addressed public meetings,
or otherwise sought to speak to (and constitute) a public considerably
larger than that actually present in the courtroom. Moreover, the Bar
(particularly, *perhaps*, the Criminal Defence Bar) provided a route to
fame or notoriety which could create a public profile sufficient to obtain
election to local or national political office. Barristers, of necessity, travelled with England's itinerant assize courts, thereby becoming highly
visible actors in the work of a centrally important seventeenth-century
political institution.

[W]hen the judges arrived on circuit in a county town, it was never purely a
judicial affair: whether or nor politics actually entered into the litigation . . . the
assize had its political dimension, for it was one of the ways in which government conveyed its views, through the mouths of the judges, to the locality; and
conversely, it was an established means of expressing local political views which
were meant to be heard by those at Westminster.[33]

[33] J. Brewer, 'The Wilkites and the law, 1763–74: a study in radical notions of governance' in J. Brewer & J. Styles (eds.), *An Ungovernable People: the English and their law in the
seventeenth and eighteenth centuries* (London, Hutchinson, 1980) 127–81, at 135.

The court circuits established networks connecting London and local elites, served as a propaganda machine and polling service for the central government, and provided means whereby radical or dissident barristers could maintain contacts with provincial allies. 'This travelling train of justice', according to John Brewer, 'linked the centre with the localities, enabling not only loyal servants of the Crown, but also radical dissidents, to publicize their views in the provinces.'[34]

The social and political significance of courts has been widely noted by historians of eighteenth- and nineteenth-century England. The criminal trial of late eighteenth-century London, for example, has been described thus:

The inherent drama of the courtroom when the confrontation between two versions of the truth took the form not of a squabble but of a game, a contest with rules, played by clever, skillful, and equally matched opponents, and a game that came quickly to a conclusion. The theatrical character of the trial was heightened in England by the provision of galleries for spectators in courtrooms open to the public . . . A further dimension was added as the trial became more structured as a conflict between prosecuting and defense lawyers and as its adversarial capacities were developed, to the extent that the rules governing defense counsel allowed that to happen. For the trial came to have some of the characteristics of a sport, a contest with a winner and a loser—and, to heighten the drama, a loser whose client might be executed in another public arena. Theatre and sport made a perfect combination for a society in which spectator sports such as horse-racing and prize-fighting were developing rapidly and becoming commercialized. The gladiators in this judicial combat became known in part for their entertainment value.[35]

Lawyers' work was thus *political* in the simple dictionary sense of obviously and unequivocally 'belonging, or pertaining to . . . the body of citizens' (Oxford English Dictionary).

If this was so of the central courts in London, it was arguably even more the case in the provinces. Quarter sessions and assize courts provided intermittent spectacles unmatched in pagentry, ceremony, display, and drama. Doug Hay has provided a compelling portrait of the drama of the courtroom in rural England in his justly celebrated article on property, authority, and the criminal law in eighteenth-century England:

---

[34] Brewer, 'Wilkites' at 135.

[35] J. Beattie, 'Scales of Justice: defence counsel and the English criminal trial in the eighteenth and nineteenth centuries', *Law & Hist. Rev.* 9 (1991), 221–67, at 247–8.

The antics surrounding the twice-yearly visits of the high-court judges had considerable psychic force. They were accorded far greater importance by contemporaries than by most historians, who have been concerned more with county government, particularly at Quarter Sessions, than with the majesty of the law. The assizes were a formidable spectacle in a country town, the most visible and elaborate manifestation of state power to be seen in the countryside, apart from the presence of a regiment. The town was crowded, not only with barristers and jurors, but with the cream of county society, attending the assize ball and county meetings, which were often held in the same week. Tradesmen and labourers journeyed in to enjoy the spectacle, meet friends, attend the court and watch the executions. And the court arrived in town with traditional, and calculated panoply . . . Within this elaborate ritual of the irrational, judge and counsel displayed their learning with an eloquence that often rivalled that of leading statesmen. There was an acute consciousness that the courts were platforms for addressing 'the multitude'.[36]

In so doing lawyers invoked the power of a public they themselves helped to constitute and re-constitute as occasion demanded. The *power* of courtroom discourses was not lost to contemporaries.

It was a power to communicate freely though free communication might otherwise meet with criminal sanction; the power to speak what dare not be spoken, to challenge those one dared not challenge. It provided opportunities to attempt social engineering through manipulation of the languages of law and provided a public platform unequalled by any other. The courtroom might either be used defensively to foist off the aggressions of the state or proactively employed to advance social visions thought undesirable by rulers and class elites. In any number of ways courtroom advocacy provided unique opportunities to advance one's own cause while embarrassing a rival. It simultaneously provided opportunity for crucial defences of dissident politics, assertion of individual right, articulation of radically democratic political visions, and moments of significant class formation. Balanced on a knife-edge between social control and 'rule of law', the courtroom might at any moment be transformed into a significant arena for counter-hegemonic struggle.[37] Moreover, it also provided a unique opportunity for the

[36] D. Hay, 'Property, Authority and the Criminal Law', in D. Hay, P. Linebaugh, & E. P. Thompson (eds.), *Albion's Fatal Tree: Crime and Society in Eighteenth Century England* (London, Allen Lane, 1975) 17–63, at 27–8.

[37] See R. Challinor, *A Radical Lawyer in Victorian England: W. P. Roberts and the Struggle for Workers' Rights* (London, I. B Tauris & Co. Ltd., 1990). It is the recognition of this which leads E. P. Thompson to describe the 'rule of law' as an 'unqualified human good' in his book *Whigs and Hunters* (London, Allen Lane, 1975). See also E. P. Thompson, 'Custom, Law and Common Right', in E. P. Thompson, *Customs in Common: Studies*

promotion of one's own career whether in electoral or patronage politics: the courtroom became a breeding ground for what was pejoratively named demagoguery.

Not surprisingly English lawyers throughout the eighteenth and nineteenth centuries both sought out a political voice on their own initiative and were enlisted by others in aid of their political causes.

The Wilkites

The followers of John Wilkes (hence 'Wilkites') were one particular group of bourgeois radicals, who consistently and effectively employed legal tactics as an indispensable part of their political strategy. The Wilkite 'Society of the Supporters of the Bill of Rights' was dominated by lawyers, who made up fully 10 per cent of its membership (the largest single group) and exerted disproportionate influence. The Wilkites 'used the law itself as a political weapon, exploiting the highly ritualized theatre of the courts and the labyrinthine complexity of the criminal law to propagandize their cause, defend themselves and wreak vengeance on their enemies.'[38] There is scarcely any imaginable legal/political strategy they did not employ. They exploited legal loopholes instrumentally and also used the opportunities law provided to promulgate their ideology, speaking through the courtroom to a wider public about grand political issues. Their activities were widely reported in the radical press as they took legal action against state officials or sought to 'shame those in authority into reformation' by publicity of 'abuses' as occasion demanded. Often they initiated litigation with respect to situations arising from their own difficulties—as when two of Wilke's supporters were killed in 1768 by Government-hired thugs. On other occasions, however, they worked with ordinary victims of mundane elite manipulation to turn private grievance into *cause célèbre*.[39] Always, they presented their causes not as 'matters of personal recrimination or vengeance, but [as] *class* actions which affected the rights and liberties of all subjects.'[40] They engaged in extensive pamphleteering

in *Traditional Popular Culture* (New York, New York Press, 1993), 97–184, esp. at 111 ff., discussing John Lewis and the legal defence of customary rights in Richmond Park in the 1750s.

[38] Brewer, 'Wilkites' at 131. Brewer identifies a number of important lawyer-activists (a category encompassing barristers, solicitors, and attorneys): John Glynn, John Reynolds, William Ellis, George Bellas, Robert Morris, Arthur Lee, Watkin Lewes, Charles Martin, Sayer, and Dayrell.

[39] Ibid. at 131–2, 135–6, 142, 148–50, 158.   [40] Ibid., 155, 163–4.

about the rule of law[41] and were not above using collusive actions in order to establish friendly legal–political precedent.[42] All of this took place in the context of more orthodox parliamentary and extra-parliamentary political activity.

Though not shy about using law instrumentally to achieve particular, limited ends, the legal vision of the Wilkites was fully part and parcel of their political positions. For eighteenth-century Englishmen law and politics collapsed 'in one on another'.[43] John Brewer explains that 'political ideology and the law as ideology were intertwined', with the result that 'legal bodies and processes (many of which had an overt political function anyway) were frequently the foci of political expression and political conflict'.[44] Liberty, the foremost political value of eighteenth-century England, was thought to be the product of law. Consequently, the making, administration, and execution of law constituted the very pith and substance of politics.[45] Wilkite views on these matters were, for our purposes, 'liberal'. Their political programme and hence their legal strategies sought to ensure the public accountability of officials, effect equality before the law for all subjects regardless of rank, wealth or personal association, advance legal due process, and minimize or eliminate official discretion. Generally, they hoped to create a state in which orderly government could be maintained by means of 'the use of the civil power on behalf of the public rather than the deployment of military power on behalf of the Crown'.[46] Government, in other words, was ultimately to rest upon the willing consent of the people, not upon the rule of force.[47]

The Transformation of Criminal Defence

There is no more important intersection of law and politics than the state trial and its next-of-kin, the criminal prosecution. Not surprisingly then, the particular legal matters of concern to Wilkites often concerned

---

[41] Ibid., 156–7.

[42] Ibid., 140 documents the case of Wheble, a printer summonsed before the House of Commons for printing its debates. Wheble was apprehended by his own servant and brought before John Wilkes who, in his capacity as City alderman and magistrate for London, promptly released him on the 'grounds that he was a London freeman, that Carpenter was not a City peace officer, and that the cause of arrest was neither a felony nor a breach of the peace. Wheble promptly counter-suited Carpenter and charged him with assault.'

[43] Ibid., 132. [44] Ibid., 133. [45] Ibid., 132. [46] Ibid., 136.

[47] Ibid., 165.

political offences or criminal prosecution. They attacked the legality of general warrants (which named no individual but authorized officals to seize *anyone's* papers and personal effects), more or less routinely prosecuted state officials for illegal conduct, defended 'seditious libel' prosecutions, opposed the 'corrupt' use of the Royal prerogative of mercy, objected to the imposition of court fees (which restricted access), insisted on strict compliance with procedural rules, strongly asserted the rights of the jury (including jury 'nullification' of odious laws), insisted on public and open legal processes, and opposed summary procedures of all sorts.[48]

The Wilkite case provides powerful illustration of several important points. First, their many efforts illustrate that the administration of justice was centrally important in modern English politics. Eighteenth-century reformers believed that the legal system and the state at large had been captured by 'oligarchy and corruption', to the detriment of 'free-born Englishmen'.[49] Legal processes were important in struggles of liberty, partly because the law was frequently used by 'Corruption' as an instrument of oppression but also, more proactively, because rights could be asserted, defended, and won in the legal arena. More importantly still, 'law' played a massive part in the discursive world of the English and was a central ingredient of true Englishness. Trials provided a highly public display of the status of English subjects *and* provided the raw material from which the languages of liberty were fashioned, adapted, moulded. The 'Englishman's' status as either a denuded subject, the victim of 'privilege', or, alternatively, as free citizen fully clothed in meaningful individual rights, was cast in stark relief in the courtroom. Immediate, often dire, consequences for the individuals concerned, captured and amplified much of importance in the invisible world of ideas, imagery, symbols, and myth which constitute the lived experience of citizenship.

Any trial seemingly contained within it the seeds from which a highly charged melodrama focused on hidden influence, the prerogatives of status or wealth, abuses of judicial discretion, corrupt process, or unfair substantive law might, unpredictably, emerge. Such matters lie especially near the surface in criminal prosecutions and throughout the eighteenth and nineteenth centuries lawyers' opinions regarding the appropriate conduct of criminal trials was strongly coloured by political conviction. Stephan Landsman asserts that English adversarial process originated in the eighteenth century:

[48] Brewer, 'Wilkites' at 165.   [49] Ibid., 145.

Criminal trials in Tudor and Stuart England were, according to J. S. Cockburn, 'nasty, brutish, and essentially short.' Counsel seldom participated, few, if any, rules of evidence constrained enquiry, judges routinely examined witnesses and defendants in the most vigorous, and at times ruthless, manner, only prosecution witnesses were allowed to swear testimonial oaths and thereby enhance the credibility of their statements, jurors were free to utilize private knowledge gained outside the confines of the courtroom, judges frequently introduced their political views into proceedings, and there was virtually no appellate procedure . . .

By the early nineteenth-century, the traditional, non-contentious approach to adjudication had been supplanted in English felony trials by a system with the rudiments of an adversarial process. Party direction and control had replaced judicial enquiry, counsel's role had expanded dramatically, and sophisticated rules to regulate courtroom conduct had been developed.[50]

So dramatic a transformation over the course of a century is remarkable. It exaggerates only slightly to suggest that the common law's much vaunted adversarial system was created in this period. The forces which produced this transformation played themselves out in reaction to diverse issues and in varied ways. The adversarial system emerged in England as advocates developed concrete responses to the exercise of state power. Their responses, conditioned by a discursive universe which included a mythologized historiography of English freedoms,[51] were broadly 'liberal' or proto-liberal in character. Several central elements of liberalism coalesced dramatically in many loosely-scripted courtroom plays: a suspicion of state power, hostility to class prerogative, faith in rationality (especially in this period as regards the processes of 'proof'), and an overall inflation in the value attached to the individual.

---

[50] S. Landsman, 'The Rise of the Contentious Spirit: Adversary Procedure in Eighteenth Century England', *Cornell Law Rev.* 75 (1992), 479–609, at 498–9 & 501–2. The quotation about Tudor and Stuart trials is from J. S. Cockburn, *A History of the English Assizes 1558–1714* (Cambridge, Cambridge Univ. Press, 1972) at 109, who indicates that trials of that period almost never took longer than twenty minutes.

[51] J. Beattie, *Crime and the Courts in England, 1660–1800* (Oxford, Clarendon Press, 1986), at 314, has put it thus '*That Englishmen enjoyed* fundamental liberties beyond the reach of government was a commonplace in the eighteenth century. It was a notion shared across society and across the political spectrum, celebrated by Whigs and Tories, by Hanoverian oligarchs and their country and radical opponents. There might be disagreements about whether those rights were being threatened and by whom, but no one questioned that Englishmen had inherited liberties won by their forefathers in the struggle against despotic governments.' (Emphasis in original.)

Landsman has argued that '[t]he rise of contentious procedure undoubtedly was associated with the historical and intellectual changes that swept English society in the seventeenth and eighteenth centuries'[52] and it is well to bear in mind that the causal relations between law, society, ideas, and economy were multiple and complex. The right to counsel, for example, though central to late twentieth-century liberal legal faith and professional myth alike, did not exist in early English criminal procedure. The enormous constitutional disruptions of the seventeenth century produced, in the Treason Act of 1696, however, an explicit parliamentary acknowledgement of 'the value of counsel to those faced with serious charges and carefully orchestrated prosecutions. It was only natural in light of that legislation for the courts to allow defendants not only to press their cases with increased vigor, but to employ counsel to do it for them.'[53] While the importance of this intellectual shift cannot be gauged with precision, it should not be underestimated. Any argument which might justify the presence of counsel in state trials *as such* slipped by inevitable analogy into a justification for the presence of lawyers in defence of non-political criminal prosecutions. Although lacking state prosecutors, English state power was directly implicated in criminal law enforcement from 1692 on through a system of bounties and rewards for the apprehension and prosecution of felons. This resulted in the 'development of a cadre of professional thief catchers'[54] or bounty-hunters who, not surprisingly, sometimes gave way to the temptation of fabricating accusations in order to gain easy convictions and quick financial return. They did so even in capital cases ('it is not every day that one gets forty pounds for hanging a man')[55] and during the 1720s and 1730s a growing awareness of these sorts of abuse resulted in judges conceding an increased role to defence counsel in more or less routine criminal cases. This awareness and the participation of counsel in turn contributed, incrementally, to the development of adversarialness, the testing of evidence, cross-examination, and all the panoply of a newly emerging, more 'liberal' form of trial.[56]

A second strong influence on the character of criminal trials in eighteenth-century England grew more directly from the activities of 'liberal'

[52] Landsman, 'Contentious Spirit' at 572.

[53] 7 & 8 Will. 3, c. 3, s. 1. (1696); Landsman, 'Contentious Spirit' at 579.

[54] Landsman, 'Contentious Spirit' at 573.

[55] So William Garrow charged in cross-examination of the victim of highway robbery during a trial in 1784. Quoted in Beattie, 'Scales of Justice' at 240–1.

[56] Landsman, 'Contentious Spirit' at 534 ff.

reformers of all stripes. Wilkite legal battles provided a training ground in vigorous advocacy and also a highly visible display of new ways of conducting court cases. 'The lessons' lawyers learned through observing or participating in those causes 'were directly imported into the criminal process'[57] where they took on a life of their own. Lawyers constantly redefined, debated, and contested the meanings of citizenship, rights, and the rule of law in innumerable large and small courtroom battles. Many causes and reformers of all colours participated in 'political' legal strategies during the eighteenth century as, time and again, 'the courts were called upon to adjudicate social conflicts and modify the law'.[58] Each had its impact on particular issues but also drew upon and contributed to wider discourses of liberal legalism and citizenship.[59]

The career of Thomas Erskine, for example, looms large. Many have accorded him pride of place in the struggle to promote what one hagiographer called 'justice and liberty—the heritage of the Anglo-Saxon!' Liberal notions of law and politics came into particularly sharp definition during the December 1792 prosecution of Thomas Paine for alleged seditious libel arising from the publication of his *Rights of Man*. The lead prosecuting barrister, Attorney-General Sir Archibald Macdonald, began his opening address by asserting his personal conviction in the guilt of Paine and suggesting he would consider it disgraceful for a barrister to represent a cause he did not believe in. Erskine responded with words which have been much repeated:

I will forever, at all hazards, assert the dignity, independence, and integrity of the English bar, without which impartial justice, the most valuable part of the English constitution, can have no existence. From the moment that any advocate can be permitted to say that he will or will not stand between the Crown and the subject arraigned in the court where he daily sits to practice, from that moment the liberties of England are at an end. If the advocate refuses to defend from what he may think of the charge or of the defense, he assumes the character of the judge; nay, he assumes it before the hour of judgment; and in proportion to his rank and reputation, puts the heavy influence and perhaps mistaken opinion into the scale against the accused, in whose favor the benevolent principle of English law makes all presumptions, and which commands the very judge to be his counsel.[60]

---

[57] Ibid., 589.   [58] Ibid., 590.

[59] Ibid., 589 ff. identifies a number of such individuals or causes including Thomas Erskine, James Stephen, Granville Sharp, and other abolitionists.

[60] L. P. Stryker, *For the Defense: Thomas Erskine, the most enlightened liberal of his times, 1750–1823* (New York, Doubleday, 1949), vii, 212, 217. See also J. A. Lovat-Fraser, *Erskine* (Cambridge, Cambridge Univ. Press, 1932).

David Mellinkoff's sensitive treatment of this exchange in *The Conscience of a Lawyer* cautions that Erskine (who has been 'draped with sufficient worshipful nonsense to distort the image of a great lawyer') probably did not intend to advance a fully liberal notion of advocacy of the sort familiar to late twentieth century US lawyers.[61] Conceding entirely that the question of how properly to locate statements such as these in their appropriate historical context is complex and multifaceted, it is none the less reasonable to think of Erskine as having advanced a 'liberal' notion of advocacy and citizenship both as that term is used in this paper and, indeed, as contemporaries and near-contemporaries perceived it. We need not, in so doing, slip unthinkingly to the conclusion that Erskine would have endorsed an adversarial ethic identical to the cynical disinterestedness which characterizes late twentieth-century US legal professionalism.

As the Erskine example suggests, wider changes in social and intellectual life which were taking place coloured many particular issues as they appeared in the courts. These larger transformations too often tended to elevate the virtues of individualism, of 'rational' processes and therefore of new notions of 'proof' and 'evidence' in the courtroom. Such processes and the interactions amongst them have been brilliantly assessed in John Beattie's discussion of the contributions of William Garrow to the development of adversarial justice (the 'liberal' trial) in the late eighteenth century. Though the precise relations between lawyers, political liberalism, and particular forms of trial in this period have yet to be fully studied, Professor Beattie's assessment of one moment in which the centre of gravity of criminal trials shifted markedly provides important evidence of a circumstantial nature:

It is an interesting question, in light of a possible connection between the increase in the number of lawyers at the Old Bailey in the 1780s and contemporary concerns about the oppressive character of the government, whether Garrow's earlier [Whig] political views and connections had also shaped his career as a lawyer at the Old Bailey. For Garrow was not only the most active barrister in the ten years he practiced in that court. What is most striking was his apparent preference for the defense side: In fully 83 percent of the cases he appeared in during his first three years of practice at the Old Bailey (1784–86), he acted for the defendant, a preference he maintained until the year before he took silk. Does that betoken a political stance, a Whig view that a corrupt government threatened to overturn liberty at home as it had in America, and that

---

[61] D. Mellinkoff, *The Conscience of a Lawyer* (St. Paul, Minn., West Publishing Co., 1973), 240–7, at 240.

the defense of the constitution could be carried on in the criminal courts as well
as in Parliament? The connection did not need to be as clear as that for the
Old Bailey to hold some attraction to a young Whig lawyer like Garrow as a
place in which political views could be expressed during the American war and
a distrust of the power and intentions of the administration registered. There is
no evidence that such views lay behind Garrow's practice. But the possibility is
clear, not only as an explanation of Garrow's career, but more generally as an
explanation of the striking movement of lawyers into the criminal courts.

That political context is at the least suggestive, especially because the greater
participation of lawyers in criminal trials in the 1780s led not merely to more
defendants being represented by counsel, but to a more committed advocacy
of their cases in the courtroom and a new emphasis on their rights.[62]

Beattie has pointed out that during the American War of
Independence many in England were concerned that the 'rights and
liberties of Englishmen' were not as secure as they should be. 'There
was widespread concern over the apparent corruption in the government, its unconstitutional behavior', and a belief that 'England was
threatened by a tyrannical and oppressive regime'. At the end of the
war various groups sought reform of Parliament or administration, and
worked to establish 'religious freedom and toleration' so that 'the full
rights of citizenship' could extend 'to those outside the Anglican establishment'.[63] Barristers could—and did—speak through the courts to a
larger public about such matters. By so doing they contributed to eighteenth-century discourses about rights, citizenship, and liberty and
simultaneously put themselves before the public in ways which could be
more directly useful to those intent on pursuing a more conventionally
political career. The political readings of criminal trials by late
eighteenth-century lawyers were quickly communicated to the larger
public through the mass media of the day. The Old Bailey Session
Papers, for example, published for nearly 250 years from 1674,
reported criminal cases tried at that court. Addressed to a lay readership, this publication put lawyers, their actions, and the criminal
process before a reading 'public'.

Nineteenth-Century Developments

The origins of both the adversarial trial and the political visions of state,
society, and citizenship which drew upon and reinforced it are, thus,

---

[62] Beattie, 'Scales of Justice' at 238.   [63] Ibid., 230.

found well before the beginning of the nineteenth century. Further, the use of trials for explicitly political purposes had been well developed during the eighteenth century. The development of 'liberal' criminal trials was not concluded by 1800 however. No point of stasis was then (or has since) been reached. Questions concerning state power, judicial discretion, individual right, and the rule of law have continued to be of importance throughout the nineteenth and twentieth centuries.

During the nineteenth century a number of *causes célèbres* focused public attention squarely on the rule of law and the evolving character of the liberal state. Nineteenth-century English barristers frequently acted much like their counterparts across the Channel: engaging in vigorous advocacy on behalf of individual clients, framing their arguments in relation to issues of great national importance, translating individual grievance into constitutional cause, and employing the privileged sanctum of the courtroom as a podium from which to address a wider public which, simultaneously, they invoked (and constituted) as a source of legitimacy. Barristers, like *avocats*, knew that in the right circumstances their words and actions would be repeated, discussed, interpreted, re-interpreted, and, sometimes, celebrated well beyond the bounds of the courtroom. They were important and self-conscious contributors to public discourse. The Press reported extensively on trials, the courtroom remained an important public forum, and barristers themselves engaged in active propaganda campaigns—writing to newspapers, addressing crowds at public meetings, and expressing their views with surprising regularity in privately printed pamphlets.[64] A high profile on circuit, at the Old Bailey, or in other London courts could provide an excellent foundation from which to launch a political career of either an establishment or a radical sort.

A wide variety of issues were charged with political importance during the nineteenth century. State trials and criminal prosecutions, of course, continued to be of importance as they had in the past. In the

---

[64] The pamphlet collection of the Middle Temple Library is a huge, much under-utilized resource. Rande Kostal has made productive use of such sources in his outstanding recent book *Law and English Railway Capitalism, 1825–1875* (New York, Oxford Univ. Press, 1994), while I have drawn somewhat unsystematically on such sources, in W. W. Pue, 'Moral Panic at the English Bar: Paternal vs. Commercial Ideologies of Legal Practice in the 1860s', *Law & Social Inquiry* 15 (1990) 49–118; W. W. Pue, 'Guild Training versus Professional Education: The Department of Law at Queen's College, Birmingham in the 1850s', *Amer. Jrnl. Legal Hist.* 33 (1989) 241–87; W. W. Pue, 'Rebels at the Bar: English Barristers and the County Courts in the 1850s', *Anglo-American Law Rev.* 16 (1987) 303–52; W. W. Pue, 'Exorcising Professional Demons: Charles Rann Kennedy and the Transition to the Modern Bar', *Law & Hist. Rev.* 5 (1987) 135–74.

repression following the Napoleonic Wars, for example, political radicals embraced the opportunities presented by their prosecutions. According to one historian of London radicalism:

All trials had educative potential, and the radicals knew this. For example, in the late autumn of 1819 Cartwright looked forward to his trial by a far from sympathetic Warwickshire jury as a chance 'to meet and remove prejudices which are opposed to freedom and our country's future welfare'. Some months later John Hunt prepared for his fifth prosecution for libels in the *Examiner* with thoroughness and the determination, as he told Place, to 'say bold things when saying them may be useful to the cause we advocate'. With the help of Place and Hone he collected materials for a defence based on 'proof of the flagrant corruption of the House of Commons' and its constant offences against Justice and Humanity. Similarly, Carlile's trials for blasphemous libel served to advertise the very things that the government sought by prosecution to suppress.[65]

Radicals of this era made the fullest use of law to advance their goals, speaking 'through' the courtroom when they were persecuted, defending themselves vigorously and with imagination, publicizing their cause through wide-circulation pamphlets, speaking of legal proceedings at public meetings, prosecuting their enemies, using the law proactively in their own interests, exposing the Government's spy system, and illustrating, when appropriate, that it was 'extremely difficult for humble persons to call the laws to their assistance in the hours of need when they are to be employed to punish powerful men'.[66]

Nineteenth-century 'liberals' thus continued to be concerned with oppressive state power exercised through political proceedings and criminal trials. They also became concerned, however, with matters arising from labour contracts, the privileges and duties of barristers, and inheritance and wills. The state writ large was sometimes the target of 'liberal' political action through litigation but on other occasions barristers turned their full rhetorical force on the lingering manifestations of 'Old Corruption', employers, or simply the pretences and prerogatives of the wealthy, noble or well-connected. Victorian England's self-understanding was based on informal though clearly understood hierarchies of class, religion, and ethnicity. Not infrequently, social

---

[65] Hone, *Radicalism in London*, 337.

[66] Ibid., 337–54. The quotation, reproduced at 341, is from Report of the Metropolitan and Central Committee, 304 n. 3. For a later period see also J. M. Fellague Ariouat (formerly Sergent), 'The Politics of Trial Procedure in the Chartist Trials in England and Wales, 1839–1848', unpub. Ph.D. diss., Univ. of Birmingham (1995).

presumptions of entitlement originating from this terrain collided in the courtroom with alternative, more liberal, notions of citizenship.[67]

One early nineteenth-century case played at centre-stage of English politics in highly charged circumstances. It generated understandings of advocacy, representation, and barristers' duties which have persisted, mutated, and provided the raw material from which others have fashioned many subsequent discussions of lawyers' professionalism. Oddly, this formative moment in the legal construction of liberal society centred on the lives of aristocrats.

On ascending to the throne at the height of the post-Napoleonic repression, George IV initiated divorce proceedings by trial before the House of Lords, claiming that his wife, Caroline of Brunswick, had behaved in a scandalous fashion and committed adultery with one of her courtiers. The general political context combined with widespread knowledge of George IV's notorious sexual indiscretions to transform the entire matter into a politically-charged morality tale about double standards, public conduct, 'privilege', and equality of justice. In Dorothy Thompson's assessment, 'the queen was seen not only, in Macaulay's phrase, as the victim of "tyrant hatred" but also as the victim of male tyranny and sexual double standards'.[68] Radicals from

---

[67] Challinor, *Radical Lawyer*, documents the extraordinary efforts of a radical barrister to give effect to workers' rights by means of vigorous advocacy before local, inferior, courts (reviewed at length by W. W. Pue in *Victorian Rev.* 17 (1991), 99–106).

For a discussion of three highly politicized cases, see Bege Bowers Neel, 'Lawyers on Trial: Attitudes toward the Lawyer's Use and Abuse of Rhetoric in Nineteenth-Century England', unpub. Ph.D. diss., Univ. of Tennessee (1984) (discussing Lord Brougham's defence of Queen Caroline (1820), Charles Phillips's defence of Courvoisier (1840), and Sir Fitzroy Kelly's defence of John Tawell (1845), Dissertation of Abstracts International, Vol. 45/10–A, p. 3136).

The cases which surrounded *Kennedy* v. *Broun* and *Swinfen* v. *Chelmsford* at mid-century were simultaneously about the privileges of barristers and about class and inheritance. I have discussed these from various perspectives in 'Moral Panic', 'Guild Training', 'Rebels', and 'Professional Demons'. Commercialized notions of legal practice represented a strongly 'liberal' vision of lawyering, representation, and rights of citizens. They ran head-long into Bar 'etiquette'. See also J. R. S. Forbes, *The Divided Legal Profession in Australia: History, Rationalisation and Rationale* (Sydney, The Law Book Co., 1979).

Towards the century's end, an extraordinary case involving a contested inheritance was reinterpreted in popular discourse as in terms of class and citizenship and raised stark questions regarding 'liberal advocacy' before launching the important populist movement which became known as the 'Kennealyites' or the 'Magna Charta Association', which found expression through a newspaper entitled *The Englishman*. A massive literature on the 'Tichborne cause' includes M. Roe, *Kennealy and the Tichborne cause: a Study in Mid-Victorian Populism* (Melbourne, Melbourne Univ. Press, 1974).

[68] D. Thompson, 'Queen Victoria, the Monarchy and Gender' in D. Thompson (ed.), *Outsiders: Class, Gender and Nation* (London, Verso, 1993), 164–86, at 171.

across England, but also many women and men who were not political radicals, petitioned on her behalf. Ultimately, the King's own title
to the throne was implicitly challenged[69] as the cause transformed into
a trial of an entire political system many thought to be corrupt and illegitimate.[70] Ironically, this aristocratic woman became 'a symbol of
many things, not the least of which were the struggles of an oppressed
people against borough-mongering despotism'.[71] Henry Brougham,
one of Caroline's three principal barristers,[72] uttered his famous, unre-
strainedly liberal, dictum regarding the duties of an advocate:

An advocate, by the sacred duty which he owes his client, knows in the dis-
charge of that office but one person in the world, that client and none other.
To save that client by all expedient means, to protect that client at all hazards
and costs, to all others, and among others to himself, is the highest and most
unquestioned of his duties; and he must not regard the alarm, the suffering, the
torment, the destruction which he may bring upon any other. Nay, separating
even the duties of a patriot from those of an advocate, and casting them, if need
be to the wind, he must go on reckless of the consequences, if his fate it should
unhappily be to involve his country in confusion for his client's protection.[73]

These words, much repeated since, were not merely empty rhetoric
in the time and place in which they were first uttered. The case

[69] D. L. Rhode, 'An Adversarial Exchange on Adversarial Ethics: Text, Subtext, and
Context', *Jrnl. Legal Educ.* 41 (1991) 29–41, at 30.

[70] H. J. Perkin, *The Origins of Modern English Society, 1780–1880* (London, Routledge &
Kegan Paul, and Toronto, Univ. of Toronto Press, 1969) at 216–17 asserts that Queen
Caroline's case in 1820 'ranked with Peterloo in crystallizing the working-class con-
sciousness'.

[71] Hone, *Radicalism in London*, 350.

[72] The others were Thomas Denman and Dr Lushington, Williams, Tindal, and Wild
joined these three in representing the Queen. Brougham was variously a Whig politician,
editor of the *Edinburgh Review*, and a writer for the *Morning Chronicle* and the *Review* and
The Times. He had little love for the leaders of his profession. At one stage his professional
career was all but brought to an end by a form of professional blacklisting for, as T. H.
Ford observes, 'No solicitor in the Metropolis or on the Northern Circuit was willing to
give him briefs because of his radical reputation. Brougham, consequently, devoted himself to promoting such radical change that the Whigs were forced to find a seat at
Camelford, a pocket-borough in distant Cornwall' (110). He was involved in Hunt's seditious libel trial (for re-publication of an article by Cobbett), advertised professional services in the *Review*, reviewed Erskine's speeches as a barrister, Stockdale's libel actions,
and worked in several liberal causes which came before the courts. He spoke against anti-
Luddite measures in Parliament, and '[i]n November 1814 occurred Brougham's famous
"dressing down" of Ellenborough for confusing counsel with a client in a case of blasphemous libel' (119). Brougham was intensely disliked by Eldon but his career advanced
through growing co-operation with Romilly (120) and he served as 'Attorney-General'
for Queen Caroline. See T. H. Ford, 'Brougham as a Barrister: Courtroom Dilemmas of
a Notorious Radical', 5: 3 *Jrnl. Legal Hist.* (1984) 108.

[73] Quoted in Rhode, 'Adversarial Exchange' at 29.

combined issues relating to gender equity, transgression of class lines, political 'corruption', tyranny, and equality before the law. Nothing less than the throne itself was at stake, the 'public'—indeed, the mob—was intensely interested in the matter, and Caroline's Whig barristers advanced her cause with unflinching nerve. Ultimately, Caroline prevailed, civil war—apparently a real possibility—was averted, and the monarchy sustained.

Caroline's advocates moved, through luck, persistence, connection, talent, and a change of administration, into positions of some prominence in the English legal system. Their vision of advocacy took root in a reforming nation and much of the nineteenth century history of the English Bar is concerned with more precisely defining the ways in which barristers in liberal society should represent clients and present themselves and their causes to judges, juries, and the wider public. It is far too early to enter any definitive assessment of the phases and stages of the processes creating liberalism but it is clear that English barristers, like French *avocats*, were much involved in all aspects of the construction of a liberal polity in the nineteenth, as in the eighteenth, century. Chartist trials, defence of the rights of workers, and proceedings involving Tawell, Courvoisier, the Swinfen estate, and the Tichborne claimant (amongst others) reflect on-going struggles of English barristers to carry a liberal vision of citizenship into the courtroom.

The 'Frenchness' of the English Bar and the Peculiarities of the English?

How, then, does the English Bar compare with Paris *avocats* in terms of overall contribution to the development of political liberalism?

The question is not easy. While it is abundantly clear that English barristers have been actively involved in 'liberal', 'reform', or 'radical' causes throughout the eighteenth and nineteenth centuries—and certainly before the eighteenth—the present state of research does not permit easy and accurate generalization. The outline sketch provided here does at least demonstrate that some individual English barristers engaged in activities analagous to that of their French counterparts—challenging authority, using their privileged positions within the courtroom in order to address a larger public, engaging in carefully chosen strategic rights-oriented 'test-case' litigation, publishing pamphlets, addressing crowds, and invoking, whether explicitly or implicitly, the unpredictable power of the mob.

A number of points of difference distinguish Paris *avocats* from English barristers, just as significant differences distinguish the broader socio-political situations in the two countries. The English Bar, divided amongst the Inner Temple, the Middle Temple, Lincoln's Inn, Gray's Inn, and Serjeants' Inn in London, was also divided, along different lines, into 'circuit messes' in the provinces. Beyond this, we simply have no idea how many barristers conducted professional work to one degree or another without any reference whatsoever to the institutions or cultural life of the Bar. Certainly, there was nothing to stop them from doing so. For its part, the organized Bar showed little inclination to political unity, much less towards cohesive political action, and less still towards disrupting the political or economic status quo of any given generation. The Inns were 'governed' (to the extent that they were governed at all) by a self-perpetuating oligarchy of elite lawyers. Unaccountable to any professional electorate, organized on hierarchical lines, buffered by corporate status from any generalized 'mood' of the profession, and dependent upon the solicitors of the rich and powerful for their briefs, the Benchers had little incentive to take bold or controversial action. Professional survivors to a man, the Benchers were beneficiaries, and potential future beneficiaries, of the distribution of lucrative legal offices. One English radical pointedly drew attention to this in his description of the Inner Temple Benchers who refused him admission to the Bar in the 1820s:

WILLIAM WELCH, Esq., an independent country gentleman.

FRANCIS MASERES, Esq., cursitor baron of the exchequer and judge of the sheriff's court.

RICHARD BAKER, Esq. (This gentleman was one of the two who decided without hearing.)

WILLIAM HOOD, Esq. a retired barrister formerly of considerable eminence at the chancery bar.

JOSEPH JEKYLL, Esq.

BARNE BARNE, Esq., a retired commissioner for the affairs of taxes, with a pension of 800L a year, and formerly M.P. for the rotten borough of Dunwich.

H. C. LITCHFIELD, Esq., formerly solicitor to the Treasury, retired upon a pension of 3000L per annum. (Vide parliamentary grants of last year.)

JAMES SCARLETT, Esq.

WILLIAM HARRISON, Esq., standing counsel to the Treasury, solicitor general to the duchy of Cornwall, and my professional opponent upon all occasions at Colchester.

JOHN GURNEY, Esq., the avowed prosecutor.

GILES TEMPLEMAN, Esq., an auditor of the public accounts.

GIBBS WALKER JORDAN, Esq., colonial agent for the island of Barbadoes. (Vide Red Book.)

SNOWDEN BARNE, Esq., chairman of the commissioners of the customs, and remembrancer of the lords treasurer's office with a deputy of 800L a year; and formerly M.P. for the rotten Borough of Dunwich; and one of the gentlemen who decided without hearing . . .

KEANE FITZGERALD, Esq., registrar of the Inrolment office, and clerk of the inrolments in the office of Custos Brevium, with a deputy.

I. E. D. E. FINCH HATTON, Esq. . . . this gentleman has as many sinecures as Christian names.[74]

Many elite barristers, in short, were thoroughly enmeshed in the formal and informal webs of political relationship, privilege, and office which reformers castigated as 'Old Corruption'. The Inns of Court were unlike the Paris *Ordre* in all essential respects.[75] English society was different too and the tremendous upheavals of these two centuries did not simply replicate French developments. To the extent—which is only partly true—that English 'liberals' confronted 'corruption' rather than a despotic monarch, their target was different and both their public and professional politics might be expected to play out in different ways. 'Corruption', but also a more generalized and genuinely held terror of the mob, fractured English professional guilds in ways that naked despotism could not.

By the nineteenth century the English Inns of Court showed every sign of decay. Their traditional programmes of education were in desuetude[76] and their minute books reveal the benchers to have been preoccupied with the maintenance of buildings, collection of rents, and the organization of dinners. The one marked exception to all of this— and it seems to continue throughout the nineteenth century—is with regard to the Inns' attitudes towards 'rebel', 'liberal', 'republican', or

---

[74] D. W. Harvey, *A Letter to the Burgesses of Colchester, containing a plain statement of the proceedings before the Benchers of the Inner Temple, upon his application to be called to the Bar, and upon his appeal to the Judges* (London, R. and A. Taylor, 1832).

[75] Bell, *Lawyers and Citizens*, 53, notes that *avocats*, 'unlike the *procureurs*, record-keepers, bailiffs, and nearly all other denizens of the *Palais de Justice*, not only never formed a *corps*, but never became venal officers'. An eighteenth-century *bâtonnier*, unlike his eighteenth-century English equivalent, the Treasurer of an Inn, existed in a professional environment in which the very idea of an 'officer', 'leader', 'register', or 'even a place of assembly' was deemed illegitimate (ibid., 52).

[76] W. R. Prest (ed.), *The Rise of the Barristers: A Social History of the English Bar 1590–1640* (Oxford, Clarendon Press, 1986); W. R. Prest, 'Why the History of the Professions is Not Written', in G. Rubin & D. Sugarman (eds.), *Law, Economy and Society*, 300–20. The state of mid-19th-cent. English legal education is canvassed in Pue, 'Guild Training'.

'reforming' barristers: there is a remarkable pattern of conduct in which the Inns of Court sought to exclude, silence, or expel any barrister whose politics—and particularly whose professional actions—exceeded the relatively narrow bounds of acceptability which circumscribed the political, social, and professional *status quo*. This is a crucially important point for it drives a wedge between the general association of lawyers with liberalism—which this essay generally supports—and the formal associations of lawyers. The latter not infrequently acted to suppress 'liberal' legal practice.

Much is made in the common law world of the social, political, and economic importance of an independent legal profession and it is not uncommon to find both historians and officers of professional organizations asserting that an independent legal profession is crucial to the preservation of the liberties of citizens—a sort of keystone of civil rights, humane governance, democracy itself. This position is traditionally defended by an interpretation which casts lawyers—since at least the time of England's century of revolution[77]—in the role of defenders of fundamental freedoms. This historiographic spin is employed to generate contemporary narratives asserting the political significance of a free and independent legal profession. Typically, the absence of an independent 'bar' is said to be a hallmark of totalitarianism. Traditional 'historical' accounts portray the lawyer as an heroic figure who stands bravely between the citizen and a rapacious state, while the institutions of the legal profession are celebrated as providing the institutional and ideological structure necessary to insulate lawyers from state control, protecting individual advocates from the vindictiveness of those who may have been offended by their actions in protecting the 'rights of the subject'. Their professional organizations are variously portrayed as bulwarks of professional liberty[78] or, at worst, as inefficient, harmless, if unhelpful, associations.[79]

---

[77] See J. E. C. Hill, *The Century of Revolution, 1603–1714* (Edinburgh, T. Nelson, 1961; New York, Norton, 1980).

[78] See e.g. J. H. Cohen, *The Law: Business or Profession?* (New York, Banks Law Pub., 1916), Chs. 4, 5, & 6, 'An Officer of the Court' (Chs. 5 & 6 are 'cont'd')—these chapters give potted accounts of the legal professions in China, Japan, and numerous European countries, illustrating the 'need' for an independent legal profession. See also the literature reviewed in Pue, 'Better Myth'.

[79] R. L. Abel *The Legal Profession in England and Wales* (Oxford, Blackwell, 1988) comes close to this second position.

The Myth of Ineffectiveness

The four Inns of Court have been given a surprisingly easy go of it in this respect by historians. Despite a wealth of primary material documenting contemporary challenges to the exercise of 'disciplinary' powers by the English Bar, the prevalent interpretation has it that the organized Bar of the Victorian period was largely uninterested in policing either admissions or the activities of its members. In an outstanding study of the Victorian Bar, Raymond Cocks asserts that for a large part of the nineteenth century the Inns failed 'to have any significant effect upon professional life'.[80] Similarly, Richard Abel concludes that 'until the end of the nineteenth century the Inns exercised little formal control over either entry into the profession or practice by barristers'.[81] Not inspiring perhaps, but this at least is a relatively benign interpretation of English forms of professional association.

Following Holdsworth,[82] Deborah Rhode has described the Victorian Bar as a sort of archetypal English institution: elitist, remarkably inefficient, blundering, disorganized, perhaps rumpled or frayed around the edges, a bit dusty, but ultimately charming, quaint, endearing, harmless:

In the early nineteenth century, the Inns began requiring applicants to obtain references from two barristers prior to admission, but there is no evidence that this mandate functioned other than to solidify the class bias of the admissions structure. Nor does it appear that barristers during this period were much interested in formally disciplining moral lapses, except where they affected the internal atmosphere of the Inns. Unbecoming behavior could trigger expulsion, but

---

[80] R. Cocks, *Foundations of the Modern Bar* (London, Sweet & Maxwell, 1983). Cocks does argue that the circuit messes of the Bar had some significant regulatory role though his only empirical evidence for this is derived from the Norfolk Circuit in the 1830s. While no thorough comparative study of the regulatory role of the 19th-cent. circuits has yet been undertaken, the Midland Circuit Mess at any rate did not assert a disciplinary function until the 1850s—by which time the authority of the circuits had, according to Cocks, been much eroded by the coming of the railways. In any event, given an absolute lack of power to prohibit barristers from practising, expulsion from a circuit Mess had the paradoxical effect of liberating the expelled individual from professional persuasion altogether: see Pue, 'Professional Demons'. Cocks reports later in the century that 'the Inns were failing to provide anything like a vigorous disciplinary system and now, by the 1880s it was very difficult indeed to argue that the Circuit Messes provided adequate supervision of the whole profession' (214).

[81] Abel, *England and Wales*, 127.

[82] W. Holdsworth, *A History of English Law*, vol. XII (London, Methuen, 1938), 3–101.

publicly sanctioned offenses typically involved breaches of etiquette rather than serious ethical lapses.[83]

The Benchers' minutes of the four English Inns of Court reveal, however, that the Inns were not *quite* as impotent as friend and foe alike would have it. The undisputed leaders of the Bar failed to even attempt to preserve the independence of the legal profession from repression. Worse, they in fact consistently exercised their power to supress those who offended powerful figures or whose legal practices were effective in challenging the *status quo.* Although individual barristers practiced within an institutional structure which might plausibly have insulated them from patronage influences, state coercion, or private corruption, it was in fact generally understood that this freedom existed within relatively narrow bounds. It took some considerable fortitude for a barrister to step outside these limits. The organized legal profession could savagely punish barristers and would-be barristers whose beliefs or practices fell without the political mainstream. There is a hidden history of professional repression which reveals the organized barristers' profession to have been antithetical to, rather than protector of, an independent Bar.

This working hypothesis seems so entirely counter-intuitive from the vantage point of the late twentieth century that a few preliminary comments are therefore in order. First, it should be noted that, in celebrating the 'independent' Bar, the question, 'Independence from whom?' is rarely raised. In *our* historical contexts (that of late twentieth-century liberal democracies) it is often simply assumed that independence from direct state regulation is all that matters. Overlooking this basic preliminary question leads to an inadvertent reinforcing of that peculiar distortion of liberalism whereby only the abuse of 'public' power can be perceived. The Bar, once located in the 'private' realm is simply assumed to be unthreatening, harmless, devoid of disagreeable consequences for 'freedom', 'liberty', political life.

This is, of course, a woefully inadequate conceptual framework. 'Private power' can clearly be as effective, intrusive, or harmful in its effects as public power. Because of this its exercise needs to be at least as carefully scrutinized as the exercise of 'public' power: neither can be *presumed* to be benign. This is perhaps especially so with regard to the regulation of the barristers' branch, a profession which—according to

---

[83] D. L. Rhode, 'Moral Character as a Professional Credential', *Yale Law Jrnl.* 94 (1985) 491–603, at 495.

conventional analyses—must *in fact* be free from interference if constitutional liberty is to survive. Though easily lost sight of in the late twentieth century, this point was readily apparent to Victorian observers. In introducing a bill to Parliament which was intended to effect major changes in the governance of the English Bar, Sir George Bowyer told the House of Commons in 1862 that the Inns of Court were subject to 'a system of absolute self-election, with an arbitrary power of exclusion, perfect irresponsibility, and perfect secrecy'. These principles, he observed, 'were repugnant to the doctrines of constitutional liberty recognized in this country, and *if the power of the Benchers extended, as it did, over a profession, it was a political power and ought not to be exercised in the dark, or without responsibility*'.[84]

To similar effect some three decades earlier, A. Baring had addressed the House of Commons and raised the question as to whether the private power of the Benchers ought properly to be permitted to exclude an individual 'for life from the practice of the higher branch of the Law'.[85] In the same year, Daniel Whittle Harvey spoke of his own exclusion from the bar, telling the House of Commons that the law is 'the people's patrimony', calling the Inns' monopoly over it 'an entire and perfect despotism'.[86]

A second problem which renders it difficult for contemporary observers to perceive the effectiveness of the exercise of bar power arises from an overly narrow focus. Many contemporary students of the legal profession begin from a perspective within liberal economics: hostility to economic monopolies and a belief that the bestowal of monopoly in any area of economic life must be off-set by regulation if the public interest is to be served. Where, as in the case of lawyers, self-regulation is at issue, there is a natural suspicion that self-regulation might serve merely as a code word for the promotion of economic self-interest. These perspectives have produced a varied and extraordinarily rich secondary literature which critically addresses questions relating to how effectively the Bar 'protects' the public from 'bad' lawyers. Valuable and full of insight though it is, this body of work has tended towards a surprisingly narrow concentration on a few concerns: the

[84] *The Times*, 26 June 1862, 10 (emphasis added).
[85] Quoted in Harvey, 'Letter to Lord John Russell', frontispiece.
[86] D. W. Harvey, *Inns of Court. The Speech and Reply of D. W. Harvey, Esq., M.P. on the 14th of June 1832, in the House of Commons, on moving for Leave to bring in a Bill to empower the Court of King's Bench to regulate the Admission of Students and Barristers* (London, James Ridgway, 1832), 6–8.

apparent inability of the legal profession to guarantee the individual 'moral character' of lawyers, or their individual technical 'competence'.

Wider questions which might arise from a focus on divisions within the profession (and the differences in outside constituencies to which various fractions of the profession wish to appeal) are too easily lost in the process of gathering statistics to assault the credibility of the legal profession as a guardian of the public interest (so conceived). When all incidents of professional 'discipline' are treated as interchangeable for this limited purpose the meaning of 'ethics' is left unproblematized.

A third feature of much contemporary research which contributes to obscuring the importance of nineteenth-century disciplinary actions of the Inns of Court also arises in the shadow of 'market control' theory. Historians concerned primarily with the parameters of professional monopoly and its public interest rationalizations concede too much to functionalist social sciences: mesmerized by an economic monopoly enjoyed by the profession *as a whole* it becomes difficult to perceive other—more important—monopolies which lurk in its shadow: discursive privilege, cultural monopoly, political monopoly, or ideological hegemony.[87] 'Discipline', including proactive policing at the point of admission, is the foundation upon which these other monopolies rest.

One further point is important. A small number of documented discipline cases does not necessarily mean that the Bar's powers are inconsequential. It is simultaneously possible that the nineteenth-century Inns failed to achieve the efficiency and regularity of a modern disciplinary apparatus *and* that they substantially inhibited the flourishing of liberal legal practices. Critics of the English Bar who argue that the barristers' profession failed to adequately 'protect' the public from 'bad' barristers, imply that more rather than less discipline was rightly called for.[88] In itself, however, the absence of any record of a large number of clear-cut 'disciplinary actions' by the Benchers is poor evidence from which to fashion any argument relating to the character, purpose, or effect of professional association.

Because there was no formalized system for recording disciplinary incidents by any of the Inns of Court, all estimates of the reach and efficacy of the Bar's disciplinary power must be rough and tentative.

---

[87] Feminist scholars, for obvious reasons, are often better attuned to issues of cultural monopoly. See, e.g., the insightful analysis of the 'benchmark man' of the legal profession in relation to 'others' in Australia in M. Thornton, *Dissonance & Distrust—Women in the Legal Profession* (Melbourne, Oxford Univ. Press, 1996).

[88] See e.g. Abel, *England and Wales*.

Many estimates are probably under-inclusive if only because it seems likely that only the most hotly contested of cases have generated significant written record: the 'gentlemanly' power of English elites has often been exercised in subtly effective ways, shielded from the prying gaze of contemporary critic and historian alike by innumerable interlocking webs of unspoken understanding. Rhode, for example, has observed that:

> Of course, the absence of recorded disciplinary cases or formal character screening cannot be taken to imply an absence of moral oversight. The Inns constituted a small, homogeneous community, in which deviant behavior was unlikely to escape notice. The requirement that students eat a number of dinners at their Inn permitted some professional socialization, as well as *de facto* screening of potential clerks. And in many instances, collegial opprobrium undoubtedly proved as effective a disciplinary mechanism as formal sanctions. What is less clear is the extent to which character mandates had content apart from etiquette and social status.[89]

More crucially however, the effectiveness of bar discipline should not be confused with its quantum. The admonishment, exclusion, or expulsion of individuals has striking symbolic importance: chilling effects ripple outwards unpredictably, affecting the character of the legal profession far more than any simple numerical tally might indicate. This is especially so in cases of 'political' repression where, of necessity, the condemned activity is very much in the public eye, highly visible.[90] Unlike 'political' representation, mere deception of adjudicative tribunals or theft from clients is best done surreptitiously—ideally in the privacy of one's own chambers where it is least likely to be deterred by even a fine-mesh disciplinary net. 'Political' advocacy, unlike simple fraud, cannot, however, be done on the sly.

Given the limitations of quantitative analysis in contributing to the study of professional culture, the very great difficulty in obtaining reliable statistics relating to nineteenth-century bar discipline, and limitations of space, I cannot here offer a case-by-case analysis or statistical summary of Bar discipline.

---

[89]   Rhode, 'Moral Character' at 495.

[90]   Cf. D. L. Rhode's observations regarding the 'moral fitness' requirement of USA legal professions: 'Throughout its history, the moral fitness requirement has functioned primarily as a cultural showpiece. In that role, it has excommunicated a diverse and changing community, variously defined to include not only former felons, but women, minorities, adulterers, radicals and bankrupts. Although the number of applicants formally denied admission has always been quite small, the number deterred, delayed, or harrassed has been more substantial.' (Rhode, 'Moral Character' at 493–4.)

Trends in 'Discipline'

A number of relatively well-documented cases of professional discipline are important, however to the extent that they serve as cultural show-pieces and are illustrative of important issues surrounding the exercise of disciplinary powers by barristers' professional organizations during the first half or two-thirds of the nineteenth century. The best documented cases of professional discipline in this period reveal certain, striking, shared features. In each case the Inns of Court effectively delimited the outer boundaries of 'liberal' advocacy by means of their powers over admission and discipline.

The first noteworthy feature of these early cases of Bar discipline is that almost all of the individuals whose careers were at stake had some affiliation with parliamentary liberals or political radicals (Horne Tooke, Wooler, Harvey, James, Seymour, Kennedy, Keneally, Claydon, Jones). The association was stronger in some cases than others, sometimes a strained alliance rather than party affiliation as such, but the recurrence of some such association is noteworthy. Second, with the exception of Charles Claydon—a rather harmless local barrister caught in cross-fire between powerful opposed forces—each of these individuals had achieved some considerable degree of national prominence either through political activity or by their conduct of famous cases. Third, it is noteworthy that the conduct for which several of these men were disciplined had either taken place some considerable number of years previously or involved continuing conduct which had been well known for some time before discipline proceedings were commenced (Harvey, James, Claydon, Seymour, Kennedy). Fourth, in most of these cases no complaint was made by any client of the individual involved. In several cases disciplinary proceedings were taken in the face of evidence that the individuals alleged to have been injured felt no sense of grievance whatsoever (Jones, James, Claydon, Keneally) or were widely acknowledged to have received exemplary professional services (Kennedy). In one case (Harvey) an individual was repeatedly denied admission to the Bar on character grounds notwithstanding a finding by the House of Commons that he had done nothing which should preclude admission.

These cases fall into two categories: refusals to admit (Harvey, Wooler, Horne Tooke) and the 'discipline' of individuals who were already barristers (Jones, James, Claydon, Seymour, Kennedy, Keneally). In most cases some 'provoking event' brought the individual barrister's conduct to the attention of the Bench of the relevant Inn of Court. This was, variously, the application for admission in the first place (Harvey, Wooler), the appointment of a new Queen's Counsel (which would normally result in promotion to the Bench of his Inn— Seymour), or the conduct of a highly public and controversial cause in court (Jones, Kennedy, Keneally). It also seems likely, though this was never unambiguously indicated in the Benchers' records, that the imminent rise of Edwin James to the office of Attorney-General for England was the 'provoking' cause lying behind his own disbarment. With regard to the cases of refusal to admit (Horne Tooke, Harvey, Wooler) a more or less direct political blacklisting by the Benchers seems indisputable despite the rationalizations offered by the Inns of Court. This, indeed, was the construction put on the Horne Tooke and Wooler cases during a House of Commons debate of the matter.

In other cases, however, it is less certain whether the benchers took offence to particular professional practices as such, or to the background political convictions which those practices reflected. Liberal free-traders engaged in professional practices which turned barristers' rules of etiquette upside-down (Kennedy, and to a lesser extent, Seymour and Claydon) while liberal and radical alike could, in the proper case, be expected to assault class hierarchy, privilege, and the vestiges of 'Old Corruption' with a virulence and lack of decorum rarely displayed in the forensic arena (Jones, James, Seymour, Kennedy, Keneally). In any case, the conduct of famous cases was clearly a large political activity in itself as trials from Queen Caroline's divorce[91] through to Courvoisier,[92] Tawell,[93] Drury,[94] and Tichborne demonstrate.

[91] E. P. Deutsch, 'The Trial of Queen Caroline', *Amer. Bar Assoc. Jrnl.* 57: 12 (1971), 1201–8; W. D. Bowman, *The Divorce Case of Queen Caroline* (New York, E. P. Dutton, 1930); Rhode, 'Adversarial Exchange'; and see also I. McCalman, *Radical Underworld: Prophets, Revolutionaries and Pornographers in London, 1795–1840* (Cambridge, Cambridge Univ. Press, 1988). Bowman suggests that the trial and Brougham's address had 'shaken the aristocracy' and discusses the political dimensions of the case in relation to Brougham's zealous Whig partisanship (254–5; 259–61). The defeat of the King was seen by Erskine as a victory for 'rule of Law' (281).

[92] See Mellinkoff, *Conscience*.

[93] 'On the Principal of Advocacy as Developed in the Practice of the Bar', 265–98. *The Law Mag.* XX N.S. (LI, 103 os) (Feb.–May 1854), 265–98 (repr. from ibid. LXXXIV). This article offers a defence of vigorous 'liberal' advocacy through a discussion of the cases of Courvoisier, Tawell, and Queen Caroline and argues that 'the writers who would uproot the profession of advocacy must seek the destruction of the Law itself'.

[94] In 1851 James acted as counsel for the defence in *The Queen* v. *Thomas Drury*. His client, Dr Simon Bernard, was accused of conspiring with Orsini to assassinate Napoleon

Bar Discipline and the Rhetorics of Liberty

The case of D. W. Harvey is illustrative of several recurrent themes relating to Bar discipline and the rhetorics which have surrounded it. Despite having been admitted as a student member of Inner Temple and fulfilling all of the normal prerequisites for call to the Bar, Harvey was repeatedly refused admission to the status of barrister. His exclusion is of especial interest for several reasons.

First, because of who he was: Harvey was a prominent democratic political activist who, at the time of his exclusion from the Inner Temple, was Member of Parliament for the radical borough of Colchester. His friends, allies, and supporters included many outstanding political radicals and reformers of his day: William Cobbett, Daniel O'Connell, John Wilks, J. Peel, George Sinclair, E. Lytton Bulwer, and Joseph Hume amongst others.[95]

Second, Harvey was peculiarly persistent in his desire to be admitted to the Bar. He pursued every avenue available to him in order to overcome the adverse decision of the Benchers. This included appealing to the judges as Visitors of the Inns *and* causing a Committee of the House of Commons to inquire into the matter. His attempts to fight the Benchers' exclusion spanned a thirteen-year period from 1821 through to 1834. Harvey published a number of pamphlets on the matter and his efforts have left an extraordinarily full documentary record.

Third, the Harvey case is revealing in the structure of the arguments which were developed. Over and above a number of specific responses to the Benchers' announced reasons for his exclusion, Harvey and his allies developed a series of directly political arguments in order to challenge the entire concept of independent professional regulation of Bar

III, a charge on which he was acquitted only by introducing evidence to show that Bernard had in fact intended to kill somebody else! Politically James made it clear that he personally endorsed the views of Orsini and Bernard, for shortly after the defence was complete he appeared on a public platform to attack Napoleon III and endorse what were then radically democratic political views. The *Law Times* abhorred his politics and commented, after that speech, that 'after the exhibition of Wednesday it will be impossible for any government, not Red Republican in its origin and objects, to give him place' and suggested that he should 'resign the office of counsel to the Queen, as being altogether incompatible with the principles proclaimed upon the platform and to which he gave his public adhesion'. 32 *Law Times*, 1 May 1858, 78.

[95] Smith, 'Harvey' at 69 describes him thus: 'the novelist, father of the first Lord Lytton. He was at that time an ardent reformer in politics, and a few years previously had stood for Southwark and issued an address, but had retired on finding his prospects hopeless.'

admissions. The power of the Bar was characterized as a manifestation of Old Corruption and it was asserted that any restrictions on the rights of citizens to practise as barristers seriously jeopardized the constitutional rights and liberties of the English people.[96]

Moreover, Harvey's challenges to the prerogatives of the Inns of Court were expressed as a matter of general principle. The discussions that arose in the context of his case involved an extensive review of the past admissions practices of the Inns of Court. The Harvey case, in short, captures much of the essence of concerns about the governance of the Inns of Court as these had developed during the period between the French Revolution and the decline of Chartism.

At a more general level, many commentators called into question the procedures and standards by which the Benchers of the Inns evaluated the appropriateness of individuals for practice at the Bar. This in turn shaded into grand-scale critiques of the appropriateness of the exercise of such powers by private bodies operating without legislative sanction (the Inns) and an extended criticism of the Benchers themselves. Generally critics of the Inns identified the Bench with 'corruption', accusing the Benchers of having unconstitutionally usurped to themselves the power of denying any Englishman his liberty or right to pursue the profession of barrister. Apologists for the Inns responded with the paternalistic argument that it was desirable to prevent inappropriate individuals from gaining admission to the Bar, that the Benchers had long exercised such a power and, in any event, that any potential abuses of this power would be curbed by the Visitorial jurisdiction of the twelve judges.

Harvey felt that his exclusion from the Bar had been 'nothing less than a political and an inveterate party proceeding throughout' and claimed to have been 'tried by a jury of Whigs and Tories, instead of by men acting in the character which they nevertheless assumed, of impartial judges of the moral and mental fitness of persons seeking to become members of the profession.'[97] His offence to the sensibilities of the Benchers had nothing to do, he felt, with the long-finished civil actions of his youth but much to do with his political career. Harvey told the House of Commons that he would have obtained a fair hearing 'had I not been a politician as well as successful [*sic*] attorney, independent in my principles, belonging to neither party, and therefore the common prey of both, the sworn foe of corruption . . . and always the

---

[96] See, e.g., Harvey, *Letter to Lord John Russell* at 7.
[97] Harvey, *Inns of Court*, 46–94, 55–6.

bold, undaunted, and uncompromising enemy of the enemies of my country.'[98]

William Cobbett concurred in this opinion, writing on 10 January 1834, that Harvey would have been called to the bar without incident had not corruption been afraid 'of your talents, and afraid, too, of her want of power to make those talents subservient to her purposes'.[99] He chided Harvey:

> You should always have taken for *granted* that those who objected to you were corruption No. 2, doing the work of No. 1, and have spoken of them accordingly . . . Hit corruption in her *soft places*, and hit her *hard*; and be delighted as I am, and laugh when she is in a *rage*.
>
> Come, come! it is time to lay upon the ruffians, and to waste no more of your precious time in efforts to obtain 'justice' from men whose *business* it is to do injustice.[100]

The 'Great Liberator' of Ireland, Daniel O'Connell, spoke to similar effect, in support of Harvey's House of Commons motion respecting admissions to the Bar. He too suggested that political malice motivated the Inns in their professional gatekeeping, and went so far as to suggest that any individual of established reputation and untraditional political conviction would be denied the right to practice as a barrister.[101]

Viewing the practice of law as 'the people's patrimony', Harvey argued that because the law 'must be obeyed by all' its practice 'should be open to all'. Any restriction on this right was 'odious' and the actual behaviour of the Inns of Court amounted, he said, to 'an entire and perfect despotism'.[102]

The clearest development of any such linkage of constitutional vision to questions of professional regulation was made during the House of Commons debate on Harvey's 1832 motion respecting the Inns of Court. Speaking to the House, Daniel O'Connell advanced a 'free-trade' vision of legal practice. Pointing out that Lincoln's Inn had once

---

[98] Ibid., 46–94, 75–6.

[99] Quoted in Harvey, *Letter to Lord John Russell* at 7–8, n. [100] Ibid.

[101] 'I say you should not shut out an individual who, instead of walking the Hall for six or seven years, and then being looked upon as a very promising young gentleman, would come to the bar with full-blown honours, with the knowledge and confidence of the public, with a steady independence, and who would make an unwilling Judge tremble on his seat I am perfectly sure that if I had not been called to the Bar previous to my entering into political life, I should never have been permitted to come to the Bar at all.' (O'Connell, quoted in Harvey, *Inns of Court*, 38–44, at 43.)

[102] Ibid., 6–8.

attempted to exclude reporters of Parliamentary proceedings from admission to the Bar, he continued, pointedly citing developments in the USA as an appropriate model:

And might not any other of these men make a similar rule to-morrow, if he chose, and exclude any other class of persons for any reason he chose to assign? Now, let us see how the law stands at present. In the case both of the attorney and the counsel, you must take the greatest care, and you must regard with the most rigid scrutiny, whoever you admit. Why, after you have admitted him, is anybody bound to employ him? There is no salary, no emolument whatever attached to a member of the profession. His only chance of reward is the confidence of the public; if he does not deserve it, he does not obtain it. Where, then, is the necessity of any tribunal to stand between the public and the practitioner? I take it to be altogether unnecessary; it has not been considered necessary in America, and its necessity does not seem to me very obvious . . . It seems to me, therefore, that you have no necessity for this tribunal. What is done by admitting a man to the Bar?—You leave it open to the public to employ him.[103]

O'Connell, like Harvey, relied on principles of English constitutionalism to conclude

that no man's rights should be taken away capriciously—that no man's property should be disposed of without trial—that you should have no secret tribunal—no base inquisition—and every secret inquisition is base.[104]

Others expressed similar opinions. John Campbell, a Bencher of Lincoln's Inn, defended the character of Benchers and Judges but agreed that 'I think it is an *arbitrary and irresponsible* power that ought not to attach to any tribunal' and admitted that the Inn's conduct of Wooler's case was '*highly objectionable*'.[105] Hunt referred to the Inns as 'this disgraceful Star Chamber Court',[106] while Lennard asserted that they had usurped 'a most unconstitutional power, and one which is contrary to the doctrines maintained in this country, that the road to professional honours is open, without distinction, to everyone'.[107]

---

[103] O'Connell, quoted in Harvey 'Inns of Court', 38–44 at 39–40.

[104] O'Connell, quoted ibid., 38–44 at 43–4.

[105] Campbell, quoted ibid., 44.   [106] Hunt, quoted ibid. 44–5, at 44.

[107] Lennard, quoted ibid., 45–6 at 45. He continued, 'arbitrary power should not be confided to any man, however respectable . . . But we are told that there is an appeal to the Judges; but be it observed that it is not to the Judges, sitting in open Court and in public, but in private. In an action for the smallest amount of property, would the public bear that the trials should be behind closed doors? Yet it appears that in a matter of far greater importance than that of mere property—namely, in a question involving a man's character and his eligibility to a profession—this may be heard in private.'

Harvey himself compared the Inns' censoring of admissions to the Bar with 'the Star Chamber, or the Spanish Inquisition' in its arbitrariness, capriciousness, absurdity' and unjustness.[108] The Inns had become, he said, 'secret and self-created tribunals . . . in the spirit of a pure and perfect despotism' which committed 'a species of moral murder'.[109]

Conclusion

The suppression of political and cultural unorthodoxy by the Benchers was possible even in times of apparent professional disintegration. In the result no English barrister could practise law 'at the edge' without fear of reprisal for actions which might cause offence to the professional establishment. The result is that a fully deliberate fettering of the independence of the English Bar by their own professional associations rendered English barristers a subservient profession by the standards of their French counterparts. If professional independence is to be given meaning the lesson to be derived from history might well be that barristers (and citizens) need independence *from* professional associations rather than the independence *of* those institutions.[110]

It is not necessary to celebrate those whose activities were questioned, investigated, or punished by the Benchers of the four Inns in order to be drawn to this conclusion. It may indeed be the case that many of them were arrogant, egotistical, deceptive, dishonest, selfish, untrustworthy, or otherwise thoroughly unpleasant individuals. They may have been wrong-headed, conspiratorial, politically incorrect. It cannot be presumed, however, that as a group these individuals were markedly more arrogant, egotistical, selfish, untrustworthy, or unpleasant than barristers at large. Judging by Bar disciplinary proceedings, it is certainly quite remarkable that such a significant portion of disciplined individuals turned out to be of radical, 'liberal', democratic, or unorthodox political persuasion. Many, though certainly not all, contemporary observers saw the hidden hand of political repression at play in the actions of the Inns of Court.

The pattern of disciplinary interventions outlined here raises some important questions with respect to those rationalizations of professional self-regulation resting on the supposed ability of self-regulating bodies to shelter unorthodox individuals from political interference or suppression. If, as seems clearly to be the case, professional

---

[108] Ibid., 46–94 at 91, 92, 93.   [109] Ibid., 46–94 at 88.
[110] Cf. Bell, *Lawyers and Citizens*, 51–3, 63–4.

organizations can themselves be employed as agents of political repression (recall that Cobbett had called the Inns 'corruption No. 2' doing the work of 'No. 1') the political underpinning for the maintenance of self-regulating professional structures is called into question. Despite longstanding and widespread assumptions about the historic roles of the English Bar in relation to the Rule of Law and British liberty, one is left to wonder if the causes of 'liberalism' might not have been better served had English barristers, like Paris *avocats*, steadfastly refused to take on the characteristics of a corporate structure.

In 1750 Chancellor Henri-François d'Aguesseau expressed his repugnance at the very notion that the *avocats*' profession should organize as a *corps*. They could, he said, 'have neither officers, nor leaders nor registers nor even a place of assembly'. The reasoning which lay behind this found expression in an anonymous 1782 pamphlet issued by the Order of Advocates and quoted by Bell:

All corps are subject to a superior authority which makes them act as it pleases,' the anonymous author declared. This reasoning runs counter to the assumptions made by some modern historians who (following Montesquieu) have assumed that corporate bodies, by providing a trade or profession with a unified voice, give its members greater autonomy than otherwise. [*Avocats*], however, clearly regarded themselves as an exception to this rule, and with some reason. Given the sensitivity of many of the cases that came before the *parlement*, it is reasonable to suppose that powerful magistrates or ministers would have used every instrument at their disposal—including the mechanisms of corporate discipline—to keep members of the bar under tight rein.[111]

Many 'liberal' English barristers of the eighteenth and nineteenth centuries would probably have agreed.

---

[111] Cf. Bell, *Lawyers and Citizens*, 52.

6   State, Capitalism, and the Organization of Legal Counsel: Examining an Extreme Case—the Prussian Bar, 1700–1914

Dietrich Rueschemeyer (Brown University)

The Problem

This is a historical sketch of the Prussian Bar spanning two centuries. Its analytic purpose is to explore how an authoritarian, modernizing state and a late-developing capitalist economy shaped the dispensation of legal counsel and how in response lawyers sought to restructure their professional organization, attempts that were part of a larger agenda of German liberalism. In a comparative perspective, Prussia is an extreme case. Yet extreme cases and their historical fate are analytically instructive.

In the early eighteenth century, lawyers in Prussia were not subject to strong regulation—be it by professional bodies, the courts, or the state. It is safe to say that they were considerably less regulated as a profession than the pre-revolutionary bar in North America.

After repeated efforts at discipline and regulation by the Prussian state and after the developments following the American Revolution, the situation was reversed. During the century that lasted from 1781 to 1878, attorneys in Prussia were a small and close-knit group of quasi-civil servants. In roughly the same period, from the American Revolution until after the Civil War, the legal profession of the United States was essentially a collection of individuals of uneven legal competence and little collective organization. In the initial stages of capitalist development, then, the Bar in Prussia, the largest of close to forty German states and sovereignties, was as different from the American bar as any profession has ever been from another.[1] From the last quarter of the nineteenth century onwards, we see developments that could be described as trends towards convergence—upgrading of education

---

[1] Both differed strongly though in different ways from the English Bar, which—as a high-status occupational group that joined autonomy from the state with a well-established collective self-organization—approximated more closely the analytic models of a profession that prevail in the social sciences than either the American or the Prussian legal profession.

and increasing professional organization in the United States, open admission and some professional autonomy in Germany; but these convergent developments never fully eliminated the contrasting patterns set in the nineteenth century.[2]

The very differences that set the Prussian story apart from the history of professions that are more often studied should be instructive. This essay will first sketch an outline of the history of the Bar in Prussia, focusing on the process of emancipation from government control during the nineteenth century, and then seek to draw some lessons about law as a profession, the Bar's relation to the state, the impact of late capitalist development on lawyers, the relationship between the Bar's struggle and bourgeois liberalism, and the embeddedness of universal aspects of law work in historically concrete social and political contexts.

Imposition of Discipline by the State

Around 1700, Prussia had about twelve hundred attorneys or a little more than one for every 2,000 people, a relative density of lawyers the country was not to see again for more than two hundred years. An earlier division between advocates and procurators—with only the latter, less educated group subject to admission in limited numbers to practise at a given court—had given way to a single occupation, to which admission was not numerically limited though it was contingent on proof of (some) university education and payment of a steep fee; 'the position of an advocate was in a certain sense bought', comments Weissler, the eminent historian of the Bar in Germany.[3] Though not very often aristocrats themselves, many attorneys were associated with aristocratic interests—as legal advisers, agents, or administrators. Frequently they did not practise law as a full-time occupation. And their qualifications were extremely uneven.

Their reputation as a group was low, so low that a dress code, which was imposed on attorneys later in the century and designed to 'make the crooks visible from afar', was felt as a real burden. This contemporary reputation of attorneys must not, however, be taken at face value, as it often was in later retrospectives. It derived in large part from the character of the judicial system in which they served. Dominated by aristocratic interests, the administration of justice was cumbersome,

---

[2] D. Rueschemeyer, *Lawyers and Their Society: A Comparative Study of the Legal Profession in Germany and the United States* (Cambridge, Mass., Harvard Univ. Press, 1973).

[3] A. Weissler, *Geschichte der Rechtsanwaltschaft* (Leipzig, C. E. M. Mohr, 1905), 296.

slow, and incomprehensible to intelligent outsiders; it was thoroughly biased and yet ideologically insistent on a clear-cut identification of 'just' and 'unjust' causes. Attorneys were blamed for the ills and contradictions of this system of justice, a system they did not control.[4]

Throughout the eighteenth century, the Prussian state sought to reform and regiment not only the system of justice dominated by the aristocracy but also the size, composition, and competence of the Bar. The first major move was dramatic indeed: in 1713, the Bar was purged of more than half of its members. The idea was not just to reduce the size of the Bar but to change its character. In particular, the policy aimed to exclude the less educated, the less economically successful, part-time practitioners who combined law with other pursuits, those of 'too despicable and poor background', and those of questionable character (which included, undoubtedly, also questionable political loyalties). Education, practical training, and court-administered examinations were restructured by state regulation. Fees were set by the state and pegged at a radically lower level than before. Severe penalties were put on the unauthorized practice of law.

One may have doubts about the realism and practicality of these policies: doubts that those who were excluded from the profession actually refrained from practice; doubts that a proper assessment of the various criteria of desirability was possible given the massive size of the purge; and doubts that a drastic reduction in numbers could be combined with an equally drastic reduction—rather than an increase—in the price for legal services. Such disregard for practicality was a standard feature of state 'policing' at the time.

But so was persistence: throughout the eighteenth century, with measure after measure, the Prussian state sought to secure royal control of the courts and to transform the Bar—reducing its size, imposing uniform standards of admission, suppressing unauthorized practice, supervising attorneys' work, and holding their fees down.

The capstone of these policies was an attempt to abolish private advocacy in court altogether. In 1781, a royal decree forbade private attorneys to appear in court. They were replaced by *Assistenzraethe*, junior judges paid by the courts, who were assigned as counsel to the parties. But this innovation simply was not viable. After only a few years, attorneys of the parties' choice were again allowed to argue in

---

[4] The official criticisms focused mainly on four points that correspond closely to the overall character of the system of justice: 'accepting unjust cases, impeding the progress of a case, lengthy and misleading arguments, and greed for fees', ibid., 253.

most proceedings, and in 1793 private advocacy was reintroduced under a new name, that of *Justizkommissar*.

The figure of the *Justizkommissar* was, however, very different from the attorney of the pre-reform period and from advocates in neighbouring countries. It defined for the next three generations how legal advice and legal representation were offered in Prussia (even though in 1849 the name was changed to the one still used today—*Rechtsanwalt*). Attorneys eventually came to share the same training with judges—university studies followed by in-service training and both concluded by state examinations. Appointments to the position of *Justizkommissar* were made by the Ministry of Justice, and they were made sparingly. The appointees were assigned to a specific location, and they were transferred at the discretion of the Ministry, in itself a powerful tool of discipline. The *Justizkommissare* were under the disciplinary supervision of the courts, courts that had been wrested from aristocratic control and become institutions routinely administering a largely codified law. The fees of attorneys were set by the Ministry. Except for the clients' free choice of counsel and the variable and substantial income chances this entailed given the restrictive appointment policy, the Prussian *Justizkommissare* came as close to being *preussische Beamte*, Prussian civil servants, as an attorney can be. And legally they were considered to be members of the royal Civil Service, with all the obligations this entailed for their professional and personal conduct, including restrictions on political activity.

The Ministry's appointment policy limited the number of lawyers drastically. In the 1850s and 1860s, Prussia had only one attorney for every 12,000 people. This compares with the following figures for other countries at the same time:[5]

England	1 : 1,240
France	1 : 1,970
Belgium	1 : 2,700
Saxony	1 : 2,600
Mecklenburg-Schwerin	1 : 1,700

These figures, especially those for the two neighbouring German states that practised a more liberal admissions policy than Prussia, suggest that the size of the Prussian Bar was completely out of line with the demand for legal services. And that is supported by other evidence.

[5] R. Gneist, *Freie Advokatur: Die erste Forderung aller Justizreform in Preussen* (Berlin, Julius Springer, 1867), 22, 69.

Max Jacobsohn reports for Berlin that speedy service required a bribe to the office manager of the attorney, and small cases were often just not taken.[6] In fact, during the 1860s Berlin had three to four hundred '*Winkeladvokaten*', admitted to the lower courts, as well as fifty-nine attorneys. *Winkeladvokat* is a derogatory term for persons without university training who served as legal advisers and were tolerated by police and the administration of justice since the needs of people with moderate means were just not met by the official Bar.[7] Before open admission was introduced in 1879, the Bar of Berlin came close to failing its broader mission and being rather a '*Rechtsanwaltschaft* for the upper ten thousand'.[8]

The state's radically restrictive admissions policy had an equally dramatic effect on the bar's material situation: it made the practice of many attorneys extremely lucrative. A contemporary observer estimated in 1835 that Prussian *Justizkommissare* earned between 2,000 and 10,000 thaler. This compared with 500 thaler for judges in the lower courts.[9] A well informed article in the *Preussische Jahrbuecher* offered a similar estimate for the 1860s: if a county judge became an attorney he could multiply his income by a factor of five, raising it from 600 to 3,000 thaler.[10]

Such income differences led to a reversal of career patterns typical of common law countries: while attorneys rarely or never became judges, judges not infrequently opted to go into private practice. In fact, from the middle of the nineteenth century until the early 1870s, *nearly all appointments to positions in the Bar were awarded to former judges*.[11] This pattern of recruitment was, of course, a powerful reinforcement of the Civil Service character of the Bar, though it must be noted that by the middle of the nineteenth century the judiciary had acquired a relatively liberal cast, distinctively set off from the administrative Civil Service.[12]

Max Jacobsohn, one of the first attorneys admitted to the Bar after emancipation in 1879, describes the bar of Berlin before its transformation:

---

[6] M. Jacobsohn, 'Einzug der freien Advokatur in Berlin', in *Festschrift zum deutschen Anwaltstage* (Berlin, 1896), 81–3.

[7] Gneist, *Freie Advokatur*, 60.   [8] Jacobsohn, 'Einzug', 108.

[9] W. Doehring, *Geschichte der deutschen Rechtspflege seit 1500* (Berlin, Duncker und Humblot, 1953), 86–7.

[10] Anon., 'Die Advokatur in Preussen', *Preussische Jahrbuecher*, 14 (1864), 430–1.

[11] Weissler, *Geschichte*, 530, 532.

[12] A. Wagner, *Der Kampf der Justiz gegen die Verwaltung in Preussen* (Hamburg, Hanseatische Verlagsanstalt, 1936).

The 93 Gentlemen . . . who formed the bar of Berlin . . . were a dignified professional group of high repute . . . Among them were quite a few eminent men of great legal as well as general importance so that true merit justified the external standing of the group. Every one of them could rightly be proud to be a member of this noble body.

Most had a very large clientele which they met with the reserved dignity of higher civil servants. The office managers mediated between these gentlemen and the clientele, and adjuncts [*Hilfsarbeiter*] formed the link between them and the court. These adjuncts had a rather different importance than now; the written Prussian trial procedure forced a very detailed—and unfortunately often very formalistic—treatment of the material . . . For such work many attorneys had neither the time nor the inclination and thus left it to their adjuncts . . . Since the written preparation of trial was done by the adjuncts and the [concluding] oral arguments were only in the more important trials of great significance, the attorneys themselves were much less involved in the conduct of trial than now. In most cases they were content to look through the papers, sign them, plead in important matters, and otherwise to operate their notarial practice and to hold office hours . . .

Most attorneys were too proud to accept small cases. That would indeed have been at odds with the public dignity and noble character of the Berlin bar before 1879. But this dignity, this elevated position, much as it adorned the profession, eliminated the closeness with clients and was thus at the same time the weakness of the profession. The so-called little people, petty bourgeois, craftsmen, and workers did not dare to approach an attorney. Thousands and thousands of potential clients, and especially those who needed the protection of law the most, never saw an attorney's office from the inside.[13]

The Prussian Bar of *Justizkommissare* and later of *Rechtsanwaelte* indeed acquired an excellent professional reputation, one in stark contrast to the vilified attorneys of the eighteenth century. Given the combination of material wealth and the status of royal civil servants, this is not astonishing.

Yet the position of Prussian lawyers in private practice was not only shaped by state regimentation. Other forces, too, contributed to the transformation of the Bar. Two developments in particular had a powerful impact: the capitalist development of the economy brought a different clientele and different legal issues to the fore. And developments in culture and education gave 'cultural capital' a new weight in societal stratification, professional relations as well as personal life.

Capitalist development created vast new legal problems and thus opportunities for law work. In contrast to the foundation of aristocratic

---

[13] Jacobsohn, 'Einzug', 80–1.

privilege in particularistic power arrangements, the overriding concern of the emerging bourgeoisie lay in predictable property and contract relations, guaranteed formally by the state but left in substance to the discretion of private parties conceived as equals. This was at the heart of the new liberal ideology. Though often pragmatically tempered by opportunities for particularist advantage, it also transformed the realities of legal work, putting a premium on efficient and competent attorneys that protected relations with customers, suppliers, and competitors from unwanted complications.

The original type of the *Advokat* that was the target of all the spiteful proverbs and bitter epigrams, expressions of popular dislike, nearly disappeared under the influence of economic conditions transformed into a larger scale and the growing power of ethical ideas.[14]

Cultural developments were another important factor. The literary and philosophical rise of neohumanism—symbolized most eminently by the idealist philosophy of Kant and the Weimar of Goethe and Schiller—came together with the restructuring and renaissance of German universities. Stiffened requirements of secondary education as a condition for university studies—the humanist *Gymnasium* became the mandated gate to university studies in the 1830s—and of university education as a condition for entering the higher Civil Service introduced these ideas and orientations into the bureaucracy and the professions.

The German ideal of *Bildung* that arose around the turn from the eighteenth to the nineteenth century had a particular character:

Bildung as conceived by the German neohumanists in the age of Lessing, Herder, Winckelmann, Goethe, Schiller, Kant, Fichte, and Humboldt, meant more than advanced school training, general and vocational. *Bildung*, no doubt, called for trained minds and for more and better knowledge, but no less for character and personality development . . . It invited man to seek happiness within himself by orienting his total life toward the harmonious blending of spiritual elevation, emotional refinement, and individualized mental and moral perfection.[15]

This conception had an impact that is of interest here in several ways. It was, first, the intellectual underpinning for the fight of bureaucratic

---

[14] E. Benedict, *Die Advokatur unserer Zeit*, 3rd edn. (Vienna, Manz, 1909), 78.

[15] H. Rosenberg, *Bureaucracy, Aristocracy and Autocracy: The Prussian Experience 1660–1815* (Cambridge, Mass., Harvard Univ. Press, 1958), 182.

officials to limit autocratic royal rule.[16] Equally important for the transformation of Prussian society, educational merit became the basis on
which university-trained commoners acquired parity with aristocrats in
the Civil Service. Finally, the ideals of *Bildung*, however diluted by 'philis-
tine' routinization and pragmatic compromise, linked personal life to
professional commitment. As such they became a central element in the
ideal self-image of German professionals, or *Akademiker*, well into the
twentieth century.

Yet if developments in the state, the economy as well as culture and
education shaped the Prussian bar in ways that were in many respects
complementary, there were also powerful tensions. True, autocratic
domination had been transformed into rule by competent bureaucrats,
and the old occupation- and birth-based status order had been modified by significant if limited infusions of educational merit and competition. But both the dominant role of the state and the remnants of a
traditional status order stood in tension with capitalist economic development, which came late to Prussia and the rest of Germany. In contrast to Britain and the United States, the bureaucratic rationalization
of rule preceded in the larger German states, and especially in Prussia,
the capitalist rationalization of economic life. The rule of a modernized
authoritarian state came into conflict with the political aspirations of
the emerging bourgeoisie and with many of its economic goals. The figure of the *Justizkommissar*, which was the product of rationalizing state
action, was not well suited to the new demands of capitalist development. If attorneys had found a place in the occupational system that
gave them honour and material security in a *Staendestaat* modernized
and dominated by government bureaucracy, this system was buffeted
by the forces of capitalist transformation; economic efficiency and functional considerations now rivalled the concerns for the public honour
of a profession. And a Bar of quasi-civil servants closely tied to the state
was at odds with the political aspirations of the bourgeoisie, which
became dominant in the clientele of attorneys.

---

[16] 'Before 1800, the doctrines of German idealism acquired political significance only
in the Prussian bureaucracy . . . To the bureaucratic disciples of Kant, individual freedom to think was the gateway to professional happiness, to self-disciplined discretionary
action, to their own political liberation, and to the replacement of erratic dynastic autocracy by a more magnanimous and more effective form of despotic government, by
humanized bureaucratic absolutism, "which will find it advantageous to itself to treat
man, who thenceforth is more than a machine, in accord with his dignity." ' (Rosenberg,
Bureaucracy, 189; the concluding quote is from I. Kant, *Saemtliche Werke*, Grossherzog
Wilhelm Ernst edn., vol. I, 171).

These shifts and tensions arising from late capitalist development powered the variegated demands of German liberals in the economy and in politics. Embedded in these liberal demands—reinforcing them as well as nurtured by them—were the more specific goals of lawyers who sought to reform the administration of justice and the role of lawyers in court as well as in economic, social, and political life. Eventually, these demands and the tensions that fuelled them led to a radical transformation of the Prussian *Rechtsanwaltschaft*.

Emancipation: Early Demands and Late Realization

It was in the 1840s, in context of developments preceding the attempted German revolution of 1848, that the Prussian (and Bavarian) construction of legal counsel delivered by a closed profession of civil servants was first explicitly attacked.[17] This is significant because it symbolizes that the debate on the shape of the legal profession was as much a political debate as it was a discussion of professional concerns.

At the third *Anwaltstag*, all-German meetings of attorneys that had begun in 1846, a speaker discussing the public role of the attorney argued that the Bar's obligation of keeping the judiciary in check also entailed the obligation to participate in political movements supporting the rule of law. Therefore, the profession had to be independent, free of civil service privileges and obligations, open to all qualified applicants, and subject to its own discipline through state-mandated *Anwaltskammern*, associations with compulsory membership.

Opening admission to the Bar ran straight against the material interests of lawyers in those German states—Prussia and Bavaria among them—that imposed tight limitations on the size of the Bar and in the process created gold mines for many of its members. Thus it is not surprising that the proposal found immediate opposition (the size of which we do not know because no vote was taken). But the demand for a free Bar, open to all who are qualified, was from the beginning a political demand rather than one inspired by professional group interest. It was part of a broader programme to secure the rule of law. This broader

---

[17] A detailed discussion of the fight for changing the structure of the legal professions in the German states is given by H. Huffmann, *Kampf um die freie Advokatur* (Essen, W. Ellinghaus & Co., 1967). Other important sources are: Weissler, *Geschichte*, and Gneist, *Freie Advokatur*. See also H. Siegrist, 'Public Office or Free Profession? German Attorneys in the Nineteenth and Early Twentieth Century', in G. Cocks & K. H. Jarausch (eds.), *German Professions, 1800–1950* (Oxford, Oxford Univ. Press, 1990).

programme was a goal that the leadership of the Bar in several states—including, significantly, Prussia—made its own.

What was this broader programme? Advancing towards a unified law across the thirty-odd sovereignties, large and small, that made up Germany was one goal, inspired by economic developments as well as by the work of the law faculties in the various state universities that prepared such unification in their scholarly work, and served students who often studied at different universities and outside their own state. For the administration of justice, the demands included above all the independence of the judiciary, which was achieved—in a long drawn-out process—by 1848.[18] Other demands were public court proceedings with more room for oral argument rather than a concentration of written submissions, lay participation in adjudication (*Schwurgerichte*), a greater role in trial for initiatives of the parties, state attorneys representing the state as other attorneys represented private parties, and a self-employed, open Bar administering its own professional discipline. While many of these demands were at least partially met by mid-century, a 'free Bar' was found only in some states, many had complex intermediate arrangements, and two of the largest, Prussia and Bavaria, held on to a closed profession of civil servants.[19] That other German states had a largely self-governing Bar free of Civil Service privileges and obligations was, in conjunction with the aspirations towards unification, a major support for similar developments in Prussia.

A free bar was, then, part of the liberal demands for a *Rechtsstaat*, and it was the part on which Prussia had conceded least. This idea of a *Rechtsstaat* can reasonably be translated as 'a state in which the *rule of law* prevails', that is, in which the actions of the state apparatus especially are subjected to law, secured by an independent administration of justice. Yet it must also be noted that in nineteenth-century Germany this conception was often not only seen as compatible with a quite autocratic pursuit of the common good by a competent Civil Service but also as in tension with, and in a sense a substitute for, democratic demands for popular control of the state.

Why was a free bar a significant part of the overall liberal programme? The closed Bar, first of all, offered insufficient legal protection to the population. It was not only that people of limited means were ill served. Many lawyers were also rather removed from the concerns of business. 'Ask our businessmen how few *Rechtsanwaelte* there are

---

[18] Wagner, *Der Kampf.*   [19] Weissler, *Geschichte*, 528.

who are able to draft the statutes of a business corporation, a bank or a loan association.'[20]

Equally important politically, supervision by the state bureaucracy kept lawyers from engaging in political activity, especially from associating with liberal movements aimed at limiting the power of the state. In 1844, the Prussian Minister of Justice decreed that Prussian *Justizkommissare* were not to participate in the first German Bar meetings that were then planned, because to participate in discussions of unifying German law would exceed the bounds of their role as Prussian civil servants; in fact, it would constitute a criminal offence since all societies and associations aiming to change the constitution or administration of the state were outlawed since 1798. As late as 1861, to cite another example, the Prussian Minister of Justice took the occasion of forthcoming elections to remind the officers of the court that they were not to give any support to parties seeking to weaken the powers of the king. Five attorneys who objected with indignant, but moderate liberal arguments were indicted for insulting the Minister and the Court President.[21] Overall, the insistence of the state on abstinence from politics seems to have been effective; Prussian lawyers were said to participate less in politics than their colleagues in other states, and Weissler's explanation—that Prussia was a well-administered state—is plausible only if one takes it on its (probably unintended and at first glance hidden) double meaning.[22]

Rudolf Gneist, a conservative liberal law professor who became a leader of the movement for a free bar in Prussia and whose father had been first a Prussian *Justizkommissar* and later a judge, broadened this political rationale. He saw an independent Bar as the backbone of an autonomous civil society, which he considered a requisite for political freedom. His larger project was to recreate intermediary bodies in Prussia where they had been systematically suppressed since the eighteenth century; and for this project free lawyers would be a critical ingredient — local notables with independence, influence, and an interest in public affairs.[23]

---

[20] Anon., 'Die Advokatur', 438.

[21] They were not found guilty; the government appealed, but lost again in the appellate court. See Weissler, *Geschichte*, 532–3; for the earlier episode see 509–10.

[22] Anon., 'Die Advokatur'; on the time before 1848, see Weissler, *Geschichte*, 467–8.

[23] I thank Kenneth Ledford for emphasizing this broader concern when commenting on a first draft of this essay. On the importance of associations in local civil society dominated by liberal notables for the national political influence of liberals in the first years of unified Germany, see M. John, 'Associational Life and the Development of Liberalism

Calling the emancipation of the Bar from its Civil Service status and open admission 'the first demand of all reform of the administration of justice in Prussia', Gneist made yet another rationale central: the closed Bar of Prussia endangered the independence of the judiciary.[24] The 2,000 or so Prussian judges in the lower courts were not well paid. Promotion to higher judicial positions (all in all about 650) was in the hands of the Ministry of Justice. If this promotion was already a potential instrument of a discipline not necessarily related to merit, the assignment of judges to the 1,350 lucrative positions of attorneys was bound to evolve into a dangerous pattern of patronage since it was absurd to transfer the best judges to the Bar. 'Since neither age, nor merit, nor number of children could constitute the basis for the decision, nothing was left but purely personal discretion, favour or disfavour, personal intervention, and probably also political merits.'[25]

Gneist built on earlier calls for a free Bar that had been voiced in more liberal parts of Germany, and he buttressed his arguments with systematic comparisons across Europe. This went far beyond a few comparative statistics. 'Through extensive travels in Italy, France, England and the United States he gained profound insight into the structure of foreign legal institutions. This was particularly true of England, to whose constitutional history and government he devoted most of his chief works. Indeed, he practically rediscovered English political institutions for the European continent.'[26] Comparative law was for him at once a central intellectual project and an instrument for advancing his political pursuits and arguments. Thus English institutions implicitly became a model for his goals in reforming Prussian political institutions, including the Bar.

The emancipation of the Prussian Bar from state supervision, Civil Service status, and limited admission was grounded in the movement for self-government and self-organization of the bar. Here again, developments in other German states preceded those in Prussia, and they represented a supportive precedent for them.

---

in Hanover, 1848–66', in K. H. Jarausch and L. E. Jones (eds.), *In Search of a Liberal Germany: Studies in the History of German Liberalism from 1789 to the Present* (Munich, Berg Publishers, 1990).

[24] Gneist, *Freie Advokatur*.   [25] Ibid., 43; see also 22, 41–2.

[26] E. v. Hippel, 'Gneist, Rudolf von', *Encyclopedia of the Social Sciences*, vol. VI (New York, Macmillan, 1931), 682; see also J. Hatschek, 'Gneist, Heinrich Rudolf Hermann Friedrich v.', *Allgemeine deutsche Biographie*, vol. XLIX (Berlin, Duncker und Humblot, 1904 [1971]); E. Angermann, 'Gneist, Heinrich Rudolf Friedrich v.', *Neue Deutsche Biographie*, vol. VI (Berlin, Duncker und Humblot, 1964).

The first association of attorneys was the *Lyceum fuer Jurisprudenz* in Jena, which was founded in 1801 and met weekly to discuss problems of law and legislation.[27] The 1830s and especially the 1840s saw the creation of many more local and regional associations, which often, however, were only fleeting phenomena. They were viewed with suspicion by most state governments, and often they were outlawed.

Attorneys were among the leaders of the attempted revolution of 1848, when legislation and regulations restricting associations of any political relevance were openly flouted by the courageous few until the victorious political reaction prevailed. 'We see everywhere attorneys as leaders of the liberal movement . . . In the first German Parliament this single profession alone accounts for one sixth of the members . . . *Rechtsanwaelte* are the leaders of the parties . . . There was no city which did not see an attorney in the vanguard of the movement.'[28] This involvement strengthened the linkage between political liberalism and professional reform, even though it was an elite phenomenon, not representative of the rank and file of the profession, and Prussian lawyers were less involved than colleagues from other states.

Bar organizations declined after 1848, partly because of renewed repression, partly because Prussia and other states introduced elected honours councils with limited jurisdiction over professional self-discipline, satisfying to some extent one major demand of the bar's activists. Renewed associational activity is evident in the 1860s, when state-wide associations were founded in both Prussia and Bavaria.

The initiative for the creation of the Prussian bar association in 1860 grew out of a critique of the dependent Civil Service status of the profession. In the following seven years, state-wide meetings of the Prussian Bar—poorly attended but nevertheless representing the Bar in public—at first responded with reserve, but then voted repeatedly to demand full emancipation with open admission. Opposition to open admission was stronger in local bar associations, but the organizational elite opted for the by now firmly established liberal programme of reform rather than for the material self-interest of the profession.

The realization of these demands came much later, in 1879. The timing is of considerable political significance: the demand for emancipation emerges with the attempt at a liberal revolution; it is renewed and becomes significant within Prussia at the time of constitutional conflicts between liberalism and the Prussian state; the unification of

<hr>

[27] Weissler, *Geschichte*, 502. [28] Ibid., 501–2.

Germany under Prussian leadership in 1870–1, while it followed a victory of Bismarck's state over its liberal critics in Prussia, engendered a period of institutional restructuring, of 'internal unification', in which liberals wielded strong influence until 1878.

The emancipation of the Prussian Bar comes about as part of the introduction of uniform court procedures in the German empire. If we leave technical details aside, the new *Rechtsanwaltsordnung* met most of the old demands; it provided for self-government and (largely) for self-discipline in compulsory bar associations as well as open admission of all educationally qualified applicants, though admission remained limited to one specific court.

Victory on this plank of the liberal programme was not, however, due simply to a temporary political dominance of liberal forces. It was also the result of a conjuncture of other factors and considerations. Foremost among these was the very need for a unified German institutional pattern. The Prussian system of attorneys as quasi-civil servants would not have been easily accepted across Germany. Furthermore, it was at odds with the liberalizing, free trade thrust of much of the other unifying developments in the legal order. The reform received support from political groups other than the liberals, such as the Catholic Centre Party, who saw itself fighting a defensive battle against a hostile Protestant-dominated state and favoured areas of professional work not controlled by the government. Open admission to the Bar also served the needs of bourgeois families whose sons had trouble finding legal employment after lengthy studies and the obligatory training period.[29]

What, then, of the Bar itself? Even though other forces were important for the final realization of the call for a 'free bar', its support for reform was critical. After initial opposition from the rank and file, Prussian and more generally German lawyers supported the liberal reform programme of their leaders, even though this ran against the material interests of the bar. Their support may at many points have been lacking in depth and enthusiasm, but the leadership did win. And it won decisively: calls for a reimposition of limited admission were again and again rejected for political reasons, until the Great Depression in the late 1920s undercut this commitment.[30]

---

[29] A good discussion of this conjuncture of factors is given in the paper by H. Siegrist, 'Autonomy and Heteronomy. National Unification, Legislation, and Professional Policies in Germany in the Late Nineteenth Century', presented to Conference on Lawyers and Political Liberalism, Oñati, Spain, 1993.

[30] See K. F. Ledford, 'Lawyers and the Limits of Liberalism', chap. 7 *infra*.

Emancipation: Consequences

What were the consequences of emancipation and open admission? There was, first, a rapid growth in numbers: in Berlin, the Bar grew from ninety-three members in 1879 to 675 in 1896 and more than 1,000 in 1906.[31] The number of attorneys in all of Germany grew from 4,112 in 1880 to 12,324 in 1913, with the per capita figures increasing from 1:10,970 to 1:5,436 respectively.

The character of the bar changed radically, as one might expect. An increase in numbers of this magnitude makes institutional and subcultural continuity precarious.[32] But there were also astounding continuities. There was, for one thing, no significant increase in disciplinary activity, and it is unlikely that contemporary observers were mistaken in interpreting this as evidence of continued adherence of a much changed bar to established standards of professional conduct.[33]

The average income of Prussian attorneys declined, even though they expanded their activities into new areas. Part of this expansion was an extension of services to a less well-to-do clientele. There was also an expansion into business law and related activities, but this remained relatively weak, perhaps not even keeping up with the expansion of economic activity in the thirty-five years before the First World War. In addition, it seems that only parts of the enlarged bar succeeded in entering the field of corporate and other business law. For others, the hold of a more traditional pattern of legal work was stronger. As a consequence, different segments of the bar increasingly represented different patterns of professional experience and orientation.

---

[31] Jacobsohn, 'Einzug'; J. Magnus, (ed.), *Die Rechtsanwaltschaft* (Leipzig, W. Moeser, 1929), appendix.

[32] A parallel distant in time and location can illustrate that: after the American Revolution, many old-time lawyers retired or emigrated to England or the Canadian provinces, while in the following few years large numbers of newcomers entered the profession—in New York City, the numbers changed from 40 in 1785 to 290 in 1818. See C. Warren, *A History of the American Bar* (Boston, Little, Brown, 1911), 212–13, 214, 295, and 301. This radical discontinuity of personnel—even more radical than the changes in Berlin and Prussia a hundred years later because here the old elite did not disappear—holds the key to understanding the rapid change in the character of the profession, from a quite effective autonomous professional self-control based on informal local organization before the Revolution to a loose aggregation of unorganized practitioners of very uneven competence and equally uneven adherence to professional standards only a short time later. See R. Pound, *The Lawyer from Antiquity to Modern Times* (St. Paul, Minn., West Publishing Co., 1953); Rueschemeyer, *Lawyers*.

[33] Jacobsohn, 'Einzug'.

Politically it was important that the open admission of the new *Rechtsanwaltsordnung* coincided with a turn to the right in the politics of the Prussian–German state in the years 1878–9. A major turning-point in the development of Bismarck's Germany, the new policies radically diminished the political influence of liberalism, they sought to end the fight against—and to co-opt—political Catholicism, and they initiated the repression of the Social Democratic movement. This turn of Bismarck's politics had reverberations in the administration of justice, involving official discrimination against liberal civil servants. The newly opened Bar offered a convenient dumping ground for these unwanted lawyers. While this strengthened the liberal forces within the Bar, the political environment of the Bar had decisively turned against liberal ideas.[34]

In conjunction with an increasing official anti-Semitism in the 1880s, the opening of the Bar led also to a dramatic increase of the number and proportion of Jewish attorneys—from virtually none in the 1870s to half of the bar in Berlin, a quarter in Prussia and 15 per cent in Germany as a whole by the beginning of the twentieth century. Anti-Semitism at the bar was said to be weak in the 1880s,[35] while from the 1890s onwards a more generally increasing anti-Semitism took hold among attorneys, too, and became associated with complaints about overcrowding, ruthless competition, and commercialization of the profession. 'The bar was in this period liberal against the wishes of its non-Jewish majority,' said one knowledgeable observer in retrospect.[36]

By the years preceding the First World War, then, the Prussian Bar had acquired a structure that was more similar to the legal professions in other advanced capitalist countries than it had ever been in the hundred years between 1781 and 1878. It experienced a radical change which had been advocated for more than a generation by liberal politicians and Bar leaders. Yet the old patterns of a Civil Service orientation persisted in parts of the bar. Furthermore, together with a weakening of the liberal forces in German politics, the Bar exhibited internal fissures and antagonisms that we may see as indications of the difficulty of adjusting to the transformation of the old order. The weak-

---

[34] See J. Ziekursch, *Politische Geschichte des neuen deutschen Kaiserreiches*, Sozietäts-Druckerei, vol. II (Frankfurt, Frankfurter, 1927), 385; E. Kehr, 'Das soziale System der Reaktion in Preussen unter dem Ministerium Puttkamer', in Kehr (ed.), *Der Primat der Innenpolitik* (Berlin, de Gruyter, 1965), esp. 75–6; and Rueschemeyer, *Lawyers*, 175.

[35] Jacobsohn, 'Einzug'.

[36] S. Feuchtwanger, *Die freien Berufe. Im Besonderen: Die Anwaltschaft. Versuch einer allgemeinen Kulturlehre* (Munich and Leipzig, Duncker und Humblot, 1922), 165 f.

ening of liberalism, splintered internally and unable to come to terms
with the rising socialist movement, as well as the rising anti-Semitism
inside the Bar and outside foreshadowed the catastrophic developments
in Germany another long generation later, though there is nothing in
the politics of Imperial Germany nor in its legal profession that made
that outcome inevitable.

Reflections and Comments

Why should anybody be interested in the Prussian Bar and its development over a period of two centuries? Even the effort of reading a
brief essay must be justified by broader concerns. What, then, are some
of the wider implications of the story told—for our understanding of
the law as a profession, of the role of the state in structuring law work,
of the impact of capitalist development, of the relation between law
work and a liberalization of politics, and of the historically specific contexts in which these developments take place?

1.   The failed experiment of 1781—of excluding attorneys chosen
by the parties from court proceedings—shows that removing legal
counsel from the choice and trust of the parties simply does not work.
The episode has a parallel in the failed attempts to abolish the self-
employed Bar in the Soviet Union.
The fact that attorneys mediate between parties and the authoritative
system of adjudication gives them a basis of independence and autonomy that is separate from the explanations of professional autonomy
in the various available theories of the professions as expert occupations.
2.   That the Prussian Bar was for more than a century a body of
quasi-civil servants is an illustration of the provincialism of much
(Anglo-American) theorizing about the professions, be it of the structural–functional or the more conflict- and market-oriented variety.
State control is an important alternative to collective self-organization
and to control by customers and the market.[37] To point to the drawbacks and tensions of this structure, particularly evident in the case of
legal counsel, does not diminish the point; rather, such arguments
typically betray a mistaken simplistic functionalism by presupposing
that a tension-ridden arrangement must be unstable.

[37] T. C. Johnson, *Professions and Power* (London, Macmillan, 1972); Rueschemeyer,
Lawyers, chap. 1.

3.   The tensions between bourgeois interests and the ideals of liberalism as well as the professional tasks of lawyers in the emerging capitalist society on the one hand and authoritarian state control on the other did eventually—beginning in the middle of the nineteenth century—lead to the movement for a 'free Bar'. Yet while the leadership of the Bar, together with other liberal political elites, demanded the change, emancipation was not granted in direct response to these demands. It came about as part of the restructuring of the German state after unification. Even aside from that, we must note that the Bar's leadership and its allies acted out of political motivations and for state-structural reasons.

That means that even the emancipation of the Prussian Bar, the major development in the history of the German legal profession that could be interpreted as a convergence towards professional self-control in response to capitalist development, was in significant part the result of relatively autonomous state action as well as political movements.

4.   The emancipation from state control coupled with open admission did, however, have increasing support within the profession, even though it obviously went against the financial self-interest of the profession. That the Prussian Bar followed its leadership in demanding the abolition of its privileged status puts into question the validity of market-oriented theories of the professions which see 'professional projects' as singularly motivated by material self-interest.

This actually has an echo in the history of the American bar: access to night schools was defended for long because law work was seen as politically significant and relatively open access to it was considered essential in a democratic society.

5.   The movement for the emancipation of the Bar has an interesting international dimension. Gneist especially, the most important leader of the movement in Prussia, had strong English orientations. Such an openness for, and orientation towards, foreign models is remarkable and must not be taken for granted. Law is, after all, a field closely tied to the particularities of state organization, and there were powerful movements in the nineteenth century, powerful both intellectually and politically, that viewed law and political structure as expressions of an organically grown national character and considered 'alien' imports and impositions with hostility.

Among the likely factors that supported taking foreign institutions as positive reference points, the following seem especially important:

(1) Due to the contrast between the political splintering of the German territories and the development of large-scale economic exchange, there was a sense among German intellectuals that a new legal–political order had to be prepared; this rendered the status quo less legitimate and its future peculiarly open.

(2) The opportunity for comparison inherent in the contrasts between different German states was equally important. It was enhanced by a university system that served all German territories and saw considerable circulation of students. Such intra-German comparisons could be extended to other states in Europe.

(3) Higher levels of wealth gave the institutions of England and France the prestige that goes with success and—in a historicist intellectual world—with being 'ahead' in social development.

(4) The universalism inherent in the ideas of liberalism made liberals more open to international comparison than conservatives emphasizing the organic growth of particular traditions.

6.   The fact that the movement for a 'free Bar' was embedded in the much broader liberal demand for a *Rechtsstaat* and that both were influenced by the international context suggests that most theories of the professions seek to explain professional projects in too narrow a fashion. Professions and professional politics must be seen in contexts that are both wider, more complex, and more variegated than the conditions and factors considered by the dominant positions in the analysis of the professions. The Prussian story suggests that the changing shape of the bar cannot be understood in isolation from the emergence of the bourgeoisie in the course of late capitalist development and its struggle to define its position vis-à-vis a powerful state ready to repress the political self-organization of society.

7.   The timing and sequence of historical developments matters. It was of critical importance for liberalism as well as for the Bar that bureaucratic rationalization of the state preceded general capitalist rationalization of the economy in Prussia and Germany.

It is this difference in sequence that seems to hold the key for the explanation of most contrasts between Anglo-American and continental European patterns in the organization of legal counsel as well as of other professional work. It explains why in the critical initial stages of capitalist development in Prussia legal counsel took a form seemingly at odds with the requirements of these developments in the economy.

That during the very constitutive phases of German capitalism the Prussian Bar was accused of a peculiar incompetence in business matters should give also pause to those who are inclined to make too simple functionalist inferences on what is *needed* for capitalist development.

8.   A related lesson concerns historical persistence. Once an institutional pattern is settled, it often persists beyond the conditions that brought it about and it may continue to shape attitudes and behaviour even after it has formally been abolished.[38]

The relative separation of Prussian (and German) lawyers in private practice from business involvement persisted beyond open admission and the attendant pressures to open new fields of practice. Patterns of practice forged in the years of the closed Civil Service Bar continued to shape later developments in spite of some changes (that are not as yet very well understood). The German Bar stayed much more closely to court-related work than the American Bar, and it retained significant traces of its civil service orientation.[39]

9.   The peculiar sequencing of different transformations in state, economy, and society probably also holds the key for explaining the development of German liberalism, a subject that is of central importance for understanding the changing shape of the Prussian legal profession but that clearly exceeded the space limitation of this brief essay.[40]

Aside from the fact that the bourgeoisie that emerged with late capitalist development had to face a strong and highly rationalized state bureaucracy, two other developments seem critical. First, the goal of overcoming the particularism of thirty-odd German states and sovereignties had to be pursued at the same time as the liberalization of political life. That probably accounts for a good deal of the failures, compromises, and splits which the liberal movement experienced in 1848, 1867, and in the 1880s and 1890s. Second, late and fast capitalist development as well as compromises with the ruling elites of the state made it more difficult for Prussian and German liberalism to come to terms with the rising power of the working class. German liberalism

---

[38] J. A. Schumpeter, *Capitalism, Socialism and Democracy*, 3rd edn. (New York, Harper and Row, 1950), 12.

[39] Rueschemeyer, *Lawyers*.

[40] Jarausch and Jones offer an excellent overview of the changing historiography of German liberalism and its relation to conceptions of the historical roots of National Socialist Germany. See K. H. Jarausch & L. E. Jones, 'German Liberalism Reconsidered: Inevitable Decline, Bourgeois Hegemony, or Partial Achievement?' in Jarausch & Jones (eds.), *In Search of a Liberal Germany*.

never made the transition that in the United States gives the 'L-word' its progressive character detested by the right. This is also reflected in the orientations of the Prussian and, more generally, the German Bar.

10.   The story of the Prussian Bar has perhaps also implications for the discussion about the German '*Sonderweg*', that is, about the question to what extent German nineteenth-century history already prefigured the later catastrophe of National Socialism. In the nineteenth century, many lawyers in Prussia and other German states, and especially many leaders of the Bar, showed an impressive commitment to liberal ideas. At the same time, the aftermath of open admission in a Bar accustomed to protection, a Civil Service ethos, and the attendant high standing led to developments in the Bar that fed eventually into the rejection of democracy and anti-Semitic Nazi policies. Yet one must be careful to resist a retrospective determinism that forgets the difficulty of predicting the future. In 1847, in 1867, in 1878, and even in 1918, the future was experienced as open, much as it is today, and more open than it may appear in retrospect. Bismarck's defeat of the liberal opposition in Prussia in 1867 was, after all, followed by ten years of impressive liberal achievements in the institutional construction of unified Germany.

7 Lawyers and the Limits of Liberalism: the German Bar in the Weimar Republic

Kenneth F. Ledford (Case Western Reserve University)

On Saturday, 22 April 1933, members of the lawyers' chamber for the Court of Appeal district of Celle convened in Hannover for a special meeting to elect a new Executive Board (*Vorstand*).[1] This extraordinary and irregular assembly met at the order of the Prussian Ministry of Justice in Berlin, which since 30 January had fallen under the control of the National Socialist party.[2] The sitting Executive Board had on 3 April refused the Ministry's demand to resign *en masse*, and it had further declined to accept the tendered resignation of its single Jewish member, 'in consideration of [his] long years of meritorious service'.[3] As a result, the Ministry of Justice had deposed the Executive Board and appointed a local National Socialist lawyer, Focko Meiborg, as 'Commissar' to run the lawyers' chamber until the 22 April meeting could be held to choose a new Board that would presumably be more

This paper is much revised from the version presented at the Oñati Conference in 1993, and I would like to thank the participants and other contributors to this volume for their helpful comments and suggestions. I wish also to thank my colleagues Catherine Kelly, Alan Rocke, and Jonathan Sadowsky, as well as Douglas Klusmeyer, for their close readings of earlier drafts.

[1] The lawyers' chamber (*Anwaltskammer*) for the Court of Appeals district (*Oberlandesgerichtsbezirk*) of Celle included all lawyers in the Prussian province of Hannover and the two principalities of Lippe. On 1 Jan. 1933, its total membership was 820 lawyers; 350 attended the meeting, an unusually large number. The summons to the meeting is found in Niedersächsisches Hauptstaatsarchiv Hannover (NHStA), Hann. 173, Acc. 30/87, Nr. 30, 'Geschäftsberichte', unnumbered loose leaves at front of folder. Accounts of the meeting may be found in the annual report of the lawyers' chamber for 1933, authored by the new National Socialist executive board, ibid., 110–19, 112, and in H. Mundt, *100 Jahre Rechtsanwaltskammer für den Oberlandesgerichtsbezirk Celle* (Hannover, n.p., 1979), 43–8.

[2] The history of the Reich and state Ministries of Justice is beginning to be told in extensive detail. See the massive work, L. Gruchmann, *Justiz im 'Dritten Reich' 1933–1940. Anpassung und Unterwerfung in der Ära Gürtner*, 2d edn. (Munich, Oldenbourg, 1990), as well as more focused contributions such as E. Nathans, *Franz Schlegelberger* (Baden-Baden, Nomos, 1990). For an overview of National Socialist attitudes towards law and justice, see D. L. Anderson, *The Academy for German Law, 1933–1944* (New York, Garland, 1987); see also K. C. H. Willig, 'The Theory and Administration of Justice in the Third Reich', unpub. Ph.D. diss., Univ. of Pennsylvania (1975).

[3] Vorstand der Anwaltskammer Celle an den Herrn Oberlandesgerichtspräsidenten (OLGP) Celle, 3 Apr. 1933, NHStA, Hann. 173, Acc. 30/87, Nr. 30, 91.

willing to 'take its part in the fulfilment of the great tasks that face the administration of justice in the new state'.[4]

At the express order of the Justice Minister, the assembly was open to the public, and in the intimidating presence of a large number of *Sturmabteilung* (SA) brown-shirts who lined the back of the courtroom where the meeting was held, the members of the lawyers' chamber elected a National Socialist-dominated slate, chaired by Meiborg.[5] Although a conservative lawyer from Hannover protested beforehand that the extraordinary meeting was irregular and illegal, particularly because it would be open to the public, and a second lawyer from Göttingen afterwards published an open letter to Meiborg declaring that the meeting violated all procedural rules, the new Executive Board remained in place.[6]

Similarly, the national organization of lawyers in private practice, the German Bar Association (*Deutscher Anwaltverein*, (DAV)) experienced 'co-ordination' (*Gleichschaltung*) at the hands of the National Socialists. Although the DAV had refused on 26 March to merge with the Nazi lawyers' auxiliary because DAV members who were Jewish would be excluded, Jewish members of the DAV executive board responded to requests from the non-Jewish members and resigned on 7 April. On 18 May the DAV corporately joined the Nazi group, and the bar association formally dissolved itself on 27 December 1933.[7]

---

[4] OLGP Celle an den Herrn Vorsitzenden des Vorstandes der Anwaltskammer Celle, 3 Apr. 1933, NHStA, Hann. 173, Acc. 30/87, Nr. 30, 88, and OLGP Celle an den Herrn Preußischen Justizminister (PJM) in Berlin, ibid., 92; the quotation comes from PJM an den Herrn OLGP, 11 Apr. 1933, ibid., unnumbered loose leaves.

[5] For the order that the meeting be open to the public, see PJM an den Herrn OLGP, 11 Apr. 1933, ibid., unnumbered loose leaves, see also the invitation to the meeting, ibid., and the results of the election reported to Berlin on 24 Apr., ibid. 102–3. A useful account can also be found in Mundt, *100 Jahre Rechtsanwaltskammer*, 47–8.

[6] Rechtsanwalt Otto Kleinrath an den Herrn PJM, 20 Apr. 1933, Ibid., 97; and Briefwechsel mit dem Kommissar für den Vorstand der Anwaltskammer Celle, Herrn Rechtsanwalt Meiborg in Celle, zur Kenntnis. Rechtsanwalt Friedrich-Karl Walbaum, ibid., 104. Kleinrath specifically added that his objection was lodged 'with the consent of the [local] leadership of the German National People's Party [*Deutschnationale Volkspartei* (DNVP)]'. Gripping accounts of co-ordination of the lawyers' chamber in Berlin, and a summary of events elsewhere, can be found in Tillmann Krach, *Jüdische Rechtsanwälte in Preußen. Bedeutung und Zerstörung der freien Advokatur* (Munich, Beck, 1991), 215–23.

[7] The National Socialist lawyers' auxiliary, the Federation of National Socialist German Jurists (*Bund nationalsozialistischer Deutscher Juristen* (BNSDJ)), never had a very large membership prior to 1933. Only 253 lawyers had joined by 1 Oct. 1931, and Konrad Jarausch estimates that only 5% of the members of the bar, fewer than 1,000, had joined prior to 1933; K. H. Jarausch, *The Unfree Professions: German Lawyers, Teachers, and Engineers, 1900–1950* (Oxford, Oxford Univ. Press, 1990), 102, 109, Table A.16 at

Like many aspects of the National Socialist seizure of power, the easy success of the co-ordination campaign aimed at German lawyers in private practice has puzzled historians. Lawyers in Germany had long been allied with political liberalism, conceiving of themselves, and being perceived by liberals, as the particular bearers and guarantors of the main achievement of German liberalism, the *Rechtsstaat*, the state ruled by law. For lawyers to succumb so easily to the procedural irregularity and illiberalism of National Socialist co-ordination, something must have gone powerfully wrong.

Some historians seek an explanation in the link between German Jews and liberal doctrine, contending that elimination of Jewish leaders of the bar decapitated the liberal leadership among practitioners and placed the rudderless bar at the mercy of National Socialist activists.[8] Others lump private practitioners in with the broader class of university-trained jurists, steeped in monarchist and nationalist culture through university life and military training, most of whom were at best only temporarily reconciled to the Republic and at worst actively hostile to it.[9] Finally, more recent studies of the experience of professionals through the Second Empire, Weimar Republic, and Third Reich emphasize the very real financial distress of lawyers caused by the general economic exigencies of the 1920s and early 1930s, which coincided with professional overcrowding caused by vastly increasing numbers of

254. Krach, *Jüdische Rechtsanwälte*, 146–51, concludes that: 'The resonance [for the foundation of the BNSDJ] was apparently slight.'

Accounts of the co-ordination of the DAV can be found in F. Ostler, *Die deutschen Rechtsanwälte, 1871–1971*, 2d edn. (Essen, Juristische Fachbuchverlag, 1982), 229–35; Krach, *Jüdische Rechtsanwälte*, 223–36, esp. 223–32, H. Göppinger, *Juristen jüdischer Abstammung im 'Dritten Reich'. Entrechtung und Verfolgung*, 2d edn. (Munich, Beck, 1990), 118–21; and Jarausch, *Unfree Professions*, 116–19, concludes, 'In order to preserve their profession, lawyers sacrificed their liberal tradition and vaunted autonomy with astonishing alacrity.'

[8] I. Müller, *Hitler's Justice: The Courts of the Third Reich*, D. L. Schneider (trans.), (Cambridge, Mass., Harvard University Press, 1991), chap. 8, 'Purges at the Bar', 59–67.

[9] The focus on the political conservatism of the German judiciary during Weimar dates to contemporary observations; see E. Fraenkel, *Zur Soziologie der Klassenjustiz* (Berlin, 1927; repr. edn., Darmstadt, Wissenschaftliche Buchgesellschaft, 1968) and T. Rasehorn, *Justizkritik in der Weimarer Republik. Das Beispiel der Zeitschrift 'Der Justiz'* (Frankfurt, Campus, 1985). See also R. Angermund, *Deutsche Richterschaft 1919–1945. Krisenerfahrung, Illusion, politische Rechtsprechung* (Frankfurt, Fischer, 1990), and R. Dreier & W. Sellert (eds.), *Recht und Justiz im 'Dritten Reich'* (Frankfurt, Surhkamp, 1989). For radical nationalism and the illiberal milieu of university life, especially in the legal faculties, see K. H. Jarausch, *Students, Society and Politics in Imperial Germany: The Rise of Academic Illiberalism* (Princeton, Princeton Univ. Press, 1982).

legal graduates and private practitioners.[10] Konrad Jarausch argues that the alliance between German lawyers and liberalism dissolved amidst cumulative crises of hyper-inflation, stabilization, and depression. Lawyers abandoned liberal practices in their professional governance, embraced neo-conservative and even *völkisch* ideas in the general cultural realm, and rejected liberalism in the political realm.[11]

Focus upon the drama of the first months of 1933 and upon the economic dislocations of 1929–33 has masked the larger story of the relationship of the German bar in private practice with political liberalism from the 1830s to 1933 and the generalized crisis of liberal ideologies and institutions in the 1920s. This essay will argue instead that German lawyers did not abandon liberalism so much as they ran out of solutions when their liberal practices failed at every turn to protect their professional interests. Swift co-ordination occurred because the ideological and institutional structures of the bar, like those of political liberalism, proved incapable of accommodating new substantive notions of justice, unfamiliar activism from different government agencies, and paralysing conflict in internal professional affairs. The procedural approach of lawyers to problem-solving and the elite-dominated institution of the bar, both products and symptoms of liberalism, simply failed to offer effective solutions to the wide array of conflicts that confronted lawyers between 1919 and 1933.

Two factors united the trajectories of the legal profession and political liberalism. The first was the crucial importance to each of proceduralism, most succinctly expressed in the German conception of the *Rechtsstaat*, the aim of which was to bind actions of the state within prescribed rules that would render its acts predictable, universal, and certain.[12] In fact, a workable definition of liberalism is the political doctrine that stresses the creation of a set of more or less fair, but uni-

---

[10] Jarausch, *Unfree Professions*, and C. E. McClelland, *The German Experience of Professionalization. Modern Learned Professions and their Organizations from the Early Nineteenth Century to the Hitler Era* (Cambridge, Cambridge Univ. Press, 1991).

[11] K. H. Jarausch, 'The Decline of Liberal Professionalism: Reflections on the Social Erosion of German Liberalism, 1867–1933', in K. H. Jarausch & L. E. Jones (eds.), *In Search of a Liberal Germany: Studies in the History of German Liberalism from 1789 to the Present* (New York, Oxford, and Munich, Berg Publishers, 1990), 261–86 at 284.

[12] The standard work on the equivocal nature of the German conception of the *Rechtsstaat* remains L. Krieger, *The German Idea of Freedom: History of a Political Tradition* (Chicago, Univ. of Chicago Press, 1957), esp. 252–61. See also E.-W. Böckenförde, 'The Origin and Development of the Concept of *Rechtsstaat*', in E.-W. Böckenförde, *State, Society, and Liberty: Studies in Political Theory and Constitutional Law*, J. A. Underwood (trans), (New York, Berg Publishers, 1991), 47–70.

form, known, and certain, procedures to constrain the state and within which many competing notions of justice or the good life can compete.[13] The centrality of the *Rechtsstaat* to the German liberal project constructed an affinity between the procedural analytical idea-systems of legal practitioners and the proceduralism of political liberalism.[14] Liberals seized upon the importance of an independent private legal profession to a liberal political culture as they pursued a legal reform programme to secure the *Rechtsstaat*, and lawyers in turn embraced and promoted the belief that their campaign to reform the structure of their profession advanced the general interest of society. The liberal agenda of lawyers as social bearers of the *Rechtsstaat* complemented the aspirations of private practitioners for increased status and independence; lawyers' professional project merged with liberalism's social and political project.[15]

In 1877–9, the Reichstag enacted into law the Imperial Justice Laws, which embodied profound reforms of court organization, civil and criminal trial procedure, and the structure of the legal profession.[16] But this great legislative victory proved to be the high-water mark of the power of political liberalism in Germany after unification.[17] In 1878

[13] M. J. Sandel, *Liberalism and the Limits of Justice* (Cambridge, Cambridge Univ. Press, 1982), 113–22. Sandel's book is an extended critique of the liberal doctrine of J. Rawls, *A Theory of Justice* (Oxford, Oxford Univ. Press, 1971). This very constrained definition of liberalism is advanced as an alternative to dismissing the term as meaningless or arbitrary by J. Breuilly, 'State-Building, Modernization and Liberalism from the Late Eighteenth Century to Unification: German Peculiarities', *European Hist. Q.* 22 (1992), 257–84 at 277.

[14] D. J. Gerber, 'Idea-Systems in Law. Images of Nineteenth-Century Germany', *Law & Hist. Rev.* 10 (1992), 153–67, uses the term 'idea-system' to denote a relatively autonomous, systematically-related set of ideas that can be conceived of as an organic entity. I use it here simply as shorthand for the procedural analytical approach of modern lawyers.

[15] The concept of 'professional project' comes from the structuralist sociological account, M. Sarfatti-Larson, *The Rise of Professionalism: A Sociological Analysis* (Berkeley: Univ. of California Press, 1977). Interesting reflections on the connection between the 'middle-class project' of liberalism and the professional project can be found in H. Siegrist, 'Bürgerliche Berufe. Die Professionen und das Bürgertum', in H. Siegrist (ed.), *Bürgerliche Berufe. Zur Sozialgeschichte der freien und akademischen Berufe im internationalen Vergleich* (Göttingen, Vandenhoeck & Ruprecht, 1988), 11–48.

[16] For a discussion of the background to the adoption of the Imperial Justice Laws, see K. F. Ledford, 'Lawyers, Liberalism, and Procedure: The German Imperial Justice Laws of 1877–79', *Central European Hist.* 26 (1994), 165–93.

[17] D. Langewiesche, 'German Liberalism in the Second Empire, 1871–1914', in Jarausch & Jones (eds.), *In Search of a Liberal Germany*, 217-35, 218, argues that: 'The normalization of political life in the German national state meant that the liberals could lose their exceptional position, that they would be transformed from the embodiment of the whole national movement to simply one party among others.'

and again in 1879, German political liberalism suffered new and deeper fissures in debates over the adoption of protective tariffs and repressive legislation against emergent Social Democracy, and the deeply divided movement suffered shattering electoral reverses that caused it to fragment further and weakened its influence decisively. For the bar in private practice, though, 1879 signalled the beginning of their new institutional history and the second vital link between lawyers and liberalism. The private bar built for itself institutions that mirrored the strengths and weaknesses of those of German liberal political parties. Both shared the elite, deference-based structure of the organization of notables.[18] From this institutional framework, lawyers constructed a liberal professional ideology and established comfortable relations with bureaucracy and legislature before 1918 that brought predictability and a high degree of success to their efforts to promote the interests of the profession. The organization of notables signified the conviction and posture of lawyers that they stood above interest and represented the common good rather than private gain, specifically that they were the Hegelian 'general estate'. This elitist and deference-based institutional structure, however, proved inadequate to an age of special-interest-group politics.

The same reforms of the profession brought about great change within the profession. Open admission led to rapid growth of the bar and to new concerns about overcrowding.[19] Social groups that had formerly been excluded or that had formerly avoided legal study now flocked to the bar.[20] Social change and market pressures forced lawyers

[18] The term in German is *Honoratiorenorganisation*, and the concept is defined best by T. Nipperdey in 'Verein als soziale Struktur im späten 18 und frühen 19. Jahrhundert', in H. Boockmann *et al.* (eds.), *Geschichtswissenschaft und Vereinswesen im 19. Jahrhundert* (Göttingen, Vandenhoeck & Ruprecht, 1972), 1–44. This builds upon his analysis of the structure of political parties, *Honoratiorenpolitik* in H. Boockmann, *Die Organisation der deutschen Parteien vor 1918* (Düsseldorf, Droste, 1961). G. Eley explicates the challenges confronted by liberal parties organized on the basis of the politics of notables in 'Notable Politics, the Crisis of German Liberalism, and the Electoral Transition of the 1890s', in Jarausch & Jones (eds.), *In Search of a Liberal Germany*, 187–216; and G. Eley, *Reshaping the German Right. Radical Nationalism and Political Change after Bismarck* (New Haven, Yale Univ. Press, 1980), 19–40.

[19] The number of lawyers in Germany expanded from 4,091 in 1880 to 6,800 in 1901, to 12,297 in 1913, to 18,036 in 1932; see Table A.5a, 'Increase in Attorneys: German Lawyers', in Jarausch, *Unfree Professions*, 238. See also K. F. Ledford, *From General Estate to Special Interest: German Lawyers 1878–1933* (Cambridge, Cambridge Univ. Press, 1996).

[20] Although the story of the social diversification of the bar is complex, it may be summarized as an increase in the proportion of sons of businessmen and university-trained professionals other than lawyers, and a decrease in the proportion of sons of lawyers and government officials, especially in district court towns and large cities; see Ledford, *From General Estate to Special Interest*, Tables 5.3–5.6, 147–50, and text at 143–9. For the influx

into new career paths, which led to internal conflicts within the bar. Contradictory interests among different groups of lawyers began to emerge, giving rise to competing and conflicting special-interest organizations which challenged existing arrangements within professional institutions. These competing interest groups began to seek resolutions to the conflicts, both within the profession and by resort to institutions of the state, bureaucracy, and legislature. The upheavals and dislocations of the First World War and the revolution ensured that during the Weimar Republic, the bar would have to come to grips with the new realities of its composition and of the circumstances in which it had to operate.

During the Second Empire (1871–1918), the German bar maintained comfortable relations with the monarchical state. Legislation that affected the profession emerged from the Imperial Office (later Ministry) of Justice, although most of the drafting occurred in the Prussian Ministry of Justice. The bar cultivated close relationships with both bureaucracies, and the important role of lawyers in the leadership of the liberal parties in the Reichstag ensured them a second line of influence on any legislation in that body.[21] When the empire collapsed in November 1918 and the Weimar Republic came into being in 1919, the upheaval not only swept away the monarchies and the comfortable relationships that had developed between the bar and the Ministries of Justice but also had profound political consequences for the liberal parties with which lawyers had been most closely identified. The Social Democratic Party of Germany (*Sozialdemokratische Partei Deutschlands*, (SPD)), whose constituency consisted almost entirely of industrial workers, and the Catholic Centre Party (*Zentrum*) constituted the largest parties of the Weimar era, and neither had strong appeal for lawyers. The two liberal parties, the German Democratic Party (*Deutsche Demokratische Partei*, (DDP)) and the German People's Party (*Deutsche Volkspartei*, (DVP)) drew significant initial electoral support, especially the DDP in 1919 and the DVP in the mid-1920s, but by 1932 and the economic crisis, the two parties between them drew less than 2 per cent of the

---

of Jews to the bar after 1878, because of continued discrimination in other fields of practice such as administration and the judiciary, see Krach, *Jüdische Rechtsanwälte*, 14–32, and K. H. Jarausch, 'Jewish Lawyers in Germany, 1848–1938—The Disintegration of a Profession', *Leo Baeck Institute Year Book* 36 (1991), 171–90.

[21] Lawyers regularly discussed any proposed revisions to procedural law and the lawyers' code in their biennial conventions, and the executive board of the DAV made formal submissions to the Imperial or Prussian Ministries of Justice; see e.g. Ostler, *Die deutschen Rechtsanwälte*, 39–46.

popular vote.[22] During the Weimar Republic, then, German lawyers faced a political situation in which the two largest parties pursued either socialist or organic-corporatist policies in the interests of electoral constituencies alien to lawyers. Moreover, the liberal parties that had provided lawyers both an ideological home and a springboard into public life suffered severe erosion of their electoral and social bases and hence their governmental influence. The story of the travails of the German liberal political parties between 1871 and 1933 is familiar and well-told.[23] This essay will focus instead upon the less-well-known but parallel story of lawyers in private practice.

Lawyers, Liberalism, and Procedure: the *Rechtsstaat*.

When Hegel, in *The Philosophy of Right*, identified state officials as the 'universal class' or 'general estate', representing the 'universal interests of the community' in both civil society and state, Prussian law already required higher state officials to possess university training in law.[24] But the retreat from state-initiated reform begun in 1819 sent liberals looking for another social bearer of the general interest, one more independent from political control and tutelage. Some fastened upon the judiciary, building upon separation-of-powers arguments in favour of judicial independence.[25] Others, from the 1830s into the twentieth cen-

---

[22] The definitive work on the liberal parties during Weimar is L. E. Jones, *German Liberalism and the Dissolution of the Weimar Party System 1918–1933* (Chapel Hill, Univ. of North Carolina Press, 1988). See also D. Langewiesche, *Liberalismus in Deutschland* (Frankfurt, Suhrkamp, 1988), 240–86, and Table 16: 'Reichstagswahlen in der Weimarer Republik', 334.

[23] Besides Jones, *German Liberalism*, and Langewiesche, *Liberalismus*, for the period up to 1918, see also J. J. Sheehan, *German Liberalism in the Nineteenth Century* (Chicago, Univ. of Chicago Press, 1978).

[24] See R. Koselleck, *Preußen zwischen Reform und Revolution. Allgemeines Landrecht, Verwaltung und soziale Bewegung vom 1791 bis 1848* (Stuttgart, Ernst Klett, 1967), esp. 87–115; G. W. F. Hegel, *Hegel's Philosophy of Right*, T. M. Knox (trans. and ed.), (Oxford, Oxford Univ. Press, 1952), ¶¶ 205, 303, (at 132, 197–8). Hegel published *Philosophy of Right* in 1821; all candidates for higher administrative positions in the Prussian bureaucracy were required from 1817 onwards to have completed at least three years' study of law at a German university. For the history of the requirement that state officials be trained as lawyers, see W. Bleek, *Von der Kameralausbildung zum Juristenprivileg*, Historische und Pädagogische Studien, Bd. 3 (Berlin, Colloquium, 1972). See also J. R. Gillis, *The Prussian Bureaucracy in Crisis 1840–1860: Origins of an Administrative Ethos* (Stanford, Stanford Univ. Press, 1971).

[25] C. von Rotteck voiced his belief in the central importance of an independent judiciary to freedom: '[I]f the independence of the courts and the secure position of the judge ever ceases, . . . then it would be better that society dissolved itself and that its members sought in the rights of self-defence that exist in the state of nature substitutes

tury, came to be convinced that lawyers in private practice, once established as independent from state control, could tutor Germans in the
skills of citizenship, reform German society, and fulfil a natural affinity
for political leadership.[26]

Carl Josef Anton Mittermaier stressed in 1832 that through their
professional role as advocates, each lawyer served 'as adviser to those
in need of aid, as representative of the afflicted, as control of judges, as
eternally watchful protector of all oppressed, as translator of judgments
once handed down, as explicator of the law'.[27] But lawyers' liberal
political role did not stop with their professional practice. Experience
gained in practice, Friedrich List argued in 1834, gave lawyers 'the high
calling to instruct the people in their rights and duties, to perfect the
state of the law, to develop legal doctrine ever further, and always to
keep it attuned to the general culture of the people'.[28] By 1867, Rudolf
von Gneist, a chief theorist of the *Rechtsstaat*, contended that lawyers in
private practice were 'the Archimedian point' from which German
society would be moved towards self-government. '[T]he free practising bar means nothing less than the precondition for all independence
of communal life, of self-government, of constitutional life on the largest
scale.'[29]

If liberalism had need for lawyers, nineteenth-century observers
firmly believed that lawyers conversely had an affinity for liberalism.[30]

for the guaranties of rights that the state has failed to give.' (C. von Rotteck, 'Justiz', in
C. von Rotteck & C. Welcker (eds.), *Staats-Lexikon oder Encyklopädie der Staatswissenschaften*,
(15 vols., Altona, Verlag von Johann Friedrich Hammerich, 1834–43), vol. VIII (1839),
720–56, 756).

[26] L. O'Boyle describes the normative argument about the political role of lawyers in
the *Vormärz*: 'For both liberals and democrats, the case of the lawyers became the focus
of wider political considerations. An improvement in the lawyers' status was seen as inseparable from the extension of political liberty . . . [O]nly an honored and independent
legal profession could teach the public the meaning of government under law. The
lawyers came to be regarded by many not only as possible but as necessary allies in the
struggle for free government.' (L. O'Boyle, 'The Democratic Left in Germany, 1848',
Jrnl. Mod. Hist. 33 (1961), 374–83 at 379.)

[27] C. J. Anton Mittermaier, 'Die künftige Stellung des Advokatenstandes', *Archiv für die
civilistische Praxis* 15 (1832), 138–50 at 138–9. (Author's translation.)

[28] F. List, 'Advokat', in von Rotteck & Welcker (eds.), *Staats-Lexikon*, vol. I (1834),
363–77, 366.

[29] R. Gneist, *Freie Advocatur. Die erste Forderung aller Justizreform in Preußen* (Berlin, Julius
Springer, 1867), 49, 70. (Author's translation.) Gneist was Professor of Law at Berlin,
National Liberal delegate to the Reichstag, and a founding member of the *Verein für
Sozialpolitik*.

[30] Observers since Burke and Tocqueville have been convinced that French lawyers
as a group supported the Revolution; E. Burke, *Reflections on the Revolution in France* (Garden
City, NY, Anchor Books, 1973), 54, and A. Tocqueville, *Democracy in America*, J. P. Smith

This conviction persisted into the twentieth century, with some evidence. Lawyers had played a prominent role in the German National Assembly of 1848–9, and many leaders of the National Liberal and Progressive Parties (the two principal liberal parties in the German political spectrum) prior to the First World War were private practitioners.[31] Thus lawyers very much embraced the programme of political liberalism as the vehicle to attain personal and professional security in a realm safe from the interfering reach of the tutelary state. At the beginning of the 1920s, Max Weber still believed that lawyers had a particular calling for politics and for political liberalism:

[L]egal rationalism had its great representative in the lawyers in private practice of the era of the French Revolution. The modern lawyer in private practice and modern democracy plainly belong together since that time . . . The importance of lawyers in private practice since the rise of political parties is no accident. The management of politics through political parties simply means management by interest groups . . . And it is the craft of the trained lawyer in private practice to conduct a case effectively for an interested party.[32]

(ed.), G. Lawrence (trans.), (2 vols., New York, Anchor Books, 1945), vol. I, 284–5. For more nuanced arguments, see L. R. Berlanstein, *The Barristers of Toulouse* (Baltimore, Johns Hopkins Univ. Press, 1975), 148–82; M. P. Fitzsimmons, *The Parisian Order of Barristers and the French Revolution* (Cambridge, Mass., Harvard Univ. Press, 1987), 196–8; D. A. Bell, 'Barristers, Politics, and the Failure of Civil Society in Old Regime France', chap. 2 *supra*; and D. A. Bell, *Lawyers and Citizens: The Making of a Political Elite in Old Regime France* (New York, Oxford Univ. Press, 1994). See also A. Weißler, *Geschichte der Rechtsanwaltschaft* (Leipzig, Pfeffer, 1905), 458.

[31] At the German National Assembly in Frankfurt in 1848–9, 445 of the 812 delegates and substitutes were *Volljuristen*, who had completed legal studies and pursued some kind of legal career. W. Siemann, *Die Frankfurter Nationalversammlung 1848/49 zwischen demokratischem Liberalismus und konservativer Reform. Die Bedeutung der Juristendominanz in den Verfassungsverhandlungen des Paulskirchenparlaments* (Frankfurt, Peter Lang, 1976), 33-4. See also F. Eyck, *The Frankfurt Parliament 1848–1849* (London, Macmillan, 1968), 57–102, esp. Table 1 at 95.

Among the liberal parties in the Reichstag, the preponderance of lawyers was striking. Out of the 120 National Liberal deputies in the first Reichstag (1871), 17 were lawyers in private practice; 19 of 152 in the second (1874); 12 of 127 in the third (1877) and 10 of 98 in the fourth (1878). The numbers fell in the 1880s but rose again to 9 out of 44 in 1912. Similarly, 12 out of 42 Progressive Party deputies in the Reichstag in 1912 were private practitioners. W. Kremer, 'Die soziale Aufbau der Parteiein des Deutschen Reichstages von 1871–1918', unpub. Dr. jur. diss., Univ. of Cologne (1934), 13–14, 46–47. See also the summary tables drawn from Kremer in Langewiesche, *Liberalismus*, Table 7, 312–13, and in Sheehan, *German Liberalism*, 239–41.

[32] M. Weber, 'Politik als Beruf', in J. Winckelmann (ed.), *Max Weber. Gesammelte politische Schriften*, 5th edn. (Tübingen, J. C. B. Mohr [P. Siebeck], 1988), 505–60, 522–3, 524 (Author's translation). The trans. by H. H. Gerth & C. Wright Mills does not effectively highlight the distinction that Weber is making between persons trained at university in the law, only roughly one-quarter of whom engage in private practice in Germany

Thus, by the very nature of their professional training, in modern society lawyers had a special role to play in political leadership and more specifically in the leadership of liberal political parties.

Besides the affinity of lawyers for liberalism, both the profession and the ideology shared an emphasis upon proceduralism, upon formalism, and the junction of professional and political discourse lay in the *Rechtsstaat.* Modern Western legal systems make a fundamental distinction between substance and procedure in law. Substantive law defines the rights and duties of individuals towards each other and the state and prescribes the rules of conduct that promote the welfare and security of society. Procedural law sets out the process by which substantive law is enforced; it does not define rights or duties, but merely specifies the procedures to implement them, providing predictability and regularity of outcome.[33] Lawyers accept substantive law as a given, provided by the legislature or by jurisprudence. Their job as lawyers is to find the applicable substantive law, but most importantly to manoeuvre their client's case, through skilful manipulation of procedural law, into the posture that presents it in the best light and offers the greatest chance of success.

In modern systems of formally rational law, the regularity, uniformity, and generality of procedure legitimates the entire legal order.[34] Theories of the rule of law central to liberalism emerged in the nineteenth century as profoundly procedural constructs.[35] As Niklas

(Juristen) and lawyers in private practice *(Advokaten)*. M. Weber, 'Politics as a Vocation', in H. H. Gerth & C. Wright Mills, *From Max Weber: Essays in Sociology* (Oxford, Oxford Univ. Press, 1946), 77–128, 93–4, 94–5.

[33] M. D. Green, *Basic Civil Procedure*, 2d edn. (Mineola, NY, Foundation Press, 1979), 5–6. In German, the distinction is framed in the opposition of *materielles Recht*, material law, the norms that order the law as such, and *formelles Recht*, formal law, the norms that serve to carry out the material law; the former corresponds to substantive law and the latter to procedural law. See the entry 'Recht', in C. Creifelds, *Rechtswörterbuch*, 8th edn., (Munich, Beck, 1986), 897–8 at 898.

[34] Although J. Habermas criticized Weber's conception of the modern legal order in *Theory of Communicative Action*, T. McCarthy (trans.), (2 vols., Boston, Beacon Press, 1984), vol. 2, *Reason and the Rationalization of Society*, 254–71, esp. 264–5, as overly-formal, Habermas's own reading of Weber's sociology of law is subject to challenge: S. Ewing, 'Formal Justice and the Spirit of Capitalism: Max Weber's Sociology of Law', *Law and Social Inquiry* 21 (1987), 487–512, 506–11.

[35] The principal English theorist of the Rule of Law argued that the essence of that concept was the provision of procedures to pursue remedies to vindicate individual rights: 'The *Habeas Corpus* acts declare no principle and define no rights, but they are for practical purposes worth a hundred constitutional articles guaranteeing individual liberty.' A. V. Dicey, *Introduction to the Study of the Law of the Constitution*, 3rd edn., (London, Macmillan, 1889), 184–9, 187. Judith Shklar pointed out that regularity of criminal

Luhmann argues, procedure serves the same role in the public sphere of the state that contract serves in the private sphere of society: it is the magic formula that assures the greatest measure of security and freedom.[36] Liberalism enshrines procedural right over substantive determination of good as the chief goal of the state, increasing the affinity between legal forms of thinking and liberal doctrine.[37] The importance of procedure in the legal thought in which German lawyers were trained and in the legal order in which they were socialized combined with the procedural nature of liberalism to reinforce their affinity to identify with political liberalism.

The German conception of the *Rechtsstaat* shares the substantive-procedural dichotomy.[38] Emerging in German political and constitutional theory after 1815, *Rechtsstaat* doctrine had shifted by the middle of the nineteenth century from the prescription of the purposes of the state to the prescription of the outer forms of state action.[39] Even liberals accepted the distinctly procedural formulation of conservative theorist Friedrich Julius Stahl: '[The *Rechtsstaat*] signifies above all not the aim and content of the state, but only the method and nature of their real-

---

procedure was what Montesquieu's Rule of Law was all about, and that Dicey hollowed the inquiry out even further, to look only at the forms of juridical rigour rather than its structure or purposes; J. Shklar, 'Political Theory and the Rule of Law', in A. C. Hutchinson & P. Monahan (eds.), *The Rule of Law. Ideal or Ideology* (Toronto, Carswell, 1987), 1–16 at 5, 6.

[36] N. Luhmann, *Legitimation durch Verfahren* (Neuwied, Luchterhand, 1969), 7, and esp. 55–135 on 'Gerichtsverfahren'.

[37] M. J. Sandel, 'The Procedural Republic and the Unencumbered Self', *Political Theory* 12 (1984), 81–96, reprinted in S. Avineri & A. de-Shalit (eds.), *Communitarianism and Individualism* (Oxford, Oxford Univ. Press, 1992), 12–28.

[38] The most accessible brief history of German *Rechtsstaat* doctrine is Böckendörde, 'Origin and Development of the *Rechtsstaat*'. The concept of the *Rechtsstaat* is similar to, but distinguishable from, the Anglo-American doctrine of the rule of law; ibid., 48, n. 3. For the importance of this distinction, see H. J. Berman, 'The Rule of Law and the Law-Based State with Special Reference to the Soviet Union', in D. D. Barry (ed.), *Toward the 'Rule of Law' in Russia? Political and Legal Reform in the Transition Period* (Armonk, NY, M. E. Sharpe, 1992), 43–60.

[39] In addition to Krieger, *The German Idea of Freedom*, 252–3, see F. Neumann, *The Rule of Law. Political Theory and the Legal System in Modern Society* (Leamington Spa, Berg Publishers, 1986), 179–82, 180. For a discussion of the legalism of German liberal theory, especially the 'Juridical Conception of the State', see G. de Ruggiero, *The History of European Liberalism*, R. G. Collingwood (trans.), (Oxford, Oxford Univ. Press, 1927; reprint ed. Gloucester, Mass., Peter Smith, 1981), 251–64. O. Pflanze makes a similar argument about German liberalism in 'Juridical and Political Responsibility in Nineteenth-Century Germany', in L. Krieger & F. Stern (eds.), *The Responsibility of Power: Historical Essays in Honor of Hajo Holborn* (New York, Doubleday, 1967), 162–82.

ization.'[40] By the 1870s, the *Rechtsstaat* meant 'simply the kind of state whose power was articulated in legal modes of action—that is, in measures which conformed to general rules'.[41] The procedural conception of *Rechtsstaat* doctrine held by German liberalism thus meshed neatly with lawyerly emphasis on the primacy of procedure. With the enactment of the Imperial Justice Laws in 1877–9, almost entirely the handiwork of lawyer-politicians in the National Liberal and Progressive Parties, the work of liberalism in creating the *Rechtsstaat* reached its first climax.[42]

Institutions of the Bar

The Imperial Justice Laws of 1877–9 consisted of a uniform, national court organization law, national codes of criminal and civil procedure, and a lawyers' statute governing the organization of the bar, and they represented the culmination of thirty years of agitation and eight years of hard legislative work. The Lawyers' Statute had been a particular goal both of lawyers and liberals, for Gneist and others had seen in the reform of the legal profession the key to the reform of German state and society. In the eyes of both groups, the German bar needed profound reform. Even after unification, each of the multifarious German states had a separate system of governance of lawyers, and the largest state, Prussia, maintained strict limitations upon the number of practitioners admitted to the bar at each court (a system called *numerus clausus*), subjected lawyers to demeaning discipline at the hands of the judiciary or the Ministry of Justice, limited their fees to amounts decided upon at the discretion of judges, and treated lawyers as state-official-like (*beamtenähnlich*) and hence an appendage of the state justice

---

[40] F. J. Stahl, *Die Philosophie des Rechts*, vol. 2, *Rechts- und Staatslehre auf der Grundlage christlicher Weltanschauung*, 3rd edn., (Heidelberg, J. C. B. Mohr, 1856), 137, quoted in Neumann, *The Rule of Law*, 180, n. 6.

[41] Krieger, *German Idea of Freedom*, 459–60, quotation from 460. Others share this criticism of Gneist's narrow conception; see E. J. C. Hahn, 'Rudolf Gneist and the Prussian *Reichsstaat*: 1862–1878', *Jrnl. Mod. Hist.* 49 (Dec. 1977), D1361–81, and at greater length, E. J. C. Hahn, 'Rudolf von Gneist (1816–1895). The Political Ideas and Political Activity of a Prussian Liberal in the Bismarck Period', unpub. Ph.D. diss., Yale University (1971).

[42] See Ledford, 'Lawyers, Liberalism, and Procedure', and Michael John, *Politics and the Law in Late Nineteenth-Century Germany: The Origins of the Civil Code* (Oxford, Clarendon Press, 1989). The title of John's earlier dissertation, 'The Final Unification of Germany: Politics and the Codification of German Civil Law in the *Bürgerliches Gesetzbuch* of 1896', unpub. D.Phil. diss., Univ. of Oxford (1983), captures for substantive law the same sense of accomplishment that liberals felt with regard to procedural law with the enactment of the Imperial Justice Laws.

apparatus.[43] Lawyers quite naturally chafed under many of these restrictions, not without perceiving the benefits as well as the detriments of the *numerus clausus*, but their desire for professional self-governance and administration of discipline combined with their general attraction to liberal economic and political doctrine to cause them to agitate for change.[44] To liberals, the need to create an independent, self-governing, and self-reliant bar appropriate to the great normative role of lawyers as educators of the German people appeared self-evident.

The fundamental principle upon which the Lawyers' Statute was based was freedom of advocacy, *freie Advokatur*: abolition of the *numerus clausus* and free entry into the profession for all who had completed three years' study of law at a German university, passed two state bar examinations, and fulfilled a three-year period of unpaid practical legal training (*Referendariat*); organization of the lawyers in the district of each court of appeals into lawyers' chambers, membership in which was mandatory, and which had powers of self-administration and of disciplinary jurisdiction over their members; and fees based upon a legislatively-adopted statute for lawyers' fees, freeing lawyers from judicial discretion in awarding fees.[45] Upon admission to the bar, each lawyer could choose freely to practise before any court in Germany, but the law also required that lawyer to live in the city or town in which that

[43] For the development of the private practice of law in Germany, see the early history by Weißler, *Geschichte der Rechtsanwaltschaft* and Ledford, *From General Estate to Special Interest*, see also D. Rueschemeyer, *Lawyers and Their Society: A Comparative Study of the Legal Profession in Germany and the United States* (Cambridge, Mass., Harvard Univ. Press, 1973), and Ostler, *Die deutschen Rechtsanwälte*. See also H. Siegrist, 'Public Office or Free Profession? German Attorneys in the Nineteenth and Early Twentieth Centuries', in G. Cocks & K. H. Jarausch (eds.), *German Professions, 1800–1950* (Oxford, Oxford Univ. Press, 1990), 46–65.

[44] M. John, 'Between Estate and Profession: Lawyers and the Development of the Legal Profession in Nineteenth-Century Germany', in D. Blackbourn & R. J. Evans (eds.), *The German Bourgeoisie. Essays on the Social History of the German Middle Class From the Late Eighteenth to the Early Twentieth Century* (New York, Routledge, Chapman, and Hall, 1991), 162–97, gives a nuanced discussion of the ambivalent attitude of many German private practitioners to the end of the *numerus clausus*.

[45] On the long campaign for *freie Advokatur*, see H. Huffmann, *Kampf um freie Advokatur* (Essen, Juristischer Verlag W. Ellinghaus & Co., 1967); L. Müller, 'Die Freiheit der Advokatur. Ihre geschichtliche Entwicklung in Deutschland während der Neuzeit und ihre rechtliche Bedeutung in der Bundesrepublik Deutschland', unpub. Dr. jur. diss., Univ. of Würzburg (1972). For a description of the modern training procedure for the German legal professions, see Erhard Blankenburg & Ulrike Schultz, 'German Advocates: A Highly Regulated Profession', in R. L. Abel & P. S. C. Lewis (eds.), *Lawyers in Society*, vol. 2, *The Civil Law World* (3 vols., Berkeley, Univ. of California Press, 1988), 124–59.

court was located.[46] The Imperial Justice Laws, particularly the Lawyers' Statute, thus established the bar upon the framework sought by liberals and practitioners alike, in which lawyers could structure their own professional affairs.

While lawyers' chambers were innovative institutions that lawyers had long sought, lawyers had created other institutions for themselves during the long wait for legislative action.[47] First, since the 1820s, lawyers in good *bürgerlich* fashion had formed local voluntary bar associations.[48] The aims of the local voluntary associations were both public and private: to exercise disciplinary authority over those who joined; to represent the interests of the private Bar; and to provide a forum for sociability. Under the harsh conditions of state suspicion of public activity during the 1830s and again in the 1850s, local associations could aspire to no more.

Beginning in the 1840s and again in the 1860s, lawyers began to form regional, provincial, and finally state-wide voluntary bar associations. In some instances organic ties existed between local associations and larger ones, but more often parallel organizations emerged. Except for a brief moment during 1848, reactionary governments thwarted efforts to hold a national congress of lawyers. Unification in 1870–1 changed the picture. In August 1871, lawyers responded to the call of the Bavarian and Prussian Bar Associations to attend a national congress to found a nation-wide bar association, the DAV. The DAV became in many ways the archetypal professional organization.[49]

---

[46] By 1915, there were 29 courts of appeal, 176 superior courts, and over 1,950 district courts in Germany. Reichs-Justizministerium, *Deutsche Justiz-Statistik* (Berlin, 1915), 17, Table IV, 22–5. Lawyers could not freely choose to practice before the Imperial Supreme Court (*Reichsgericht*), which had a closed bar of 25 lawyers chosen by the judges of that court. Moreover, candidates for the Bar had no absolute right, but rather a permissive right to enter practice in a state *other than* that in which they had passed their Bar examinations and completed their *Referendariat*.

[47] For a more detailed account of the complex interrelations of the various institutions of the bar, see Ledford, *From General Estate to Special Interest*, chap. 4.

[48] Weißler, *Geschichte der Rechtsanwaltschaft*, 502, puts it this way: 'It is self-explanatory that, in the century of association, the practising bar would also seize this mighty lever of public effectiveness.' (Author's translation.) For a more expansive consideration of the phenomenon of the association in the 19th cent., see W. Hardtwig, 'Strukturmerkmale und Entwicklungstendenzen des Vereinswesens in Deutschland 1789–1848', in O. Dann (ed.), *Vereinswesen und bürgerlich Gesellschaft in Deutschland, Historische Zeitschrift* Beiheft 9 (Neue Folge) (Munich, Oldenbourg, 1984), 11–50, and K. Tenfelde, 'Die Entfaltung des Vereinswesens während der Industriellen Revolution in Deutschland (1850–1873)', ibid. 55–114.

[49] From 1871 to 1933 the DAV published, at first bi-monthly and then weekly, a professional newspaper aimed at lawyers in private practice and other legal scholars called

Similarly, lawyers structured it as a typical, elite-dominated, liberal organization of notables. From its inception until the early twentieth century, the DAV consisted of two organs, a biennial bar convention (*Anwaltstag*), which each member was entitled to attend, and a seven-member executive board which represented the association between conventions. Although in 1881 only 37.8 per cent of German lawyers were members of the DAV, by 1915 over 80 per cent were members, a figure that remained remarkably constant through the 1920s and early 1930s.[50]

Thus, each German lawyer had the opportunity to be a member of three organizations: a local voluntary organization, the national DAV, and the lawyers' chamber prescribed by the Lawyers' Statute. No organic ties existed among the three levels. Moreover, each set of organizations was dominated by an elite of lawyer-notables. The Executive Boards of lawyers' chambers tended to consist primarily of lawyers who practised before courts of appeal and superior courts.[51] Lawyers who practiced before the Imperial Supreme Court and the *Kammergericht* in Berlin dominated the Executive Board of the DAV, which had its headquarters in Leipzig, site of the Supreme Court.[52] Local associations also tended to be run by leading lawyer-notables. The only opportunities for wider participation in professional governance by rank-and-file lawyers were the annual plenary meetings of the lawyers' chambers and the

Juristische Wochenschrift (*JW*). Beginning in 1914 and running through to 1933, it published another newspaper aimed only at its own membership and discussing matters of internal governance of the legal profession and other issues of concern mainly to practitioners, at first called *Nachrichten für die Mitglieder des Deutschen Anwaltvereins* and later simply *Anwaltsblatt* (*Abl*).

[50] Ledford, *From General Estate to Special Interest*, Table 4.1, 102.

[51] S. 8 of the by-laws (*Geschäftsordnung*) of the lawyers' chamber in Celle, e.g., required that the chairman and secretary of the executive board 'shall regularly be elected from among the members of the chamber living at the seat of the chamber', i.e., from among the court of appeal lawyers in Celle: Geheimes Staatsarchiv, Preußischer Kulturbesitz, Berlin-Dahlem (GStA), I HA Rep. 84a, Nr. 21912, 'Jahresberichte, Rechtsanwaltskammer Celle', 9–27. Of the 32 lawyers who served on the executive board in Celle between 1881 and 1900, 8 practised before the court of appeal in Celle and 9 in Hannover, while only one practised before a district court. Of the 31 who served between 1901 and 1930, only 5 were in Celle and 6 in Hannover, while 4 practised before district courts. Ledford, *From General Estate to Special Interest*, Table 5.19, 165.

[52] Of the 52 members of the executive board of the DAV between 1871 and 1920, 10 practised before the Imperial Supreme Court in Leipzig, 4 before the superior court of Leipzig, 8 before the *Kammergericht* in Berlin, 17 before some other court of appeal, 10 before some other superior court, and only 3 before a district court. Ibid., 138, n. 37, calculated from Heinrich Dittenberger, 'Fünfzig Jahre Deutscher Anwaltverein 1871/1921'. *JW* 50 (1921), 990–1.

biennial bar conventions of the DAV. Lawyers from the city in which the bar convention convened often predominated.

Already before the First World War, some lawyers, especially those who practised before district courts in small towns, felt that the institutions of the bar left them unrepresented. These lawyers felt in particular that none of these institutions represented with sufficient vigour the economic interests of lawyers.[53] In 1907–9, a crisis erupted within the DAV over the refusal of the Executive Board to convene an extraordinary bar convention to debate proposed procedural reforms, despite the fact that half of the membership had petitioned for one.[54] After heated criticism of the DAV Executive Board as being composed of elite lawyers, far removed from the concerns of the rank-and-file, and of the bar conventions as consisting of 'accidental majorities' (*Zufallsmehrheiten*) of local lawyers, the insurgent lawyers succeeded in 1909 in forcing the DAV to change its constitution to create a representatives' assembly, elected by the DAV membership in districts, which was to be more representative than the Executive Board but less cumbersome and expensive than the bar convention. This reform of professional structure, however, proved unsuccessful in reducing the power of the professional elite. District court lawyers, after founding their own special-interest professional association and running a designated slate of candidates for election to the representatives' assembly, succeeded in increasing their representation at the expense of superior court lawyers, but the gradual equation of strength of those two constituencies only *increased* the power of the elite court of appeal lawyers who held the balance of power.[55] This institutional reform simply provided another arena for groups of lawyers to turn the professional organization into the terrain for their struggles for power.

The Multi-faceted Crisis of Weimar

In the 1920s and early 1930s, the German bar in private practice confronted a wave of crises and challenges that contested its fundamental

[53] See especially H. Soldan, *Neue Ziele, Neue Wege. Ein Vorschlag zur Hebung des deutschen Anwaltstandes* (Mainz, Verlag des Wirtschaftlichen Verbandes deutscher Rechtsanwälte, 1909), 2–4; Soldan's concern led him to form a separate lawyers' association for the express purpose of promoting their economic security, the Economic Association of German Lawyers.

[54] For a fuller account of this crisis, see K. F. Ledford, *From General Estate to Special Interest*, 103–12, and Ostler, *Die deutschen Rechtsanwälte*, 90–2.

[55] Ledford, *From General Estate to Special Interest*, 112.

assumptions about itself. Newly-enfranchised voices raised claims of substantive justice that challenged the comfortable proceduralism with which lawyers conceived of their professional sphere and the public political sphere. Lawyers also found that they had to negotiate with different and newly-assertive governmental bodies over issues of importance to the profession and to individual practitioners, and those different agencies, which answered to constituencies other than lawyers, listened to lawyers with less deference. Finally, the bar struggled with internal challenges to its professional structure, as traditional elites sought to adapt enough to prevent schism yet also to maintain power, and dissident groups of lawyers made recourse to outside agencies to attain their goals. Together, these crises revealed deep fissures within the bar, unmasked lawyers' pretensions of being the 'general estate', representing the common interest, and revealed lawyers, and subgroups of the bar, to be merely another of the many special-interest groups that struggled to survive in the Weimar political landscape. Lawyers' experience during Weimar, then, mirrored to a remarkable extent the experience of political liberalism itself.[56]

The early 1920s confronted lawyers with a substantive claim of justice that contested their claim to represent the general interest and to serve as guarantors of the *Rechtsstaat*. The Constitution of the Weimar Republic extended guarantees of equal rights to women (Art. 109) for the first time in German history. Article 128 provided further that 'All citizens of the State, without distinction, are eligible for public office, as provided by law and in accordance with their qualifications and abilities. All exceptional provisions against women officials are annulled.'[57] On its surface, this would seem to have admitted women to all positions in the administration of justice, but lawyers made it clear that they opposed admission of women to their profession. On 13 June 1919, the Executive Board of the lawyers' chamber in Celle resolved by a vote of 10 to 1, 'As a matter of principle, women ought not to be admitted to the bar'. The reasons advanced expressed both economic and ideological-essentialist objections to women's participation in the

---

[56] For a more detailed discussion of several of the issues discussed in this essay, see K. F. Ledford, 'German Lawyers and the State in the Weimar Republic', *Law & Hist. Rev.* 11 (1994), 317–49.

[57] The translation is taken from the text of the Weimar Constitution that can be found in E. Hucko (ed.), *The Democratic Tradition. Four German Constitutions* (Oxford, Berg Publishers, 1987), 149–90 at 177.

administration of justice.[58] Similarly, the Executive Board of the DAV, as well as the representatives' assembly, expressly and consistently, between 1919 and 1922, rejected the admission of women to the private practice of law.[59]

Not surprisingly, given this opposition, the constitutional provisions that seemed clearly to require the admission of women to bench and bar were not interpreted as self-executing, and the Reichstag had to enact a statute that admitted women to the bar and the judiciary on 11 July 1922.[60] In the course of the Reichstag debate, lawyers found themselves arrayed against a unified group of women members, from various parties, and the SPD, under the leadership of Gustav Radbruch, a lawyer and briefly, in 1922, Reich Minister of Justice. Lawyers thus found their attempts to block the admission of women into the profession thwarted by substantive claims of equal justice championed by women themselves and by Socialists. This unpalatable alliance contested lawyers' claim that the professional *status quo* represented the common good, and lawyers' commitment to a procedural liberalism proved insufficient to resist under the new political realities of Weimar.

Another issue in the early 1920s revealed the declining ability of the leadership of the bar to persuade the membership that a given course of action was in the profession's best interests. The discourse that surrounded the question of enactment of a mandatory retirement insurance scheme, and the reversal of opinion from initially favourable to ultimately unfavourable, show that enthusiasm for mandatory retirement insurance by state bureaucracies with which lawyers were not previously accustomed to dealing triggered suspicion among the bar about

[58] 'Economic reasons were chiefly those mentioned, especially the extraordinarily bad circumstances of judicial officials and lawyers that already now prevail. But the opinion was also voiced that women are ill-suited to these positions and professions.' (Mundt, *100 Jahre Rechtsanwaltskammer*, 25–7.) See also GStA I HA Rep. 84a, 21913, 'Jahresberichte, Rechtsanwaltskammer Celle', 'Geschäftsbericht der Anwaltskammer zu Celle für das Jahr 1919', 207.

[59] Ostler, *Die deutschen Rechtsanwälte*, 169–74; the arguments advanced echoed the essentialist ones voiced by the executive board in Celle.

[60] Deutscher Juristennenbund (ed.), *Juristinnen in Deutschland. Eine Dokumentation (1900–1989)*, 2d edn. (Frankfurt, J. Schweitzer, 1989), 1–16. Following this legislation, the first woman private practitioner in Germany, Dr Marie Otto, was admitted to practice in Munich on 7 Dec. 1922; the first woman in Prussia was Dr Maria Munck in 1924; the first woman admitted to the bar in the province of Hannover was Berta Schmidt of Duderstadt, whose father was a lawyer there, who swore her admission oath in September 1927. In 1931, 3 other women effected their admission to the bar, 2 in the city of Hannover and one in Lüneburg, but the total of 4 was only a tiny portion of 820 lawyers in the province. Mundt, *100 Jahre Rechtsanwaltskammer Celle*, 26–7.

the aims of the 'democratic-social' republic and concerns for how to maintain the profession's special status and disinterested pose.

Soon after 1871, lawyers created an 'Assistance Fund for German Lawyers' to collect voluntary contributions from individuals, voluntary bar associations, and lawyers' chambers.[61] A number of local charitable and need-based funds also continued to exist.[62] Although the Assistance Fund proposed creation of a mandatory 'Retirement, Widows', and Orphans' Fund' in 1894–5, a lively debate about the feasibility and desirability of such an institution lasted for years.[63] After several considerations of the issue and rejection of a mandatory system, a voluntary fund came into being, but membership remained quite low.[64]

During the First World War, the question of how to care for lawyers wounded in action and for surviving relatives of those killed, combined with the disruptions of professional income and security caused by military service and wartime inflation, led to renewed consideration of mandatory retirement insurance. In March 1918, Adolf Gröber (a superior court judge) introduced a resolution in the Reichstag that called for the government to draft a bill to provide for the 'social organization of the German bar in private practice', by making membership in the existing two funds mandatory for all lawyers.[65] Although many leaders of the bar greeted this overture as a great opportunity to advance the social security of lawyers, others rejected the proposal, which for the first time extended 'mandatory insurance, which has been

---

[61] Ostler, *Die deutschen Rechtsanwälte*, 87, 89, 200–1.

[62] See the reports of the activities of the local funds in the province of Hannover recorded in the annual reports of the *Anwaltskammer* in Celle, GStA, I HA Rep. 84a, Nr. 21912 and 21913, 'Jahresberichte, Rechtsanwaltskammer Celle'. Healthy funds in smaller cities fell into extinction after the inflation of 1923.

[63] Useful here is the historical outline provided in H. Cahn, 'Denkschrift des Bayerischen Anwaltsverbandes zur Herbeiführung einer Pensionsversicherung der Deutschen Anwaltschaft', *Abl* 9 (1922), 92–104, 92–6.

[64] Proponents of mandatory plans in the 1920s interpreted this rejection as indicative of a certain doctrinaire economic liberalism on the part of lawyers in the two decades around 1900: 'Indeed, these bodies [the DAV executive board and the bar conventions]—whose composition and votes were left to chance—normally treated the problem with a certain reserve. This can be explained by the prior character of our profession and the—pardon the expression—plutocratic composition of its congresses. My but we were really inclined toward Manchesterism then! A commitment to *"laisser faire laisser aller"* that is incomprehensible today characterized the attitude of the majority.' (Ibid., 94.)

[65] Ibid., 95–6; the resolution is also reprinted in the legislative justification for the draft insurance bill, 'Das Versicherungsgesetz für Rechtsanwälte', *Abl* 13 (1926), 31; on the Gröber resolution, see also Ostler, *Die deutsche Rechtsanwälte*, 120–2.

limited only to workers and employees (*Arbeitnehmer*), to a free profession'.[66]

After the turmoil of defeat and revolution, the issue lay dormant until 1922. As inflation continued to erode the value of retirement savings, interest increased among lawyers in some sort of retirement insurance fund that could shelter retirement funds effectively. The DAV again addressed the question of mandatory retirement insurance. In early 1923, the DAV created a committee to produce a draft bill. The DAV committee consulted with the Executive Boards of the various lawyers' chambers, compiled a draft law, and on 2 January 1924 forwarded it to the Reich Ministry of Justice.[67]

The hyper-inflation of 1923 had prepared the ground for a generally favourable reception for the DAV's draft, and the Executive Boards of sixteen lawyers' chambers endorsed the draft. At the March 1924 meeting of the representatives' assembly of the DAV, however, Hamburg lawyers opposed it:

By means of retirement insurance, the bar would fall into a dependence upon the state that is inconsistent with the freedom of the legal profession. Because the national government would permit the bar to pass on the costs of retirement insurance to its clients, the bar would submit itself into a dependent relationship unworthy of itself. It would submit itself voluntarily to the yoke of social insurance, thus into relations that ought to be eliminated, but not extended.[68]

Nevertheless, the representatives' assembly endorsed the draft. Officials in the Reich Ministry of Labour greeted this as an important moment: 'The draft before us ventures into new territory, because it represents the first attempt to incorporate a free profession into the social insurance system.'[69]

[66] Cahn, 'Denkschrift', 95–6. Germany had, of course, developed the most comprehensive system of accident, sickness, and old-age pension insurance in the world since the 1880s, but its coverage had begun with industrial workers and only gradually been extended to other groups, including the 'new middle class' of white-collar employees in 1911; see G. A. Ritter, *Social Welfare in Germany and Britain: Origins and Development*, K. Traynon (trans.), (Leamington Spa, Berg Publishers, 1986), 17–130, esp. 91–5.

[67] Dr Strauder, 'Pensionsversicherung für Rechtsanwälte', *Abl* 9 (1922), 30–2; Dr Schweer, 'Geldentwertung und Allgemeine Pensionskasse der Rechtsanwaltschaft', *Abl* 9 (1922), 37–8; 'Aus der Vereinstätigkeit', *Abl* 10 (1923), 24–6, 25; 'Entwurf eines Gesetzes über die Pensionsversicherung der deutschen Rechtsanwälte. Nebst Erläuterungen. Aufgestellt vom Deutschen Anwaltverein Dezember 1923', *Abl* 11 (1924), 15–20.

[68] '17. Vertreterversammlung des Deutschen Anwaltvereins', *Abl* 11 (1924), 59–64, 62.

[69] 'Aus der Vereinstätigkeit', *Abl* 12 (1925), 32. The editorial staff of the *Anwaltsblatt* considered this novelty, inclusion of a free profession in a social insurance scheme, to be one of the strengths of the bill; 'Die Aufgaben des Jahres 1926', *Abl* 13 (1926), 1–3, 2.

As the draft law ground slowly through the bureaucracies of the Reich Ministry of Justice and the Reich Ministry of Labour, lawyers' attitudes toward mandatory retirement insurance began to change.[70] Private insurance companies bombarded lawyers with advertisements, arguing that lawyers would receive higher benefits at lower costs by purchasing coverage individually rather than by the profession acting collectively.[71] Continued consultation with the Executive Boards, and annual assemblies of the lawyers' chambers made possible by the delay, also permitted second thoughts to emerge. For example, the lawyers' chamber in Celle, which had endorsed the mandatory retirement insurance scheme in 1923, rejected it in 1925 (Executive Committee) and 1926 (plenary assembly), arguing that state intrusion into professional affairs through legislation that mandated retirement insurance would limit the freedom of the legal profession.[72] The representatives' assembly of the DAV met in March 1926 to consider the draft that had by now emerged from the Reich Ministry of Labour, and it found that the attitude of the bar had changed fundamentally since the previous year. Out of seventy-five local associations that had passed resolutions on the subject, thirty-four supported the draft legislation while forty-one opposed it.[73] At the conclusion of the debate, the assembly rejected the draft mandatory retirement insurance law by a margin of thirty-eight to forty-eight, and the issue of mandatory retirement insurance was dead.

The evolution of lawyers' attitudes toward mandatory retirement insurance reveals an erosion of the ability of the leadership of the DAV to impress its vision of what was best for the profession on the rank-and-file membership. DAV Executive Board members and the editorial boards of the two bar newspapers never wavered in their conviction that mandatory insurance would serve most lawyers best. They could

---

[70] For the progress of the bill through the two Ministries, see the reports 'Aus der Vereinstätigkeit', *Abl* 12 (1925), 10 (Feb.); 17 (Mar.); 32 (Apr.); 97 (June); 145 (Nov.); 167 (Dec.).

[71] See the complaints by the editor of the *Anwaltsblatt* and by other supporters of mandatory retirement insurance, arguing that the claims by the insurance companies were false; 'Die Pensionsversicherung', *Abl* 12 (1925), 97–8, 97, 'Pensionsversicherung', *Abl* 12 (1925), 115–16; H. Cahn, 'Zwangspensionsgesetz und Lebensversicherungsanstalt', *Abl* 12 (1925), 134–6; 'Pensionsversicherung', *Abl* 12 (1925), 163.

[72] See the annual reports of the *Anwaltskammer* in Celle, GStA, I HA Rep. 84a, Nr. 21913, 'Jahresberichte, Rechtsanwaltskammer Celle.' The action of the executive committee was in 1925, I HA Rep. 84a, Nr. 21913, 235, and that of the plenary assembly in 1926, I HA Rep. 84a, Nr. 21913, 241 ('rejected by an overwhelming majority').

[73] 'Die 19. Vertreterversammlung', *Abl* 13 (1926), 118.

not, however, withstand the misgivings of the rank and file. The turning point was when a new and alien bureaucracy, the Ministry of
Labour, assumed jurisdiction over the matter. This equated lawyers
with other groups subject to social insurance and hence challenged their
special status as the 'general estate', guarantors of the *Rechtsstaat*. Such
a derogation of status was a sacrifice German lawyers were not prepared to make in 1926.[74]

As in the question of women's franchise, another issue of substantive
interest to the SPD conflicted with the symbolic and material interests of
the bar. One of the chief items on the legislative agenda of the SPD in
the 1920s was the enactment of a comprehensive system of labour law
(*Arbeitsrecht*). In pursuing this end, the Social Democrats built upon a legislative foundation that lawyers already hated for both its symbolic and
material impact upon their profession. Prior to the enactment of a comprehensive code of labour law, the heavily Roman character of German
law provided very little guidance for an emergent labour law at a time
when that field began to assume greatest significance for a majority of
the German population. The feeling grew among employees and others
that justice in labour law cases was slow and expensive, that courts and
judges helped only the wealthy, and that they were hostile to the interests of workers. Not only did the worker have to hire a lawyer and face
a lawyer representing the employer, but the losing party, in accord with
civil law practice, would have to pay both sets of attorney's fees.[75] Many
believed that lawyers only worsened the process and rendered it more
expensive. Schooled in dialectical argument, they simply muddied the
waters rather than clarifying the state of the facts and the law. Their
focus upon legal formalities and procedure obscured the content, substance, and social spirit of labour law.[76] The conviction spread that the
exclusion of lawyers from labour law cases would promote speed, economy, simplicity, and 'naturalness' of decision-making.[77]

[74] A nuanced discussion of the status concerns of middle-class groups and the circumstances under which they will behave in 'solidaristic' ways appears in P. Baldwin, *The
Politics of Social Solidarity: Class Bases of the European Welfare State 1875–1975* (Cambridge,
Cambridge Univ. Press, 1990), esp. 1–54. German lawyers only joined the state-run
retirement system in 1957; ibid., 277.

[75] §87 (later §91) of the Code of Civil Procedure requires the losing party to bear all
the costs of the successful party, including lawyers' fees.

[76] L. Bendix, 'Richter, Rechtsanwälte und Arbeitsgerichte', *Die Justiz* 1 (1925–6),
186–93 at 187. See also the arguments in Lothar Engelbert Schücking, 'Leitwort zur
Verabschiedung des Arbeitsgerichtsgesetzes', *Die Justiz* 2 (1926–7), 273–7.

[77] Bovensiepsen, 'Das Verbot der Zulassung von Rechtsanwälten vor den Gewerbe-
und Kaufmannsgerichten', *JW* 42 (1913), 729–30 at 729.

After a great wave of strikes in 1889, legislation in 1890 had created industrial courts (*Gewerbegerichte*) with exclusive jurisdiction over employment disputes between masters and journeymen or apprentices, and it excluded lawyers from practice before them.[78] Industrial courts consisted of panels of workers and employers, chaired by an impartial judge. Male workers (or employers) over the age of twenty-five elected lay judges by direct, secret suffrage. Exclusion primarily hurt the incomes of district court lawyers, but restrictions on appeal also had a negative effect upon superior court lawyers.[79] More important was the blow to the prestige of lawyers, for this was the first deviation from the principle of representation by lawyers. In 1904, despite renewed protest from the Bar, the Reichstag created a second court of special jurisdiction in 1904, commercial employment courts (*Kaufmannsgerichte*) with exclusive jurisdiction for employment disputes between commercial employers and employees; lawyers were excluded.

Social Democrats and trade unions quite naturally benefited from the political mobilization that surrounded election of lay judges and from the role of union or party officials in representing the interests of their constituents before the industrial and commercial courts. Lawyers just as naturally continued to reject the principle that they could be dispensed with, that they were harmful to the efficient and economic administration of justice. In the Weimar Republic, the SPD and the trade unions sought, as part of the codification of labour law, to expand the jurisdiction of the special courts to encompass all labour disputes by creating labour courts (*Arbeitsgerichte*).[80] Work began in the Reich Ministry of Labour on a draft of a labour court law. Lawyers responded sharply. On 2 November 1920, the Executive Committee of the DAV protested to the Reich Ministry of Justice and began to seek support for its position from local bar associations and lawyers' chambers, from state Ministries of Justice, and from members of the Reichstag.[81] The representatives' assembly of the DAV resolved in 1922 that

[78] The most comprehensive work on the history of courts of special jurisdiction for labour disputes in F. Wunderlich, *German Labor Courts* (Chapel Hill, Univ. of North Carolina Press, 1946). Ostler, *Die deutsche Rechtsanwälte*, 39, discusses the attitude of the private Bar towards creation of the trade courts in 1890.

[79] Ostler, *Die deutschen Rechtsanwälte*, 40–1.

[80] See the discussion at Wunderlich, *German Labor Courts*, 40, and Ostler, *Die deutschen Rechtsanwälte*, 179–81. The Weimar Constitution provided that the federal government should adopt a uniform labour code (*Arbeitsrecht*), Art. 157.

[81] 'Zum Entwurf eines Arbeitsgerichtsgesetzes', *Abl* 7 (1920), 210–11; see the descriptions of the efforts of the executive committee of the DAV in 'Sitzung des Vorstandes des Deutschen Anwaltvereins vom 4. und 5. Dez. 1920', *Abl* 7 (1920), 227–31 at 227; and

[T]he exclusion of lawyers from the special courts represents a serious blow to the justice-seeking public, employee and employer alike, who would be denied justice by the extension of special jurisdiction to the entire field of labour law. The exclusion of lawyers from the special courts is an unprecedented and unjustified insult to the legal profession.[82]

Proponents of labour courts and the exclusion of lawyers built upon a growing hostility towards lawyers and the entire legal system on the part of the working class, exacerbated by the political justice of the Weimar era.[83] Part of the expression of this suspicion was the fact that the draft labour court law emerged from the Reich Ministry of Labour, with jurisdiction over labour and other social questions, rather than from the Reich Ministry of Justice, with jurisdiction over courts, lawyers, and legal reform.[84] Lawyers harshly criticized the fact that the Social-Political Committee of the Reichstag conducted the hearings and debate on the bill rather than the Committee on Law; not only was the former Committee less sympathetic to lawyers' interests, but only two or three of its twenty-eight members were themselves legally trained.[85] Lawyers bitterly denounced the draft as 'doctrinaire' and 'hostile to lawyers', but despite their opposition, it passed on 13 December 1926, by a vote of 210 to 140.[86] With a last burst of recrimination against political parties who sought to ingratiate themselves with the bar with claims that they had fought the exclusion, lawyers in

---

'Aus der Vereinstätigkeit', *Abl* 8 (1921), 3–5 at 4. See under 'Aus der Vereinstätigkeit', *Abl* 9 (1922), 3–5, 3–4, outlining the position of the DAV taken in discussions with the Reich Ministry of Justice.

[82] 'Entwurf eines Arbeitsgerichtsgesetzes, insbesondere; die Angliederung der Sondergerichte an die ordentliche Gerichte, Zulassung der Rechtsanwälte', *Abl* 9 (1922), 19–20 at 20; resolution passed at the 14th Representatives' Assembly in Braunschweig, 28 Jan. 1922. (Author's translation.)

[83] This attitude is accepted as axiomatic by H. Sinzheimer, 'Zum Entwurf eines Arbeitsgerichtsgesetzes', *Die Justiz* 1 (1925–6), 6–12, 8. See also the observations on this suspicion and hostility by M. Hachenburg, *Lebenserinnerungen eines Rechtsanwalts und Briefe aus der Emigration*, J. Schadt (ed.) (Stuttgart, W. Kohlhammer, 1978), 164.

[84] Wunderlich, *German Labor Courts*, 55–6.

[85] Ibid., 121; see the express lament by H. Dittenberger, '1927', *Abl* 14 (1927), 1–3 at 1.

[86] Out of many examples, see A. Engel, 'Zum Entwurf eines Arbeitsgerichtsgesetzes', *Abl* 12 (1925), 152–6 at 152, 153. For a description of the system created by the labour court law, see H. B. Davies, 'The German Labor Courts', *Polit. Sci. Q.* 44 (1929), 397–420, and especially his examination of the exclusion of lawyers, 414–16, in which he concludes that their admission would not make much difference as to comparative advantage between capital and labour but does not evaluate the issues of increased expense or delay.

private practice had to accommodate themselves to this blow to their dignity and expanded encroachment upon their field of action.[87]

Traditional and comfortable state agencies that had long been familiar negotiating partners, especially the Reich Ministry of Justice, no longer held unrivalled power over issues of importance to lawyers. Other, newer ministries, particularly the Reich Ministry of Labour, with competing if not contradictory policy goals, now entered as actors whose decisions affected lawyers. Parties in the Reichstag, especially the Social Democratic Party, with constituencies and agendas hostile to lawyers, acted in newly assertive and independent ways in the legislature. Under these circumstances of the Weimar Republic that were changed from those of the Empire, lawyers had suffered a humiliating political defeat that reduced their incomes, revealed their lessened political clout, and further eroded their disinterested pose as the 'general estate'.

By the turn of the twentieth century, the professional structure created by the Lawyers' Statute had also created a problem unforeseen in 1879.[88] The law permitted each lawyer to choose freely the court before which to practise but required each to reside permanently in the town where that court was located (*Lokalisierung*). The civil procedure code required that parties in cases before superior courts (and courts of appeal) be represented by lawyers admitted before that particular court (*Anwaltszwang*). That same requirement did not exist for the district courts, which had exclusive initial jurisdiction for cases involving relatively small amounts in controversy. Parties in district court cases thus could hire any lawyer, even those admitted before superior courts or courts of appeal. Conversely, district court lawyers could *never* plead before superior courts, even in appeals of cases that they had handled initially before the superior courts. As the number of district court lawyers grew, they found this limitation demeaning.[89] They possessed the same qualifications and had undergone the same neo-humanist

---

[87] See the remarkable exchange between the DAV and the DDP, in which the DDP tried to undermine the claim of the DVP that it supported the interests of lawyers in the whole episode; the DAV rejected the DDP's claims, noting that *both* parties failed to protect the interests of lawyers; 'Zum Arbeitsgerichtsgesetz', *Abl* 14 (1927), 57–8.

[88] For a discussion of the problem caused by the increasing tension between district court and superior court lawyers, see K. F. Ledford, 'Conflict Within the Legal Profession: Simultaneous Admission and the German Bar 1903–1927', in Cocks & Jarausch (eds.), *German Professions*, 252–69.

[89] In 1880, there were only 165 district court lawyers in all of Germany (out of 4,091 total lawyers); by 1915, there were 3,123 out of a total of 13,051; Ledford, *From General Estate to Special Interest*, Table 7.2, 219.

classical secondary school study, university education, and practical legal training as their superior court colleagues, and thus they reasoned that they should have the same privileges. The remedy that they sought was simultaneous admission; each district court lawyer should be admitted as a matter of right both to his own district court and to the superior court within whose jurisdiction the district court fell.[90]

The Prussian and Bavarian Ministries of Justice resisted simultaneous admission, arguing that no lawyer can serve clients in two places at the same time. Simultaneous admission, the ministries contended, would result in delay and increased cost, so they refused to exercise their discretion to permit it.[91] District court lawyers decided to seek legislation to amend the Lawyers' Statute to create the right to simultaneous admission. They raised the issue with the DAV beginning in 1903, and DAV conventions in 1905 and 1907 endorsed amendment of the Lawyers' Statute to permit simultaneous admission as a matter of right. District court lawyers even founded their own bar association in 1909, the Association of German District Court Lawyers, to advance their particular interests.[92]

But the interests of district court lawyers threatened markets for professional services previously reserved for superior court lawyers and galvanized them into opposition to simultaneous admission. They launched their counter-attack in the professional Press, and the debate raged. At the DAV convention in 1913, superior court lawyers succeeded in referring the question of simultaneous admission to a DAV committee for study, where it rested until after the First World War. Wartime and post-war inflation intensified the economic rivalry between the two groups of lawyers, as it caused cases to 'migrate' upward from district to superior courts as the nominal amount in controversy increased. District court lawyers raised the matter anew with

[90] The dispute over simultaneous admission filled the periodical literature of the practising bar between 1903 and 1927, and the debate persisted even afterwards. A complete, albeit partisan, history of the debate can be found at Verein Deutscher Amtsgerichtsanwälte, e.V., ed., *Simultanzulassung. Handbuch zum Reichsgesetz vom 7. März 1927* (Berlin, Franz Vahlen, 1931), and 'Bericht des Referenten Justizrat Schatz, Leipzig', Anlage B, in Deutscher Anwaltverein (ed.), *Um die Simultanzulassung. Bericht über die Ausschußverhandlungen im Deutschen Anwaltverein (Erster Teil)* (Leipzig, Oscar Brandstetter, 1925), 22–43. See also Ostler, *Die deutschen Rechtsanwälte*, 67–78.

[91] See the explanation for refusal to permit simultaneous admission provided by the Prussian Ministry of Justice to Chancellor Caprivi on 23 May 1894, GStA, I HA Rep. 84a, Nr. 10346, 'Gesetzliche Ordnung der Verhältnisse des Anwalts- und Advokatenstandes, Bd. VI, 1888–1902', 223–9.

[92] For a summary of the arguments, see G. Reidnitz, *Lokalisation und Simultanzulassung* (Mainz, Verlag der Zentralbuchhandlung Deutscher Rechtsanwälte, 1911).

both the DAV and the Reich Ministry of Justice in 1920, and the DAV
Executive Board renewed its support for legislation to introduce simultaneous admission.[93] Superior court lawyers retaliated by forming their
own association in 1921, the Association of German Superior Court
Lawyers.[94] The DAV tried to broker an agreement between the two
contending sub-groups, but with no success. Polarization of the bar into
district court and superior court factions paralysed both the DAV and
the local lawyers' chambers, rendering them incapable of anything but
lamenting the acrimonious nature of the dispute. From 1922 onwards,
both special-interest associations bombarded the Prussian and Reich
Ministries of Justice with petitions and publications calling for legislation to support their positions.[95] Rebuffed there, each began to
approach members of the Reichstag directly, seeking to use the parliament to attain their goals. In March 1925 a district court lawyer who
was a delegate of the German National People's Party introduced draft
legislation providing for simultaneous admission as a matter of right.
After a rehearsal in committee and on the floor of the Reichstag of the
arguments that had raged among lawyers since 1903, the law passed
on 7 March 1927, and entered into effect on 1 January 1928.[96]

The internal struggle over simultaneous admission further reduced
the credibility of the organized bar's claim to represent the common
good of society, for it made plain that lawyer-notables could not speak
convincingly even for all lawyers. Even the institutions of the bar itself
became the terrain upon which competing groups of lawyers struggled
for their interests, contesting elections to professional bodies with rival
slates of special-interest candidates.[97] Moreover, traditional institutional
supports for the interests of the bar leadership proved lacking; neither
the Prussian Ministry of Justice nor the liberal political parties could

[93] Schatz, 'Bericht', 24. See also the petition by the Verein der Amtsgerichtsanwälte
des Oberlandesgerichtsbezirks Düsseldorf to the Reich Ministry of Justice, 6 July 1920,
in GStA, I HA Rep. 84a, Nr. 71, 'Gesetzliche Ordnung der Verhältnisse des Anwalts-
und Advokatenstandes, Bd. XII, 1920–23', 127–8, calling for the introduction of simultaneous admission.

[94] The superior court lawyers sent an announcement of the formation of their associ-
ation in Jena on 22 May 1921, to the Prussian Ministry of Justice; Verein Deutscher
Landgerichtsanwälte to Prussian Ministry of Justice, 2 June 1921, GStA, I HA Rep. 84a,
Nr. 71, 259–61.

[95] See e.g. the petitions reproduced in Verein Deutscher Amtsgerichtsanwälte (ed.),
Simultanzulassung, 193–315, and the submissions in GStA, I HA Rep. 84a, Nr. 71, 225–30,
307, Nr. 72, 571–85 & 589–607.

[96] The DAV felt itself quite irrelevant to the final outcome of the dispute over simultaneous admission; see the account by Hachenburg, *Lebenserinnerungen*, 163.

[97] Ledford, *From General Estate to Special Interest*, 111–12.

help the leadership mediate the dispute, leaving the legislative initiative to non-liberal parties, especially the DNVP. At the end of the battle, both district court and superior court lawyers resented bar leaders for having failed to support their interests fully, and they retained their special-interest organizations, showing that the 'general estate' claim had been permanently eroded.

The inter-War era also saw further state intervention into lawyers' lives through the inclusion of income from legal practice within the scope of the trade tax. Normally used to finance the functioning of local (*Gemeinde*) government, the hard-pressed governments of the early 1920s tried to expand the definition of what constituted a trade in order to offset their diminishing incomes. In 1921, a proposal by the state government of Saxony to subject income from all free professions to the trade tax drew the comment and opposition of the DAV.[98] The DAV argued first that the inclusion of free professions violated federal law, which reserved taxation of income to the federal government, and second that free professions were not 'trades' within the legal definition of that term and cited limitations upon competition such as prohibitions upon advertising and upon combining law practice with other occupations, which they claimed flowed naturally from 'professional morality' (*Standessitte*).[99] Nevertheless, in the course of 1921, Saxony, Baden, and several smaller states swept professional income into the purview of the trade tax.[100]

The years of economic stability in the middle 1920s saw a decline in governmental efforts to include the incomes of free professions under the trade tax.[101] Depression again reduced the incomes of localities and ended the respite for lawyers. By 1929, the battle raged both on the national level, where draft 'framework' legislation for the trade tax expressly *excluded* the incomes of free professions, and on the state level, particularly in Prussia, by far the largest state in Germany, where the ruling coalition, led by the Catholic Centre Party and the SPD, moved

---

[98] 'Aus der Vereinstätigkeit', *Abl* 8 (1921), 3–5, 3–4. The submission by the DAV to the Saxon government is reprinted at ibid., 19–21.

[99] Wassertrüdinger (Nürnberg), 'Gewerbesteuer vom Anwaltseinkommen?', *Abl* 8 (1921), 182–4 at 184.

[100] 'Aus der Vereinstätigkeit', *Abl* 8 (1921), 104–7, 105–6; the DAV indicated that it would rely upon local bar associations to combat introduction of the trade tax on lawyers in their states.

[101] For the larger political context of governmental fiscal policy during the financial crisis at the end of Weimar, see D. Orlow, *Weimar Prussia 1925–1933: The Illusion of Strength* (Pittsburgh, Univ. of Pittsburgh Press, 1991), esp. 165–72.

to *include* free professions under the tax.[102] The DAV once again mobilized lawyers' chambers and local bar associations to oppose the change, and it also staged a protest assembly and demonstration in Berlin.[103] Although lawyers avoided subjection to the trade tax in 1929, they were not so lucky in 1930. As economic conditions worsened, the search for tax revenues became more desperate, and the trade tax presented itself once again. Tradesmen and their organizations campaigned to have free professions included in hopes that the effective rates of taxation on their own incomes would be reduced.[104] Despite arguments by lawyers that their profession was not a trade, despite warnings that the revenues would not be significant, and despite warnings that the added burden might crush the already beleaguered profession, the Prussian parliament adopted a new trade tax law in March 1930 that included income from the practice of free professions.[105]

The DAV continued its resistance to the trade tax on two fronts. First, it recommended to the local bar associations that the increased financial burden of the trade tax be passed along to clients through an agreed-upon 10 per cent surcharge to the statutory attorneys' fees.[106] The local associations declared use of this surcharge to be a 'professional duty' (*Standespflicht*), and they imposed the surcharge despite objections by organizations of clients, until the government outlawed the practice by decree in 1932.[107] Second, the DAV challenged the legality of the trade tax in two sets of legal cases. One challenge before the national constitutional court (*Staatsgerichtshof*) contested the constitutionality of state taxation of professional income under both the Weimar Constitution, which reserved the income tax to the federal government, and the Prussian Constitution. The second set of challenges came through resort to appeal of tax assessments through the state

[102] 'Aus der Vereinstätigkeit', *Abl* 16 (1929), 76–80 at 78.

[103] Ibid, 116–18, 116–17; over 1,500 professionals attended the Berlin protest.

[104] 'Vereinsnachrichten', *Abl* 17 (1930), 97–100 at 99.

[105] For lawyers' arguments as to why they should not be included in the tax, see P. Marcuse, *Die freien Berufe und die Gewerbesteuer* (Leipzig, Oscar Brandstetter, 1929), and P. Marcuse, 'Die preußische Gewerbesteuer', *Abl* 17 (1930), 116–20.

[106] Ostler, *Die deutschen Rechtsanwälte*, 208; see also 'Die Abwälzung der Gewerbesteuer', *Abl* 17 (1930), 174–6; by 15 June 1930, 54 local bar associations had adopted 'pass through' provisions. The device of uniform surcharge tariffs was a reversion to war-time and inflation devices that permitted fees to keep pace with inflation through self-help measures without resort to legislation.

[107] See the exchange of letters between the Reichsverband der Deutschen Industrie and the DAV in May 1930, *Abl* 17 (1930), 175–6. As to the outlawing of the policy, see Ostler, *Die deutschen Rechtsanwälte*, 209.

finance courts (*Finanzgerichte*).[108] Both challenges wound their way up through the judicial system over the course of 1930 to 1932. In both instances, the organized bar met with no success. The constitutional court ruled in 1931 that extending the trade tax to include professional income did not violate the Weimar Constitution.[109] After lawyers achieved initial success on the intermediate appellate level, the Prussian Supreme Administrative Court ruled on 5 April 1932 that the Prussian trade tax law could legally be applied to professional income.[110] With that decision, legal action was at an end, and Prussian lawyers, the majority of all German lawyers, continued to operate under the burden of the trade tax.

The financial blow of subjection to the trade tax certainly was important to lawyers, but more important was the blow to their prestige, to their claim to special status. Despite their best efforts in legislature and courts, lawyers found their profession classified as a 'trade'. The power to make this decision lay in the increasingly polarized legislatures, where the parties of political liberalism, with which lawyers identified, found their numbers and hence their influence sharply reduced. Financial need on the part of localities, whose governing bodies were no longer the exclusive preserve of liberal parties, caused them to seek access to new sources of revenue and to pursue lawyers' incomes in a way that was insulting both to their economic and status security. The organized Bar and its liberal allies proved impotent to protect its own interests.

Finally, economic crisis forced lawyers to abandon one of the most cherished tenets of their professional ideology in order to solve the problem of overcrowding of the profession. Concerns about overcrowding had been raised as early as the debates over the Lawyers' Statute in the 1870s.[111] The end to limitations upon admission, some argued, would attract too many and unsuited candidates, lowering standards and damaging public esteem for the profession. Although initial

---

[108] 'Preußische Gewerbesteuer', *Abl* 17 (1930), 227.

[109] 'Aus der Vereinstätigkeit', *Abl* 18 (1931), 172–4 at 173.

[110] 'Aus der Vereinstätigkeit', *Abl* 19 (1932), 229–30 at 229; the opinion is reprinted at *JW* 61 (1932), 2113.

[111] Especially useful here is E. Fließ, 'Der Kampf um den numerus clausus in der Rechtsanwaltschaft', unpub. Dr. jur. diss., Freiburg i. B. (1933). For the consistent fears of overcrowding of the legal profession, see T. Kolbeck, *Juristenschwemmen. Untersuchungen über den juristischen Arbeitsmarkt im 19. und 20. Jahrhundert* (Frankfurt, Peter Lang, 1978), and H. Titze, 'Die zyklische Überproduktion von Akademikern im 19. und 20. Jahrhundert', *Geschichte und Gesellschaft* 10 (1984), 92–121.

increases in the size of the bar were not dramatic, many remained concerned. In 1885 and again in 1894, the Prussian Ministry of Justice inquired of lawyers' chambers and court of appeal presidents whether overcrowding existed in their districts. The Ministry even suggested the reimposition of a *numerus clausus* limiting the number of lawyers, but after gathering information on the question it took no action.[112]

The DAV consistently resisted all proposals to place any limitations upon admission to the bar. Invoking memories of the political persecution of lawyers and judges in the 1850s and 1860s, speakers and writers resisted calls for limitation upon the number of lawyers, not only in terms of economic liberalism ('free path to talent'), but by arguing that a state-imposed limitation upon the number of lawyers would lead to some system of state selection of whom to admit, resulting in the opportunity for, if not the reality of, political vetting. Despite agitation that emerged in the decades that surrounded the turn of the century, including the formation of special-interest associations of lawyers dedicated to reducing overcrowding, bar conventions in 1894 and 1911 rejected limitations upon admission.[113] Lawyers' chambers in most districts also opposed any imposition of limits upon admission to the bar.

After the First World War, economic dislocation, the influx of lawyers whose candidacy and training had been interrupted by the War and hence their admission delayed, together with the general expansion of higher education, led to renewed fears of overcrowding in the profession.[114] Many blamed overcrowding for the profession's general economic distress. Under the new circumstances of the 'democratic-social' republic, some argued, the state had the right, even the duty, to tighten the qualitative selection process for lawyers in order to protect the com-

[112] For the circular inquiries of the Prussian Ministry of Justice to the presidents of each court of appeal inquiring as to whether the practising bar was overcrowded, see GStA, I HA Rep. 84a, Nr. 36, 'Revision der Rechtsanwaltsordnung', 33–40 (11 April 1885) and 67–90 (19 Mar. 1894).

[113] 'Verhandlungen des XII. deutschen Anwaltstag zu Stuttgart', *JW* 23 (1894), Beilage zu Nr. 55; and 'Verhandlungen des XX. deutschen Anwaltstages zu Würzburg', *JW* 40 (1911), Zugabe zu Nr. 20, 50. See also Ledford, *From General Estate to Special Interest*, chap. 8, 245–73.

[114] For a useful survey of the perception and reality of overcrowding in the academic professions during the Weimar Republic, see M. Beatus, 'Academic Proletariat: The Problem of Overcrowding in the Learned Professions and Universities during the Weimar Republic 1918–1933', unpub. Ph.D. diss., Univ. of Wisconsin (1975). For a briefer summary, see W. M. Kotschnig, *Unemployment in the Learned Professions: An International Study of Occupational and Educational Planning* (Oxford, Oxford Univ. Press, 1937), 117–21.

mon welfare of the state, even if its actions circumscribed the rights of individuals:

Only Nature can allow herself the extravagance of lavishing thousands of seeds so that one can grow while the others may wither. Perhaps Manchesterite political theory can permit itself to take an analogous position on the question of the over-production of productive forces, but never the democratic-social republic. The social republic bears the responsibility of finding employment for willing labour forces.[115]

Leaders of the DAV, however, resolutely resisted calls for limitation upon admission. Proponents of limitation viewed the leaders of the bar as the problem, arguing that opposition to limitation came from the older, more established, and more economically secure segments of the profession. These members of the 'lawyers' upper class' controlled the institutions of the practising bar, the DAV, the Executive Boards of the lawyers' chambers, and the disciplinary panels, and they imposed their ideas and ideals upon younger and more economically vulnerable colleagues.[116]

Lawyers concerned about overcrowding ran slates of candidates in elections to the representatives' assembly of the DAV, and by the time of the economic crisis from 1928 to 1932, they possessed a greater voice in professional institutions. In November 1928, the assembly defeated a motion to reject all limitations upon admission, but it could not unite behind any specific mode of limitation.[117] In 1930, it endorsed a *numerus clausus* for *Referendare*, that is, a quota for those entering the period of practical legal training, which lay between the two bar examinations

---

[115] S. Feuchtwanger, *Die freien Berufe. Im besonderen; Die Anwaltschaft. Versuch einer allgemeinen Kulturwirtschaftslehre* (Munich and Leipzig, Duncker & Humblot, 1922), 150–1. (Author's translation.)

[116] The concept of an 'upper class of lawyers' stemmed from M. Rumpf, *Anwalt und Anwaltstand. Eine rechtswissenschaftliche und rechtssoziologische Untersuchung* (Leipzig, Oscar Brandstetter, 1926), 31–2. The idea of their remoteness from the day-to-day struggle of the younger, rank-and-file lawyers was elaborated by R. Bauer-Mengelberg, *Standesgefühl und Solidaritätsgefühl gesehen von der Psychologie des jungen Anwalts* (Leipzig, 1929), 58–9; he repeated this claim that the leadership was out of touch with the economic concerns of the average lawyer in 'Die Abgeordneten', *Abl* 18 (1931), 237–40, esp. 238, accusing the leaders of the DAV of being 'unrepresentative'.

[117] 'Vereinigungen Deutscher Anwaltverein', *JW* 57 (1928), 3094–5. The assembly defeated the rejection of all limitations by a vote of 61 to 56; it defeated a call for a waiting period by Assessoren by 68 to 49 and for a *numerus clausus* for Referendare by 64 to 52 (with one abstention). 'Stenographischer Bericht über die 22. Abgeordnetenversammlung vom 3. und 4. November 1928 im Hotel "Frankfurter Hof" zu Frankfurt a.M.', *Abl* 16 (1929), Beilage zu Heft 2, 115–18.

and was required for all legal careers, not just private practice.[118] Finally, in December 1932, at the depth of the world economic crisis, the assembly called for a three-year freeze on new admissions to the bar, proposing to use that time to draft a plan for a workable *numerus clausus* for lawyers, regardless of any risk of tutelage to the state.[119] Although no legislation was forthcoming prior to the advent of the National Socialists and their far different criteria for how to reduce overcrowding in the bar, the decision by the assembly to endorse an admissions freeze and *numerus clausus* represented a final effort by the DAV to prove its mettle as defender of the interests of the bar.

Conclusion

The events of April and May 1933 demonstrate beyond question the inability of the German bar to withstand the profound illiberalism of the National Socialist movement. But the co-ordination of the bar was neither a sudden capitulation in the face of Nazi militancy and coercion nor a mysterious abandonment of long-held lawyerly liberalism. Lawyers shared the fate of a liberalism whose claims to be the 'general estate' had long since lost plausibility in the face of an eroding social basis of support.[120] The roots of the response of lawyers to the changed circumstances of the Weimar Republic and Third Reich lay in pre-War ideologies, institutions, and structural changes. The six issues confronting lawyers under Weimar that are discussed in this essay illustrate the limited utility of lawyers' liberal professional structure and ideology under those changed circumstances.

Just as the leaders of German liberal political parties failed to convince the German people that their platforms advanced the general

---

[118] 'Beschlüsse der 25. Abgeordneterversammlung des Deutschen Anwaltvereins vom 22. und 23. März 1930 zu Leipzig', *JW* 59 (1930), 1036. The vote to control overcrowding by limitations upon admission was 65 to 50. 'Stenographischer Bericht über die 25. Abgeordnetenversammlung vom 22. und 23. März zu Leipzig', *Abl* 17 (1930), Beilage zu Heft 6, 99–102; the vote to adopt the *numerus clausus* for Referendare was 63 to 52, ibid., 102. Max Hachenburg noted with surprise that the chief proponents of the *numerus clausus* came not from the large cities, where the overcrowding was most pronounced, but from medium and smaller districts; 'Juristische Rundschau', *Deutsche Juristen-Zeitung* 35 (1930), 539–44 at 542.

[119] The votes on the 3-year freeze were 127 to 19 in favour; on the *numerus clausus*, 115 to 31 in favour; 'Stenographischer Bericht über die 29. Abgeordnetenversammlung von 4. Dezember 1932 zu Berlin', *Abl* 20 (1933), Beilage zu Heft 3, 70–2.

[120] The parallel to the analysis of the fate of the liberal parties is striking; see the conclusion in Jones, *German Liberalism*, 476–82.

interest, leaders of the bar failed both to make the case to the public that lawyers represented the interests of all of society and to maintain their own claim to be the 'general estate' of private practitioners, representing the interests of all lawyers. Lawyer-notables who practised before the Supreme Court and the Berlin *Kammergericht* dominated the Executive Board and Representative Assembly of the DAV; superior court and court of appeal lawyers controlled lawyers' chambers; and well-to-do local practitioners led local voluntary associations. Claims of these leaders to represent the interests of all lawyers succumbed to outsiders' conviction, which emerged in the debates surrounding retirement insurance, simultaneous admission, and limitations upon admission, that they were unrepresentative, a 'lawyers' upper class'. Moreover, leaders of the bar failed to convince the larger public of the legitimacy of lawyers' claims to special status and special control of their own affairs, as should be the due of the 'general estate', losing battles to exclude women, to ensure lawyers' practice before labour courts, and to avoid the trade tax. Repeated legislative campaigns unmasked the bar's posturing as the 'general estate' and revealed it as one of many competing interest groups.

In the same way that the challenges of Weimar exposed the bar to be just another special-interest group representing its narrow social basis, the proliferation of special-interest bar associations transformed professional institutions into a terrain upon which those groups struggled with each other for hegemony. The reaction of the leaders of the DAV was to attempt to create new procedural avenues through which interests could be expressed. Procedural reforms, such as broader representation for excluded voices, did not resolve substantive claims of justice but only restructured the terms of debate. As the leadership sought to hold liberal institutions together, special interests began to look to outside agencies in order to attain their goals. Status concerns loomed at least as large as economic interest in such disputes as that over simultaneous admission, and the inability of the institutions of the bar to mediate those disputes called into question both the legitimacy of bar leaders to represent the interests of the profession *and* the claims of the bar as a whole to special treatment as the 'guardians of the law'.

Lawyers who turned to the state for assistance, both leaders of the bar and insurgents, found that their influence in the 1920s and early 1930s did not extend as far as it had before the First World War. By 1922, only eleven lawyers in private practice served in the Reichstag, and by 1932 only fourteen.[121] Similarly, city councils, formerly a preserve of liberal influence and a stronghold of lawyers as members, became more competitive electoral arenas under the reformed suffrage of the republic, and lawyers lost ground.[122] The political voice of lawyers in elective bodies fell with the fortunes of the liberal political parties.

After 1918, lawyers also encountered new, unfamiliar, and less friendly bureaucracies. The Reich Ministry of Justice, previously the principal and usually sympathetic bureaucratic contact, was no longer the sole arena in which lawyers had to contend. Many lawyers cooled in their support of mandatory retirement insurance when the Ministry of Labour eagerly embraced the idea, and that same Ministry steadfastly pursued the Social Democratic programme of labour law reform, despite the resistance of the organized bar and its insistence that the Ministry of Justice should have jurisdiction.

Lastly, the narrow proceduralism of professional ideology, closely linked with liberal *Rechtsstaat* doctrine, offered no solutions to conflicts within the bar or in German society. Like liberalism, professional ideology fundamentally *denied* the legitimacy of interest groups. It refused to prescribe substantive bases to decide among competing claims, instead focusing upon procedures that avoided addressing the heart of issues. The final refuge of the organized bar was to seek to change the procedural ground rules of entry into the profession by endorsing a *numerus clausus*.[123] They thus prepared the ground for convincing themselves in 1933 that they could remain true to their formal commitment to liberty even while they acquiesced in injustice. Remaining within their framework as the paradigmatic independent, liberal, 'free' profession, lawyers demonstrated the limits of procedural liberalism.

[121] J. Curtius, 'Anwaltschaft und Parlament', *JW* 51 (1922), 1289–91 at 1289. See also complaints about too few lawyers in the Reichstag in '1927', *Abl* 14 (1927), 1–2 at 2, and 'Aus der Vereinstätigkeit', *Abl* 19 (1932), 188–91 at 189–90 (only 14 out of 560 deputies in the just-dissolved Reichstag). For the centrality of political activity and parliamentary service to the self-conception of lawyers in France during the late 19th and early 20th cents, see L. Karpik, 'Lawyers and Politics in France, 1814–1950: The State, the Market, and the Public', *Law & Social Inquiry* 13 (1988), 707–36 at 719–20.

[122] H. P. von Strandmann, 'The Liberal Power Monopoly in the Cities of Imperial Germany', in L. E. Jones & J. Retallack (eds.), *Elections, Mass Politics, and Social Change in Modern Germany: New Perspectives* (Cambridge, Cambridge Univ. Press, 1992), 93–117; W. Hardtwig, 'Großstadt und Bürgerlichkeit in der politischen Ordnung des Kaiserreichs', in Lothar Gall (ed.), *Stadt und Bürgertum im 19. Jahrhundert* (Munich, Oldenbourg, 1990), 19–64.

[123] While Tilmann Krach concludes that anti-Semitism among lawyers did not play a significant role in the decision in Dec. 1932 to endorse a *numerus clausus*, the decision nevertheless 'objectively facilitated the National Socialists in their measures against Jewish lawyers', Krach, *Jüdische Rechtsanwälte*, 75.

8 Making the Courts Safe for the Powerful: the Commercial Stimulus for Judicial Autonomy in Reforms of the United States' Bankruptcy Law

Terence C. Halliday and Bruce G. Carruthers

> The complete independence of the courts of justice is peculiarly essential in a limited Constitution.—Alexander Hamilton, *Federalist* 78, 1788

The institutional foundation of limited government in the United States received its most eloquent early defence by New York lawyer, Alexander Hamilton, later to be founder of the Bank of New York and an architect of the national banking system. Writing in *The Federalist Papers*, a widely circulated tract that sought to persuade New Yorkers to ratify the new federal constitution, Hamilton averred that 'courts of justice are to be considered as the bulwarks of a limited Constitution against legislative encroachments'. Against the legislature, the courts provided a balance against majoritarian tyranny; against the executive—and, formerly, the monarchy—independent courts erected 'a barrier to despotism'.[1]

Chief Justice Marshall's Opinion in *Marbury* v. *Madison* [1803], which allowed courts to strike down a constitutionally repugnant piece of legislation, enormously expanded, at least in principle, the putative power of courts. By so doing, it presaged an arena of conflict in which lawyers, judges, and political parties all had stakes. Since the formative years of the new republic, this distinctive institutional matrix heralded a form of politics in which political parties would regard courts as a prize to be controlled or contained, and lawyers would be caught in a perpetual tension between their own constitutional status as officers of the courts, and thus as putative champions of the rule of law, and their everyday obligations to clients and political parties, in which substantive commitments sat uneasily with much vaunted legal neutrality.

---

[1] A Hamilton, J. Madison, & J. Jay, *The Federalist Papers* (New York, The New American Library, 1788 [1961]), No. 78: 465, 469.

In the United States lawyers have heavily invested in political struggles over independence of the courts. The condition of the judiciary in state and federal governments has been a primary preoccupation of bar association collective action since the last quarter of the nineteenth century and, indeed, was one of the founding *raisons d'etre* for a revival of bar associations in the 1870s. An alliance of bar elites with civic reformers sought to widen the distance between party control of the courts and judicial self-determination and self-expression. That this movement coincided with the profession's own efforts at self-determination was no accident. But the legendary diversity of American lawyers has made internal professional politics over the courts almost as byzantine as its struggles with parties, and sometimes, with judges themselves. Judicial independence has historically been an elite political project, and some of its strongest foes have come from within the legal profession itself. Thus the outcome of professional conflicts with political parties has been partially contingent on the resolution of conflicts among lawyers over who should control the courts and who will have access to judicial posts.

Alongside what might be called a 'civic' push for judicial autonomy exists another powerful impulse for independent courts. We shall show that the reproduction of the moderate state may rest as heavily on commercial interests as on constitutional doctrine. Lawyers historically may have advanced judicial independence for reasons as diverse as legal ideology, class interest, antipopulist defence, or professional self-protection. Their motivations were sometimes principled and sometimes base. But commercial and financial industries, too, can be heavily invested in the neutrality, competence, and efficiency of a justice system whose rulings affect not only individual corporations, but may establish rules of the game for fundamental economic practices, such as corporate reorganization and liquidation. Commercial interests will not always find courts important enough to warrant their attention, nor find autonomy of the courts to be in their favour. But in those circumstances when far-reaching court judgments reach to the core of commercial practice, and the very structure of court administration itself affects the predictability and quality of justice, then it is most probable that financial industries will mobilize to ensure their interests are protected. That mobilization, necessarily, will engage legal professions. Just as lawyers have split over their support for court autonomy in the reform movement for merit selection of judges, so, too, lawyers divide over the institutional form that will be taken by adjudicatory and administrative institutions that deal with financial regulation. And just as individual firms represent corporate clients in individual cases, so also can collective organizations of lawyers be called to represent industries in fundamental restructuring of laws and legal institutions.

We can therefore identify a double movement for judicial independence in the American courts, fuelled by different interests, but in both cases resting on external alliances that divided the bar against itself. In one, a strong alliance between the elite founders of major bar associations and civic reformers sought a restructuring of the state to attenuate party control over judicial recruitment and management. This movement was central to the collective reorganization of the profession from the 1870s, and stimulated (together with a reorganization of bar associations) the founding of the American Judicature Society, a successful reformist group that has consistently, and often effectively, pushed for judicial autonomy since 1913. The other movement was fuelled by changes in the economy and practice. As the relative importance of commercial practice and the power of corporate clients has expanded into the last quarter of the twentieth century, a powerful segment of the profession that is organized to serve corporate interests, aided by academic lawyers, has joined an effective *de facto* partnership with finance capital to ensure that courts, so far as possible, function to advance their model of an efficient market.

This double movement for judicial independence masks two complex variations that distinguish the means of action, even if the ends remain functionally identical. In the movement for civic independence, the organized bar as a whole, at least insofar as it was represented by major metropolitan and state associations, adopted the goals for independence that came to be championed by the American Judicature Society. This orientation towards judicial independence initially coincided with the organized bar movement, which lasted from the 1870s through to the mid-1930s, to draw all lawyers into effective, inclusive associations for collective action. The bid for restructuring of the state occurred concomitantly with consolidation of the profession as a unitary political actor. In the movement for commercial viability of the courts, however, which comes to be manifest much later in the twentieth century, the exponential growth in the size of the legal profession has been accompanied by a correlative segmentation into a vast array of specialty, gender-based, race-based, client-based lawyer groups, where the principle of segmental identity predominates over unitary state and national associations. The politics of lawyers and the courts consequently permits sub-groups of lawyers and judges, represented by their sectional associations, to negotiate over legislative reforms, with putative external partners, relatively independently of the bar as a whole.

This double movement does not imply a simple historical sequence from civic to commercial interests. Clearly the behaviour of courts was of great importance to major corporate clients in the mid-nineteenth century, for the case law that emerged constituted the economic environment in which the powerful thrived.[2] But while bar associations were non-existent, or in their infancy, and courts were responsive to the instrumental interests of corporations, it made little sense for business to mobilize through lawyers' collegial organizations. The late twentieth century presents a significant contrast. Civic efforts at judicial reform still thrive and rank highly in the goals of major professional bodies. But courts, too, have commensurately grown in importance, and their judgments affect both the survival of large corporations and the viability of financial and other markets. Alongside civic movements for independence, therefore, have grown less concerted, less coherent, and less unified *ad hoc* alliances between industry groups and segments of the profession.

This paper illustrates the financial push for judicial independence through the politics of the 1978 United States Bankruptcy Code, a legislative innovation that has had far-reaching effects on corporate reorganization, labour relations, business strategy, bank lending, and managerial control. The bankruptcy legislation demonstrates that the independence and power of the courts can be critical to banks, investors, and the financial industry. But just as the struggle for autonomy of the courts cannot be separated from the interests of powerful commercial actors, neither can it be detached from the internecine politics of lawyers and judges, generalists and specialists, legal academics and bankruptcy practitioners. Hence in yet another historical moment and national venue, the alliances of fractions of the legal profession with external actors provide a further, albeit economic, incentive for the production of the moderate state.

We begin by reviewing the first movement for judicial independence, which began following the Civil War and continues until the present. We shall then look more intently at one case—the reform of American bankruptcy legislation—and consider how one fraction of the legal profession found common cause with the banking and financial industries to advocate a radical reorganization of bankruptcy courts.

---

[2] See, e.g., L. M. Friedman, *A History of American Law*, 2nd edn. (New York, Simon & Schuster, 1982), 202–47, 359–501; M. J. Horwitz, *The Transformation of American Law: 1780–1860* (Cambridge, Mass., Harvard Univ. Press, 1977).

The Politics of Judicial Autonomy

Since the founding of the American Republic, judicial autonomy and Bar politics have lived together in uneasy co-existence. The frame of that cohabitation can be narrowed to the method of appointing judges, which has been the paramount indicator of judicial autonomy from executive, legislative, and party control; or it can be widened to embrace the full panoply of structural initiatives that differentiate courts and judges from any form of direct political intervention. Both set a context for the growing significance of commercial interests in judicial independence. And each implicates the legal profession on national and local stages.

A. Judicial Selection

Five major methods for appointing judges have predominated at different points in the last two centuries.[3] During the colonial period, appointment by the executive (usually the governor) and the legislature were the primary means of ascending to the bench, although elections were not unknown. After the Revolution, however, the appointment of judges was progressively replaced by popular election. The extension of the suffrage to election of judges moved slowly from the early 1800s until it became a flood by mid-century. Courts and bar associations alike were caught in the same levelling surge of populist sentiment that insisted on broader popular control of public offices. Jacksonian Democrats and their successors swept away most vestiges of executive and judicial appointment. New York took the lead to elect judges in 1848, and by the middle 1850s, fifteen of the existing twenty-nine states had adopted this method. Moreover, virtually all new states entering the Union after 1846 also adopted a method of popular election of judges who ran on partisan ballots.[4] Bar associations, too, were entangled in the outburst against privileged statuses. Tocqueville had styled lawyers as the new American aristocracy. After Jackson, this was not an epithet to be celebrated. The once robust and active associations of

---

[3] R. A. Watson & R. G. Downing, *The Politics of the Bench and the Bar: Judicial Selection Under the Missouri Nonpartisan Court Plan* (New York, John Wiley, 1969), 2 (n. 8), 7; L. M. Friedman, *History*, 124–38.

[4] J. W. Hurst, *The Growth of American Law: The Law Makers* (Boston, Little, Brown, 1950), 138–61; Watson & Downing, *Politics of the Bench and the Bar*, 7. On the early post-revolutionary struggle over law and politics, as it was refracted through the institutional structure of the courts, see K. L. Hall, *The Magic Mirror: Law in American History* (New York, Oxford Univ. Press, 1989), 67–88.

lawyers in many major cities and counties were extinguished entirely. Lawyers were left with only a handful of the clubs or associations that Tocqueville had so vaunted as a notable feature of political organization in the United States. The courts became the locus of professional activity and the core of professional identity.[5]

It is more than an historical accident that the second wave of collegial organization by lawyers should coincide with the broad disgruntlement among elite lawyers over the condition of state and local courts. After the Civil War, the development of the big city political machines—where a dominant party controlled government institutions and rewarded party loyalists with patronage appointments—knit politics and the courts even more tightly together. Party bosses were the new patrons of 'justice' and their family, friends, supporters, and other recipients of political largesse moved from the precincts to the bench. To elite lawyers, estranged from urban machine politics, this abuse of the high institutional order envisaged by Alexander Hamilton was deeply offensive. The political manipulation of the courts became so blatantly scandalous that it precipitated, in no small measure, the new wave of lawyers' professional organizations; since the former groups had been so completely devastated in the years leading up to the Civil War.

The formation of the Association of the Bar of the City of New York (ABCNY) in 1870 established a pattern that would be reproduced in major cities and states across the continent in the ensuing decades. An explosion of bar organizations had its stimulus not merely in the political rape of courts, but it became the *raison d'être* for many fledgling groups. By 1920, the United States was exhaustively peppered by national, state, county, and metropolitian associations, virtually all giving priority to problems of court organization and judicial appointment.[6]

[5] For an interpretation of legal professions and Jacksonianism in the context of political revolutions more generally, see M. Burrage, 'Revolution as a Starting Point for the Comparative Analysis of the French, American, and English Legal Professions', in R. L. Abel & P. S. C. Lewis (eds.), *Lawyers in Society*, vol. 3, *Comparative Theories*, (Berkeley, Univ. of California Press, 1989), 338–51. The demise of lawyers' collective associations should not be overstated for the court remained as a centre of professional activity. On a small scale, the circuit, and local collegial ties of practitioners could retain a sense of identity and some measure of control.

[6] On the foundings and failures of state associations, see T. C. Halliday, M. J. Powell, & M. W. Granfors, 'Minimalist Organizations: Vital Events in State Bar Associations, 1870–1930', *Amer. Sociol. Rev.* 52 (1987) 456–71. The rise of the American Bar Association is documented sympathetically by Rutherford in and sceptically by J. S. Auerbach, *Unequal Justice: Lawyers and Social Change in Modern America* (New York, Oxford Univ. Press, 1976). Major studies on metropolitan associations include G. Martin (see n. 7 *infra*), M. J. Powell, on the New York city bar, and T. C. Halliday on the Chicago bar (see n. 8 *infra*).

As the pioneer, the ABCNY well exemplifies the power of revulsion and reaction against the deformity of the courts to animate collective action. Two years before the new wave of bar organization began, a leading New York lawyer and master of florid alarmist prose, George Templeton Strong, told his diary that 'bench and bar settle deeper in the mud every year and every month. They must be near the bottom now.' By the end of 1868 he confessed to have grossly underestimated the baseness of his fellows and community. 'The New Yorker', he lamented, 'belongs to a community worse governed by lower and baser blackguard scum than any city in Western Christendom, or in the world.'[7]

Organization for purposes of reforming the courts was not for the faint-hearted. Lawyers were afraid to criticize the bench for fear of retaliation. Nevertheless, at an early organizational meeting, William Evarts, an eminent trial lawyer destined to be first President of the ABCNY, told his audience that the traffic of the courts with patronage, influence, and political authority had brought them into disrepute. And Samuel Tilden, a political opponent of Boss Tweed, the corrupt machine overlord of New York City, called both for an elevation of the bar, and to have 'the administration of justice made pure and honourable'. More pointedly, he avowed that 'the City of New York is the commercial and monetary capital of this continent. If it would remain so, it must establish an elevated character for its Bar, and a reputation throughout the whole country for its purity in the administration of justice.'[8] The commercial current, however understated, ran beneath the surface of bar reform politics in the nation's leading financial centre. In 1872, an enormous scandal put four New York judges on trial for corruption and launched the city bar on the first of many major campaigns. Bar leaders agreed that the problem was patronage and political 'appointments' through partisan elections. Only appointment by the Governor, with the approval of the Senate, would solve the problem. This proposal formed the heart of the 1873 referendum campaign by the neophyte association—a noble effort defeated by 319,979 votes to 115,337.[9]

---

[7] G. Martin, *Causes and Conflicts: The Centennial History of the Association of the Bar of the City of New York, 1870–1970* (Boston, Houghton Mifflin, 1972), 3.

[8] Ibid., 16, 36, 38; M. J. Powell, *From Patrician to Professional Elite: The Transformation of the New York City Bar Association* (New York, Russell Sage, 1988); T. C. Halliday, *Beyond Monopoly: Lawyers, State Crises, and Professional Empowerment* (Chicago, Univ. of Chicago Press, 1987).

[9] Martin, *Causes and Conflicts*, 109–19.

The New York experience was replicated across the country. The organized bar—as the complex network of associations came to be called—undertook two broad strategies of change and control. The first operated within the parameters of popular judicial elections. This approach sought to make the best out of a bad situation by minimizing political party influence on judicial selection. Through a variety of ingenious devices, such as non-partisan ballots, separate judicial nominating conventions, and polls of lawyers about preferred judicial candidates, bar associations gamely stepped into the ring with political power-brokers and almost invariably took a severe beating.[10]

The more muscular approach to judicial selection aimed at changing the parameters of elections altogether. But if mounting decades of defeat over the lesser goal were any precedent, bold ventures towards structural change that required the acquiescence of politicians in the destruction of one element of their power base seemed vainly foolish. Part of the problem—a large part—arose from the weakness of the profession itself. Although bar associations covered the entire map of the US with voluntary organizations, most associations at the turn of the century were puny and several had expired altogether. An inability to attract and hold members, limited incentives for membership, problems of bringing widely dispersed lawyers together in the same body—these and other deficits provided limited force for confrontation with parties and legislatures. Moreover, the divisions between the upper and lower reaches of the profession that had stalked professionalism through the nineteenth century eroded collective action from within. For every elite lawyer who wanted to keep parties at arms' length were three or four professional artisans whose only hope for ascending to the bench lay through party sponsorship.

The turning-point in state bar organization, which had enduring repercussions for national and local bodies as well, came with the founding of the American Judicature Society by Herbert Harley in 1913. Like other perceptive observers of the professional scene in the United States, Harley recognized that most realistic hopes of reformed judicial administration, quite apart from professional self-regulation, rested on the robustness of professional associations. No other groups had such a symbiotic and sustained interest in the character of judges and courts. Voluntary bar associations had proved disappointing. Many

---

[10] For a detailed account of such initiatives by the Chicago Bar Association after 1887, which also illustrates the Herculean task facing the organized bar, see E. M Martin, *The Role of the Bar in Electing the Bench in Chicago* (Chicago, Univ. of Chicago Press, 1936).

had failed. Between 1877 and 1902 eighteen state associations collapsed and were subsequently revived. But even those associations that did not fail were frequently so anaemic that they had paltry resources to mount effective campaigns of court reorganization and judicial reforms.[11]

Harley found a solution across the border in Ontario, Canada. Following in the mould established by its English progenitor, the Upper Canada Law Society required that all lawyers be members as a condition of practising in the jurisdiction. This model was imported by the American Judicature Society and widely disseminated under the label of the bar integration or unification plan. Although slow to take root, the bar integration movement gathered rapid momentum during the fallow years of the Great Depression and by 1950 included more than half of all state bar associations in its ranks.[12]

Court reform stood at the apex of goals awaiting pursuit by exercise of the organized Bar's newly-flexed muscle. But to what particular end? Roscoe Pound, a young law professor destined to be Dean of Harvard Law School, delivered a watershed speech to the American Bar Association in 1906 in which he cautioned that popular election of judges was destroying the reputation of the judiciary, a refrain taken up by former US President Taft, and the founders of the American Judicature Society. While the American Judicature Society had a manifesto for court reorganization much broader than judicial selection, the modes of appointing judges remained its highest visibility issue.

But quite how to remove politics from judicial appointment remained obscure. The new model of merit selection—the Missouri Plan, named after the first state to adopt it in 1940—gestated for some twenty-five years, following a series of intermediate proposals, not least of which was offered by English socialist, Harold Laski, in 1926. The Missouri Plan refined and distilled earlier versions into a pure model of appointment that had three elements. A panel of lawyers, judges, and laymen would select three nominees for a judicial position, based on merit. The Governor would choose one of the three. The judge would subsequently run in an election for re-appointment, but unopposed.[13]

---

[11] Halliday, Powell & Granfors, 'Minimalist Organizations'.

[12] On the founding and expansion of Bar integration, see D. McKean, *The Integrated Bar* (Boston, Houghton Mifflin, 1963); T. J. Schneyer, 'The Incoherence of the Unified Bar Concept: Generalizing from the Wisconsin Case', *Amer. Bar Found. Res. Jrnl.* (1983), 1–108; T. C. Halliday, M. J. Powell, & M. W. Granfors, 'After Minimalism: Transformations of State Bar Associations from Market Dependence to State Sponsorship, 1917–1950', *Amer. Sociol. Rev* (1993), 515–35.

[13] Watson & Downing, *Politics of Bench and Bar*, 8–14; Friedman, *History*, 690.

The movement to upgrade courts, attenuate political influences, professionalize judging, and legitimate the justice system percolated up to the American Bar Association, which persuaded the federal government and the Senate that all federal judges should be screened by the bar before nomination. State and metropolitan associations also shared in the drive for court reform. A survey of all major state and metropolitan associations in 1980 found that more than 60 per cent had mounted campaigns over the past year to institute merit selection in the courts.[14]

The chequered political successes of bar campaigns for merit selection resulted not only from political opposition outside of the profession, but from political differences within it. When the New York City Bar pushed for merit selection during a 1967 Constitutional Convention, professional class warfare broke into the open. Like Chicago, and the entire institutionalized system of electoral judicial politics, local political parties had high stakes in local courts because they provided patronage posts for the party faithful. For small town and community lawyers, a politically-sponsored path to a local judgeship was the only means of obtaining the security and prestige of what many regarded as the capstone of a legal career. Moreover, lawyer-legislators, themselves, commonly had aspirations to reach the bench. According to a former President of the New York City Bar, 'nearly every member of the legislature who is a member of the bar has such aspirations'. And as representatives of their constituents, they were also mindful of the political mileage to be gained from appointments of ethnic and black judges. Local and ethnic Bar groups therefore came out in opposition to merit selection. Proponents of merit selection, by contrast, were drawn disproportionately from the corporate and defence bars, a finding that could be replicated in Chicago, Missouri, and across the nation.[15]

B. *Autonomy of the Courts*

By the middle 1950s, the narrower frame of judicial independence—the merit selection of judges—had broadened into a much more global effort by major bar associations to produce a greater measure of institutional autonomy from politics. Analytically, these initiatives had two

[14] J. Grossman, *The American Bar Association and Judicial Selection*; Halliday, *Beyond Monopoly*, 294–8.
[15] Powell, *From Patrician to Professional Elite*, 206; Halliday, *Beyond Monopoly*, 148–58; Watson & Downing, *Politics of Bench and Bar*.

principal components: structural differentiation of the court system from embedding organizations, whether political parties, state legislatures, or local municipal councils; and bureaucratization of the judicial institution itself.[16]

Structural differentiation of the courts from political control took two forms. On the one hand, differentiation occurred through the separation of organizational responsibilities (such as the setting of court procedures and the making of court rules) from legislative intervention.[17] For instance, in the Civil Procedure Acts in 1933 and 1955, the Illinois bar associations succeeded in reforms that vested greater powers in the Illinois Supreme Court to make court rules, rather than leaving them in the hands of the legislature. After much heavy politicking by the Chicago and Illinois bar associations, the 1964 and 1970 reforms of the Judicial Article of the Illinois Constitution permitted the Supreme Court of Illinois to decide what cases it should hear and which should be heard at lower levels in the system.[18] Throughout the United States during the 1970s, more than 40 per cent of major bar associations sought to replace local financing of municipal and county courts, which often bred political interference, with state-wide financing; around one-third of associations sought to limit legislative rule-making authority; and between 15 and 25 per cent fought to give courts far more independent control over their financial affairs. On the other hand, between 25 and 40 per cent of major lawyers' associations sought to professionalize legal and judicial roles by abolishing the Justice of the Peace system, excluding non-lawyers from judicial offices, and resisting part-time judging.[19]

Bureaucratization of the courts complemented differentiation for it consolidated the institutional coherence of the court system throughout an entire state and thereby created an administrative hierarchy that was

[16] Halliday, *Beyond Monopoly*, chap. 6.

[17] By structural differentiation we refer to the process whereby one organization or role bifurcates into 2 organizations, or roles, but the performance of both structures, at least initially, is functionally equivalent to that performed by the original structure. In general on structural differentiation in the general theory of rationalization of law and other institutions, see W. Schluchter, *The Rise of Western Rationalism: Max Weber's Developmental History* (Berkeley, Univ. of California Press, 1981).

[18] The New York City bar also sought to rationalize and modernize rules by ridding them of inconsistencies, obsolescence, and disorganization and to attenuate the power of the legislature. They actively worked against the provisions of the New York Civil Practice Act of 1921, which allowed the legislature to make court rules. Powell shows that the city bar sought consistently 'to separate the political and judicial spheres'. See Powell, *From Patrician to Professional Elite*, 196–200.

[19] Ibid., 294–303.

much more resistant to local political pressures. For example, after the Second World War, ABCNY leaders railed against overlapping jurisdictions and a profusion of courts that had few unifying organizational mechanisms or centralized authority. Local courts and judges were essentially autonomous, at least from other courts, and 'local financing meant local control of the courts' which hardly aided their independence. No systematic or comprehensive reforms had taken place since the Field Code in 1848.[20] The New York bar associations joined with local crusading groups in the 1950s and 1960s to transform court administration, recommending 'a simplified, unified court system with a central administrative office as a necessary rationalization of the numerous courts with overlapping jurisdictions and without any centralized authority'.[21] In 1962 the New York state legislature passed a Court Reorganization Act which created a centralized state-wide court administration, although financing remained local. Significantly, the courts with the most 'immense patronage power', the Court of Claims and the Surrogates Courts, remained untouched. Powell concludes that a centralized court system threatened local control over courts and judges' previous discretion to run their courts as they wanted.[22] But New York was not alone in its push for unification of the courts: in the 1970s, bar associations in more than two-thirds of the states engaged in some form of political initiative to organize their courts in a rational hierarchy independent of legislative and executive constraints.[23]

Divisions within the bar recurred on this wider political front as surely as they were evident in campaigns for merit selection of judges. In the 1961 effort of New York bar leaders to wrest control of court rules away from the legislature, trial lawyers, who represented plaintiffs, were pitted against big-firm lawyers, who represented corporations. The plaintiffs' lawyers, who styled themselves as defenders of the weak and poor, and who were often drawn from ethnic and working-class communities, viewed efforts to change pre-trial procedures as an establishment assault on their practice and clients. Plaintiffs' lawyers had been excluded from the revision process, and they resented the refusal of reformers to hear their contrary point of view. Lawyer-legislators were responsive to these concerns. In many respects, they identified more with the plaintiffs' than the elite bar. And apart from their generic

---

[20] Powell, *From Patrician to Professional Elite*, 196–200.
[21] ABCNY, *Bad Housekeeping: The Administration of the New York Courts* (1955,) 197.
[22] Powell, *From Patrician to Professional Elite*, 200–4.
[23] Halliday, *Beyond Monopoly*, ibid., 299.

disquiet with a loss of statutory control over rules, they feared the rule-making judges might also side with elite defence lawyers against the plaintiffs' bar. Eventually the Act passed the legislature, but only after it had been purged of its controversial provisions, and most notably, the threat to weaken political control over judicial rule-making.[24]

This inherent conflict between small town, ethnic lawyers who represented individual clients, and the large-firm corporate leaders who controlled the major bar associations is played out across the entire panoply of the politics of judicial autonomy. Indeed, it has been shown that political takeovers of major bar leadership by marginalized lawyers, or breakaway movements to form counter-associations, have frequently been propelled by the need to control collective resources in order to influence the courts.[25] For the lawyers, as for politicians, judicial autonomy has been an historic battleground, whose repercussions reach ultimately to the shape of the moderate state.

A Professional–Financial Alliance for Judicial Reform

The continuing engagement of legal professions with courts is not confined to the ostensible politics of judicial reform, with its frontal assaults on the prerogatives of parties and patronage, but it extends into substantive law reforms where the texture of politics is highly complex, for it involves some of the most powerful and sophisticated collective actors in advanced industrial societies. Even in areas of commercial law, where statutory revisions had implications for the calibre of justice available to litigants, the status of courts is thrust into the bargaining arena. Indeed, given the potential power of courts in the institutional form of American government, the courts are a point of contention in rough proportion to the stakes of issues resolved in them, and this pertains as much to commercial as to party political interests.

At first blush, the 1978 United States Bankruptcy Code presents an unlikely instance in which a variant on the historical struggle over the definition of courts should be re-enacted. Broadly acknowledged as one of the more arcane and marginal areas of legal specialty, bankruptcy has traditionally existed in the nether regions of legal practice, only

---

[24] For the views expressed by ABCNY leaders over the issues at stake in the reforms, see Annual Reports of the President, *Record of the Association of the Bar of the City of New York*, no. 17, 1962: 374–410; & no. 16, 1961: 350–84.

[25] M. J. Powell, 'Anatomy of a Counter-Bar Association: The Chicago Council of Lawyers', *Amer. Bar. Found. Res. Jrnl.* (1979), 501.

rarely bursting into the public eye, swiftly to recede again out of public consciousness. This borderline existence changed radically after 1970.[26] In the past two decades, bankruptcy law arguably has experienced the most meteoric climb in professional status of any specialty over the modern history of the legal profession. Within its transformative restructuring can be detected a double movement of change where lawyer-led reforms influenced not only economic behaviour, but the wider institutional framework of justice.

One movement within the bankruptcy reforms was consistent with the historical trend to attenuate political influence and patronage in the functioning of lower courts, whether in state or federal jurisdictions. Indeed, the status of courts threatened to overwhelm all the sweeping substantive changes that were generated by the principal reforms. Another movement had less symbolic notability, but potentially greater practical import—the attraction of courts for corporations as a forum of dispute resolution and a haven for financial reconstruction. As the major financial industry groups told Congressional hearings, their willingness to aid in the rehabilitation of financially disabled companies turned as much on bankruptcy administration as well as substantive revisions. Major credit institutions signalled their reluctance to use the institutions of justice as a forum of last resort for saving high risk companies unless the courts made significant changes in the ways they treated business.

Although several bankruptcy bills were introduced to Congress between 1974 and 1978, we focus on the penultimate bills before the House of Representatives, HR 8200, and the United States Senate, S 2266, in which lines of conflict and points of consensus are clearly delineated and all parties were in play. We focus on two aspects. First, the demand by the financial industry, led by national associations of bankers, for changes in the court system that would ensure the efficiency, the neutrality, and the competence of commercial courts. These issues quickly devolved into patterns of discourse reminiscent from earlier epochs of court reform in which matters of court jurisdiction, patronage influences, quality of judges, and modes of judicial appointment were highly contentious. Second, the legal profession and judges had a pervasive influence in these reforms, but it was highly segmented and often conflictual. The forms and factions of professional politics

---

[26] See Y. Dezalay, *Marchands de droit* (Paris, Fayard, 1992); and B. G. Carruthers & T. C. Halliday, *Rescuing Business* (Oxford, Oxford Univ. Press, expected 1998).

therefore demonstrate the contingency between the institutional expression of justice and manifestations of lawyers' collective action.

A. *The Prelude to Bankruptcy Reforms*

A report from the independent Washington think-tank, the Brookings Institution, flags most visibly a rising tide of discontent with bankruptcy law and practice, which culminated in the 1978 Bankruptcy Code.[27] The Brookings' investigators recognized that changes in the economy, most particularly in the explosive growth of consumer credit, had created an economic environment that built up enormous pressures on a governmental apparatus that threatened to buckle under the strain. Prodded into action by a request from the federal judiciary, public administration expert David Stanley directed case studies of eight federal judicial districts, interviewed some 400 debtors and bankrupts, conducted a Gallup poll of the public, and mailed 1,000 questionnaires to attorneys.[28] Based on these empirical materials, the Brookings Report identified deficiencies in bankruptcy administration that were to be echoed incessantly over the next seven years. Without mincing words, the Report bluntly concluded that although the bankruptcy system muddles through, 'it is a dreary, costly, slow, and unproductive process. Compared to what the system might be, the present reality is a shabby and indifferent effort.' The multiplicity of courts, and the lack of consistency among them produced 'baffling inequities' from court to court.

As the Brookings Institution Report moved towards publication, heightened concerns with bankruptcies engaged the interest of Congress, which established a Commission in 1970 to undertake a comprehensive review of bankruptcy law and administration. The nine commissioners comprised three appointed by the President, two appointed from the Senate, two from the House, and two federal judges appointed by the Chief Justice of the United States. While all branches of government were represented, lawyers dominated. The Chairman, Harold Marsh, was one of California's leading commercial lawyers; Professor Seligson was reputedly America's most distinguished bankruptcy law professor; and both judges had extensive experience with

---

[27] D. T. Stanley & M. Girth, *Bankruptcy: Problem, Process, Reform* (Washington, DC, Brookings Institution, 1971), vii ('Brookings Report').

[28] Interestingly enough, Brookings overcame conventional parochialism in the US by conducting a brief study of other national bankruptcy systems, but they found 'no general cure for the weakness of our system and few ideas for greater efficiency, lower cost, or more equitable treatment of debtors and creditors'. Brookings Report, App. B, 241.

bankruptcy. As important, perhaps, was the influence of two law professors, Professor Vern Countryman of Harvard, and Professor Lawrence King of New York University, both of whom prepared several position papers, assisted in the drafting of Report chapters, and participated in Commission meetings. Significantly, there was not a strong commercial or financial representation on the Commission.[29]

Although the Bankruptcy Commission had humble beginnings, reputedly in a conversation between a farmer and Senator Burdick of North Dakota, it responded generically to the 1,000 per cent increase in bankruptcies over the previous twenty years, the pervasive expansion of credit in all sectors of the economy, and general problems of bankruptcy administration. Moreover, with giant corporations such as Penn Central and Chrysler Motor Corporation facing radical financial restructuring, it was becoming increasingly clear that a downturn in the economy would require corporate reorganizations of unprecedented size and complexity. The Commission recognized that a great deal of effective financial reorganization goes on outside bankruptcy, which has the merits of 'relative simplicity, speed, low costs, and administrative flexibility'. But the changing structure of modern business increasingly demonstrated that informal arrangements are much less effective when there are very large numbers of creditors spread over many jurisdictions and a wide territory and some creditors refuse to go along.

Criticism of the system penetrated deeply into the core of court organization and practice. The Bankruptcy Commission directed close attention to the major confusions, terrible time-wasting, and procedural squabbling over the court jurisdictions in which bankruptcy proceedings were held. The Commission was acutely sensitive to problems that provoked lawyers—the sense of bias and conflicts of interest that bedevilled bankruptcy courts and undermined their neutrality. But of greatest relevance to the financial industry, the Bankruptcy Commission recognized that the prevailing system actively discouraged business from using the law for company rehabilitation. Lack of rational order and predictable adjudication ramified through the system.

Confronted with a system so compromised in its organization and personnel, the Commission essentially echoed Stanley's judgement that minor palliatives would not serve to remedy what needed major

---

[29] Report of the Comm. on the Bankruptcy Laws of the United States, HR Doc. No. 137, Part II, 93 Cong., 1st Sess. 1973, xv (Bankruptcy Comm. Rep.; Minutes, Comm. on the Bankruptcy Laws of the United States, Washington and Lee University ('Bankruptcy Comm. Mins').

surgery. In a series of bold measures the Commission Report redesigned the principal foundations of the system. Filed with Congress on 30 July, 1973, the Commission's Report, and the draft bill that accompanied it, expressed a broad consensus that had emerged among the lawyers and politicians who dominated the Commission's deliberations.

B. *Lawyers and Bankers in the Reform of Federal Bankruptcy Courts*

The general orientation to court autonomy in the judicial selection literature emphasizes the incipient conflicts between political parties and their allies in the legal profession, on the one side, with the elite lawyers who historically have controlled bar associations, on the other side. But in the field of corporate law, a third party has a major interest in the character of courts, namely, business and the financial industry.[30] Passage of the 1978 United States Bankruptcy Code was consequently framed by the sometimes confrontational differences among judges, various groups of lawyers, and the financial interest groups on a Congressional terrain effectively controlled by the Democrats.

The potential repercussions of changes in bankruptcy law for credit institutions brought three enormously powerful financial peak associations into play. Alongside the umbrella organization, the American Banking Association, stood the Robert Morris Associates, a national association of more than 6,000 bank loan and credit officers, who could boast that they represented some 1,650 banks holding 78 per cent of all US commercial banking resources. In case their political weight was underestimated, they informed each subcommittee of Congress that their banks lent in excess of $190bn. to business firms. Joining the banking groups was the American Council of Life Insurance, which also reminded Congress that they spoke on behalf of 473 life insurance companies which carried more than 90 per cent of life insurance in the US. Their assets exceeded $312bn. and they had $87bn. in private pension plans, quite apart from the $265bn. they held in corporate securities, mortgages, and other loans.

The judiciary was sundered along lines of power and status. At the lowest rank of judges—forced to fight even to keep this elevated title—the National Association of Bankruptcy Judges was dedicated to the interests of referees, bankruptcy courts, and the bankruptcy field. While they and the trustees they usually appointed appeared weak in the

---

[30] In some of the earlier campaigns for merit selection, business was an ally of the bar on behalf of merit selection.

hierarchy of federal courts, they had strong local political connections. Convinced that they could never get proper respect or even response from the federal judges, they chose to mobilize through Congress, where they anticipated more respect, by introducing a competing bill through the auspices of the National Conference of Bankruptcy Judges.

Disdainfully confronting them was the federal judiciary, which usually directed its collective activity though its Judicial Conference. The minority report to the Bankruptcy Commission, which was filed by federal Judge Weinfeld, signalled that an impending attack might be anticipated from the federal judiciary, who vigorously opposed the elevation of bankruptcy courts to the level of federal district courts, whose status was codified in Article III of the United States Constitution. Given the responsibilities of the Senate for appointment of federal judges, the federal judiciary looked to the upper chamber for political allies. Consequently, it was not surprising that the legislation introduced as HR 8200 in the House of Representatives was much more sympathetic to bankruptcy judges than the Senate bill S 2266, which championed the cause of the federal judiciary.

Practising lawyers mobilized on three fronts. Leading the charge for the lower bankruptcy and debtor–creditor specialists was the Commercial Law League of America. Founded in 1895, the 6,000-member League boasted its own journal and a long, strong connection with the bankruptcy courts on the private side of practice. Having profited from the specialized character of bankruptcy practice, their inclinations were to keep it a relatively private domain of action. Ostensibly representing the bar at large were the national, state, and metropolitan associations, such as the American Bar Association, the Minnesota State Bar Association, and the Dallas Bar Association. Who they were representing, in fact, was a little more difficult to discern. As often as not the resolutions emerging from the broadly inclusive associations came from the corporate end of the practising profession, although these were frequently kept in tension with the views of bar committees on court reform. Carrying the torch for lawyers who specialized in litigation was the highly resourceful and effective lobbying organization, the American College of Trial Lawyers. Their implacable resistance to any moves that would segregate specialist courts from general trial courts brought them directly into confrontation with advocates of specialization.

Standing rather aloof from the lurking partisanship of respective lawyers' and judges' groups was a very small, but enormously influential group of bankruptcy specialists. The National Bankruptcy Conference described itself to Congress as a 'a nonprofit unincorporated organization composed of representatives of different groups who are interested in the administration of bankruptcy law and practicing attorneys who specialize in this area. There are 58 full members and 11 associate members.' The self-perpetuating elite of judges, academics, and lawyers had been operating since the 1930s. According to some observers, they were the almost-hidden hand guiding the reform cycle from its inception.[31]

In a bid to bring unity to potentially warring parties within the bankruptcy field—a dispute that could derail the entire process—Congressman Edwards of the Bankruptcy Commission, together with the Chair of the House Judiciary Subcommittee responsible for passage of the bill in the House, urged the National Conference of Bankruptcy Judges to sit down with representatives of the National Bankruptcy Conference and forge a mutually acceptable piece of legislation. The compromise bill they produced split the differences between them and led—via two intervening bills—to a new legislative proposal that incorporated the compromises into a modified version of the Commission's bill, itself amended by the House subcommittee, to produce HR 8200.[32] On 31 October 1977 the Chair of the Senate Judiciary Committee, Senator Dennis DeConcini, introduced a bill into the Senate, S 2266, which was much more amenable to the federal judiciary.

The House Subcommittee and its Senate equivalent invited submissions from interest groups on the bills before their respective chambers. These submissions, and the exchanges between the politicians and the interest groups, reveal in rich detail both the dispositions of key groups to the prevailing bankruptcy system, and their views on change. The rhetoric of representation displays three clusters of values which formed the normative battleground on which differing groups fought for advantage: the efficiency of justice, the neutrality of justice, and the competence of the justice system.

---

[31] R. I. Aaron, 'The Bankruptcy Reform Act of 1978: The Full-Employment-for-Lawyers Bill: Overview and Legislative History', *Corporate Practice Commentator* 22: 2 (1980), 201.
[32] J. R. Trost & L. P. King, 'Congress and Bankruptcy Reform Circa 1977', *Business Lawyer* 33 (1978), 489–557 at 493–5.

Efficiency of justice

In bankruptcy cases, delay permits the remaining assets of the bankrupt corporation to run down thus impairing chances for corporate turn-arounds. Delay and speed in the disposition of bankruptcy cases were affected by three factors:

(1) jurisdiction of the court;
(2) the constitutional powers of the court; and
(3) the degree of court specialization.

Jurisdiction. Among the bankruptcy specialists—lawyers and judges—the need for broadening the bankruptcy court's powers was a primary arti-cle of faith. The strong representation of lawyers and judges on the Bankruptcy Commission had placed court jurisdiction high on its reform agenda. The awkward delegation of most bankruptcy proceed-ings to inferior bankruptcy courts, where authority was derivative, resulted in a perpetual uncertainty over the limits of the powers that were delegated to the bankruptcy court. The law made a distinction between plenary and summary powers of the court. The former were the province of bankruptcy courts; the latter were the dominion of the federal district courts. But which was which? 'Frequent, time-consuming, and expensive litigation' over this issue made it 'one of the most involved and controversial questions in the entire field of bank-ruptcy'.[33]

Moreover, the jurisdictional time bomb bedevilled any party that urgently required swift resolution of creditors' claims while the assets of the bankrupt ran down. Thus any party that had an interest in delay found jurisdictional issues a godsend because they could trigger appeals all the way through the appellate courts, to the immense frustration of the expedient parties.[34]

Jurisdictional disputes also lurked in the shadows of corporate bank-ruptcy law, where the unwary could find themselves ambushed by liti-gation to switch Chapters. Since the 1938 Chandler Act permitted various kinds of business bankruptcy to be handled in any one of three Chapters—X, XI, and XII—their detailed and overlapping rules pro-

[33] Bankruptcy Comm. Rep., xv.
[34] Ibid., see 14–17. The Commission notes the problems that companies have previ-ously had with the Act, including the pervasive problem of delay through the use of jury trials, or need to prove acts of bankruptcy, not to mention awkward and costly steps between filing and answer of the petition. All these delays ran down the assets so that creditors got little.

duced so much 'pointless litigation' that 'the patient will probably die while doctors argue over which operating table he should be on'. Hence jurisdictional disputes and delay fed off each other to mire any contested bankruptcy in debilitating obstacles of successive appeals. And as the Commission noted, while delay in any court is a matter of regret, in bankruptcy issues it is especially critical because the chances of rehabilitating companies in financial distress may depend on the rapid disposition of its financial assets. Decline in value of the estate can be arrested; dissipation of resources can be blocked. Creditors can be held at bay, or new agreements can be negotiated. But time and flexibility are key. Moreover, the time-value of money is compounded by the administrative costs of litigation itself, which can run down the assets available to creditors or for rehabilitation. Jurisdiction, therefore, was a key that unlocked the log jam.[35]

The problem of jurisdiction was more than perverseness. A derivative bankruptcy court simply could not exercise powers that the Constitution reserved to federal district courts and presidentially-appointed judges.[36] A derivative court, for instance, could not conduct jury trials. Moreover, for a trustee to bring legal actions against various parties to retrieve assets for the debtor's estate[37] it was too often necessary to scramble from court to court in various parts of the country in order to patch together all outstanding debts. In addition, plaintiffs could bring suits against trustees—and those, too, in courts other than the bankruptcy court. Derivative courts with limited and uncertain jurisdiction consequently multipled confusion, increased delay, and compounded costs in litigation.

In their bill, the bankruptcy judges had offered Congress a stark alternative:

Either [1] a forum of disputed, arguable jurisdictional authority—one operating within the shadow of a supervising court so burdened with other responsibilities and interests as to have neither the time nor expertise to contribute meaningfully, or [2] a forum of clearly defined, true bankruptcy jurisdiction— one operating as a court of identifiable stature equipped with adequate

---

[35] Ibid., 23, 89.

[36] The difference between Art. I versus Art. III courts had substantially to do with the breadth of jurisdiction and powers that can be given a court (cf. Bankruptcy Comm. Mins, 17–19 May 1973, 3).

[37] An 'estate' in bankruptcy law refers to the total pool of all items of value either remaining in, or owed to, the corporation.

personnel and expertise to give 'one-stop' service to the nation's bankruptcy needs.[38]

On this problem, federal district court Judge Shirley Hufstedler agreed: 'the idea of requiring poor litigants, bankrupt litigants, to litigate about jurisdiction, to me, is utterly repugnant.'[39]

All the lawyers' groups concurred. For the Commercial Law League, vesting the court with complete jurisdiction for all matters that arose in it was 'an absolute prerequisite'.[40] The corporate lawyers in the American Bar Association agreed that 'enlarged powers' of a court with expanded jurisdiction was critical. The professional authority of the elite National Bankruptcy Conference weighed in with the pronouncement that 'the present summary–plenary jurisdictional dichotomy is illogical, wasteful, and archaic; it spawns litigation and causes delay and unnecessary expense.' It also made for the 'uncertainty presently plaguing the system'.[41]

Representatives of corporate America offered vivid accounts to put evidentiary flesh on the dry bones of procedural discussions. 'If you want delay in the bankruptcy court,' stated Stanley Shaw, President of the Bohack Corporation, 'the byword is, file a motion and contest the jurisdiction of the court. Everything stops. The red lights go up. And the hearing must be held on jurisdiction.'[42] The bankers, too, forcefully demanded 'a strong independent bankruptcy court capable of exercising a broad jurisdictional grant'.[43]

Only the federal judges demurred. The Judicial Conference was somewhat alarmed by a proposed jurisdiction so broad that it would embrace securities, patents, and civil rights law, among others, thus effectively giving the court a breadth of jurisdictional reach identical to the district courts. And their ally in the Department of Justice, Attorney-General Bell, while acknowledging the value of some wider jurisdictions, none the less thought it should remain narrower than the district courts. The judges and Bell recognized that a jurisdiction this

---

[38] Bankruptcy Reform Act of 1978: Hearings before the Subcomm. on Improvements in Judicial Machinery of the Senate Comm. on the Judiciary on S 2266 and HR 8200, 95th Cong., 1st Sess. 440 (1977) (S 2266).

[39] Bankruptcy Court Revision: Hearings before the Subcomm. on Civil and Constitutional Rights of the House Comm. on the Judiciary on HR 8200, 95th Cong., 1st Sess. 87 (1977) (HR 8200).

[40] S 2266, 601.   [41] S 2266, 831–2.   [42] HR 8200, 18–27.

[43] Ibid., 193; submns by the Amer. Banking Assoc./Robert Morris Associates.

broad would sustain the call for bankruptcy courts to be raised to full Article III status.[44]

Constitutional status of the bankruptcy court. It was the powers of the court itself, above all else, that aggravated the federal judges. Greatly increased court powers inevitably raised the constitutional status of the court. Four models of a bankruptcy court were proposed by parties to the reform. First, courts might be given much broader jurisdiction and made independent of the federal district courts, but have a somewhat circumscribed status defined by Article I of the United States Constitution, a standing held by certain specialized courts, such as the Tax Court. This was the model advanced by the Bankruptcy Commission, after long internal debates over the sufficiency of Article I courts to handle the breadth of powers envisaged by reformers.[45]

At the other extreme was the model advanced by the House Judiciary Committee, which decided that bankruptcy courts should be raised to the highest level of Article III courts. This would not only solve jurisdictional problems, but its standing would attract judges of the very highest calibre and be appealing to business. But it would be a court specialized in bankruptcy alone. Harold Marsh, Chairman of the Bankruptcy Commission, and some of its other members preferred an Article III court. Bankruptcy specialists leaned also in this direction, as did some bar groups.[46] Not unexpectedly, the bankruptcy judges pressed energetically for the Article III model, complete with an appellate division.[47]

Unequivocal advocacy for fully-fledged Article III courts was expressed by the financial community. For the most part, this support sprang from frustration with the cost and delay of endless litigation over jurisdiction. John Ingraham of Citibank, and a prime mover in the gargantuan reorganization of the Penn Central railroad, declared that,

> We do try to help a company, but sometimes it's darn difficult, particularly if you see, from a financial standpoint, that putting new money at risk to a company that gets into difficulty, and where you're going to be tied up in knots, and waltzed around the maypole on appeals.[48]

---

[44] HR 8200, 154–8; oral test., Judicial Conf. of the US Federal Cts; Att.-Gen. Bell S 2266, 484.

[45] Bankruptcy Comm. Mins.

[46] S 2266, 438 (submn by Commercial Law League), ibid. 956 (submission by Minnesota Bar Assoc.).

[47] HR 8200, 166. [48] Ibid., 211.

Moreover, prospective litigation over the constitutional status of Article I courts with exceptionally wide jurisdictions greatly troubled the bankers. Constitutional appeals 'will unquestionably paralyze the rehabilitation process . . . . There are financial interests, who have been largely silent, who really cannot afford to have reorganization efforts delayed while constitutional issues are litigated'.[49]

In general, said a spokesman for the Robert Morris Associates, 'it is hard for members of the banking community with hundreds of millions of dollars invested in debtors who have invoked the jurisdiction of the bankruptcy court, to sympathize with the positions taken by the opponents of Article III status'.[50]

Faced with growing momentum for an Article III court with powers comparable to their own, the federal judiciary at the penultimate moment eventually awoke to the threat posed by this unlikely coalition of law reformers, low-prestige bankruptcy judges, and the entire national banking industry. In March 1977, the Judicial Conference adopted a resolution opposed to Article III courts and it charged a committee of federal judges to formulate a response to Congress.[51] Armed with votes from Judicial Councils around the country, and its own hardline document, federal judges appeared before House and Senate Committees to argue passionately for continuation of the present system, with some modest changes.

The federal judges were not alone in stolid resistance to change. The American College of Trial Lawyers maintained that apppointments of hundreds more Article III judges would dilute the prestige of the federal judiciary. Coincidentally, it would place great pressure to appoint current referees to the new courts—one reason why they had so vigorously supported the legislation, charged Judge Rifkind, a name partner of a leading New York litigation firm.[52] Welcome support came from the United States Attorney-General, who expressed the view that bankruptcy courts should remain in their current status as adjuncts of the district court—the so-called 'step-child' status so excoriated by reformers.[53] Most critically, however, key allies of the federal judges emerged from the Senate Judiciary Committee, whose chairman, Senator

---

[49] HR 8200, 203–4, 210.   [50] Ibid., 195.

[51] V. Countryman, 'Scrambling to Define Bankruptcy Jurisdiction: The Chief Justice, the Judicial Conference, and the Legislative Process', *Harvard Jrnl. on Legislation* 22 (1985) 1–45.

[52] HR 8200, 9.   [53] S 2266, 216.

DeConcini, applauded the Senate Bill 2266, which kept 'referees' as adjuncts of the district courts.[54]

Specialization. One element of resistance by lawyers derived from fears of specialization. The American College of Trial Lawyers strenuously resisted any hint of barriers that would exclude generalist litigators from trying cases before a major court. Their spokesman, Judge Rifkind, expressed it most colourfully:

I've watched it all of my professional life—that at the bar there is a parochial hunger which keeps recurring and reexpressing itself periodically for the practitioners in a particular field to get themselves a little courthouse of their own, a little bar of their own, a little judiciary of their own so that they become the ministers of a private temple in which they are the priests and nobody else knows how to function. That gives them a little bit of a monopoly in a field of practice.[55]

According to the American Bar Association, 'the entire judicial reform movement in this century has been in the direction of consolidating courts', by eliminating specialized courts in favour of general jurisdiction trial courts.[56] For the litigators, undoubtedly, the preferred solution was a powerful court that would attract litigation, but not so particular a court that their services would be made superfluous.

Neutrality of justice

Alongside the need for rapid judgments by an empowered court, lawyers and the banking industry vigorously pressed for a decisive resolution of the patronage, partisanship, and conflicts of interest that bedevilled the bankruptcy courts.

This 'personal-political-patronage' basis of appointment, as Stanley and Girth styled it, suffused all levels of the system. For instance, when bankruptcy judges were asked how they came to be appointed, 25 per cent said they were recommended by political party officials, 46 per cent were known to the judges, and only 21 per cent had applied. In Chicago the patronage link was so tight that referees kept office for only so long as their appointing judge; when he retired, so did they. Compounding the classic conflicts that are inherent between patronage and partisan intrusions into the court system and the vaunted neutrality of justice was a system of 'mutual accommodations' and 'exchanges of favours' that brought all players in the system into a tight coalition

---

[54] Ibid., 878.   [55] HR 8200, 16.   [56] Ibid., 16.

of mutually protective practitioners. Their loyalties, charged the Brookings Report, lay rather more to each other than creditors or debtors.[57]

Two elements of this 'bankruptcy ring' of private practitioners and public officials derogated the bankruptcy court.[58] On the one hand, an appeal made by a lawyer against a referee's decision was decided as often as not by the judge who had appointed the referee in the first place. As two-thirds of these appeals were decided in favour of the referees, it was not surprising that lawyers saw 'a natural inclination' of judges to back up their appointees. Moreover, the referee had future leverage over lawyers both for approving fees and for making new appointments of trustees. There was therefore a double incentive for lawyers not to ask for reviews, which probably helps account for the fact that never more than 2–3 per cent of all cases were appealed. On the other hand, the Brookings Report saw a fundamental disjunction between the essentially routine administrative character of the 200,000 or more uncontested cases and the prevailing adversarial system that seemed to add layers of personnel and costs to a process better fitted to a bureaucracy.[59]

According to Brookings, the core of the rot lay in the system of political and personal patronage that permeated the lower reaches—and everyday practice—of consumer and business bankruptcies. In a hierarchy of patronage appointments, prestigious federal district court judges (who themselves were often 'political' appointees) had complete discretion to appoint bankruptcy judges or 'referees', to whom were then delegated virtually all the 250,000 bankruptcy cases that flooded into the federal courts each year. Distributed across 90 district courts, the 218 referees in turn appointed trustees to sell or abandon the assets of the bankrupt person or company. Trustees, too, had their little fiefdoms of patronage, since they had discretion to retain lawyers as counsel, together with appraisers, auctioneers, accountants, and others.[60]

---

[57] Brookings Report, 160, 164, 197.

[58] The term 'bankruptcy ring' was probably first coined by a New York bar association study of insolvency, where they demonstrated that administration of insolvent estates was 'cozily distributed' among a handful of attorneys. W. Collier, *Collier on Bankruptcy*, 14th edn. (Albany, M. Bender, 1976), 4. 03.

[59] Brookings Report, 153 ff., 200.

[60] Brookings Report, 197, 147, 122-6. Stanley & Girth reiterated that the judicial branch championed independence of courts at the expense of central management. It was little wonder that 'patronage [political or personal] is securely established in the judiciary as a method of personnel selection'. Ibid., 200.

This blurring of administrative and adjudicatory responsibilities by referees drew condemnation from the Bankruptcy Commission:

When litigation does arise, there are substantial reasons for not entrusting its determination to bankruptcy judges involved in the prior administration of these litigated estates. It is necessary and important that the adversaries have confidence that their controversy will be determined by evidence adduced by them and presented to the trier of the law and the facts. The Commission is convinced that referees' participation in administrative aspects of bankruptcy proceedings tends to impair the litigants' confidence in the impartiality of the tribunal's decision. In particular, adversaries of the trustee in bankruptcy tend to doubt that the referee who appointed the trustee can insulate himself from at least a suspicion of partiality when he may have previously been involved in any and all of a range of prior actions concerning the estate.[61]

Congressional hearings echoed the findings of Brookings and the Bankruptcy Commission that methods of appointment and work organization permitted politics to intrude into the courts in ways that made certain litigants doubt they could get a fair hearing. Stanley and Girth, authors of the Brookings Report, again urged Congress to design a system 'free of cronyism'.[62] Even Attorney-General Griffin Bell reminisced that when he was a young lawyer, he was told by an older lawyer that 'the bankruptcy court was run for the benefit of the referee and the trustee, and the referees' pension fund . . . People wonder who gets all these trusteeships. Whose friends are they?'[63]

[61] Bankruptcy Comm. Rep., 5. That patronage was pervasive was not doubted by most Commissioners. Chairman Marsh noted that in Los Angeles 'demonstrated ability and expertise are not so important as personal relationships to the judges who have appointing authority'. And Judge Will agreed that 'political factors were significant in referees' appointments in Chicago and elsewhere', a point that the New York lawyers and judges were not so ready to concede. (Bankruptcy Comm. Mins, 13–14 Nov. 1972, 2, 13.) Bankruptcy Commissioners Prof. Seligson of New York and Judge Will of Chicago both agreed that there were kickbacks of fees by district attorneys to trustees in New York and Chicago. When this was placed alongside the 'unseemly and continuing relationship between the referees and the members of the . . . so-called "bankruptcy ring" of specialist bankruptcy lawyers', who were essentially 'private contractors seeking business with the BR court' the entire sphere of practice emitted 'a bad odor'. (Bankruptcy Comm. Mins, 15–17 Jan. 1973, 42; Bankruptcy Comm. Rep., 95; Bankruptcy Comm. Mins, 13–14 Nov. 1972, 6.)

[62] S 2266, 1081.

[63] HR 8200, 224. This was not simply a matter of personal patronage, which could be problematic enough. Professor Vern Countryman, bankruptcy specialist from Harvard Law School, entered a *Boston Globe* article into the Congressional Record to exemplify longstanding complaints about politics and competence in bankruptcy court appointments. US district court judges in Massachusetts had appointed a former US attorney-general to the position of bankruptcy judge, even though he had no prior bankruptcy

Political partisanship melded into localism. Parties who entered a court from out of state, or another community, felt especially vulnerable to the vagaries of local loyalties against 'outlanders'. In smaller cases, observed the bankers' group, the Robert Morris Associates, when a banker-creditor

leaves his own district, his own home base, he does not believe that he is in a fair court. He may be in a fair court, and it may be that no bias exists or it may be that a bias exists only unconsciously, but the confusion of the roles has led many members of the American Bankers' Association and the Robert Morris Associates to complain of the type of justice that can be meted out in a bankruptcy court context.[64]

Bankers were adamant that they would offer endorsement of increased court jurisdiction only if the new court was independent and administrative and judicial roles were segregated. In oral testimony, the spokesman for Robert Morris Associates quoted sympathetically a bankruptcy judge's statement that

the bankruptcy court is a departure from the traditional Anglo-American concept of a trial court; an impartial arbiter who receives evidence in accordance with procedure and evidentiary rules of ancient vintage; and who receives no evidence or communication except on the record and in the presence of both parties. The administrator-judge does not and cannot fulfill this image.[65]

The American Bankers' Association categorically stated that 'we view separation of judicial and administrative functions as a vital part of bankruptcy reform'.[66] The refrain of court independence recurred incessantly among all interest groups, except one.

Despite the consensus among the professionals and bankers who wanted an independent court engaged only in adjudication, the federal judges thought the problem was much overstated. So express was their denial of major difficulties in the *status quo* that the Chairman of the House Judiciary Subcommittee expostulated in frustration that

experience. But it was the political overtones that captured the *Globe*'s attention. Mr Gabriel succeeded, reported the article, because he had the backing of US Sen. Brook, who had more support for the appointment among sitting judges than his political rival, Sen. Edward Kennedy. 'Because the district judges are nominated for their own jobs by one or the other United States senator, they are vulnerable to political pressure and may feel inclined to endorse a nominee who has been proposed by their own sponsor . . . Ideally, the judges would resist naming hacks to bankruptcy judgeships . . . In reality, however, there is no insulation between judges and the political process of nominating and promoting candidates for judicial positions.' (HR 8200, 259.)

[64] HR 8200, 205–6.   [65] Ibid., 195.   [66] S 2266, 574.

we are in a quandary, of course, because for the last 5 or 6 years we have been hearing witnesses—banks, commercial law representatives, merchants, business people, and the general public—complaining about the referee system. Actually, we have not had one witness, except you gentlemen [federal judges], who have said that it is working well and that we should be proud of it.[67]

Eventually the judges did offer a compromise proposal—that a local bankruptcy administrator be appointed for each court for five years at a time and he would free the judge to engage entirely in adjudication. But this fell far short of the Brookings' civil service option, and indeed of a nationally organized system of administration within the judiciary that would avoid any more appearance of patronage and favouritism in appointments of administrative personnel.

Quality of justice

Calibre of Judges. The Brookings Report had lamented the quality of bankruptcy referees, later to be called bankruptcy judges. The position required no formal qualifications, apart from those common to all lawyers. And it demanded no prior experience in bankruptcy. Even the latter was not a guarantee of quality or respect, as the bankruptcy bar itself was held 'in low esteem'. Terms of appointment were limited to six years and salaries were low. None of these factors provided inducements to highly qualified practitioners.

Quality of recruitment to the bankruptcy bench was also criticized by the Bankruptcy Commission. Everything conspired against highly qualified bankruptcy judges—patronage appointments, short-term tenure, low salary, and diminished powers of the court, where nearly all of the most stimulating and far-reaching issues would be siphoned off to a higher court. According to Chairman Marsh,

fundamentally the public has a right to have issues adjudicated by a full-fledged court and not some subordinate functionary. Perhaps the problem is one of status or maybe pride but in order to attract and hold the right people a new image must be projected . . .The community at large . . . needs to have confidence in the judiciary. At the moment that confidence rests uneasily on the shoulders of referees.[68]

Accusations of 'second-rate justice' and 'second-class courts' were levelled at the bankruptcy courts by Congressmen Drinan and Edwards of the House Judiciary subcommittee. As the National Bankruptcy Conference put it, the bankruptcy court 'is without prestige and

---

[67] HR 8200, 151.   [68] Bankruptcy Comm. Mins, 4–5 Dec. 1972, 8, 13.

ordinarily does not attract highly qualified attorneys to accept appointments on the bench. The best lawyers do not want to be assistants to district judges.' All the lawyers' groups supported either life tenure comparable to federal court judges, or very long term appointments of twelve to fifteen years. For most appointees, only two such appointments would bring a judge to retirement. It could serve as a career, thus avoiding the inevitable conflicts of interest that arise in revolving doors between judiciaries and private practice.[69]

The arguments for life tenure were consistent with those for Article III judges and Alexander Hamilton's original commentary on the US Constitution. Life tenure insulates judges from political control, or as Father Drinan commented during the hearings, it makes judges more courageous. This was more than a rhetorical veneer that permitted the ambitious lawyer-members of the Commercial Law League to proclaim their advocacy of long-term appointments for reasons of independence of the courts. Bankers, too, were convinced that the status and method of judicial appointment was 'of grave concern to commercial lending institutions throughout the country'.[70] In a joint submission, the American Bankers Association and the Robert Morris Associates wanted length of appointment, salary levels, and other benefits sufficient to 'guarantee a first rate court'.[71] By the time the House and Senate bills came to Conference in late 1977, all parties agreed that terms should be at least twelve years, in the case of federal judges, through to life, in the case of those who favoured Article III courts.

Independence and quality depended as much on who did the appointing as on the length of the appointment. The strongest proposal was for the President to make either life tenure or fifteen-year appointments as he did for sitting federal judges and the Article I Tax Court respectively. This not only moved appointments away from local patronage relationships, but it endowed the bankruptcy judge with all the charisma of presidential recognition. While most professional groups preferred presidential appointment, the Commercial Law League preferred appointments to be made rather closer to the local situation. They suggested that the local federal Judicial Council or Court of Appeals could do the appointing. This would strengthen the local connection—and their chances of making it to the bench—but it would compromise rather less the relationship between district and bankruptcy court judges.

---

[69] S 2266, 950, 98, 831–2.   [70] HR 8200, 194.   [71] S 2266, 574.

Here again the dissenters were the federal judges. Since 1960 they had asked for referees' terms to be extended from six to twelve years, and this they had recommended to the Bankruptcy Commission.[72] But they resisted energetically any notion that the appointment process parallel their own. They much preferred to maintain some local judicial control—and thereby perpetuate an attenuated patronage—while most other observers sought to abolish it. From Congressman McGlory their position drew the sarcastic retort that 'one very good reason why district court judges don't want to change the system . . . is that they enjoy appointing the referees . . . I'm very sorry to infringe on their very long time enjoyed prerogatives, but I think this is part of the problem we have.'[73]

Appeals. The mode of appeals from bankruptcy courts further divided lawyers and judges. While appeals' prerogatives appear as bureaucratic technicalities, like so much else about courts (and indeed any other organizations), the structure of the system carried powerful symbolic overtones. As the National Bankruptcy Conference observed, appeals to circuit court judges do little for the dignity of bankruptcy courts. 'It is anomalous, and detracts from the dignity of a trial court, for appeals from its orders to run to another single judge court, particularly if that court is essentially a trial court itself.'[74] Appeals directly to an appellate court was also the position taken by the Commercial Law League, because perpetuation of the present system simply preserved 'both the second class status of bar judges and the unnecessary expense and delay of a 3-tier appellate system'.[75]

The financial industry lent its weight to exactly the same end—direct appeals to appellate courts elevated the dignity of the courts and provided an expedited mechanism to provide prompt relief.[76] For bankers and secured creditors, decisive decision-making that permitted predictable outcomes from the extension of credit was a primary goal for legal change. The principal dissent came again from the federal judges who, ironically, borrowed the bankers' reasoning and turned it against them. In response to an explicit question posed by the House Subcommittee counsel, the Chairman of the Ad Hoc Committee on Bankruptcy Legislation of the Judicial Conference wrote that it 'recommends that bankruptcy cases continue to be under the jurisdiction of the district courts, with appointment of bankruptcy judges by the

---

[72] HR 8200, 115.   [73] Ibid., 50.   [74] Ibid., 239.   [75] S 2266, 601.
[76] Ibid., 574; submission by Amer. Banking Assoc./Robert Morris Associates.

district councils. The Committee sees no need for a separate court system which would inevitably create jurisdictional conflicts and would be very costly.'[77]

House Bill 8200 passed on 1 February 1978. Senate Bill S 2266 passed the Senate in September 1978. But the wide differences between them required intense negotiation between the two chambers to produce several compromises.

1. The expanded jurisdiction sought by virtually all parties was to be lodged in the circuit court of appeals, but bankruptcy courts were directed to use all of that jurisdiction.
2. The bankruptcy court would be retained as an adjunct court to the district court and not attain the Article III or Article I status advocated by the most active interest groups.
3. But to compensate for the loss of Article III, the two Houses agreed to fourteen-year appointments that would be made by the President on the advice of the Senate.
4. Salaries were to be substantially improved—only marginally below those of federal district court judges—and bankruptcy judges would be added to the federal Judicial Conference.

Rather remarkably, these apparently 'watered-down' proposals were still too radical for the Chief Justice of the Supreme Court, who intervened directly by calling on key senators to block the bill unless it diluted further three provisions on the status of the bankruptcy courts, presidential appointment, and membership in the Judicial Council. With the Chief Justice's Senate allies holding the bill to ransom, intense negotiations, which also involved the Attorney-General, took place with the clock slowly running out of parliamentary time for passage in the current legislative session. In a last minute bid to find acceptable middle ground, an amended version of HR 8200 downgraded the bankruptcy courts from adjuncts of appeals courts to ordinary district courts, although the expanded jurisdiction would remain in place. Moreover, presidential appointment would 'give due consideration' to any nominees that might be proposed by local Judicial Councils. With hope gradually dimming that passage of the bill could make it in the 95th Congress, the House settled for the compromise and the bill was forwarded to the President for signature. Again the Chief Justice intervened, this time calling the President directly to urge that he veto the

[77] HR 8200, 155.

bill. On the very last day on which the bill could be signed into law, 6 November 1978, President Carter ignored his Chief Justice and placed his signature on the bill.[78]

Banking, Legal Rationalization, and the Constitution of Liberal Politics

Because the enormous diversity of the American legal profession is refracted through a profusion of cross-cutting lawyers' organizations, the bankruptcy reforms display a kaleidoscope of sectional differences. The 'class' divisions between upper and lower strata of lawyers and judges, and the tension between generalist and specialist practitioners, replay in this arcane area of lawyers' law many of the same battles over independence of the courts that have punctuated the history, and defined the identity, of the American legal profession. Yet intra-professional conflicts represent only one dimension of historic shifts in court organization. Less readily identified or acknowledged by commentators on judicial reforms are the interests of corporate America in the form of justice offered under the mantle of the courts.

While the most ubiquitous actors in the bankruptcy reforms undoubtedly were the lawyers' and judges' organizations, it is manifestly clear that the financial industry saw any modifications of bankruptcy law—and the arrangements for corporate liquidation and administration—as integral to commercial lending and practice. We have seen that the commercial community had decided views on what it wanted from bankruptcy reforms. Speed and decisiveness depended on powerful courts with embracing jurisdictions that minimized debilitating procedural manoeuvrings through appeals. Neutrality and absence of bias demanded sharp segregation of politics and personal patronage from judicial decision-making. Quality and expertise of judicial personnel would proceed from presidential appointment of long-tenured judges with benefits comparable to those of the federal bench.

In short, the bankers held Congress to a principle of *implied commensurability* as a condition of their co-operation in riskier corporate rehabilitations. Unless the power and quality of justice was commensurate with the scale of financial risk, bankers swore either to handle their

---

[78] K. N. Klee, 'Legislative History of the New Bankruptcy Code', *Amer. Bankruptcy Law Jrnl.* 54 (1980), 275–97 at 281–94; M. C. Butler, 'A Congressman's Reflections on the Drafting of the Bankruptcy Code of 1978', *William & Mary Law Rev.*, 21 (1980), 557–74; V. Countryman, 'Bankruptcy Jurisdiction'.

affairs outside the reach of the courts, or to forswear the sorts of commercial risk that economic policy-makers hoped would facilitate widespread corporate reorganization. The courts, in other words, could conform to the expectations of the financial industry, or lose their business. The economic threat was even more palpable: in the face of industry shake-outs in an increasingly competitive economy, the bankers intimated that they could either limit risk and permit widespread company failure, or they could extend credit further and aid reconstruction. The quality of justice factored significantly in the global strategy of the financial industry.

This powerful impulsion towards court independence and competence melded with a generic impetus towards *rationalization of law*. Bankruptcy judges and lawyers decried the variability among jurisdictions in the ways that judges handled corporate reorganizations. The Bankruptcy Commission Report forthrightly acknowledged that the 'open credit economy' demands an 'orderliness' which it is a primary function of the bankruptcy system to provide. And the National Bankruptcy Conference insisted that the 'inconsistencies, uncertainties, and illogic inherent in the present system of three separate reorganization chapters' needed to be purged and replaced by a rational system consistent with the high dollar-value of assets and claims, the need to preserve ongoing value of assets, and the impact of corporate failure on the economy.[79]

Pleas for uniformity and consistency from commercial lawyers found ready response from the financial sector. The American Council of Life Insurance expressed it best with a call for a law that will 'assure fair and predictable treatment of claims of long-term lenders and investors. In a free enterprise system where private capital investment is an important component, the law should not provide too many surprises and be so unpredictable that long-term investors cannot cope with the uncertainties . . . ' And to remind legislators again of the stakes, the Robert Morris Associates reinforced their earlier testimony that 'we have repeatedly articulated our feelings that the existing structure for reorganizations, particularly Ch. X, overwhelms most corporate debtors, with the result that corporations which could be reorganized die under the surgeon's hand during the pendency of such proceedings'.[80]

---

[79] S 2266, 400; submn by National Conf. of Bankruptcy Judges; Bankruptcy Comm. Rep., 68–71; ibid., 833–4; submn by National Bankruptcy Conf.

[80] Ibid., 855; submn by Amer. Council of Life Insurance; ibid., 194; submn by the Robert Morris Associates.

Invocation of uniformity, consistency, predictability, and legal protection as standards of legal regulation manifestly reflect a principle of formally rationalized law. This resonates clearly with the Weberian propositions that 'increased calculability' in the functioning of the legal process, and the 'purely formal certainty of the guaranty of legal enforcement', are integral to markets ruled by contract. While not unmindful of law's illogics, nor of anti-formal tendencies in the interests of substantive expediency, Weber's depiction of the efficient bureaucracy—with application to the courts—might readily have been submitted to Congress by the financial interest groups: 'the utmost possible speed, precision, definiteness, and continuity in the execution of official business' is vital for the modern capitalistic economy.[81]

Formally rationalized justice, by definition, requires attenuation of political connections. As Rueschemeyer has indicated, judicial autonomy requires that courts must persuade all parties that their standing is equalized and that outside political interference would be intolerable because 'it would seriously disturb the predictable functioning of the legal system'.[82]

Nevertheless, the rationalization of law and justice will not suit all commercial actors. Indeed, access to local justice for many local companies will be more appealing when there is less autonomy from party control and less professional detachment in judicial decision-making. As the battle for control of the Erie Railroad demonstrated in mid-nineteenth century New York, corporations may prefer courts that can be bought or politically controlled, just so long as political and corporate principals are confident that their judicial agents will deliver tendentious 'justice'.

When commercial enterprises are not confident that they control or can predict the inclinations of judicial authorities, and indeed when they suspect that such control might be exercised by rivals, then formal justice and level playing fields represent a more rational expedient. The multiplication of court jurisdictions alongside corporations that operate in scores and hundreds of markets pose precisely such enormous difficulties of control over legal and market environments. Formal rationalization of justice, and uniformity of law and practice, stabilize credit

---

[81] M. Weber, *Economy and Society*, vol. 2 (G. Roth & K. Wittich (eds.), (Berkeley, Univ. of California Press, 1978), 883; *Max Weber on Law in Economy and Society*, M. Rheinstein (ed.), (New York, Simon & Schuster, 1954), 350.

[82] D. Rueschemeyer, *Lawyers and their Society: A Comparative Study of the Legal Profession in Germany and the United States* (Cambridge, Mass., Harvard Univ. Press, 1973), 69.

environments and facilitate the extension of credit, and predictability about its protection, across multiple jurisdictions.

Paradoxically, therefore, the safety of courts for powerful commercial interests inverts the conventional orientation towards access to justice. Critics of the courts have demonstrated that high entry costs, or jurisdictional restrictions to exclude certain types of cases, effectively disenfranchise the poor or weak from high quality justice. Less seldom is recognized that the obverse also occurs. Courts only capable of dealing with low level, limited jurisdiction and mundane cases, effectively reduce their appeal to potential 'clients' with high property rights' stakes. In the absence of alternative forms of control, major financial institutions will accept courts as potential arenas for dispute resolution only when principles of rationality and commensurability are patently operational. Without these assurances, the strong are effectively 'disenfranchised' by the courts. Without meeting the criteria implicitly established by the financial community, courts marginalize themselves from powerful actors that demand high expertise and extensive, binding jurisdiction.

The bankruptcy reforms can therefore be seen not only as a struggle among professional groups for occupational advantage, but also as a drive for extended corporate 'citizenship' in the courts. The *de jure* standing inscribed in law will only begin to match the *de facto* standing in practice when the courts can convince the financial community that their risks are made safe by confidence in the quality of commercial justice. The financial peak associations, and their agents in the legal profession, essentially made independence and quality of courts a precondition for dispute resolution and rehabiliation under the mantle of public justice.[83]

If these were the imperatives of the financial sector, the courts had their own compelling reasons for responding in kind. Courts in the United States have historically confronted a problem of legitimation peculiar to this 'weakest' branch of government. Unlike the legislature, with its mandate from the voting citizenry, or the executive, with presidential elections and control over the instruments of coercion, the courts have neither popular mandate nor enforcement apparatuses. Some of their legitimacy they may borrow from other branches.

---

[83] In the US, the rapid expansion of private justice systems, ranging from arbitration to private adjudication services, effectively parallel the public court system. But as Garth has argued, the defection of major corporations from the judiciary effectively deprives the common law of cases and decisions that serve to consolidate an area of law.

Presidential appointment of judges, or derivation of rule-making powers from legislatures, permit some underwriting from more conventional forms of democratic authority. The Jacksonian experiment with election of judges can be understood as one such search for an alternative means of endowing courts with greater authority.[84] But the rise of party control of judicial nominations and large city machines doomed the Jacksonian experiment to base authority on popular representation. The more closely courts are identified with political parties, machines, or ideologies, the more vulnerable they are to capture by particular constituencies that effectively then alienate less well-connected groups from the courts. Manifest tendentiousness causes a loss of credibility, most especially to parties that demand a formally rational model of justice.

Providing access to justice for any group thereby complicates a pattern of legitimation that is constantly in the process of redefinition. Excessive identification or sympathy with some litigants inevitably gives pause to others. Consequently, higher courts in the United States seized upon legal formalism as an ideology that distinguished them clearly from political or economic ideology. Indeed, the history of US courts can be read as an odyssey among shifting ideologies and external sources of authority in order to maintain the singularity of justice as a distinctive principle of authority.[85]

By bringing their disputes or transactions to the courts, rather than resorting to purely market expedients or some forum of private justice, major commercial actors legitimate the independent standing of the courts and justice as a principle of social ordering. Drawing the largest corporations into courts to solve problems that they would otherwise manage less satisfactorily outside the courts can underwrite the independence of a branch of government sometimes wanting for external legitimation. Indeed, for reformist lawyers and judges committed to

---

[84] Although political accountability and judicial independence are conventionally thought to be at odds, Kermit Hall suggests that mid-nineteenth-century courts went to the voters in order to strengthen the stature and independence of courts. See 'The Judiciary on Trial: State Constitutional Reform and the Rise of an Elected Judiciary, 1846–1860', *The Historian*, 44 (1983).

[85] See works by C. McCurdy, H. Hovenkamp, M. Keller, and M. Horwitz, on the ebb and flow of the courts' centrality to the purposes of modern corporations in the US. In some periods, this has been defined in terms of courts' ability to draw corporate activity into the sphere of justice; in other periods, most notably after the New Deal, it has frequently been expressed in terms of a rivalry between the judiciary and the executive branch of government over 'jurisdiction' of corporate activity.

formal rationality of the courts, the coincidence of interest among major financial actors provides them with a compelling pragmatic argument for independent and powerful courts. Courts that attract the largest economic organizations, of course, concomitantly have the not unwelcome side-effect of generating more intellectually stimulating and remunerative legal practice.[86]

It is here that the historic engagements of lawyers and bankers with the courts converge again to common purpose. Removal of the local bankruptcy courts from party control, or the appearance of political influence and patronage relationships, strengthens the constitutional structure of liberalism on two counts. Its direct effect is to strengthen the independence of the judiciary and hence the formal rationality of the court system. This provides more autonomy for law and thus affirms the rule of law, and procedural neutrality, as an independent principle of social ordering. Its indirect effect is that the purging of political 'contamination' makes the judiciary more attractive for large corporations with very substantial property rights at stake. Corporate recourse to the judiciary for reorganization thereby adds another increment of authority to the institutions of justice as autonomous centres of power.[87]

This affinity between economic rationality in the market and formal rationality in the court system has more than symbolic significance for the institutional order of political liberalism. To the extent that the resolution of lawyers' internal struggles facilitates formal rationalization of the courts—in tandem with economic actors—the legal profession makes a dual contribution to a configuration of political institutions amenable to this particular form of liberalism. On the one hand, they make the courts safe for the powerful, with their correlative effects on

---

[86] This argument does have to cope with the rather inconvenient fact that the federal judges opposed making the courts safer for the powerful, at least in the manner proposed by most other parties to the reforms. Curiously enough, the financial industry identified problems that federal judges were unwilling to acknowledge, and pressed for changes that federal judges were loath to permit. At this particular moment, therefore, it appears that the federal judges did not consider legitimacy issues to be nearly so important as did their potential clients.

[87] On a relationship between the formal rationality of a system of justice, and its implications for liberal politics, see D. N. Levine, 'Rationality and Freedom, Inveterate Multivocals', in D. N. Levine (ed.), *The Flight from Ambiguity: Essays in Social and Cultural Theory* (Chicago, Univ. of Chicago Press, 1985), chap. 7. The formal rationalization of law and legal systems more generally is treated in W. Schluchter, *Rise of Western Rationalism*, 82–138; M. Rheinstein, 'Introduction', in Rheinstein (ed.), *Max Weber*; A. Kronman, *Max Weber* (Stanford, Stanford Univ. Press, 1983), 72–95.

court legitimacy.[88] On the other hand, they reinforce the independence of the courts from majoritarian (that is, legislative) and imperative (that is, executive) influence, thus dividing power and reconstituting the institutional liberal order dimly envisaged by the Federalists.

[88] Note that this identification can also have delegitimating effects. Just as excessive identification of courts with civil rights may alienate courts from those whose rights they believe are infringed, so undue identification of the courts with big business will render them unpalatable to other parties.

9 The Politics of Professionalism: the Creation of Legal Aid and the Strains of Political Liberalism in America, 1900–1930

Michael Grossberg (Indiana University)

In 1869, Philadelphia lawyer and pioneering bar ethicist George Sharswood expressed his hope that 'the time will never come at this or any other bar in this country, when a poor man with an honest cause, though without a fee, cannot obtain the services of honorable counsel in the prosecution of his rights'.[1] Less than a decade later, however, the leaders of a New York City immigrant aid society decided that just such a time had come; they felt compelled to add legal assistance to their array of services. And by the first years of the next century securing legal counsel for poor clients had been transformed into a full-blown national movement, legal aid.

Legal aid in the United States emerged in a moment of significant professional discontinuity for American lawyers. Around the turn of the twentieth century a conscious sense of sweeping change, even crisis, compelled legions of the bar to defend the liberal legal order by grappling with basic issues from the nature of representation and the organization of the courts to the content of legal doctrines and the training of fledgling attorneys. Legal aid was a direct product of the strains produced by this moment of crisis in American political liberalism. And thus while in many ways legal aid was then, as it has remained ever since, a rather marginal movement among American lawyers, its creation provides a revealing perspective on the larger political context within which the profession operated. Specifically it reveals the centrality of the politics of professionalism in struggles over the changing place of the bar in the American liberal order. By that phrase I mean to distinguish contests over professional place and power from electoral politics. Though inextricably linked, particularly in the case of lawyers, the two should be separated analytically. The politics of professionalism involves struggles among professionals and between professionals and laypeople over the scope and authority of a profession. American legal aid is the result of one such struggle.

[1] G. Sharswood, *Essay on Professional Ethics* (Philadelphia, 1869), 153.

Legal aid's champions made it a part of the bar's political project to reconstruct the liberal state and preserve the powerful particular place of lawyers in it. As a result, the key issues of political liberalism dominated their movement, especially conflicts over the authority of the moderate state, the extent of citizenship rights, and the scope of civil society. At the heart of their building project was the fundamental liberal conviction that for the benefit of both the bar and the republic, law must be an autonomous profession and the law itself a distinct realm of society. Convinced that the necessary independence of the law and the profession of law were under attack, they used the fight for legal aid as a form of political engagement against internal and external critics. The character and meaning of their two-front struggles can be recovered in an examination of three critical components of the movement.

First, the sources of American legal aid disclose the time-bound context of its creation. As has happened at other times, conditions distinctive to the era compelled lawyers to pursue professional political actions like the creation of legal aid. Equally important, though legal aid movements emerged throughout Western Europe and North America, neither the effort in the United States nor in any other country can be understood simply as the inevitable product of changes wrought by industrial capitalism or as a functionalist response to swelling popular demands for representation. On the contrary, each movement had its sources in both common developments as well as the particular experiences of individual nation–state bars.[2] In the United States, lawyers created legal aid in a conscious attempt to stake out new boundaries for legal practice in an era when the existing ones had become uncertain. They did so as self-styled legal reformers and participants in a new wave of humanitarianism, one dominated by professional interests and methods. Legal aid became, in short, a lawyers' reform that mediated the forces of change by emphasizing the continued saliency of the liberal ideals of procedural justice and equality before the law, while defending the legitimacy of the liberal legal order itself. Equally important, legal aid represented an attempt to redefine individual rights by detaching those rights from their traditional American mooring to property ownership. By creating a new form of representation legal aid

---

[2] For an overview of the movement see M. Cappelletti, 'Legal Aid: The Emergence of a Modern Theme', *Stanford Law Review* 2 (1972), 357–86; M. Cappelletti, J. Gardley, & G. Johnson (eds.), *Toward Equal Justice: A Comparative Study of Legal Aid in Modern Societies* (Dobbs Ferry, NY, Oceana, 1975).

participated in the era's redefinition of citizenship rights by helping to rearrange the relationship between individuals and the state.

Second, the relationship between legal aid and the organized bar in America proved to be critical and revealing. As self-styled lawyer reformers, legal aid lawyers considered ties to the bar their most important connection. Purposefully labelling their effort a professional reform, they used their newly created role representing poor clients to police the profession's lower reaches. In doing so, they embraced the right of professional self-government to protect the bar's autonomy from increased state supervision and from the interference of non-legal professionals also working to aid the poor. Particularly important, most legal aid lawyers founded and worked for private societies and the movement itself resisted the direct provision of legal services by the state. As part of their professional commitment to the moderate state and thus to limits on public authority, legal aid lawyers made staking out and defending the line between public and private spheres of American life one of their most important responsibilities. This self-assumed task reveals their dedication to preserving what has come to be called civil society, a changing set of institutions and practices that occupied the space between the state and the family. Despite these commitments, however, legal aid lawyers found themselves under attack from fellow attorneys as well as from other reformers. These internal and external conflicts became skirmishes in what would be long-running battles over the role of law and lawyers in the slowly emerging American version of the European welfare state.

Finally, the development of new forms of representation by legal aid lawyers demonstrates how the movement translated its assumptions and commitments into everyday professional practices. They did so by trying to implement an idealized form of legal practice that emphasized compromise and education rather than adversarial conflict. And they dealt with bulging caseloads by establishing elaborate procedures to screen clients and cases. The result of these practices was the establishment of a new professional responsibility and the legitimation of a two-tiered legal system that sanctioned adversarial solutions for those who could pay, and alternative forms of dispute resolution for those who could not. As such, the practice of legal aid law highlights some of the implications, particularly some of the limits, of legal liberalism.

Taken together, an examination of these three facets of the first American legal aid movement document how and why legal aid lawyers succeeded in making representation of the poor a new and particular kind of professional responsibility. Their achievement becomes a vivid illustration of the politics of professionalism. It helps us identify some of the distinctive realities of this particular form of political strife while suggesting as well the legacy of this critical era in the history of lawyers and American political liberalism.

Sources

In 1919, Reginald Heber Smith published *Justice and the Poor*. The book capped forty years of legal aid development and quickly became the movement's manifesto. Its author, the director of the Boston Legal Aid Society, was a graduate of Harvard Law School and a disciple of its reformist dean, Roscoe Pound. Funded by the Carnegie Foundation, *Justice and the Poor* offered a comprehensive rationale for legal aid and in doing so expressed the basic assumptions of legal aid lawyers. These assumptions, in turn, help contextualize the movement as the product of a particular moment in the history of American liberal legal order.

Justice and the Poor indicted the American urban legal system. 'The administration of justice', Smith declared and then documented, 'is not impartial, the rich and the poor do not stand on an equality before the law, the traditional method of providing justice has operated to close the doors of the courts to the poor, and has caused a gross denial of justice in all parts of the country to millions of people.' The result was not only injustice and further exploitation of the poor, but also severe unrest, mounting dissatisfaction, and torrents of criticism against the nation's legal system. The real tragedy, proclaimed Smith, was that the growing complaints were well founded: 'the distrust of lawyers today is marked, but it differs from the dissatisfaction of earlier times in that it is not the product of jealousy or fear of a new ruling class, but proceeds from intelligent criticism founded on the facts.'[3]

Even so, Smith absolved the system from blame. Like many other reformers in the era, he attributed the problems to the uncontrollable forces of modernity that raged outside the law: immigration, the rise of a wage-earning class, and the startling growth of urban populations.

---

[3] R. H. Smith, *Justice and the Poor. A Study of the Present Denial of Justice to the Poor and of the Agencies Making More Equal Their Position Before the Law With Particular Reference to Legal Aid Work in the United States* (New York, Carnegie Foundation, Bull. no. 13, 1919), 8, 228; for Smith's explicit evocation of Pound, see 8–9. Pound had identified the poor's lack of access to the urban legal system as one of its major failings, see R. Pound, 'The Administration of Justice in the Modern City', *Harvard Law Rev.* 26 (1912–13), 302–28 at 315; R. Pound, 'Social Justice and Legal Justice', *Missouri Bar Assoc. Proc.* 30 (1912) 112.

These forces of change had destroyed the former homogeneity of a rural nation and led to the inhumanity and complexity of the modern city. Naturally the legal system reflected these new tensions. Adopting what would later be called 'gap analysis', he argued that the legal machinery had broken down under the new stresses; it badly needed overhaul. The barriers preventing the poor from using the legal system were caused by 'gaps, or flaws, or outworn parts, or imperfect adjustment in the organization of our administration of justice'.[4]

Most critically, Smith gave no ground to external critics who charged that injustice was intentional. To those who argued that exploitive labour contracts, racial and ethnic discrimination, inhumane working conditions, and low wages were condoned by current legal practices, Smith countered with a defence of the legal realm of the liberal state and insisted that 'the substantive law, with minor exceptions, is eminently fair and impartial'. This assertion, he confidently proclaimed, was supported by the judgement of 'our greatest scholars, and most searching critics of our legal institutions; of men such as Roscoe Pound, John H. Wigmore, and the group who comprise the membership of the American Judicature Society'. The existing denial of justice, he concluded, 'is not attributable to any injustice in the heart of the law itself. The necessary foundation for freedom and equality exists. The immemorial struggle is half won.'[5] Rather the sources of problems lay outside the legal system, tremendous changes had overtaken the nation and led inexorably to a procedural breakdown resulting in a system that denied access to those without money.

Emphasizing procedural reform like other legal defenders of the liberal state, Smith singled out three structural defects as the main culprits: delay, court costs and fees, and the availability of counsel. By eliminating each deficiency the urban administration of justice could be re-opened to the poor and the liberal ideal of equal justice restored without the distortions in the law that he feared would be the inevitable result of the creation of new substantive rights. Barriers created by delay and costs could be remedied by implementing procedural and administrative reforms championed by other legal reformers. Among these he cited simpler procedural rules, lower court costs, speedier services, and alternative remedial bodies.[6] Yet even these remedies were

[4] Smith, *Justice and the Poor*, 6–7, 224. For a discussion of gap analysis see Austin Sarrat, 'Legal Effectiveness and Social Studies of the Law', *Legal Studies Forum* 9 (1985) 23.

[5] Ibid., 13–14, 15.

[6] Smith, *Justice and the Poor*, 16, 17–30. These topics will be discussed below as part of the discussion of legal aid and remedial reform.

only partial correctives. In the remaining areas of legal action the services of a lawyer were essential for the poor to exercise their legal rights. Only two solutions occurred to Smith: abolish the bar or provide lawyers for the poor.[7] The choice was obvious: 'since we cannot eliminate the need for lawyers without overturning our legal institutions, the only possible alternative is to eliminate the expense.'[8]

This was legal aid's role. It would resolve the most significant failure of the urban legal system by offering low-cost legal services to the poor. Explicitly delegating the abolition of poverty to others outside the legal realm, Smith stayed within his profession to place on the bar the responsibility of minimizing the legal effects of poverty.[9] 'Our duty,' he declared, 'is to do our part in our field.'[10] Legal aid, he urged, 'was not to be regarded as a thing apart or as a thing unto itself', but as part of a general professional reorganization of the urban administration of justice necessitated by massive social changes and by the need to maintain the nation's commitment to equal justice.[11]

Though he predicted dire results if his reform project failed, throughout this structural analysis Smith did not question the social or economic values and ends of the liberal legal order. Nor did he advocate a significant expansion of state welfare services. On the contrary, he explained the existence of urban injustice in the politically neutral terms of modernization. Social change had thrown a fundamentally just urban legal system out of balance, legal aid societies and kindred legal reforms would make the necessary modifications to restore its equilibrium. Smith defined the problem in ostensibly value-free craft terms; its solution in craft responsibility and expertise.[12]

---

[7] Smith to US Comm. on Industrial Relations, 24 Jan. 1914, Boston Legal Aid Society, 1914 Files, 4-5.

[8] R. H. Smith, 'The Relation Between Legal Aid Work and the Administration of Justice', *Reports of the Amer. Bar. Assoc.* 45 (1920) 223.

[9] R. H. Smith, 'An Introduction to Legal Aid Work', *Annals* 124 (1926) 2.

[10] *Report of the Proceedings of the Fourth Conference of Legal Aid Societies* (1916), 64.

[11] Smith, *Justice and the Poor*, 149. See also M. J. Horwitz, *The Transformation of American Law, 1870–1960: The Crisis of Legal Orthodoxy* (New York, Oxford Univ. Press, 1992), 187–9.

[12] For Smith's warnings about the consequences of failure see, Boston Legal Aid Society, *Annual Report* (1915–16), 8; and R. H. Smith, 'Denial of Justice', *Jrnl. Amer. Judicature Soc.*, 3 (1919), 126; and R. H. Smith, 'The Relationship Between Legal Aid Work and the Administration of Justice', *Central Law Jrnl.* 91 (1920), 378. For a different analysis of *Justice and the Poor*, see J. S. Auerbach, *Unequal Justice: Lawyers and Social Change in Modern America* (New York, Oxford Univ. Press, 1976), 59–61. Unlike this essay, which considers the tract an intra-professional critique, Auerbach argues that it was a direct attack on the legal order itself.

Justice and the Poor expressed conclusions legal aid lawyers had reached from their experiences representing poor litigants since 1876, when the German Society of New York City, fed up with the exploitation of their immigrant countrymen by 'runners, boardinghouse keepers and a miscellaneous coterie of sharpers', formed *Der Deutschutz Rechtsschutz Verein* to 'render legal aid and assistance, gratuitously', to Germans in need.[13] In 1896 the Society opened its doors to all impoverished New Yorkers and by 1910 fourteen organizations existed. In 1910 Kansas City opened the first publicly sponsored legal aid bureau. When Smith surveyed the movement, it had grown to forty-one societies in cities across the North and on the West Coast.[14]

Legal aid lawyers sustained this growth by using the Magna Charta, the Sixth Amendment to the United States Constitution, and the newly adopted canons of the American Bar Association (ABA) to forge a lawyerly responsibility to come to the legal aid of the poor. Though they repeated the professional folklore that in the past aiding the poor had been a natural role of all lawyers and pointed to the little-used *in forma pauperis* procedure through which courts could appoint counsel to impoverished litigants as evidence of a tradition of such professional responsibilities, legal aid lawyers argued that times had changed. To achieve equal justice now required a revision of the traditional procedural tenet of liberal legalism that the right to counsel simply meant the state could not bar a litigant from obtaining counsel. As Smith had explained, in a modern complex and interdependent society all litigants needed legal counsel and thus representation must be made an active, not a passive, professional duty and a permanent part of the American administration of justice.[15]

Legal aid lawyers reached that conclusion because, as Smith had repeated in *Justice and the Poor*, the conditions and crises of their times had made them conscious of change and convinced of the need to take collective political action. The rippling impact of industrial capitalism not only produced the kinds of dislocating changes that Smith had chronicled, but also compelled the wholesale re-evaluations of existing forms of knowledge and practices, as his argument for legal aid made clear. Most important for understanding the sources of legal aid,

[13] J. MacArthur Maguire, *The Lance of Justice, A Semi-Centennial History of The Legal Aid Society, 1876–1926* (Cambridge, Mass., Harvard Univ. Press, 1928), 18–19.

[14] *History of the New York Legal Aid Society* (New York, 1912), 15; Smith, *Justice and the Poor*, 140–8.

[15] Ibid., 1-5; Maguire, *Lance of Justice*, 1–9; J. MacArthur Maguire, 'Poverty and Civil Litigation', *Harvard Law Rev.*, 36 (1923), 361–404.

Smith's analysis represented one product of a larger reconceptualization of the relationship between strangers that expanded the boundaries of individual responsibility and launched a second wave of American humanitarian reform. Locating law reform within this larger reform drive is critical not only to an understanding of its fundamental assumptions but also to avoid the reductionist tendency to explain such social activism simply as the product of benevolence or social control. It also suggests why legal aid ought to be considered what Michel Foucault and Jacques Donzelot have called 'discursive movements'. By that they mean that at particular times new ways of perceiving social conditions give rise to new forms of knowledge and, in turn, that knowledge compels attempts to apply it through movements that share common priorities, assumptions, and tactics.[16] Late nineteenth- and early twentieth-century American humanitarianism was one such movement. And classifying it as such compels consideration of the time-bound creation of what anthropologists call social knowledge, or the operational understanding of particular groups. In these terms, the turn-of-the-century American legal aid movement blended aspects of the larger reformist knowledge of the era with the legal profession's own understanding of social problems and legal practice.

The first wave of American humanitarianism had rolled through the Republic early in the nineteenth century. Its primary expressions had been a variety of mass movements in which voluntary associations attacked social ills from slavery and women's subordination to alcoholism and crime, and relied on moral suasion as their primary instrument of change. The various reform campaigns had also shared a romantic optimism that sprang from faith in the possibilities of human self-transformation and social reorganization and that fostered toleration for diversity.[17] The second wave too found numerous expressions

---

[16] See M. Foucault, *Power/Knowledge: Selected Interviews and Other Writings, 1972–1977*, Colin Gordon (ed.), (New York, Pantheon, 1980), J. Donzelot, *The Policing of Families* (New York, Pantheon, 1979).

[17] Thomas Haskell analyses the emergence of American humanitarianism between 1750 and 1850 by focusing on the issue of abolitionism. He locates the movement in the reverberating impact of market capitalism and the changes enforced in social conventions. In particular, he argues that extended economic relations and other features of the new order encouraged a new sense of moral responsibility to strangers evident in the growing ideological and experiential reliance on contract law. He points to abolitionists as an example of a group that took the new sentiments to their greatest extent. 'Capitalism and the Origins of Humanitarian Sensibility, Part I', *Amer. Hist. Rev.*, 90 (1985), 339–61; 'Part II', ibid., 547–66. And for a debate about Haskell's argument see David Brion Davis, 'Reflections on Abolitionism and Ideological Hegemony', ibid., 92

and had much in common with the first. But differences, as always in comparisons, are the most revealing. And among the most significant differences between the two was that the second humanitarian movement was dominated by a much greater tendency to turn to public authority and the authority of experts to ameliorate problems. Equally telling, the massive social and economic dislocations of the later era fed fears about the fate of American society that bred intolerance and demands for the imposition of order and uniformity.

Accordingly, legal aid lawyers ought to be understood as one of the cadres of this second wave of American humanitarian reform produced by a new professional, urban middle class. The fundamental ambiguities of its organizing assumptions were in many ways a direct product of the uncertainties of that class's outlook on cities. An optimistic faith in social justice, modernization, and controlled human progress intermixed with incessant fears about endangered professional authority, cultural heterogeneity, and social fragmentation. As Smith's words had suggested, proponents of legal aid accepted the new industrial order and the need to reform it, but sought to use their specialized knowledge to preserve continuity with older values and create social bonds across the classes. They saw legal aid as their contribution to the construction of a new consensual social order within a reconstructed liberal state. They shared this complex mix of forward- and backward-looking goals with other members of the instrumental, social-engineering vanguard of urban reform.[18] As sociologist John Sutton has argued in a history of juvenile delinquency, '[a]lthough concern for order was not new in American history, a characteristic feature of Progressives sought to depoliticize the growing demands for the protections of a welfare state by promoting reforms that emphasized administrative efficiency and professional expertise rather than substantive changes in the allocation of rights and economic resources.'[19]

However, the differences among the various forms of humanitarian reform, like differences between eras, are revealing as well. Indeed, too many analyses of late nineteenth- and early twentieth-century America

(1987), 797–812; John Ashworth, 'The Relationship Between Capitalism and Humanitarianism', ibid., 813–28; and Haskell, 'Convention and Hegemonic Interest in the Debate over Antislavery: A Reply to Davis and Ashworth', ibid., 829–78.

[18] For a particularly insightful assessment of the literature on the reforms movements of the era see Daniel Rodgers, 'In Search of Progressivism', *Reviews in Amer. Hist.* 10 (1982), 113–32.

[19] J. R. Sutton, *Stubborn Children. Controlling Delinquency in the United States, 1640–1981* (Berkeley, Univ. of California Press, 1988), 124.

tend to lump reformers together with generalizations like the organizational synthesis or corporate liberalism that conflate results such as growing bureaucratization or corporate ascendancy with causes.[20] Instead, as Smith's arguments made clear, legal aid was first and foremost a lawyerly expression of the era's social knowledge. Legal aid lawyers' advocacy of an expansion of the boundaries of their profession's moral responsibilities disclosed that the changes of the era forced a previously unarticulated ideal to the surface of professional consciousness. They relied on expertise and professionalism to make representation of the poor a test of the bar's commitment to equal justice. And to legitimize the organized provision of counsel for the poor as a new professional responsibility they purposely accentuated legal aid as a lawyers' reform. Staking out such professional boundaries became defining, and thus contested, issues in this reformist era.

Equally important, particularly for understanding legal aid as a collective professional political action within the liberal legal order, Andrew Polsky has cautioned that in their conception of discursive movements neither Foucault nor Donzelot fully appreciate the power of politics, and especially the state, in such efforts. He argues that discursive movements create policy entrepreneurs whose goals and tactics generate conflicts over the definition of state authority and responsibilities.[21] Legal aid is a case in point. Disagreements about the state's role in the administration of justice were indeed critical to the development of legal aid as a professional reform. They helped define the nature of the professional politics that engulfed the bar in this and other issues.

At the heart of these debates were perennial concerns in American legal and political theory about the proper division of authority into public and private realms. American lawyers had long had a potent voice in such matters. Most arguments about the relatively underdeveloped nature of the American state in comparison to those of Western European nations highlight the republic's limited public bureaucracies, decentralized political structures, and the policy-making prerogatives granted courts and lawyers in the United States. These features of the American polity combined to produce a distinctive version of the moderate state and, indeed, to make anti-statism itself a central tenet of American political liberalism. Nevertheless, the American republic,

---

[20] For a useful assessment of this issue see Alan Brinkley, 'Writing the History of Contemporary America: Dilemmas and Challenges', *Daedalus*, 113 (1984), 121–41.

[21] A. J. Polsky, *The Rise of the Therapeutic State* (Princeton, Princeton Univ. Press, 1991), 9–11.

what Sutton and Gary Hamilton call 'a weak state with strong law', had not remained static.[22] During legal aid's formative years increased governmental regulation of society and the economy, coupled with a growing tendency to devise administrative solutions to problems from railroad rates to tainted food to workplace injuries, challenged this tradition and sparked new controversies over the boundaries between public and private authority. The resulting reallocations of power redefined the authority of the moderate state within the liberal order.[23] In response, as Michael Powell argues, many lawyers defended the power and legitimacy of the bar by seeking to 'repair the situation through the restoration of the liberal legal order in which the boundaries of private and public action were clearly demarcated, individual rights well defined, and procedures regular and consistent'.[24] Legal aid became one of the panoply of law reforms with just such goals. Yet, as Smith and his allies argued repeatedly, restoration could never be complete, it could come only with change. And organized counsel for the poor was one such necessary change within a larger reorganization of urban legal institutions and practices that included corporate law firms, law schools, and professional associations as well as related reforms in judicial organization and municipal regulation.

The dual commitments of law reformers to the preservation of the liberal legal order and modernization of the legal system so evident in the legal aid movement and its kindred reforms had one other consequence as well. These goals led legal aid lawyers to champion representation as a singularly important individual right necessary for all Americans now forced to deal with the growing complexities of modern public and private life. It seemed axiomatic to legal aid lawyers that the liberal legal commitment to equality before the law could only be achieved through the provision of counsel for all who sought recourse

[22] J. R. Sutton & G. Hamilton, 'The Problem of Control in the Weak State, Domination in the United States, 1880–1920', *Theory & Society*, 18 (1989), 16.

[23] For helpful analyses of the issue of the American state and its changes during this era, see S. Skowronek, *Building A New American State: The Expansion of National Administrative Capacities, 1877–1920* (New York, Cambridge Univ. Press, 1982); M. Keller, *Regulating a New Economy: Public Policy and Economic Change in America, 1900–1933* (Cambridge, Mass., Harvard Univ. Press, 1990); M. Keller, *Regulating A New Society: Public Policy and Social Change in America, 1900–1933* (Cambridge, Mass., Harvard Univ. Press, 1994); T. Skocpol, *Protecting Soldiers and Mothers: The Political Origins of Social Policy in the United States* (Cambridge, Mass., The Belknap Press, 1992); W. R. Brock, *Investigation and Responsibility: Public Responsibility in the United States, 1865–1900* (Cambridge, Cambridge Univ. Press, 1984); Horwitz, *Transformation of American Law*, esp. chap. 8.

[24] M. J. Powell, *From Patrician to Professional Elite* (New York, Russell Sage Foundation, 1988), 10.

to the legal system. However, turning what had been a passive right into an active one meant not only reformulating professional and lay conceptions of representation but also challenging the traditional American linkage between rights and property ownership. Throughout the nation's colonial and republican past, it had been primarily through property ownership that Americans had gained standing, status, and thus rights. However not only were the forms of property being expanded in this era, but the necessary connection between property ownership and individual rights was being re-examined as well. This re-examination was part of the larger reconceptualization of citizenship taking place in the era. New ideas about legitimate individual political interests encouraged changes in this fundamental element of political liberalism. In one particularly telling example, Paul Murphy has argued that fears about the First World War expansion of state surveillance and the consequent increase of individual vulnerability to governmental scrutiny led civil libertarians to argue that all Americans were endowed with constitutional rights whether they owned tangible assets or not. The result was a transformation in the conception of civil liberties that ignited political conflict and litigation.[25] In the same manner as civil libertarians claimed the right to speak for the interests of political radicals, so legal aid lawyers voiced what they assumed to be interests of the poor by championing a right to counsel detached from an ability to pay and attached to citizenship itself. In doing so, they, like the civil libertarians, sought to preserve individual autonomy by challenging existing notions of legitimate rights and rights holders and thus they too helped spark a debate over the very nature of citizenship that became part of larger conflicts over the reconstruction and legitimation of the liberal order.

Justice and the Poor had not only laid bare the key assumptions of the legal aid movement, but like other calls for legal reform generated an intense reaction. Legal aid lawyers and many other legal reformers and their lay allies publicly and enthusiastically embraced Smith's manifesto. Indeed, it remained the movement's basic tract through the 1950s, and Smith remained legal aid's major spokesman. And the

---

[25] P. Murphy, *World War I and the Origins of Civil Liberties* (New York, Norton, 1979), esp. 42-50. And for a discussion of other changes in property law during the era see Horwitz, *Transformation of American Law*, chap. 5, and for a larger assessment of changing property regimes see Jennifer Nadelsky, *Private Property and the Limits of American Constitutionalism, The Madisonian Framework and Its Legacy* (Chicago: Univ. of Chicago Press, 1990), chap. 6.

1920s became an era of growth evident in the fact that by the start of the next decade thirty new organizations had been created and legal aid resources almost doubled.[26] But adverse reaction to *Justice and the Poor* revealed the depth of opposition to any movement that so bluntly criticized the legal system and the internecine reality of the politics of professionalism. The volume, which received wide Press and professional coverage, exposed the cleavage within the bar between reformers and what Alfred Z. Reed of the Carnegie Foundation called 'obscurantist ostriches'.[27] Most strikingly, Smith's critics did not devalue legal aid *per se* but refused to acknowledge his claim that it was necessary because of defects in the legal system. Instead, they saw legal aid mainly as a social palliative. The reaction of leading New York corporate lawyer William Guthrie, a member of the New York Legal Aid Society, was typical: 'Taken in all, the pamphlet will, I apprehend, do more harm than good in tending to create the entirely erroneous impression as to the administration of justice in this country, in so far as it relates to the poor.'[28]

Criticism like this exposed the dynamics of the politics of professionalism. Legal reformers like Smith perceived themselves as caught in a political crossfire. On the left, they attempted to defuse rising charges, primarily levied by external lay critics, of injustice in the legal order; on the right they sought to placate those, particularly within their professional ranks, who would brook no changes whatever. They sustained themselves in this two-front campaign with a dogged belief in the legitimacy of the liberal legal order and an equally fervent determination that the liberal ideal of procedural justice must be realized.

Legal Aid and the Bar

Legal aid lawyers considered themselves a flank of the organized bar and their relations with the profession the single most important defining element of their movement. They tried to carve out a place for their organizations among the various voluntary associations and state institutions that constituted the American bar within the liberal order.

[26] R. H. Smith & J. S. Bradway, *The Growth of Legal Aid Work in the United States* (US Dept. of Labor, Bureau of Labor Statistics, Bull. no. 607, Washington, DC, 1936), 55–62.

[27] Undated Memorandum, *Justice and the Poor Correspondence, 1913–1921*, Harvard Law School (unnumbered).

[28] Guthrie to Henry S. Pritchett, 6 Dec. 1919, in *Justice and the Poor Correspondence*. For further adverse reactions see the letters by Harlan F. Stone and the New York State Bar Assoc. in the same collection.

Exhortations for bar support filled their reports, speeches, and articles. They thought their arguments were irrefutable; particularly to a profession undergoing a crisis of cultural authority and suffering from public vilification.[29] In 1926 John Alan Hamilton used telling metaphors to make these points: 'The Legal Aid Bureau needs the fostering care of its spiritual parent, the Bar Association, as a boarded-out child needs its natural mother. But the Bar Association needs the Legal Aid Bureau as an aristocrat in Russia needs calloused hands.'[30] And yet the relationship between legal aid and the bar remained a tenuous one. Smith complained in 1919 that though the 'responsibilities are bilateral, the performance is still very much one-sided'. Legal aid lawyers felt the sting of accusations that they stole business from fledgling attorneys, that their services were unnecessary, and that their cause was unimportant. Even more they suffered the silent pain of the bar's indifference. The continued reluctance of lawyers to rally around the movement puzzled and angered them.

Legal aid lawyers reacted to the bar's hostility and indifference by explicitly structuring their services to meet what they perceived to be the needs and concerns of the profession and then by waging an intra-bar campaign to win support. Their struggle for professional recognition had long-lasting implications for legal aid and provides another revealing glimpse of the politics of professionalism within the liberal state. Most importantly, efforts by legal aid lawyers to secure bar endorsement demonstrate the centrality of struggles over professional autonomy in this as in the other political projects of the bar. Their campaign forced lawyers to grapple with the consequences of new forms of professional stratification, changing boundaries between the public and private realms of the American liberal order, and the place of the bar in civil society. As a result, the attempt to provide representation to the republic's least powerful citizens provoked searching debates about the independent authority of the bar to govern itself and preserve its power amidst the era's dramatic changes.

To elicit professional support, legal aid lawyers trumpeted not merely their efforts to represent poor clients, but also their many direct services

---

[29] In using the term cultural authority I have in mind the meaning developed by Paul Starr in distinguishing between social and cultural authority; see P. Starr, *The Social Transformation of Medicine* (New York, Basic Books, 1982), 13–18; and see W. K. Hobson, *The American Legal Profession and the Organizational Society, 1890–1930* (New York, Garland Publishers, 1986), chaps. 1–2.

[30] J. A. Hamilton, 'Legal Aid Work and the Bar', *Annals*, 124 (1926), 147.

for the bar. Their appeals were rooted in the period's professional controversies. Prime among these was the public and bar debate over
whether law had ceased to be a profession and had become a business.
Framing the issue were assertions that in their pursuit of the riches
available to the hirelings of industrial capitalists, leading lawyers had
abandoned traditional ethical commitments that had helped legitimate
the bar's autonomy. Legal aid lawyers refuted the charges by embracing the changed conditions of legal practice and trying to incorporate
themselves into the new professional order. Thus while Smith acknowledged that 'charity work which had always been part of the older type
of office was discarded under the pressure of the new era', Rudoph
Matz, President of the Chicago Legal Aid Bureau, explained that legal
aid fulfilled this ethical duty by bureaucratizing it and thus relieved 'the
busy lawyer' of the cases that 'they have not the time and which they
have not the facilities for taking care of'.[31] Consequently, legal aid
enabled the bar to fulfil its duties to the poor and at the same time
maintain an image of the lawyer as a minister of justice and the law as
'a profession not a business'.[32] As M. W. Acheson, Jr. of the Pittsburgh
Legal Bureau explained in 1917, 'In a word, the Legal Aid Society, is
the scientific expression of the theoretical attitude of all lawyers and the
practical attitude of many—not to charge the poor, and the Society is
enabled to live up to the ideal more efficiently than can the busy practitioner in the rush of his professional work.'[33]

And professional reorganization even worked to the poor's benefit
thanks to another welcomed aspect of the modern bar, specialization.
In the bitter intraprofessional conflicts spawned by the displacement of
general trial work by acting for corporations as the most important and
remunerative form of practice, legal aid lawyers sided with the advocates of specialization and the new professional order. In an example
of the changed professional knowledge of the era that buoyed their
movement and seemed to link it to other critical legal developments,
they joined ranks with the new corporate legal elite to contend that
modern law must be considered a science in need of specialists.[34] As
movement leader John S. Bradway claimed, using what he and many

---

[31] Smith, *Justice and the Poor*, 85; R. Matz, 'Right Before Might, Legal Aid Work in
Chicago', *The Legal Aid Review* 9: 3 (1913) 2.

[32] R. H. Smith & J. S. Bradway, 'Legal Aid and the Bar', *Tenn. Law Rev.* 5 (1927), 224.

[33] M. W. Acheson, 'Reasons for the Rise and Growth of Legal Aid Societies', *Case &
Comment* 23 (1917), 1007.

[34] For a discussion of these controversies see Michael Ariens, 'Know the Law: A
History of Legal Specialization', *S. Carolina Law Rev.*, 45 (1994), 1003–61, esp. 1015–22.

other lawyers considered irrefutable logic, '[l]egal aid work calls for specialized knowledge in a particular field of law. A lawyer who handles dozens of cases on a particular point can give an accurate opinion as to the law in a very short space of time.'[35] The welcomed and seemingly irreversible progress of specialization thus not only altered the ethical burdens of the profession, it secured expertise and efficiency for poor clients. Samuel Horovitz of the Boston Legal Aid Society proclaimed that the 'solution of the internal legal aid problem, of supplying the right lawyer for the right cause, lies in the further extension of the principles of specialization'.[36] In this way legal aid lawyers not only sought legitimacy for their movement by siding with those who argued for the authority of lawyers as disinterested scientific professionals, they laid the groundwork for poverty law as a distinct professional specialty.

Legal aid lawyers also sought professional support by volunteering for service in another one of the bar's legitimation projects. They helped deflect contentions that the corporate-lawyer-dominated urban bar was socially irresponsible by joining elite lawyers in insisting that the real culprits sullying the profession and victimizing clients were to be found in the profession's lower reaches, preying on the unprotected poor and immigrants. These were the unethical shysters, ambulance chasers, and other 'wolves in sheep's clothing who are capable of the basest sort of treachery to their clients'.[37] Those practitioners were accused of a double offence: afflicting the poor and undermining the social standing of the profession. Because of their specialized work with impoverished clients, legal aid lawyers argued, only they dealt 'with a class of attorneys who are unknown to the leaders of the bar, and they negotiate with them, try cases against them, and come into contact with them in daily practice, so they are in a position to detect improper and unlawful conduct'.[38] Through its offer of inexpensive representation, legal aid ferreted out these renegade professionals and offered itself as a professionally responsible substitute.

By uniting the defence of the profession with representation, legal aid lawyers crafted a role for themselves as the poor's guardians and the bar's 'watchdog'.[39] The societies portrayed themselves as being in 'an

[35] J. S. Bradway, 'The Function of the Modern Legal Aid Organization', *Annals*, 124 (1926), 19.

[36] S. Horovitz, 'The Need for Specialization in Legal Aid Cases', *Annals*, 140 (1929), 63.

[37] Boston Legal Aid Society, *Annual Report*, 18 (1917–18), 27.

[38] Smith, *Justice and the Poor*, 227.   [39] Ibid., 155.

impartial position' with 'no private interests at stake . . . [j]ust as they
have served to extend the administration of justice into the great field
at the bottom of society, so they have extended the watchfulness and
discipline of the bar association'.[40] This was legal aid's contribution to
the bar associations' goal of an integrated, unitary profession, whose
members had similar training, ethics, and practices.[41] Legal aid advocates thus trumpeted its service in allowing client differentiation without sacrificing some of the larger professional goals of the bar reform.
And in doing so they both exposed and endorsed the emerging system
of professional stratification based on client standing while helping to
preserve the ideal of a unified bar.

Perhaps the most significant, and the most telling, service of legal aid
to the organized bar was its direct efforts to protect the profession's
autonomy. After reading *Justice and the Poor*, Henry Taft, a prominent
New York lawyer and brother of the former President and future Chief
Justice, protested that legal aid was either 'a philanthropic undertaking
by patriotic citizens at private expense for the benefit of the poor litigant and thus is in the nature of a charity; or it is a proper subject to
be part of the machinery of the administration of justice'.[42] Legal aid
lawyers resisted this categorization and the choice it suggested. Instead,
they sought a place for legal aid as a distinctive professional undertaking that was neither a charity nor a direct state responsibility. As
they did, these lawyers had to negotiate a series of boundary disputes
that disclose the difficulties of trying to protect the bar's distinctive place
within a changing American civil society and moderate state.

Clashes occurred because persistent funding problems ignited ideological disputes about bar autonomy. Yearly reports bemoaned the lack
of funds and fretted about how limited income stunted staff development and client services. Funding difficulties exposed the basic divisions—and contradictions—of the movement. There were three main
types of organizations: independent voluntary societies, divisions of
charities, and municipal agencies. Private societies dominated the
movement. They were the most prevalent organizational form, and
their members held most positions of authority in the movement. In

[40] Ibid., 228.
[41] For a thorough examination of this effort see Auerbach, *Unequal Justice*, chaps, 4 &
5, and see Powell, *Patrician to Professional Elite* and Hobson, *American Legal Profession*. For
the most detailed analysis of bar stratification see J. P. Heinz & E. O. Lauman, *Chicago
Lawyers: The Social Structure of the Bar* (Chicago, Amer. Bar Found., 1982).
[42] H. Taft, *Law Reform: Papers and Addresses by a Practicing Lawyer* (New York, 1926),
118–19.

1919 there were twenty-five private societies of one sort or another, seventeen departments of charities, and nine public bureaux.[43]

Two controversies splintered the movement. The first concerned the relationship of legal aid and philanthropy. From the beginning, most legal aid lawyers had vehemently rejected the equation of representation for the poor with charity. It contradicted their professional commitment to the liberal ideals of equal justice and procedural rights. They argued that such an equation would have two unwelcomed consequences: first, it would undermine the basic right of the poor to counsel, threatening to equate justice with charity; and second, it would reclassify lawyers as social workers instead of independent professionals and officers of the court. Making legal aid a department of an urban philanthropy would thereby compromise the necessary autonomy all lawyers needed and thus the rights of the poor as well. Smith noted, for instance, that for 'nine years the Cleveland incorporated society published annual reports which still rank among the best contributions to legal aid literature, but since it has turned its financial control over to the Cleveland Federation for Charity and Philanthropy its annual reports have dwindled to a leaflet, and in the Federation's Year Book it occupies a scant two pages.'[44] Such events drove him to argue '[l]egal aid work is a distinct thing from general charity work, it requires the legally trained mind acting in the light of knowledge of legal affairs to understand its significance and to chart wisely its course of activity.'[45]

In part this position simply expressed a lawyerly version of the perennial American dogma that charity pauperized its recipients. According to a New York lawyer writing in the 1905 *Legal Aid Review*: 'The world owes no man a living, and to give him one has come to be recognized as unwise charity, but everyone is entitled to the preservation of his legal rights, and to enforce and protect those rights through the courts when necessary does not make our clients paupers but contented men and good citizens instead of discontented grumblers, and possible recruits to the forces of disorder.'[46] Too close an association with charities and social workers threatened to undermine this vital distinction.

Even more importantly, though, fears about the classification of legal aid as a charity exposed one of the professional boundary struggles that accompanied the birth of the American welfare state. Amid widespread agreement about the failures of existing forms of support for indigents,

---

[43] Smith, *Justice and the Poor*, 173.　　[44] Ibid., 177–8.　　[45] Ibid., 178.
[46] *Legal Aid Review*, 3: 2 (1905), 1–2.

patchwork solutions led to the creation of a variety of new welfare agencies staffed primarily by social workers engaged in their own professionalization projects. These included settlement houses, community centres, charity federations, corporate welfare departments, revamped city and county welfare agencies, and even legal institutions like juvenile and family courts. The reconstituted social services set the stage for a clash between lawyers and social workers over professional duties and responsibilities.[47]

Legal aid lawyers associated with charities faced the issue directly. They responded with declarations of independence from the social workers who ran these agencies. Some, as in St. Paul, moved their offices away from other charities; more commonly legal aid lawyers tried to secure oversight and support from local bar associations and thus construct what they considered the proper lines of support and of profession demarcation. The most extensive experience occurred in Chicago's Legal Aid Bureau run out of the city's United Charities. The Bureau was formed out of a 1905 merger of the organizations begun in the 1880s by the Women's Club and the Ethical Culture Society.[48] The origins of the agency ensured the continued dominance of social workers and compelled its lawyers to fight for internal independence. They demanded a separate voice in agency deliberations and secured direct oversight from the Chicago Bar Association and nationally prominent Northwestern University Law School Dean John H. Wigmore. As a result, in 1926 Marguerite Raeder Gariepy, the Bureau's senior attorney, contended that Smith's 1919 characterization did not apply to her organization. Indeed, she argued that 'it may be said that a departmental society is usually on a stronger financial basis than a private corporation, that it is able to do more for its clients by helping them to solve not only their legal, but also their social problems, and that it can be of greater service to family welfare

---

[47] For analyses of these issues see R. H. Bremner, *From the Depths; The Discovery of Poverty in the United States* (New York, New York Univ. Press, 1956); J. Leiby, *A History of Social Welfare and Social Work in the United States* (New York, Columbia Univ. Press, 1978); R. Lubove, *The Professional Altruist: The Emergence of Social Work as a Career* (New York, Atheneum, 1980); W. I. Trattner, *From Poor Law to Welfare State* (New York, Free Press, 1984); M. B. Katz, *In the Shadow of the Poorhouse: A Social History of Welfare in America* (New York, Basic Books, 1986); Skocpol, *Protecting Soldiers and Mothers.*

[48] R. Matz, 'Right Before Might', 1–2; J. Wigmore, 'Additional History of Legal Aid Work', *Mass. Law Q.*, 1 (1916), 288; M. Raeder Gariepy, 'The Legal Aid Bureau of the United Charities of Chicago', *Annals*, 124 (1926), 33–41; J. Katz, *Poor People's Lawyers in Transition* (New Brunswick, NJ, Rutgers Univ. Press, 1982), chap. 2.

work.'[49] Nevertheless, sociologist and lawyer Jack Katz would look back on these years and conclude that by 'official design, the Chicago Legal Aid Bureau served social work goals, attending to client problems as reflections of personal pathology rather than structural injustice'.[50] Just such a distinction and condemnation, however, represented a lawyerly judgement forged in disputes over professional identity early in the twentieth century.

A split over charity work among women lawyers provides a particularly revealing example of the deeply ingrained professional animus against the classification of legal services as philanthropic acts. Only late in the nineteenth century did women begin a sustained and difficult attempt to join the bar. They faced constant opposition and overt discrimination.[51] Charity cases exposed a raw nerve in this struggle: the essentialist gender beliefs of the era fed the assumption that women were natural care-givers who would automatically take on such tasks. And indeed some women lawyers did urge the bar to take on a greater role in addressing the legal needs of the poor. Others expressed such views as part of a larger critique of the ethical failing of their new profession. Most women lawyers, however, echoed their male counterparts in rejecting a special professional responsibility to take on charity cases. 'Charity clients should be shunned unless in extreme cases,' attorney Emma Gillett declared. 'They have no more right to a lawyer's services for nothing than a washerwoman's.' Ellen Martin agreed and insisted, '[W]hen I have anything to give away I will give it in money and not in legal services.'[52] Virginia Drachman puts these comments in context by explaining that 'to these women, charity was not simply an issue for each woman lawyer to resolve on her own. Rather, they transformed the question of charity work into a political issue, making it a test of women's commitment to the cause of women lawyers. From their point of view, the survival of a woman's lawyer's career came before the legal needs of an impoverished client.'[53]

---

[49] Gariepy, 'Legal Aid Bureau of United Charities of Chicago', 40–1, and for its general history, see 33–5.   [50] J. Katz, *Poor People's Lawyers in Transition*, 39.

[51] For particularly compelling assessments of these struggles see V. Drachman, 'Women Lawyers and the Quest for the Professional Identity in Late Nineteenth-Century America', *Mich. Law Rev.*, 88 (1990), 2414–43; and V. Drachman, 'The New Woman Lawyer and the Challenge of Sexual Equality in Early Twentieth Century America', *Ind. Law J.*, 28 (1995), 227–57.

[52] Quoted in Drachman, 'Women Lawyers and Quest for Professional Identity', 2431.

[53] Ibid. See also M. Grossberg, 'Institutionalizing Masculinity: The Law as a Masculine Profession', in M. Carnes & C. Griffen (eds.), *Meanings for Manhood: Constructions of Masculinity in Victorian America* (Chicago, Univ. of Chicago Press, 1990), 145–50.

Not surprisingly, disputes erupted every time social workers and attorneys discussed legal aid. In a 1929 edition of the *Annals* devoted to the question of 'Law and Social Work,' for instance, Alan Wardell, President of the New York Legal Aid Society, defended the necessity of a distinctively lawyers' approach to social welfare issues. Drawing clear lines of professional kinship, he maintained that where social workers' efforts were palliative, the 'legal aid worker is a lawyer, doing the work of any other member of the profession; the only distinction between him and his legal brethren is that he or the society employing him, by reason of the character of the client, receives no compensation or only nominal compensation for his work.' Wardell acknowledged that social workers were frustrated that the law was 'slow, full of complications, and often unsatisfactory results', but insisted that, as lawyers, legal aid staffers were subject first and foremost to the dictates of their profession. It could be no other way. He also detailed the results: the legal aid lawyer

is not seeking the sound social solution of the needs and difficulties of a particular client or family, but is endeavoring to obtain the enforcement of a legal right to which he conceives his client is entitled. Whether the success of his efforts will best serve his client, or perhaps his family is not his first concern. This does not mean that he differs from any other lawyer in the handling of his cases, or that he seeks to achieve academic results. It means only that he is endeavoring to solve the particular matter placed before him, and not to relate this problem to the other social difficulties of his client.[54]

The lawyers' approach continually frustrated social workers who had their own professional commitments to maintain. Besides bristling at the denigrating attitude of legal aid lawyers, they complained of the narrow approach lawyers took to the problems of the poor. In a 1928 survey of legal aid, the Association of the Bar of New York City discovered that 'half of the social agencies stated that they found the "legal mind" difficult. When the matter was delved into more deeply, it was felt that this was not due to the peculiarities of the legal mind, but to the general lack on the part of legal aid lawyers of "social mindedness" as the term is used today.'[55] For example, legal aid lawyers raised the bar's ethical commitment to client confidentiality to block sharing information with social workers. And most of the societies shunned publicity because they considered it a violation of the professional ban on advertising. Both policies, social workers argued, constricted legal aid

[54] A. Wardell, 'The Legal Aid Worker Looks at the Field', *Annals* 140 (1929), 12, 13.
[55] *Report of the Joint Committee for the Study of Legal Aid* (New York, 1928), 93–4.

and thus harmed the poor. As Robert Kelso of Boston Council of Social Agencies sadly concluded in 1926, '[t]he legal aid lawyer in common with most people looks upon constructive social work as no more than remedial charity. The social worker looks upon legal aid as an aggravating process bound in red tape and calculated to hinder rather than advance the interests of her client.'[56] This was a professional divide that could not be closed. For legal aid lawyers, the distinction between charity and justice was too important a defining element of their profession to allow compromise.

The second conflict, disagreements over law and politics caused by efforts at municipal sponsorship, raised even more troubling problems for legal aid lawyers. It brought to the fore fundamental questions about the place of the bar in the American liberal order. At the very marrow of the bar's self-identity lay the conviction that though lawyers were officers of the court their profession was a private vocation, separate and distinct from the state. This belief was an unarticulated first principle of bar claims for professional autonomy and self-governance. It was as well a basic component of their understanding of the moderate state and their conviction that bar autonomy served the interests of both the profession and the public by constraining state authority. And yet many lawyers feared that, however necessary, the reorganization of the state occurring during these years had altered inherited divisions of public and private spheres and thus threatened the bar's independence. Increasingly successful demands for new balances between public and private authority, evident most clearly in the growth of administrative agencies, not only expanded the state—they also altered civil society which had been the bar's nurturing host. In this public sphere the bar had become a key social institution exercising significant authority over the formulation and application of public and private policies dealing with issues from corporate organization to family composition. State expansion threatened to shrink the American public sphere and many lawyers resisted the encroachment in a variety of ways.[57] Opposition to publicly funded legal aid illustrates the character of this resistance and

---

[56] R. Kelso, 'Legal and Social Welfare Agencies', *Annals*, 124 (1926), 128; and see J. Hunter, 'Social Agencies and Legal Aid Theory', *Annals*, 205 (1939), 129–33; Mary Isham, 'A Social Worker in a Legal Aid Society', ibid., 134–40; Smith & Bradway, *Growth of Legal Aid Work*, chap. 17.

[57] For a general discussion of civil society, see A. B. Seligman, *The Idea of Civil Society* (New York, Free Press, 1992) and A. B. Seligman, 'Symposium: Law and Civil Society', *Ind. Law Rev.*, 72 (1997), 335–527; Horwitz, *Transformation of American Law*, 206–8.

the persistent problems American lawyers have had in trying to maintain a clear distinction between law and politics.

As was the case with legal aid and social service organizations, funding problems encouraged the turn to public support, as Smith explained in *Justice and the Poor*. 'Theoretically,' he observed, 'the argument for public legal aid is irrefutable.' By that he meant that legal aid was part of the administration of justice and the conviction that poverty should not be a bar to justice led many laypeople and lawyers to the conclusion that representation ought to be made a direct state responsibility. Moreover, in his survey Smith found that the public bureaux 'are far better known and that, because they have larger funds at their disposal, they are more nearly able to satisfy the demand'. Based on the standard of one client for each seventy-five urbanites, he calculated that public bureaux met 72.4 per cent of the need, private societies 30.6 per cent, and charity departments 18.7 per cent. However, Smith continued, '[i]n passing from the theoretical to the actual we leave an argument that is all in favor of publicly controlled and publicly supported legal aid organizations and are immediately confronted with a practical situation which gives rise to grave doubts.' He reiterated primal lawyerly fears that public control would topple a key pillar of political liberalism because it would politicize the bar by erasing the line between law and politics. Legal aid would then be subverted by inefficiency and bureaucratization, the pernicious influence of corrupt urban politics, and the loss of professional independence. Dallas and Portland loomed as tragic cases in point. In 1917 a new Dallas mayor dismissed the Director of Public Welfare and tried to place a crony in charge of the legal aid bureau. When challenged, the Mayor abolished the bureau. The same year, the Portland Public Defender campaigned against a winning mayoral candidate. The new mayor abolished the office. Smith concluded that because of 'this unhappy discrepancy between theory and fact, the only conclusions that can be drawn as to the respective merits of public and private legal aid organizations are local rather than general in application'.[58]

And yet not even the legal aid bar spoke with one voice. Proponents of municipal legal aid disputed arguments like Smith's and joined the debate over the legitimacy and efficacy of state assistance. Not surprisingly, lay supporters in particular considered public control as the only logical future for legal aid. In a 1911 study directed by influential

[58] Smith, *Justice and the Poor*, 180, 192, 185–6, 186.

labour economist John R. Commons, researcher Fred R. King lauded Kansas City for taking 'the advanced step of maintaining a legal aid bureau as a regular part of its city administration'. Though a similar effort failed in Milwaukee, King noted that since the 'coming in of the present socialist administration workingmen and women in increasing numbers have presented their private grievances at city hall, thinking that legal advice counsel were to be had for the asking'.[59] Popular belief in the inherent legitimacy of public legal aid also found expression in the words of commentator Geddes Smith: 'Private agencies lack the essential quality of this new [public] office: the recognition of the whole community's obligation to the man in court and to its own self-respect as a democracy.'[60]

Public legal aid lawyers tried to translate these sentiments into action. In 1920, Ernest Tustin, director of the Philadelphia public bureau, told ABA delegates that the recognition of legal assistance as a public responsibility made organizations like his 'superior to private organizations in the psychological results produced'. Such a recognition, he insisted, contributed greatly to public confidence in the law and its administration.[61] Six years later, Romain C. Hassrick, Tustin's successor, was even more emphatic. Citing the amazing growth of his organization, Hassrick contended that legal aid 'as a public undertaking had proved itself'. Such success, he contended, should force national leaders of the movement 'to concede with some reservations . . . that the accomplishment was distinctly favorable to legal aid as a municipally controlled agency'. Even the fear of political manipulation had been dispelled in his city though 'politics is certainly an organized business in the city of Philadelphia!' According to Hassrick, the advantages of a public agency were clear: it is part of municipal government and thus obtains greater co-operation from other agencies; potential clients see it as a public service; and it can afford a larger staff. To him, 'the future trend of legal aid work in large centers of population is toward public control.'[62]

But the future proved elusive. The 1920s turned out to be the high point of the municipal legal aid movement reaching twelve public legal

[59] *Free Legal Aid* (Milwaukee Bureau of Economy and Efficiency, Bull. no. 7, 1911), 4, 5.

[60] G. Smith, 'Making the Law Work Both Ways', *Independent*, 84 (1915), 94–5.

[61] Quoted in Earl Johnson, Jr, *Justice and Reform, The Formative Years of the OEO Legal Services Program* (New York, Russell Sage Foundation, 1974), 15.

[62] R. C. Hassrick, 'The Philadelphia Legal Aid Bureau of the Department of Public Welfare', *Annals*, 124 (1926), 42, 43, 47; and see F. C. Donnell, 'St. Louis Municipal Legal Aid Bureau', ibid., 48-53.

aid bureaux in 1932; only five remained in 1962. Public bureaux had dropped from 28 per cent of the movement in 1919 to 4 per cent in 1962.[63] The Depression of the 1930s proved the undoing of several, including the Philadelphia bureau. Smith even backed away from his earlier forecast. By 1939 he would say of the public bureaux, '[t]heir record has been a checkered one, to say the least'. Citing the closing of the Philadelphia bureau, he then commented that 'all the privately supported legal aid societies carried on. They had tightened their belts, but not one closed its doors.'[64] Conversely, the private organization found financial stability, if not full treasuries, in another critical institutional addition to American civil society during these years, the community chest movement. These voluntary organizations created non-statist bureaucracies to administer the funding of approved social services. By the late 1940s 60 per cent of all legal aid funds came from local community chests. As legal aid lawyer and future United States Attorney-General Emory Brownell presciently concluded in 1948, '[w]idespread participation in Community Chests has been of great benefit to the movement and is primarily responsible for maintaining the service as a predominantly private enterprise'.[65] Indeed, Brownell and other legal aid lawyers were so fearful of state control that they paid scant attention to the consequences of this reliance on philanthropic largesse.

The decline of public legal aid was thus in part circumstantial; but it was also rooted in the fundamental conviction of political liberalism that an expansive state posed the greatest threat to the bar's autonomy. Despite desperate funding problems and the logic of state aid, public control was put off to maintain the independent political status of legal aid lawyers as neutral experts. It seemed axiomatic to them that what Claude Clarke of the Cleveland Legal Aid Society called the 'genius of private enterprise' should lead the movement.[66] Smith explained the

[63] Johnson, *Justice and Reform*, 17.

[64] R. H. Smith, 'Interest of the American Bar Association in Legal Aid Work', *Annals*, 205 (1939), 111, 111–12.

[65] E. Brownell, *Legal Aid in the United States* (Rochester, NY, Lawyers Cooperative Publishing Company, 1951), 230, 231. And see W. J. Norton, 'The Problem of Financing Legal-Social Work', *Annals*, 140 (1929), 143–9, Smith & Bradway, *Growth of Legal Aid Work*, 130–9.

[66] C. Clarke, 'Legal Aid By Privately Supported Organizations', *Annals*, 124 (1926), 54. The New York Legal Aid Society broadcast its disdain for public funds by refusing to touch a $25,000 municipal fund created for its use. Founding President Arthur Von Briesen repeatedly threatened to resign if the money were ever used. Similarly, the 1928 survey by the ABCNY took several pages to report on the volume of what it called 'unorganized legal aid', or what now could be called pro bono work, to document the

assumptions embedded in such assertions by contending that the private societies 'possess a freedom of action, a liberty in taking risks in making experiments, which will leave in their hands for several years to come the duty of leadership in the development of legal aid work'.[67] This mix of faith in private solutions and antipathy to direct state funding intensified over time. It proceeded from the professional fear that legal aid might be used as the opening wedge for state control of the bar and the diminution of civil society as a key component of the liberal state. Indeed, privately financed legal aid can be seen as the prototypical kind of incremental reform that Marvin Becker argues has always characterized changes produced within civil society.[68] Not surprisingly, in 1950 the ABA Standing Committee on Legal Aid would declare, 'The private legal aid office, operated and supervised by lawyers . . . is, we believe, the American way to meet the need.'[69]

Legal aid lawyers' opposition to public control voiced a fear of urban politics shared with other reformers of the era. Like backers of civil service, city managers, and city commissions, they wanted to take politics out of urban affairs and replace it with rational, efficient, businesslike practices.[70] This opposition, coming as it did at the very dawn of the American welfare state, is significant. It suggests how deeply embedded was the lawyerly antipathy to expansive state authority and to the growth of substantive rather than procedural rights. And for legal aid itself, fear of public control meant the movement could never meet the needs of the indigent. Instead it remained wedded to legal representation as a private relationship that could only be entrusted to the municipality in some distant, pristine, and thus unreachable, future. The stunted development of municipal legal aid and the bitter fights that have periodically erupted over federally financed legal services since the mid-1960s suggest the long-term impact of the definition of legal aid as a professional, and thus private, responsibility.

Successful resistance to the conversion of legal practice into either a charitable or public duty was precisely the kind of service to the bar that led legal aid lawyers to expect strong support from the fellow professionals. Smith made the point explicit when he declared that since

availability of private resources for the poor, before it expressed opposition to public legal aid. *Report of the Joint Committee for the Study of Legal Aid* (1928), 42–9, 100.

[67] Smith, *Justice and the Poor*, 186.

[68] M. Becker, 'An Essay on the Vicissitudes of Civil Society with Special Reference to Scotland in the Eighteenth Century', *Ind. Law Jrnl.* 72 (1997), 463–87.

[69] Johnson, *Justice and Reform*, 18–19.   [70] Sutton, *Stubborn Children*, 127–31.

the movement performed the 'bar's responsibility to the weak and oppressed, the bar should feel that it is incumbent on it to render to the legal aid societies the services for which they stand in need.'[71] However, study after study revealed that few urban practitioners accepted that responsibility.

The subject clouded every gathering of legal aid lawyers. Bar indifference frustrated them and challenged their hopes for the movement. Refusing to conclude that the problem was the result of a professional rejection of their cause, they laid the blame on ignorance and devised educational programmes to make the bar aware of legal aid and its importance. Central to their strategy was securing the support of the organized bar, the ABA as well as state and local associations. Even though only a small portion of the bar belonged to these organizations, to the legal aid lawyers they represented the proper leadership of the profession and the most effective medium for securing support. A discussion at a 1929 conference illuminates their assumptions. In reporting on his efforts to secure the attention of the ABA, Smith told the group of his success in getting a leading Wall Street lawyer to speak to the association's meeting. He had argued, 'Mr. Wardell, you are a partner of John W. Davis, your firm is known to be the counsel for J.P. Morgan and Company, and the fact that you stand up on the platform on behalf of Legal Aid Work and you are Mr. Morgan's lawyer will impress certain members of the American Bar Association more than any other factor that I can think of.'[72]

Justice and the Poor had been written in part to win bar support. It achieved some success. In 1920 the ABA set aside a morning session for a discussion on legal aid, which included Smith, Tustin of Philadelphia, and Charles Evans Hughes, a former New York Governor and Republican presidential candidate and future Chief Justice. A special committee was then created to recommend actions for the ABA to take.[73] The following year the association created a permanent standing committee on legal aid. At the same time legal aid lawyers secured similar support from state bar associations, seventeen of them by 1930.[74] For Smith, the ABA action vindicated *Justice and the*

---

[71] Smith, *Justice and the Poor*, 234.
[72] J. S. Bradway, *Legal Aid Work and the Organized Bar: A Collection of the Deliberations of the National Association of Legal Aid Organizations Gathered from the Stenographic Record of the Conferences* (Durham, NC, Duke Univ. Press, 1939), 37–8.
[73] 'Symposium on Legal Aid', *American Bar Association Reports*, 60 (1920), 217–59.
[74] Smith & Bradway, *Growth of Legal Aid Work*, 167–74.

Poor. He took to the pages of *Survey* to proclaim the triumph, telling the readers that legal aid had 'existed in this country without being responsible to any suitable guardian' and as a result had remained 'an orphan' subject to 'local impulses'. He and others recognized 'the organized bar' as legal aid's 'natural leader'.[75] Thus by the end of the 1920s, legal aid had become an officially sanctioned movement of the organized bar.[76]

Providing Representation

'The essence of the work', Smith declared in *Justice and the Poor*, 'is the rendering of legal advice and legal assistance to the individual in the individual case.'[77] And it was in the everyday practices of legal aid lawyers that the full implications of their ideological assumptions and professional commitments became clear. Because they made their offices critical sites in the bar's political project to reconstruct the liberal order, the representation provided by legal aid lawyers offers a final means of assessing the impact of the politics of professionalism on the attempt to realize the liberal ideal of equal justice through procedural reform. Most critically, their daily work reveals some of the limits of legal liberalism.

Legal aid lawyers' self-identification as legal professionals and of their movement as the poverty arm of the organized bar determined the way they represented impoverished urbanites. No doubt Smith's strident articulation of a lawyerly approach to legal aid helped secure his authorship of *Justice and the Poor* and leadership of the movement after 1920. In a 1917 symposium on legal aid in *Case and Comment*, one of the leading general interest professional journals of the day, he used an essay with the fitting title, 'A Lawyer's Legal Aid Society', to broadcast that the 'distinguishing characteristic of the Boston Legal Aid Society is that it is pre-eminently a lawyers' institution . . . Only by appreciating the fact that lawyers have been the dominating influence throughout its history can the story of its growth, its present organization, and its strong and weak points be understood.' The Society's model of legal services was the new private corporate law firm, itself a legal clone of the business corporation. The choice resulted from the decision of the Society's governing lawyers that 'the organization of the best private

---

[75] R. H. Smith, 'The Bar Adopts Legal Aid', *Survey*, 47 (1921–2), 81.

[76] Brownell, *Legal Aid in the United States*, 230–1, 243.

[77] Smith, *Justice and the Poor*, 150.

offices represented the experience of the bar as to the method best suited to the conduct of a law practice, so that the Legal Aid Society should be conducted in a similar manner'. The only difference was to be the presence of many more clients and the fact that no bills were sent out. All else was to resemble a regular law firm: ethical responsibilities, legal tactics, regard for the client's interests, and the like. In short, '[e]very effort is made to have the applicants feel that they are in a law office—their law office.' Though the realities of legal aid made adhering to this model impossible, the constant attempt to do so made private practice—or more aptly put, an idealized vision of private practice—the standard by which legal aid lawyers assessed their services.

As Smith noted in his description of the Boston Society, bulging case loads, if nothing else, distinguished legal aid offices from those of private practitioners. Every organization compiled annual statistics on its work; each report documented the number of clients that had trooped through the office that year and classified their problems. Across the nation and in each city, legal aid caseloads grew year after year: from one society and 212 cases in 1876, the movement grew to five societies and 20,896 cases in 1900, forty-one societies and 96,034 cases in 1920, and eighty-six societies and 217,643 cases in 1930.[78] Whatever the numbers, the workload demonstrated that legal aid had indeed uncovered a vast unmet need for legal services. However, with so many clients, legal aid lawyers had little time for the intimate client contact available in the offices of their elite professional colleagues whose practices they tried to emulate. Quick solutions and rapid turnover inevitably became legal aid's hallmark.

Tremendous caseloads, the private practitioner model, and professional commitments combined to influence the choices legal aid lawyers made as they determined the kind of representation to give their clients. Tellingly, instead of advocates, they consistently selected a role for themselves as quasi-judges. Acheson of the Pittsburgh Legal Aid Society explained in the 1917 *Case and Comment* symposium that legal aid lawyers aimed 'to have the right side of a controversy, to eschew the standpoint of the partisan and approach more nearly that of the impartial judge, and to render aid to those who appear worthy and have not the means to employ counsel'.[79] Legal aid lawyers acknowledged that their judicial-like stance deviated from the approach of regular practi-

---

[78] Smith & Bradway, *Growth of Legal Aid Work*, 120–1.
[79] M. W. Acheson Jr, 'Reasons for the Rise and Growth of Legal Aid Societies', *Case & Comment* 23 (1917), 1007.

tioners. Philip J. McCook, who worked in the East Side branch of the New York Legal Aid Society, noted the difference: 'Now a lawyer in private practice is generally considered obliged, if he thinks his client has a legally enforceable claim, to obtain his results no matter where the moral right may lie. The Legal Aid Society has never felt justified in taking this attitude. It is a quasi public corporation supported by the voluntary contributions of philanthropic persons. These persons do not desire to see its power used for blackmail or even for the enforcement of what, though a legal right, may be a moral wrong.'[80] Thus legal aid allowed attorneys to ply their trade according to the ideals, not the realities, of private practice.[81]

Screening procedures were one significant result of this choice. While the decision to limit its clientele grew out of legal aid's tremendous case loads, the ideological and professional commitments of legal aid lawyers determined the exact restrictions.[82] Gate-keeping generated constant debate and controversy. Determined to represent only worthy clients, the organizations applied the distinction between the worthy and unworthy poor that had become a first principle of American social welfare policy.[83] But, as always, legal aid lawyers developed their own professional definitions. A worthy client had two major characteristics: a clear inability to afford a private attorney; and a meritorious legal cause.

Clients had to prove that they were financially eligible for legal assistance. No disagreement existed about avoiding competition with the bar. Writing as 'One Who Knows', a contributor to the 1917 *Case and Comment* assured the bar: 'Every precaution has been taken not to take from any lawyer any business which he may wish to handle for the usual or reasonable lawyer's fee. On the contrary, the legal aid society is the honest lawyer's best friend; he sends to it cases known as charity cases which are brought to him, but he cannot handle because he must derive his income from his practice and cannot afford to give his time to the poor and helpless.'[84] Senator Henry Toll of Colorado used a revealing analogy to make the same point in 1930: 'I think that we all feel that by getting as many cases as possible into private offices a more

[80] P. J. McCook, 'The Judicial Aspects of the Work of The Legal Aid Society', *Legal Aid Rev.*, 5: 3 (1907), 1.

[81] P. J. McCook, 'Attorneys for the Bottom Dog, Impressions of a Year at the East Side Office of the Legal Aid Society', ibid., 14: 3 (1916), 9.

[82] Smith, 'A Lawyer's Legal Aid Society', 1009.

[83] Smith, *Justice and the Poor*, 207.

[84] 'The Legal Aid Societies', *Case & Comment*, 23 (1917), 983.

desirable result arises, in the same way that we think it is desirable to get all children it is possible to get out of the institution, and into private homes.'[85] Legal aid organizations created complicated financial tests to realize this goal.

Finances were just one hurdle for legal aid applicants. Like other legal aid lawyers, Smith insisted that '[r]ealizing that their work was in the field of the law and that they were taking a part in the administration of justice, the organizations have wisely refrained from erecting any moral standard which applicants must satisfy before being entitled to assistance. The only test is the intrinsic merit of the claim plus a due regard for those restrictions which good ethics impose upon all members of the bar.' Smith went on to list examples of ethical violations: '[s]uits for reasons of spite, vexatious proceedings taken for delay, technical defenses to just claims, will not be undertaken.'[86]

In deciding to apply these ethical standards, though, legal aid lawyers again deviated from private practice. The distinction emerged most clearly in recurrent debates over what to do with an applicant who was 'legally right but morally wrong'. Examples included debtors trying to evade legitimate creditors, suits filed in spite against neighbours, and clients gathering witnesses of doubtful veracity. A committee of the national legal aid organization identified two basic positions on the issue. According to one view, 'the legal aid organization may take the position that if the strict letter of the law allows the step to be taken which the applicant desires, the moral or ethical side of the case should not enter in. It may be argued on this score that other lawyers take this attitude—that the legal aid society should not attempt to deal with motives in the case but merely with the machinery of the law.' On the other side, 'it may be alleged that attorneys of high ethical standing

---

[85] Quoted in Bradway, *Legal Aid Work and the Organized Bar*, 39. Disagreements often erupted in legal aid meetings over whether efforts to avoid competition with the bar produced procedures that were too restrictive. Particularly evocative was a recurrent debate over what to do with applicants turned away because a society determined the individual could afford a lawyer. Some organizations merely sent them out of the door, others referred them to the local bar association, others gave them lists of approved lawyers, and still others sent them to specific practitioners. In repeated discussions of the national conferences, those gathered at the session could not arrive at a general policy. It did become clear that most societies worried about casting applicants adrift. But they also feared criticism from the bar. Indeed, discussion at a 1927 session soon focused on what to do if during the course of a case it emerged that the client could afford a private attorney; should the case be dropped, many wondered. As in the general question no basic solution emerged, but the constant fear of competition with the bar pervaded the comments. Ibid., 95–126.

[86] Smith, *Justice and the Poor*, 162.

reserve the right to decline a case if it appears to them that their duty to the court, and through the court to the community, requires such an action.'[87]

In deciding between a '"holier-than-thou" attitude' and the 'necessity to keep the legal aid society on the highest ethical plane', the organizations generally refused such cases. The Atlanta Legal Aid Society responded to a 1926 survey by declaring, 'No case should be accepted unless the client asserts a right, both in law and in morality. This office never assists its clients in taking advantage of the Federal Bankruptcy Statutes, or State Exemption Statutes, except to prevent imposition upon the client and never to assist the client in evading any moral claim.'[88] The Rochester Legal Aid Society explained why: 'Because of our peculiar position in relation to the public, we cannot consider ourselves in a strict sense purely a law office; hence when our client is legally right but morally wrong we consider it our duty to refuse the case. Being supported, as we are, by the Community Chest, we cannot help but consider the spirit of charity and justice which prompts the public in supporting us.'[89]

The legal aid definition of a meritorious claim emerged in the refusal to accept specific kinds of cases. Criminal indictments, personal injury cases, and divorce headed the proscribed list.[90] The divorce ban illustrates how the movement's policy decisions led them to offer a particular kind of representation to poor urbanites. In an era of rising divorce rates and ever-growing claims for its need and even legitimacy, Smith reported in 1919 that there was 'a clear and well-justified rule to refuse to institute divorce proceedings. Of thirty-one organizations doing general legal aid work, twenty-two declined to represent divorce libellants, and in addition two, though accepting the cases, use every means to discourage such proceedings.' Smith endorsed the position as an expression of the 'strong public policy against making divorce easy and cheap'. He justified it by arguing that with non-support and separation proceedings available to 'protect against brutality or physical abuse', the issue was between 'legal action which breaks up the home and legal action which preserves the home and leaves the path open for recon-

---

[87] Bradway, *Legal Aid Work and the Organized Bar*, 155.

[88] R. H. Smith, cited ibid., 155; for the full results of the survey, see 155–9.

[89] Ibid., 156.

[90] For discussions of the opposition to criminal and personal injury cases see Maguire, *Lance of Justice*, 83; Smith, *Justice and the Poor*, 156–7; Mayer Goldman, 'Public Defenders in Criminal Cases', *Annals*, 205 (1939), 19; Bradway, *Legal Aid Work and the Organized Bar*, 127–38.

ciliation'. Following similar logic, the societies generally accepted defendants, almost always women, so that a household 'may be broken up
only for cause shown and not for lack of representation or for default'.[91]
Similarly, most organizations agreed to handle separations—the 'poor
man's divorce'—but would not initiate divorces considering it a luxury
that ought to be paid for. The New York Legal Aid Society laid out
general guidelines in 1904: 'it will never interfere unless the case is one
of real need, and unless some practical benefit is to be gained for the
applicant or her or his children . . . and . . . it will have its attorney
take legal proceedings only where the necessary support or protection
cannot be secured without such proceedings.' An example illustrated
the policy: an abandoned woman left to fend for herself and her children, even though 'a woman of fine character, making a splendid struggle against the hardships of life', would not be aided unless her husband
tried to take legal advantage of her or threatened to take her children.
In cases of mere abandonment, divorce was a 'luxury'.[92]

A 1923 Committee Report of the National Legal Aid Organization
forthrightly addressed the contradictions raised by the divorce policy.
'In theory,' the Committee wrote, 'a Legal Aid Organization is a poor
man's law office. If the law entitles him to a divorce, it would seem
improper to deny him the divorce merely because he is poor, when a
wealthy man, upon the same set of facts, might obtain it. If, therefore,
the Legal Aid Organization is to be the poor man's law office, it must
take divorce cases.' And yet the Committee also acknowledged that
'[i]n opposition to this line of reasoning we have certain cogent arguments. We are told that divorces should not be encouraged, and that
to open the way to a flood of divorces among the poor would go far to
disrupt the family as the basis of society'. Agonizing over the issue, the
Committee reasserted the general policy with the advice that local societies attempt reconciliation where possible, call on social workers to
assess the family, and avoid rigid policies.[93] Even so, restrictions
demonstrated the clear priority the movement placed on preserving
social order over the particular domestic difficulties of its clients.[94]

---

[91] Smith, *Justice and the Poor*, 155. For the most comprehensive discussion of divorce in
this era see Roderick Phillips, *Putting Asunder, A History of Divorce in Western Society* (New
York, Cambridge Univ. Press, 1988), chaps. 11-14.

[92] *Legal Aid Rev.*, 2: 4 (1904), 1; and see Maguire, *Lance of Justice*, 83, 171–4.

[93] Bradway, *Legal Aid Work and the Organized Bar*, 127, 127–38.

[94] For the persistence of the policy see Jerome Carlin and Jan Howard, 'Legal
Representation and Class Justice', *UCLA Law Rev.*, 12 (1964–65), 413–15.

Fees were the final hurdle. Those too impoverished were exempted. What to do with the rest split the movement. Most of the older, private societies charged both a retaining fee (which in the movement ranged from ten to fifty cents) and commissions on sums collected for clients (generally around 10 per cent). None of the public and few of the charity departments imposed such charges.[95] Fees were justified as a sign of the client's good faith, a means of eliminating unworthy cases, a rationale for examining applicants' financial affairs, and as supplemental income. Most important for the private societies, they seemed to put the legal aid lawyer–client relationship nearer to that of private offices. In their own way, private legal aid lawyers acted on the fear of many urban reformers that failure to charge fees for needed services would pauperize clients. The applicants would be led to think that aid would always be provided without cost or sacrifice, thus lowering the poor's incentives to reach for their bootstraps and pull themselves up.[96]

Fees also exposed yet another rift between social workers and lawyers. The disagreement erupted at a 1916 conference. Opponents of fees charged that they compelled legal aid to hew too closely to the practices of private attorneys and risked sacrificing the basic principle of justice proclaimed by rendering legal counsel to the poor. Critics claimed that fees also perpetuated the belief that legal rights should be paid for and protected the Bar's privileged economic position within the legal system. Maud Boyes of the Chicago Protective Agency for Women and Children declared, 'We surely believe that justice should not be a purchasable commodity but a right.' Smith replied for the private organizations. He stoutly defended the privately-paid attorney in the Anglo-American legal system. Smith argued that legal aid should not be used to undermine that professional principle. 'I think', he insisted, 'that under our present system, the way we are brought-up, the way we act and feel and live and work, we will be compelled to pay as we go, and that too seems to me to be the most helpful thing for us all.'[97]

An applicant who successfully negotiated the screening procedures met a legal aid lawyer. This lawyer tried to implement the movement's

[95] Smith, *Justice and the Poor*, 165.

[96] See, e.g., Nathan Huggins, *Protestants Against Poverty, Boston's Charities, 1870–1900* (Westport, Conn., Greenwood Press, 1971), 16.

[97] *Proceedings Fourth Conference Legal Aid Societies*, 92, 98–9, and generally 89–104; despite such debates, Smith repeatedly portrayed the dispute as one of tactics not principle: see also *Justice and the Poor*, 165–8; Smith & Bradway, *Growth of Legal Aid Work*, 126–9.

particular notion of representation. Just as legal aid lawyers decided to act the part of a judge in weighing the merits of an applicant, so they chose to revise the lawyer's role in client counselling. Rather than mere advocates, legal aid lawyers considered themselves educators. Albert Bigelow of Boston told a 1916 conference, '[i]t is our ambition not only to try and get justice for our people but also to try and show our clients where they have been wrong or unreasonable'.[98] Towards that pacific end, legal aid lawyers struggled to work out equitable solutions for all the parties, not to drive the hardest bargain for their clients. At a 1914 conference, Edward J. Fleming of the public legal aid bureau in Kansas City declared that legal aid lawyers should attempt 'to bring about a real understanding between people who are in the midst of a contro-versy with one another and establish a lasting peace which is worth as much as all the money involved'.[99] Whether clients took such a san-guine view of their funds is questionable, but in legal aid offices the indi-vidualistic justice of the common law gave way to an emphasis on compromise and social integration. Similarly, the primary commitment of legal aid lawyers to urban harmony took graphic form in the policy of avoiding litigation. Repeatedly invoking Lincoln's caution against lit-igation, annual reports trumpeted low litigation rates as evidence that legal aid stifled social conflict.[100]

These policies also followed from the movement's vision of its clien-tele. In a rephrasing of the famous characterization of slaves by histor-ian Kenneth Stampp, legal aid lawyers conceived of their clients as middle-class men and women without money.[101] Such a conception was conveyed explicitly in the way the organizations depicted their

---

[98] *Proceedings Fourth Conference Legal Aid Societies*, 121.

[99] Quoted in *Proceedings Third Conference Legal Aid Societies* (1914), 337; and see *Legal Aid Rev.*, 2: 2 (1904), 1–3.

[100] The disposition of legal aid cases demonstrated the effects of these policy choices. Smith summarized the reports of various organizations and determined that out of a typ-ical 100 applicants, the outcomes were: advice given or papers drawn, 25; prohibited by rules, 5; not entitled to aid, 3; referred to appropriate agency, 6; no legal relief possible, 10; investigated, no merit in case, 8; lapsed by client, 10; relief by settlement or adjust-ment, 25; relief by court proceedings, 7; and defeat in court proceedings, 1. See Smith, *Justice and the Poor*, 161; and see Smith & Bradway, *Growth of Legal Aid Work*, 122.

[101] K. Stampp, *The Peculiar Institution, Slavery in the Antebellum South* (New York, Knopf, 1956), vii–viii. As the 1914 *Legal Aid Review* reported: 'The average poor man applying for legal aid . . . has been ascertained by the Cleveland Legal Aid Society to be a man that earns on the average of $11 a week and has a wife with anywhere from three to eight children, verily not a man that can afford to spend much for law, and yet a man in need of justice more than almost any other mortal, the father-less, the mother-less, helpless child alone excepted.' *Legal Aid Rev.*, 12: 2 (1914), 3.

clients to the profession and the public in their annual reports. These volumes were critical public-relations volleys in the movement's campaign for support and legitimation. Reports contained general observations, summary statistics, and then several pages of sample cases. The showcased cases emphasized several themes: economic dependency; struggles between good and evil; virtue redeemed; and the educational and moral results of legal aid work. A sample of the case titles listed in the July 1911 edition of the *Legal Aid Review* is illustrative: 'One Way of Defrauding An Immigrant'; 'Crime: A Case of Mistaken Identity'; 'In Trouble Through Other's Mistake'; 'The Society's Moral Effect'; 'A Grateful Applicant'; 'A Grasping Landlord'; 'A Misplaced Trust'; 'An Ungrateful Daughter-in-Law'; 'Speedy Justice for Working Girls'; and 'The Society's Methods Approved'.[102] Through such descriptions, as in their advising, legal aid lawyers lumped their clients together as the objects of their services and refused to distinguish between them on cultural, ethnic, or class grounds. Such was, they broadcast, the lawyer's role to secure equal justice for all.

Yet even though they claimed the authority to determine the proper representation for a group that they had created—impoverished legal clients—legal aid officials could not run their offices entirely as they wished. Instead, they had to confront two other realities of the politics of professionalism that consistently challenged the bar's larger political project: client aspirations and power, and intra-bar dissension and independence. These two realities complicated the implementation of legal aid policies by enlarging the cast of actors participating in struggles over the reconstruction of the liberal order and by thwarting the creation of uniform, consensual policies.

Though quite different from the alliances that lawyers had consistently formed with their most powerful clients as a means of preserving the bar's autonomy within the liberal order by checking the growth of state authority, legal aid lawyers also had to work with their clients to maintain their movement. And, like their wealthier fellow citizens, legal aid clients often resisted the role of passive recipients of lawyerly largesse. It is very difficult to recover the reaction of legal aid clients to 'their' law office, but enough evidence bursts out of reports and conferences to make it clear that they had their own ideas of proper and effective legal representation. Despite the efforts of legal aid lawyers, clients consistently challenged their policies. The constant discussion of

---

[102] *Legal Aid Rev.*, 9: 3 (1911), 7–15.

screening procedures suggests the determination of the poor to resist or evade the restrictions. Smith, for example, noted that legal aid organizations in Boston and Jersey City had at one point been more open to divorce cases but 'found that their assistance was abused, and so have changed their tactics'.[103] Clients also used the rhetoric of legal aid, like its assertion of equal justice and the common law adage of innocent until proven guilty, in their own fashion. At a 1927 conference, Wardell of New York noted with seeming amusement that 'you can very rarely induce negroes to take a plea; they always want to try their cases out, on the chance of getting out'. Another lawyer agreed, and regaled the gathering with the observation that 'there was a negro in our town; and the attorney asked him if he was guilty, and he said, "How can I tell until I hear the evidence?"' [104]

Contrary to the assumptions of legal aid lawyers, clients pursued their own ideas of justice. Committed to a belief in uniform legal values, the lawyers failed to acknowledge the existence, let alone the legitimacy, of differing legal visions in urban America. After her own survey of the movement, one critic, sociologist Kate Holiday Claghorn, author of the influential 1923 volume, *The Immigrant's Day in Court*, castigated the legal aid societies for their 'failure to take account in the treatment of clients of differences in nationality [which] may lead to the same hindrances to justice as we have noted in the connection with court action'. She wondered how legal aid lawyers could successfully negotiate settlements 'if the personal peculiarities of clients and their opponents are not taken into account?' On the contrary, her study led to the conclusion that the 'parties must be approached on the basis of their own feelings and prejudices about the matter in hand. How can this be done if the differences are not thought important and are not seen?'[105] Comments like Claghorn's sprang from the conviction that immigrants

---

[103] Smith, *Justice and the Poor*, 155.

[104] Bradway, *Legal Aid Work and the Organized Bar*, 203, 204.

[105] K. H. Claghorn, *The Immigrant's Day in Court* (New York, 1923), 472–3, 473. In a similar study, New York attorney John H. Mariano also emphasized differences that seemed to elude the bar. Describing an Italian immigrant's reaction to an American court, Mariano observed: 'He sees but little show and no seeming authority. The judge gives his decision in a matter of fact way. No uniforms are in evidence that betoken authority except the plain black robe of the Judge. There is an entire absence of atmosphere befitting a place where judgments deciding rights, duties, and obligations of all sorts, are permanently passed upon. All of this of course to his bewilderment! Thus his thoughts need guidance or they will soon lapse from mere indifference into contempt and disdain.' J. H. Mariano, *The Italian Immigrant and Our Courts* (Boston, Christopher Pub. House, 1925), 34–5.

understood the difference between procedural and substantive justice without the instruction of legal aid lawyers. Claghorn even posited the existence in urban America of various conceptions of substantive justice, for example contrasting Russian peasant courts with American urban lower courts, and argued that judges and lawyers needed to be aware of such differences.[106] Legal aid lawyers responded that justice was uniform and social problems were for social workers not lawyers. Yet daily work in legal aid offices may well have tempered that conviction.

It certainly had an impact on the lawyers who met with these clients. Again, the daily nature of such a practice is difficult to recover, but it is apparent that despite the model of a regular private practice the societies became particular kinds of legal offices. Especially important to the character of the movement, legal aid offices became approved professional havens for reformers and outsiders. That reality also distanced legal aid from its professional model. Socially concerned lawyers like Smith, who left the Boston Legal Aid Society early in the 1920s to join the prestigious firm of Hale and Dorr, were attracted by the opportunity to engage in professionally related social service before beginning careers in private practice. Legal aid was attractive to reform-minded lawyers because it was so clearly a front in the larger effort to reconstruct the liberal legal order. Adopting the techniques of incremental reform so central to civil society, legal aid lawyers were thus inclined to add remedial reform to their counsellor role. Imbued with ideas of preventive action by experts so prevalent in professions of the era, they eagerly adopted the guise of legal scientist. Legal aid allowed them to seize the responsibility for empirically diagnosing and then expertly attacking the areas where poverty undermined legal procedures. They did so in campaigns for remedial legislation such as the regulation of loan sharks and for judicial reform such as the creation of small claims courts. In these drives legal aid lawyers saw themselves as responsible professionals.[107] 'The ideal corollary to relief against past evils', John Maguire declared in his 1928 history of the New York Legal Aid Society, 'is the prevention of like evils in the future.' All 'public-spirited lawyers today', he went on to argue, 'carry on a preventive practice'. They try 'by sound advice, by the enforcement of existing laws, and by procuring the enactment of new laws to keep others out of the pitfalls

---

[106] Claghorn, *Immigrant's Day in Court*, 151–3.

[107] For thorough discussions of legal aid and remedial reform see Smith, *Justice and the Poor*, Part II; Smith & Bradway, *Growth of Legal Aid Work*, chaps. 6–10.

from which they have rescued or tried to rescue unfortunate clients.'[108] Such a role enticed countless lawyers into the legal aid movement. Yet such overt reformist efforts also alienated some of the bar and became a source of the movement's persistent marginality.

Others lawyers took jobs in legal aid offices for lack of other professional opportunities. This latter function was underscored by the role of women, ethnics, and students in legal aid. Smith, for example, shared the gender biases of his profession and opposed the presence of women in private law offices (except as secretaries). Nevertheless, he, like many others, decided that the 'legal aid office is different. It is much easier for them to practice in such an office and they seem to get along alright.'[109] Much the same was true for Catholic, Jewish, and other ethnic practitioners who found themselves locked out of most elite urban law firms and yet wanted to avoid careers as solo practitioners. Students too were encouraged to participate in legal aid through internships and newly-created law school legal aid clinics. The Boston Legal Aid Society, for example, supervised the Harvard Legal Aid Bureau, the first such student organization. Others followed as legal aid served the bar in a different capacity by providing practical experiences lost in the transition from apprentice training to law school training. The influx of students, in turn, helped the movement by staffing its overloaded offices. Legal aid thus offered reformers, women, ethnics, and students, one of the few professionally sanctioned outlets for their services.[110]

Staff lawyers themselves mixed idealism with the realities of legal aid practice. A chief attorney in the New York Legal Aid Society described legal aid practice as 'deadening, routine work, which would kill any sensible, ambitious man in two months'. Rapid turnover and use of legal aid as a training ground for later practice became the consequences of the burdens and possibilities of its form of practice.[111] Legal aid, despite the triumphant rhetoric of its leaders, remained less professionally

[108] Maguire, *Lance of Justice*, 105.

[109] Smith to Dean Theodore W. Swan, Yale Law School, 12 June 1924, Boston Legal Aid Society, 1924 Files; and see Grossberg, 'Law as a Masculine Profession'.

[110] For discussions of student legal aid see J. H. Wigmore, 'Legal Aid Clinics, The Student's Point of View', *Case & Comment*, 23 (1917), 973–9; J. H. Wigmore, 'The Legal Aid Clinic and What it Does for the Law Student', *Annals*, 125 (1926), 130–5; J. S. Bradway, 'Legal Clinics and the Bar', *S. Calif. Law Rev.*, 3 (1929–30), 386–94; and see L. Brown, *Lawyers and the Promotion of Justice* (New York, 1936), 99–101; Maguire, *Lance of Justice*, 177, 193, 197.

[111] See, e.g., Maguire, *Lance of Justice*, 288–9; Horovitz, 'Need for Specialization in Legal Aid Cases', 66–7.

rewarding and less remunerative than private practice. Dean Pound, for example, wrote to Dean Harlan Stone of Columbia Law School, 'I have observed this legal aid business here pretty carefully, and am still firmly of the opinion that giving advice to and prosecuting petty cases for the type of person who applies to a legal aid society is no legitimate part of the training of the sort of men to whom we appeal and whom we seek to turn out.'[112] And yet legal aid also inspired devotion. Three staff attorneys of the Chicago Legal Aid Bureau added their own sentiments to the organization's 1916 report:

Your attorneys feel that the opportunity they have to look at the law from the viewpoint of the proletarian gives them an appreciation of his attitude towards the law, government, and society. We also appreciate the responsibility resting on our shoulders; in many cases it is a heavier responsibility than rests on the shoulders of the attorney to whose hands has been entrusted the affairs of a large corporation, because a mistake on our part may mean much more serious consequences to our client than a corresponding mistake on his part, though the amounts involved in the litigation carried on by us are relatively insignificant. Our close association with the social service department of this office gives us a much keener insight into the sociological problems of poverty, disease, and destitution than a much longer time spent cloistered in a University study or law.[113]

The commitment of legal aid lawyers was strained by the conditions of their work. And yet they, too, like the clients and the movement's leaders, played critical roles in the daily operation of legal aid offices and thus in the professional struggles that engulfed legal aid.

These men and women left their own impact on the movement and its approach to legal practice. Again the exact nature of the impact is not certain, though the discretion granted attorneys in the screening mechanisms suggests that it could have been quite significant. And by the 1940s and 1950s commentators would note growing conflicts between staff lawyers and the practitioners on the boards of legal aid societies. These differences were not so apparent in the first decades of the movement, but staff lawyers were in the process of becoming a particular kind of legal practitioner. These incipient poverty lawyers were creating a specialty in the sense recognized by the bar and being broadcast by legal aid leaders and yet also laying the foundation for a kind of practice at odds with such pronouncements. Skirmishes over law

[112] *Roscoe Pound Mss*, Gen. Corr. 1917, Paige Box 8, 13 July 1917, Harvard Law School.
[113] Chicago Legal Aid Society, *Annual Report*, 31 (1916), 30.

reform, legislative lobbying, and mass lawsuits suggested the potential of new forms of professional political conflict.[114]

Freed from the constraints of regular practice, but weighted down by the tremendous demand they unleashed and the professional commitments they had made, legal aid lawyers created a new form of legal representation. It combined aspects of traditional client counselling with social integration and professional protection. And yet because of the conflicts legal aid itself generated, legal aid offices became sites of struggle where clashing ideas of justice and legal practice were fought out. The general goals of the movement to create law offices like those of their brethren in private practice and to aid only worthy clients structured, but did not always determine the outcome of, individual cases. Instead, the everyday practices of legal aid proved to be quite complicated. Most critically, despite its professed liberal ideals of uniform legal rights and procedural equality, the legal aid movement helped create and legitimate a dual system of justice in which those who could afford a lawyer proceeded with adversarial dispute resolution while those who could not were ushered into a system that prized education and conflict resolution over individual legal triumphs. This reality, though, faced constant challenge from clients and even staff lawyers. The result was to make being a legal aid lawyer a more and more distinct form of legal practice despite the professed goals of legal aid's creators.

Conclusion

In a 1926 article, 'Introduction to Legal Aid Work', Smith declared unequivocally: 'The aim of legal aid work is to improve the position of the poor before the law by making it more nearly equal to the position of all other citizens.'[115] He could look back and identify three notable achievements: recognition that poverty effectively barred large segments of the population from legal institutions; persuasion of significant portions of the legal profession and laity that the legal system should be open to the indigent; and creation of broad programmes that sought to open the urban legal system to the poor. As a result of the movement, legal aid had become an urban fixture and an accepted part of the profession. But the movement's lofty goals could not be realized. Its inability to end the effects of poverty on the legal process are not mere examples of the gap between rhetoric and reality or the inevitable

---

[114] Katz, *Poor People's Lawyers in Transition*, 45–9.
[115] R. G. Smith, 'Introduction to Legal Aid Work', *Annals*, 124 (1926), 2.

limits of social control. Instead, despite their persistent, and heartfelt, commitment to equal justice, the attempts of legal aid lawyers to combat poverty underscore some of the realities of the liberal legal order. The goals, the means created to achieve them, and the results, must all be understood as the products of their professional commitments to political liberalism. It was as a lawyers' reform that legal aid tackled poverty; and it was a lawyers' vision that structured its achievements and limitations.

As a result, the struggles over legal aid illuminate the particular kinds of contests spawned by political liberalism. Compelled to act by a sense of interconnected professional and social crises, legal aid lawyers considered themselves the allies of other legal reformers campaigning to make the necessary changes that would adapt and yet preserve the liberal legal order. In doing so, they struggled to give new meanings to the moderate state, citizenship rights, civil society, and the other central elements of political liberalism. Their success is evident in the forms of legal representation they created for the poor. As a result of their movement, legal aid revealed the faith so many American lawyers placed in procedural reform and their overriding commitment to preserving the autonomy and authority of the bar. Indeed, as their arguments for legal aid made clear, legal aid lawyers—like of much of the bar—equated the protection of their independence with the preservation of political liberalism and its fundamental components, most notably a reconstructed but not transformed civil society and moderate state. Convinced that the bar's fate was inextricably linked to the fate of the republic, legal aid lawyers, their allies, and kindred legal reformers entered the lists of the politics of professionalism determined to succeed in a double legitimation project: making representation a fundamental right of all citizens and protecting the independent authority of the bar. Earl Johnson, Jr. concisely summarizes the consequences:

It is difficult to detect much sympathy for the social and economic deprivations of the poor in the writings of the leaders of legal aid, but their sensibilities as lawyers clearly were shocked by the deprivations of due process caused by poverty. An abiding concern with the integrity of the legal system and threats to its survival pervade the pronouncements of the movement. Each man, rich or poor, deserves his day in court; that is what this country is all about; and besides, if we do not insure that access, the masses will revolt and tear down our system of government. Entirely missing is an evident stake in the outcome of the poor man's day in court and its implications for his other social and economic problems. Legal aid discharges its responsibility and satisfies its ultimate goal if a poor man is provided reasonably qualified legal counsel. Apparently, lawyers must bear the guilt for inequality in the administration of justice but need not share the guilt for the existence of poverty. These attitudes generally were not a product of insensitivity on the part of those who supported legal aid but rather the result of a failure to appreciate any close connections between a denial of equal justice and the perpetuation of economic inequality.[116]

And thus, however marginal to the bar, the creation of legal aid is an apt illustration of the sources and the results of the politics of professionalism at a time of severe strain within American political liberalism. It documents the primacy of politics in struggles over the changing composition of the liberal order.

Like so many other reforms of the early twentieth century, legal aid lingered on after its formative era. The private societies continued to do their work and to maintain a rigid faith in the movement's formative concepts. Controversy would erupt again in the 1960s when during another moment of crisis in American political liberalism a new brand of legal aid—federally financed legal services—challenged the basic premises of the movement. Until then, legal aid occupied a distinct but marginal place at the bar. Raynor Gardiner, head of the Boston Legal Aid Society from 1926, lamented in the early 1950s that highly qualified legal aid lawyers were viewed as eccentrics by their professional peers and just 'not taken very seriously by members of the bar'. He thought that it would be well to 'face the fact that legal aid is the poor relation of the bar'.[117] Despite such misgivings, the first American legal aid lawyers exposed a glaring injustice of the liberal legal order even if securing equal justice had proven to be much more complex and elusive a task than their professional predilections would allow.

---

[116] Johnson, *Justice and Reform*, 12–13.
[117] R. Gardiner, 'Defects in Present Legal Aid Service and the Remedies', *Tenn. Law Rev.*, 22 (1951–53), 566; and see Brownell, *Legal Aid in the United States*, 246–8.

Postscript: Lawyers, Political Liberalism, and Globalization

Terence C. Halliday and Lucien Karpik

Introduction

The political transformations towards democracy in the last two decades, from Latin America to Central and Eastern Europe, raise the connection between lawyers and liberalism to a new level of immediacy. For societies seeking to adopt liberal forms of politics, the form of the moderate state, the constitution of civil society, and rights of citizenship rank highly on the agenda of political and legal reconstruction. The case studies in this book demonstrate that historically all three elements of liberalism have depended in various degrees on the actions of legal professions. But these analyses have dealt mainly with the internal processes, as did our Introduction, which proceeded methodologically by cross-national comparisons. However, we are confident that for the past, as well as for the present, national changes cannot be separated from transnational developments: they were and are parts of more global transformations, yesterday, in Continental Europe, North America, and the former British Empire, and, today, in other countries across all continents.

Scholarship on legal professions has rarely held in tension the interplay of national and transnational forces of stability and change. Where it has done so, it has tended to extremes. On the one hand, in a field driven largely by case studies, historical and developmental accounts of professionalization have remained doggedly internalist. They are overwhelmingly bounded by the nation-state. On the other hand, much recent commentary that does treat globalization swings too far in the opposite direction, for it reduces the nation-state, and local politics and markets, to ciphers in the global economy and emerging transnational regulatory and political structures, such as the European Community, or the World Trade Organization. In their frame, international markets subjugate national markets. The new focus on globalization therefore has begun to move the market theory of professions away from parochialism, though it, too, tends to homogenize global impacts within national states, thereby minimizing the adaptations forced by local politics on global movements.

It is not necessary to assume that the characteristics of economic globalization are general to other institutions, such as politics. On the contrary. In this Postscript we will seek to identify the *specificity* of political globalization around legal professions and to distinguish (if necessary) between its present and its past forms. At the outset we present the caveat that this analysis has to deal with an empirical reality that until now has been largely ignored and, consequently, we do not have, at hand, the studies that could have laid a stronger foundation for a refined analysis. Nevertheless, within these constraints, we present a sociological essay that builds on what piecemeal evidence we have available from our collaborative project.

Transnational movements of people, commerce, ideas, institutions, and laws are hardly new. As Roehl has observed, globalization was anticipated in the ancient empires of Mesopotamia and the Mediterranean, in Roman law, and in the 'universal common law of the international trader class' that existed in the Middle Ages.[1] The medieval Roman Catholic church and its extension across Europe to the New World and Asia; the great seventeenth- and eighteenth-century trading companies that extended from the Netherlands to the Dutch East Indies and from London to Bombay; the European empires that colonized sections of every other continent; even the global differentiation of legal systems into civil and common law jurisdictions—all point to the integration of regions and continents into world systems with discernible cultural, economic, and political ties of affiliation and dominance.

Yet while national cases cannot be segregated from transnational movements, and contemporary globalizing movements cannot be divorced from historical precedent, it does not follow that economic and political patterns of globalization display the same dynamics or outcomes. The critical historical moments for political liberalism, the circumstances that precipitated changes in political regimes, and the conditions under which new liberal institutions were created, may have substantially different historical trajectories from those that accompanied the modern transformations of economic liberalism. For instance, after arguing that 'in the case of liberalism, a narrowing of the subject

---

[1] Klaus F. Roehl, 'The Globalization of Legal Phenomena', presented at the Joint Meeting of the Law and Society Assoc. and the Research Committee on the Sociology of Law, Amsterdam, 1991, 7–8.

to national societies . . . is hardly justifiable', Voegelin maintains not only that 'all the regional phases of liberalism are parts of a common Western movement', but that the phenomenon of liberalism can only be understood 'in the context of its struggle with other movements of the nineteenth century—reaction, restoration, conservatism, social-ism'—and in the context of watershed developments of the twentieth century—the welfare state, and the rightest and leftist reactions to lib-eralism of fascism and communism respectively.[2]

If this holds for liberalism, it also holds for lawyers' engagement in regional and international politics since the eighteenth century. That the English Glorious Revolution of 1688, the American Revolution of 1776, and the French Revolution of 1789 should all be associated with the abolition of the bar indicates that convulsive political change was neither entirely local, nor irrelevant to professions of law, which also became caught up in later revolutions, whether of the left in 1830 and 1848, or the right in 1933.[3] Not only did revolutions place a similar stamp on aspects of legal organization, but the path of military con-quest endowed a legal legacy on countries exposed to Napoleon's administrative innovations. The imposition of the Napoleonic Code was greeted as an emancipatory document by many German princi-palities because it weakened local and traditional norms and instituted certain rights. Neither were lawyers immune from the European sweep of liberal politics, reflected through suffrage movements, unionism, the advent of socialism, and the ideal of the rule-governed state. Communism and fascism, too, confronted lawyers with ideologies in direct opposition to legal liberalism. In short, national Bar politics have been moulded in the matrix of revolution, war, social movements, and nationalism—and their encounters with those forces shaded the land-scape of liberalism in European politics.

National lawyers' movements around liberal politics are thus part of a political globalization whose singularity can be captured by its differences with the dynamics of economic globalization. Three dis-tinctive differences can be identified. These are expressed through three related propositions which delineate the framework that will orient our essay.

---

[2] E. Voegelin, 'Liberalism and its History;, *Rev. of Politics*, 36 (1974), 504–20.
[3] M. Burrage, 'Revolution as a Starting Point for the Comparative Analysis of the French, American, and English Legal Professions', in R. L. Abel & P. S. C. Lewis (eds.), *Lawyers in Society*, vol. 3, *Comparative Theories* (Berkeley, Univ. of California Press, 1989), 322–74.

First, although both political and economic globalization implies at least some kind of convergence between the phenomena that are part of the whole, a significant difference between economic and political globalization inheres in the nature of their respective stakes and in the logic of change. On the one hand, the issues that can become the basis of globalization are much more heterogeneous in politics than in economics: for example, civil rights and environmental issues are quite independent of each other. Because terms like 'civil rights' or 'moderate state' and the like take on different meanings in very different national and historical contexts, they in fact designate very different realities that can only be subsumed under the same label by moving to a level of high abstraction. However, goods on the same market are largely interchangeable. On the other hand, the logic of change between economic and political globalization is quite different. Although market globalization has experienced interruptions, and even regressions, nevertheless it makes sense to think of market globalization as a complex process of extension, incorporation, and 'mondialization'. There is a 'sameness' in the direction or the trend that gives unity to all particular changes. The same cannot be said for political globalization. Nazism and the experiences of Latin American countries during the last decades demonstrate that political liberalism can disappear and reappear. The drive to liberal politics is much more contingent. Therefore we should more readily expect surprises and unanticipated outcomes in the trajectories of political globalization.

Second, political globalization is the product of mechanisms whose influences are determined by the choices of political actors. In contrast to *homo economus* (which is everywhere conceived of as a rational actor exclusively driven by egoistic motives), the political actor in general, and the lawyer in particular, cannot be assimilated or reduced to a common set of aims. On the contrary, the lawyer must be viewed as an active agent with diverse orientations, values, and political ideologies and with at least some freedom of choice. Consequently, in political globalization, the mechanisms through which knowledge, information, and ideologies spread cannot be assimilated to deterministic mechanisms. Influence is a constructive process through which those who are influenced concomitantly are transforming, sometimes widely and creatively, the objects of their influence. In our perspective, the study of globalization strongly links the mechanisms of political globalization to the diverse interpretations of its receivers.

Third, contrary to economic globalization, which is strongly driven by an economic competition that tends to homogenize goods and services, political globalization creates weaker constraints on political formations. Combined with the diversity of orientations and the margins of manoeuvre that characterize political actors, political globalization produces (or is compatible with) a much larger variety of particularisms. In other words, if economic globalization maintains some diversity, which is expressed through the various models of the Japanese, American, and German economies, nevertheless the tendency towards homogeneity is much stronger in the economic sphere, especially when competition is based on prices, than in the political sphere, where actors engage foreign models through complex interpretative processes.

Political transnational movements, therefore, are very much more entangled in localism than is ever the case with the market. Whereas markets universalize, politics particularize. They look less contemporaneously to other nations than historically to their own traditions. This polarity is intensified in the case of lawyers, whose matter is grounded in precedent, codes, and the heavy hand of prior judgments. Through their partial incorporation into the state, and their participation in the inertial weight of legal tradition, lawyers are significantly more local in their orientation than any other profession, excepting the military. Our analysis of the enlargement of political liberalism reflects on the singularity of political globalization. We will first consider the process of globalization (the mechanisms of transmitting and thus purveying knowledge and ideologies as well as the ways the content of these ideologies have been interpreted and reinterpreted by national professions) and then its historical products. We conclude with some observations on the tensions for legal professions that result from the contemporary interplay of economic and political globalization, from the universality of economics and the particularity of politics.

The Process of Political Globalization

The most important and durable movement of political globalization around legal professions began in the eighteenth century and lasted during a 'long' nineteenth century. It pivoted on the English and the French Bars. The general reasons for their respective influence are quite clear: they were the first two bars that were well organized and founded on a prestigious medieval past. Both belonged to the liberal sphere of politics, although each incarnated a different type of liberalism. Each can be considered as a specific model (of organization and commitment) that became, through sometimes complex influences, a reference for reform and more generally for action, all the more as each of them incarnated, as a result of the interpretations by recipient countries, two different forms of liberalism. It must be emphasized that these models are not sociological typologies but rather ideal types perceived and created by legal professions themselves and legal elites in other countries. Therefore the links of the models with the historical reality of professional action may be quite indirect.

The apolitical model

Best exemplified by Britain, barristers are mutually constitutive of liberal movements from time immemorial. Barristers' independence has its medieval origins in civil society, not the state. Indeed, barristers' autonomy, and those of other 'little commonwealths' in civil society, are entrenched in the unwritten English constitution. Significantly, lawyers' establishment and maintenance of their constitutional status are rarely punctuated by political struggles. Barristers have not traditionally needed to mobilize themselves as a collective actor either to fight for a moderate state or to defend their constitutional perquisites. The struggles of the English Bar to maintain its independence during Mrs Thatcher's reforms should not distract from the singular rarity of such a confrontation with the English state. Lawyers may be deeply embedded within the state—as judges, imperial administrators—but their historical identity, collegial institutions, and practices exist significantly independent of it. And from this *locus* in civil society, the profession has managed an autonomy from the state that it is rarely observed, let alone brought into question. Indeed, as Burrage argues, their independence has been fundamentally threatened only twice since the seventeenth century. The singularity of the British profession lies in the fact that the profession as a collective institution has never been committed to politics, especially against the state. [4]

There is a corollary to the embeddedness of a profession in the deep structure of constitutional life: a profession that has not periodically been required to fight for itself, or for liberal ideals, may never have learned the art nor practised the skills of political mobilization. When suddenly threatened with encroachments on its autonomy, or assaults on liberal institutions, its capacity to mobilize will be impaired. In particular, it may have very limited resources to act as a spokesman for the

---

[4] Burrage, 'Mrs Thatcher Against Little Republics'. chap. 4 *supra*.

public, whose goodwill will have been assumed rather than regularly reproduced.

The political model

Best exemplified by France, the political model requires explicit political action by a collective body against an absolutist or antagonistic state. Its constitutional status must constantly be defended. Its fortunes ebb and flow as political regimes and ideologies wax and wane in their commitment to a liberal politics that tolerates, indeed demands, powerful professional groups that stand outside the state, but which defend some pillar of liberal legalism.

The defining moment for the French political model over the *longue durée* is best represented in the eighteenth and nineteenth centuries when the profession, as a collective political actor, was compelled to act as a disinterested proto-political party, developing and articulating a set of ideals and speaking on behalf of a broader public. At that historical moment the *avocats* recognized that they were powerful enough to press for a transformation of the French political system, to fight against absolutism and for civil rights. The Paris Bar took upon itself the role of spokesman for French society. For French lawyers before the twentieth century, politics was a noble calling and their standing in politics was a defining attribute of the profession's success. Lawyers were the voice of the public they helped to constitute. In contrast to the apolitical model, French lawyers repeatedly mobilized as a political actor and their standing in French society, their role in the construction of liberalism, and their autonomy all turned on their capacity to engage in collective action, to engage directly in politics.

By their position, their prestige, and their power, these nations became the centres of power from which other models of political liberalism were derived and adapted. Britain and France are the two 'first nations' of liberal politics and they become the reference points for others. While that influence has long been recognized, what remains more obscure are the ways through which that influence was realized. In that process, we can distinguish first, the mechanisms by which those models have expanded, and second, the ways that national professions reacted to the respective models.

A. *The Mechanisms*

Britain and France were the two first nations to adopt significant liberal elements and to lead the fight against absolutism. But little direct relationship existed between them, except for the value the British conservatives derived from the use of France as a negative model of despotism. Yet it was the French model that became most important on the Continent, despite the fascination of nineteenth-century German observers with Britain's parliamentary institutions and its robust civil society. Ultimately, however, the British form of liberalism was too peculiar, its conditions too specific, its institutions too grounded in an unwritten constitution that could not readily be exported to the Continent. The British constitution, and the role of the Bar within it, was turned west to the colonies and imposed on the conquered territories, through military might and emigration, in North America, Asia, Africa, and Australasia. From 1810 to 1914, the French model, with its emphasis on autonomy of the bar, the capacity to act against the state and to engage in political action, was more readily adapted to other Continental countries where the relationship between the state and civil society more closely paralleled France.

These two models became known and variously influential through different combinations of means—between violent mechanisms and peaceful mechanisms, between imposition and voluntary choices.

Violent mechanisms

Imposition through political violence historically represents a ubiquitous mode of exporting models of political organization. Since the seventeenth century, European powers exported models of politics and law either by colonial conquest of a society without a developed state apparatus (for example, Australia), or military conquest of a state with a developed apparatus (for example, German principalities in the early nineteenth century). And the most powerful of them sought to impose their legal institutions on the entire Continent.

Britain's great colonial empire achieved astonishing success as an exporter of political ideas. The principal movement of ideas and models occurred as professions followed the path of colonial settlement and conquest. Colonizers brought legal systems that either existed independently of indigenous customary law, as in North America, or added a layer of British common law over local customary and written law, as in India. In the latter circumstance, however, the imposed law bound the colonized by both, whereas the colonizers bound themselves only by common law and the regulations of the great trading companies.

The significance of professionalization for Britain's imperial power is well explicated in Terry Johnson's accounts of ways the metropolitan regime confronted 'the task of rendering spatially and socially distant cultures amenable to government'. Imperial rule was made possible, in part, by professions, whose 'expert communities developed the capacity to universalize standards, unify goals, and create coherent interests and affiliations, and tap into and transform local aspirations, so linking the colonies to the metropolitan centres'. Professions co-opted local elites, instituted imperial systems of qualifications and examinations, and developed imperial professional societies. Professions harmonized law, engineering, transport, and education across the globe.[5]

In the case of the Napoleonic Code, imposition occurred over competing systems of modern law, just as the Occupation Forces in 1945 imposed modified forms of professional organization on defeated Nazi Germany. After the Second World War, the Western model became the normal type which influenced all of Europe. But the Americans, British, and French dealt with the Germans very differently. France left the corporatist form in place and the British, too, left the *kammer* mostly intact. Only the Americans were vigorously opposed to compulsory lawyers' chambers, and they forbade them in favour of free associations.[6]

Peaceful mechanisms

Although it is quite clear that lawyers, in the period of liberal upheavals, conflicts, and emancipation, were part of a larger movement—reading the news, following events, sharing national reactions—it is also clear that lawyers had their own, informal, and perceptible means of extending their influence and views, of discovering, knowing, checking, and debating foreign experiences. They did so through the mobilization of their national and transnational networks.

The spread of political models therefore also occurs voluntarily. Networks operate through exchanges among professional associations, and in various parliamentary and other political associations. Networks also function through publication, economic and political debate, travel, and international conferences. The circulation of critical commentaries on foreign systems conveyed Montesquieu's interpretation of British constitutionalism to the French, Tocqueville's views of American

[5] T. Johnson, 'The State and the Professions: Peculiarities of the British', in A. Giddens and G. McKenzie (eds.), *Social Class and the Division of Labour* (Cambridge, Cambridge Univ. Press, 1982).
[6] H. Siegrist, 'Lawyers and Liberalism on the Continent', commentary at Conf. on Lawyers and Political Liberalism, Oñati, 1993.

political organization to the French, Blackstone's and Bryce's writings to the United States, Blackstone's writings to Germany by courtesy of Gneist, Harley's writings on Canada to the American West, and Aitkin's writings on Britain and the United States to his Canadian constituency.

German lawyers, for instance, looked overtly to British and covertly to French models of liberal constitutionalism and professional organization. German professor and visionary liberal politician Rudolph Gneist was much impressed by English institutions of civil society in the 1830s and sought to recreate intermediary bodies in a Prussia where they had been systematically suppressed since the Great Elector, Frederick William. Unremunerated English justices of the peace and bodies of local notables, together with a self-regulating guild of lawyers, exemplified Blackstone's philosophy that free peoples need self-governing bodies, a civil society, and a public sphere. A free bar reinforced all these and presented an ideal that Gneist sought valiantly to implant in Germany.[7]

German lawyers could not visibly model themselves on French institutions in the aftermath of the Napoleonic Wars. Nevertheless, the indirect influence of France was significant, most importantly through Rhenish Prussia and Hannover, which had much closer ties with France and acted as bridgeheads for French ideas. Elements of French professionalism were incorporated into the 1878 Imperial German Justice statutes. Before German unification, the movement of law students across dozens of sovereign principalities cross-fertilized a nascent, national, legal culture that was realized in the unification of law and politics after 1869. Germany also looked to Britain, for even after the Justice Acts were adopted, Germany and Britain learned intensely from each other about unions, guilds, corporations, and the role of jurists in the rise of law schools.[8] It was not simply coincidental that Max Weber should contrast Germany with Britain as he sought to understand the interplay of economic and legal rationalization in either country. Together they sought to sustain a certain vision of civilization, custom, national identity, in contra-distinction to the French, whom the British cast as absolutists. None the less it remains an open question whether Germany seriously learnt from England, or whether it merely used English institutions to legitimate German institutions.[9]

[7] See K. F. Ledford, chap. 7 *supra*; D. Rueschemeyer, chap. 6 *supra*.
[8] Siegrist, 'Lawyers and Liberalism on the Continent'.
[9] The US also served as a negative exemplar—a warning of what can happen if a state does not have a well-developed civil service.

Lawyers are inveterate travellers, and invariably they cross-pollinate societies with ideas and observations. If their fortunes permitted it, colonial American barristers travelled back to the Inns of Court to complete their studies, a pattern imitated into the mid-twentieth century by barristers and solicitors from the old and new British Commonwealth. Small states, like Switzerland, characteristically observed what their larger neighbours did. Large numbers of Continental law students today travel to Britain and the United States for a year or more of study or internship. Similar patterns can be observed for Spanish-trained jurists in Latin America, who formerly travelled to Spain and, increasingly, are studying law in the United States.

The two mechanisms for spreading models of legal professions and politics fall into a rough historical sequence. State imposition of models that generate liberal regimes begins with British colonization in the seventeenth century and continues through the nineteenth century, while its Continental corollary, on the heels of the French Revolution and French conquest, begins in the late eighteenth century and continues into the second decade of the nineteenth century. The mobilization of social networks, principally through travel, networks, and publications, becomes notable from the 1830s, and continues at a faster rate through the nineteenth century to the present day.

B. Reactions to Foreign Models

It is one thing to discover and learn, be fascinated or repulsed, by other experiences; it is another thing to do something with them. That complex process combines personal and collective orientations, and specific and changing circumstances. It stimulates, in a very general way, three sorts of reactions: rejection, indifference, and compromise.

Rejection occurs for reasons of fear, national pride, or the preservation of local identity. Thus a previously conquered Prussia could not turn to its conqueror for inspiration, just as the smaller German states refused to bow to the Prussian model, though in this case a fear of domination united with their exposure to alternative, more liberal, and enlightened models outside Germany. But rejection occurs not only in the wake of war and conflict. A tension endures between globalism and localism in many circumstances. Lawyers' work tends to be more nation-centric than that of many other professions. This is particularly true for lawyers closely integrated into the fabric of the administrative state. Their identity with core institutions of the nation-state makes it difficult to unify professions voluntarily.

Resistance inheres therefore in the very constitution of the profession itself. Contemporary globalization of trade forces only a partial qualification of this thesis, for even after the ratification of the Maastricht Treaty for political union of Europe, large parts of national professions remain effectively untouched. And while it is true that the tiny number of mega-law firms that serve multinational clients have conveyed some Americanization and Anglicization of corporate practice in Europe and Asia, this occurs only at the apex of the profession. Although it is a disproportionately influential fraction of the profession, the fact remains that most lawyers in even the advanced industrial countries are only slightly affected by global commercial traffic. It is an illusion that it is possible to homogenize a lawyer's profession in an entire country, let alone easily effect the same end across a continent.

Rejection may occur more subtly. By appearing to accept a foreign model through the adoption of its label, and some semblance of its reality (for example, a 'constitution', or 'democracy', or 'bar association'), political leaders can seek both to satisfy those constituencies (foreign and national) that advocate the label, while simultaneously subverting the concepts in practice. According to Olgiati, for instance, Fascist professions appropriated the compelling liberal ideal of public service from free professions and converted it into a totalitarian doctrine for professionals who were yoked to the interest of the state.[10]

Indifference to the immediate pressures of transnational change characterizes the vast majority of national professionals. Unless their practice intersects with areas in which there are strong global currents of change, everyday local practice proceeds with relative autonomy. Of course, within groups of nations that are seeking formal degrees of economic and political integration, such as the European Union, and the North American Free Trade Association, administrative regulations and national statutes will be progressively homogenized, though here it is done imperatively from a political centre (that is, the relationship between Brussels and, for example, France), rather than voluntarily (for example, the relationship between American legal practices and responses by the French *avocats*). Even in this case the degrees of freedom at the local level may not be so different, in practice, than those observed in the clashes between customary law and colonial law in former colonies.

Compromise represents an innovative response to global pressures that follows from two circumstances. On the one hand, compromise occurs

---

[10]   Olgiati; Siegrist, 'Lawyers and Liberalism on the Continent'.

when political actors acknowledge some value in an exogenous model of politics, but recognize that its adoption will not take place smoothly or legitimately unless it is made consistent with national traditions and institutions. On the other hand, compromise takes place when an external model is not particularly liked, but it cannot be escaped. At some point, compromise of this sort becomes a form of resistance.

Compromise that leans more to adaptation of foreign models occurs when both the local model becomes dislocated or destabilized, and an alternative model is at hand. Awareness of the alternative model requires ready exchange of information, and adoption of an alternative model requires some identification between the original and host institutions. Models are rarely adopted from enemies, though the presence of a powerful contrary model can serve well to focus a reaction.

Innovative compromise is often the result of transnational and global forces acting on the internal politics of professions. Globalization may precipitate internal political struggles over the goals, identity, and control of the profession, usually between segments of professions differently exposed to the force of transnational developments. On occasion, adaptation of foreign concepts takes the form of insurgency, when marginal segments of the profession see global or regional changes as opportunities to alter the balance of power either in work jurisdictions or in collegial associations. The efforts of Continental notaries to take over functions of business advice and law are a notable case in point. Thus the impact of globalization in a national setting will be influenced by a national profession's ability to mobilize in ways that resist, adapt, or appropriate global changes in ways consistent with national or sectional interests.

The juxtaposition of global trends and national professional politics introduces an often missing tension into understandings of globalization itself. Globalization is a trend towards universality; but frequently it encounters reactions to reverse, or contain, its universalizing tendencies. Market and economic forces readily transcend national boundaries and therefore have a greater tendency towards universality. But national politics domesticate the general mechanism of globalization, and through resistance, conflict, translation, and innovation produce either variants on global themes, or original syntheses of global and local models. This explains why the globalization process surrounding the two models of lawyers' politics of liberalism produces such a diversity of reactions within the liberal political universe.

The Results of Political Globalization

The dynamics of political globalization produce distinctive historical products. More precisely, depending on national and historical situations, the different types of mechanisms and the different modes of reception have together oriented themselves more towards certain solutions than towards others. The picture is even more complicated for two different reasons. On the one hand, the separation between the British and French models was dynamic, as they were sometimes in competition. On the other hand, some historical products, such as the legal profession in the United States, can themselves become paradigmatic over time. While the profession in the United States combines elements of its colonial past, the English Bar, and the Canadian profession, it simultaneously managed to mask, then meld, its origins into a new coherent model that it made available for export. The American model has come to encroach on the English and the French as it has gathered momentum since the Second World War.

Germany represents an important test case for reactions to foreign forms of politics because German lawyers in the 1830s were faced with two radically different models. France had the appeal of its Revolution—a revolt in favour of freedom and individual rights. But it was the English model which looked so appealing to the German middle class. German reformers such as Gneist dreamt of an apolitical model. It appealed to professionals for it did not require political action; indeed, political action seemed antithetical to the professional model. German reformers sought a professionalism anchored in civil society, a sentiment that had an affinity with the rise of the *burgertum* and *bildungsburgertum*. Therein lay the paradox. How was it possible to purposefully create a civil society, complete with intermediate associations, autonomy, and the dignity of English lawyers—that is, the apolitical model—without proceeding politically, through legislation and political struggle? In the event, since German lawyers could not assume the constitutional status that English barristers could take for granted, they were forced into electoral and party politics, not as collectives, but as individuals. It was a strategy that seemed to work well until the highpoint of liberal political parties in the 1870s. Thereafter it backfired and the political influence of lawyer-liberals faded along with the fates of liberal political parties.[11]

---

[11] See Ledford, chap. 7 *supra*; Rueschemeyer, chap. 6 *supra*.

Siegrist argues that from the 1860s to 1914, there was a period of convergence on forms of bar organization. All European countries became nation-states and variously liberal. International Bar Congresses made lawyers feel rather similar because they were all liberal professionals. Following the xenophobia engendered by world war, communications among national professions increased again in the later 1920s, only to be interrupted by the illiberal fascist German and Italian regimes, who readily adapted the service principle of professionalism as service to the commonweal. Fascist models were promoted and imposed over much of Europe. After 1950 a revival of the liberal model of the bar occurred, a model that was Western and grounded in earlier liberal traditions, though its contemporary manifestation was heavily indebted to American influence.[12]

In Britain's colonial empires, Britain merely transplanted its apolitical model of legal professionalism to the fallow soil of New World colonies. Indeed, Britain essentially transferred much of its political society, of which the professions were an element, to rest on top of and alongside whatever indigenous traditions were officially acknowledged and co-opted by the imperial authorities. Consequently, colonial administrators faced very little resistance. Colonial professions were subsequently institutionalized not through their historical reliance on medieval English traditions, but through statutory legislation in progressively more independent former colonies. But this political institutionalization does not negate the point that the British professionals, in what came to be the Old and New Commonwealth, still maintained an essentially apolitical character. Their statutory recognition was less a matter of political struggle than a technical implementation or ratification of a transplanted, and somewhat adapted, version of the 'natural' social order extant in the heart of the empire.

England's influence on the United States is refracted through a colonial heritage. But the creation of 'the first new nation' demanded an explicit constitutionalism in which the moderate state, civil society, and citizenship all factored strongly at the point of political independence. Lawyers infused the process of constitutional reconstruction, but diffusely, not through the representations of their collective associations. After the Civil War, however, the American model comes to look more like France, for while American corporate lawyers were busily expanding the legal ligaments of commerce, bar leaders throughout the United

---

[12] Siegrist, 'Lawyers and Liberalism on the Continent'.

States were engaging in a frenzy of associational formation in cities, counties, states, and the nation as a whole. Lawyers constituted themselves as collective actors explicitly to ensure that they would help constitute political society, and fight for judicial independence from party control.[13] Courts, and later a narrow sense of citizenship rights, became part of an ostensible political struggle by American lawyers.[14] They could never represent themselves as spokesmen for the public with the same assurance as eighteenth-century French lawyers, but they could mobilize their associations on behalf of ideals variously in their own or the public interest. Their appearance, in one guise, as an interest group, and in another guise, as a quasi-public resource for governability, aligns them more closely with the Continental than the English model. But with the English they do share a deep embeddedness in civil society, as American lawyers penetrate political and civic associations of every stripe.

But the English influence went even more deeply and took a more structural form. The United States has historically developed two co-existent forms of collegial organization. The first, voluntary associations of lawyers, requires no state mandate. The voluntary city and state bar associations are concentrated in major cities and more populous, industrial states. Several of them, most notably, the Association of the Bar of the City of New York, have mobilized their independent collective voices against the state in times when certain liberal-legal rights have come under assault.[15] These associations are embedded in civil society and in that respect owe their cultural heritage more to the tradition exemplified by the ancient English Inns of Court, and their American colonial offspring, than to state-mandated organizations. Their independence from the state endows upon them some added measure of autonomy.

The second form in the United States relies on state-mandated membership and functions. The so-called 'integrated bar' is concentrated in newer, more rural states where the population is widely dispersed. It

[13] T. C. Halliday, *Beyond Monopoly: Lawyers, State Crises, and Professional Empowerment* (Chicago, Univ. of Chicago Press, 1987); T. C. Halliday & B. G. Carruthers, chap. 8 *supra*.

[14] M. Grossberg, chap. 9 *supra*.

[15] M. J. Powell, *From Patrician to Professional Elite: The Transformation of the New York City Bar Association* (New York, Russell Sage Foundation, 1988); T. C. Halliday, 'The Idiom of Legalism in Bar Politics: Lawyers, McCarthyism, and the Civil Rights Era', *Amer. Bar Found. Res. Jrnl.* (Fall 1982), 911–89; T. C. Halliday, M. J. Powell, & M. W. Granfors, 'Minimalist Organizations: Vital Events in State Bar Associations, 1870–1930', *Amer. Sociol. Rev.*, 52, 456–71.

was inherited from the English model of the Law Society, modified and refracted through the Law Society of Upper Canada in Ontario, and then imported into the United States. But because they are formed through state-mandated compulsory membership, there have been distinct limitations on their degree of political activism, so much so, that some integrated bar associations have been the subject of court cases brought by members disgruntled at the mobilization of their association on behalf of causes with which they disagreed.[16]

In short, just as the English profession divides between barristers, who ground their politics in the ancient prerogatives of civil society (and whose members could be actively involved in liberal politics even against the bar itself, as Pue argues),[17] and solicitors, who rely on parliamentary statute for their self-regulatory powers, so, too, an importer (albeit suitably adapted) of organizational models, such as the United States in the nineteenth and first half of the twentieth century, can incorporate contrasting models of professional organization which result in variable capacities for political mobilization in defence of liberal ideals. The American case shows quite clearly that apolitical professions whose legitimation derives from civil society may be better positioned to defend liberal ideals than those professions whose existence depends on the goodwill of state—which may withdraw its mandate should a profession exceed the bounds of what state authorities consider to be acceptable political resistance.

Nineteenth-century Canada is an important case of a combined influence. During that period, lawyers found themselves initially tied by the imperial knot to Britain, but they could not remain unconscious of developments in the United States, especially in the wake of the American Revolution, when many loyalist lawyers fled north. The porous border between Canada and the United States in the prairies and western regions of both countries guaranteed that political ideas and movements would flow back and forth, relatively unrestrained by the supposed national frontiers. Pue shows that for lawyers in the prairie province of Manitoba, a unique ideal of Western Canadian professionalism emerged from a unique political culture. Substantially

---

[16] T. C. Halliday, M. J. Powell, & M. W. Granfors, 'After Minimalism: Transformations of State Bar Associations from Market Dependence to State Reliance, 1918–1950', *Amer. Sociol. Rev.* (Aug. 1993), 58, 515–35; Dayton McKean, *The Integrated Bar* (Boston, Houghton Mifflin, 1963); Theodore J. Schneyer, 1983, 'The Incoherence of the Unified Bar Concept: Generalizing from the Wisconsin Case', *Amer. Bar Found. Res. Jrnl.* (1983), 1–108.

[17] W. W. Pue, 'Lawyers in C18th and C19th England', chap. 5 *supra*.

antagonistic to English influences, and eager to emancipate themselves from the overwhelming influence of the metropolitan province of Ontario, lawyer-politicians saw themselves creating a new industrial metropolitan centre for a Canada which was, 200 million people strong. The Progressive ideal of an expert legal profession, using its technical proficiency for construction of a rational social order, appealed greatly. Melded with elements of the Law Society of Upper Canada (Ontario), this unique amalgam of British and American with indigenous elements of professionalism held the promise of professional leadership in a body politic that viewed mass politics with high anxiety.[18]

The complex of political liberalism therefore presents an intertwining of sameness with particularism that bears little resemblance to the impact of economic globalization. It cannot be separated from the large movement towards political liberalism in all these countries. But within that framework, globalization of the legal profession shows quite distinctive characteristics, both through the crucial mechanisms used for the displacement of information and knowledge and through the complex interpretive reconstructions that gave birth to different variants that moved according to their own internal dynamics. What is clear is that the double extension of the apolitical model and the political model cannot be viewed exclusively as the end of internal dynamics; it was also the product of a transnational movement that put limits to the variability of the lawyers' organizations and forms of action.

Conclusion

We have presented three related arguments. First, there has been more than one model of lawyers' engagement in the construction of liberal politics. Second, the international convergences and divergences of national legal professions around political liberalism must be understood concomitantly as national and transnational phenomena. Third, political globalization remained relatively untouched by international economic forces until the second half of the twentieth century. It is true that the development of capitalism in the late nineteenth century created new legal needs and new lawyers to serve them, business lawyers who placed some restrictions on forms of professional political action. Particularly manifest in the United States, and to a lesser extent in

---

[18] W. Wesley Pue, 'Lawyers and the Constitution of Political Society: Containing Radicalism and Maintaining Order in Prairie Canada, 1900–1930', paper presented to Conf. on Lawyers and Political Liberalism, Oñati, 1993.

England, the evolution of business law remained substantially within their national borders and reinforced the comparatively apolitical character of lawyers' politics. But this limited influence of economic globalization on political globalization has been changing since the 1950s and 1960s. For the last two or three decades, legal professions have been in the middle of two distinct, sometimes contradictory, but nevertheless intertwined processes—both political and economic globalization.

More and more contemporary national professions are becoming, willingly or not, part of transnational economic exchanges that have most dramatically expanded in the past twenty years. The internationalization of commerce, the expansion of multi-national corporations, the burgeoning of corporate mergers and acquisitions (now increasingly accompanied by multi-national corporate collapses), the great expansion of international financial institutions, and the flow of professional labour across national and even continental boundaries penetrate more and more deeply into the organization of national professional bodies.

The impact of these trends on the organization of legal work has not yet been well documented, but there is clear evidence of the growth of multi-national law firms, the homogenization—and perhaps Americanization—of corporate legal practice, and the development of global legal practice and a transnational bar, complete with associations and networks. This has been accompanied by greater competition among occupations, most notably between the global accountancy firms and large corporate law firms. International legal institutions and forms of dispute resolution have sprung up alongside the internationalization of business, and these in turn have had significant effects on national legal and regulatory systems. Some even see the emergence of a global legal culture, with its supranational organizations, international law, international treaties, and the global diffusion of legal and organizational innovation.[19]

It would be surprising if these global developments did not trigger crises and struggles over adaptation by national legal professions and their most vulnerable segments of practice. The demands of multi-national

[19] Y. Dezalay, *Marchands de Droit* (Paris, Fayard, 1992); Belmont Report of the National Science Foundation, 'Law Beyond the Nation State: Global Perspectives on Sociolegal Studies', Conf. Procs. (1990); Roehl, 'The Globalization of Legal Phenomena', Conf. Procs. (1991); V. Gessner, 'Introduction', and 'The Institutional Framework of Cross-Border Interaction', in V. Gessner (ed.), *Foreign Courts: Civil Litigation in Foreign Legal Cultures* (Aldershot, Dartmouth, 1996), 1-42; Y. Dezalay, 'The Big Bang and the Law: The Internationalization and Restructuring of the Legal Field', *Theory, Culture and Society* 7 (1990), 279–93.

corporate clients, the Americanization of legal practice, the threat of alien forms of practice entering a national market, competition from multi-national professional competitors such as accountancy firms, exposure to greater competition as trade barriers are lowered within economic blocs—all present challenges to national and local parochialism. The capacity for professional mobilization—that is, the constitution of lawyers as political actors, even, if only in the first instance, on commercial matters—determines significantly their ability to defend local work juris-dictions or to equip themselves with resources to compete in new juris-dictions inside or beyond their own juridical frontiers. In turn, we must understand how far a capacity for mobilization of behalf of work juris-dictions can also be deployed on behalf of political institutions and citi-zenship.

On this issue, it is clear that the major international forces of eco-nomics indirectly but forcefully are playing against national and local politics. This occurs everywhere in two ways. First, the extension of business lawyers and their numerous specializations advance the global progress of differentiation within the bar and contribute to the creation of divergent outlooks within the profession. Legal professions are increasingly torn between different segments whose orientations—polit-ical or market—become not only different, but sometimes conflictual. It is quite clear that economic globalization contributes significantly to changing patterns of dominance within the bar and, as a result, to the changing dominance of the two 'projects'. And at the present, eco-nomics leads.

Yet in a large number of countries, and within significant fractions of professions, the task of constructing a liberal society is still consid-ered a worthy cause, and lawyers still actively participate in political mobilization and action. Not only are these commitments found within countries, but in fact they are spreading because they are reinforced by a form of political globalization. The fight for liberalism continues and general patterns of political commitment over, for example, the Civil Rights movement or the fight for citizenship on behalf of immigrants in several countries, expresses the continued, even invigorated, presence of a globalizing political movement.

Thus modern lawyers confront a problematic situation. Concomitantly, they face the tasks of building a liberal polity and extending the legal business market and these two orientations are rein-forced by two distinct and sometime contradictory globalization processes. Consequently, the interpretation of the political commitment of contemporary lawyers cannot escape the new form by which transnational forces are influencing national practices. Indeed, in several countries it appears that the historical streams of legal politics have flowed together. The international conflicts among models of professional political engagement are perceptibly internalized within national professions and their resolution crafts the future structure of liberalism. All bars now contain within them some measure of forces that orient themselves to two different types of political action and democracy.

On the one side, the apolitical politics of an earlier era have largely disappeared and have been replaced by a procedural legal politics that valorizes fairness. Since this model of politics has an affinity with market norms, it appeals to commercial lawyers; it provides a common ground for the mobilization of professional sentiment on behalf of procedural democracy. Distinctively lawyers' politics are the politics of proceduralism, which offers a form of political liberalism that accords with economic liberalism.

On the other side, a substantive politics of liberalism remains in segments of national professions which is the direct heir of the classical substantive politics of professions recounted in this volume, a politics engaged by the ideals of the moderate state, civil society, and the substantive values of citizenship. These substantive politics advocate particular rights that are attached to citizenship. But their championing of substantive rights brings these lawyers into heavy conflict with the commercial bar. Thus the economic and political division within the bar gives rise to two kinds of politics that comport with two concepts of democracy—one procedural and the other substantive.

As a result of these struggles within the bar, contemporary professions confront the problems of political liberalism with much ambivalence. At no moment in history has there been such an international movement for the spread and defence of rights, for the valorization of the rule of law. Yet the same bars that take positions of international leadership in the globalization of liberal-legal politics themselves are weakened: the leadership of the profession cannot assume unequivocally that it speaks for the entire bar. Further, lawyers themselves walk on a fine edge between their political action on behalf of constructing fundamental liberal institutions and a slide into partisan party politics which again subverts a profession from within. As a result, the bar as a coherent political actor remains under heavy pressure. It remains to discover whether professions can reconcile these conflicting concepts of politics and act as collective agents of political reconstruction or whether lawyers will fracture into incipiently conflictual segments with very different aims and strategies towards the constitution of liberal politics. The form of that political settlement within and across professions will determine how far the countervailing pressures of economic and political globalization permit lawyers to continue some measure of their historic role as builders of the liberal state.

Index

221–2, 235, 238, 245, 248, 260;
Weimar Republic 31–2, 50,
245–64; Great Depression 220,
273, 329; National Socialism 10–11,
31–2, 227, 229–31, 262, 352
United States: American Revolution
207, 351; Civil War 207, 268,
270; Civil Rights era 17, 46;
McCarthy period 17, 46
Hobson, W. K. 318 n.
Holdsworth, W. 194 n.
Hone, J. A. 169 n., 187 n., 189 n.
Horovitz, S. 320
Horwitz, M. J. 268 n., 315 n., 316 n.
Howard, J. 337 n.
Hucko, E. 246 n.
Huffmann, H. 242 n.
Hufton, O. H. 106 n.
Huggins, N. 338 n.

Inns of Court *see* Bar Associations
Intermediate Groups *see* Interest Groups
Interest Groups, non-legal; Voluntary
Associations, Intermediate Groups
generally, interest groups 21, 57; *corps
intermediaires* 21
England, action by, Chartered Institute
of Management 165; Charter
Management Initiative 165;
Committee of Vice-Chancellors
and Principals 134; Confederation
of Health Service Employees 129;
Doctors' Party, 155–6; National
Union of Public Employees 129,
130; trade unions 155–64; Royal
College of Nurses and Midwives
129
United States, action by Brookings
Institution 279, 290–1, 293;
American Banking Association
281, 292, 294; American Council
of Life Insurance 281, 298;
Carnegie Foundation 317;
Chrysler Motor Corporation 280;
Citibank 287; League of Women
Voters 40; Robert Morris
Associates 281, 288, 292, 294, 299;
United Charities of Chicago 323

Jackson, A. 169, 301
Jacobins 99
Jacobsohn, M. 211–12
Jaratt, A. 134–5

Jarausch, K. 67 n., 101 n., 226 n., 230 n.,
231 n., 232, 234 n., 235 n.
Jenkins, P. 126 n.
Jenkins, S. 126 n., 141 n., 142 n., 161 n.
John, M. 217 n., 241 n., 242 n.
Johnson, E. 328 n., 346–7
Johnson, T. 55 n., 101 n., 223 n., 356–7
Jones, E. 236 n., 262 n.
Jones, K. 131 n.
Jones, L. E. 226 n.
Justice, Courts *see* Courts, Justice

Kagan, R. L 106 n.
Kammen, M. 150 n.
Kant 35, 213
Karpik, L. 7 n., 25 n., 26 n., 44 n., 59 n.,
66 n., 68 n., 73 n., 99 n., 100 n.,
102 n., 103 n., 108 n., 169 n.,
171 n., 264 n.
Katz, J. 323 n., 324, 345 n.
Katz, M. B. 323 n.
Kavanagh, D. 126 n.
Keane, J. 86, 86 n.
Keller, M. 315 n.
Kelley, D. 65 n., 70 n.
Klee, K. N. 297 n.
Knight, C. 131 n.
Kocka, J. 67 n.
Koselleck, R. 119, 236 n.
Kostal, R. 186 n.
Kotschnig, W. M. 260 n.
Krieger, L. 232 n., 240 n., 241 n.

Landsman, S. 180–2
Langewiesche, D. 233 n., 236 n.
Laumann, E.O. 321 n.
Lavoir, L. 76 n.
Lawyers:
definition, 18; barristers, France, 68 *et
seq.*; solicitor, France, 68; specialization, 289; Lawyers' Statute,
241–4, 254, 259; *Rechtsanwalt*, 210,
212
see also Bar Associations; Lawyers' collective action; Legal aid
Lawyers' collective action:
general:
boundaries of liberal action 52–6;
dimensions of political action
56–8; economics, politics versus
53–4; limits to liberalism 50–2;
proceduralism 21, 57; procedural
democracy 6; profiles of political